Casualties of War

Casualties of War

An Investigation

From Vietnam Atrocity to the Making of Brian De Palma's Masterpiece

Nathan Réra

Sticking Place Books
New York

Outrages – de Daniel Lang à Brian De Palma, Une enquête
© Rouge Profond 2021

Translation by Paul Cronin © Sticking Place Books 2024

Design by Goran Tovilovic

www.stickingplacebooks.com

All rights reserved.
No part of this book may be reproduced, stored in or introduced into a retrieval system, or transmitted, in any form or by any means (electronic, mechanical, photocopying, recording or otherwise) without the written permission of the publishers, except in the case of brief quotations embodied in critical articles or reviews.

ISBN 978-1-942782-82-7

Contents

Introduction	1
Prologue	13
Part 1: From Headlines to the Screen	
A Test of Conscience, 1966 – 1969	19
From the Forests of Bavaria to the Snows of Connecticut: Variations and Extensions, 1970 – 1972	63
Casualties of War in Hollywood: On Some Inadaptations, 1970 – 1980	111
Part 2: The Making of Brian De Palma's *Casualties of War*	
Revisiting *Casualties of War*	169
Pre-production, October 1987 – March 1988	217
Storyboards by Brian De Palma	247
Filming *Casualties of War*: A Ground-Level Chronicle, April – July 1988	263
Post-Production to Critical Reception, August 1988 – January 1990	335
Epilogue	405
Chronology	417
Acknowledgements	423
Notes	427
Bibliography	457
Photo Credits	471
Index	473

To my grandfather Joseph Réra (1922 – 1974),
who, in the face of brutality, had the courage to say no.

In memory of Ennio Morricone (1928 – 2020).
My need to write this book arose from the
profoundly moving experience of listening to
his music for *Casualties of War*.

"And let me speak to th' yet unknowing world
How these things came about."
Shakespeare, *Hamlet*, Act V, Scene II

Introduction

A book inspired by an image: Brian De Palma, his eyes flooded with tears, unable to continue his exchange with Bernard Benoliel about his nineteenth feature film, *Casualties of War*, released in 1989. This intense moment took place during De Palma's June 2018 visit to the Cinémathèque française in Paris. It was one of the few times – to my knowledge, the *only* time – when De Palma, known for being a filmmaker reluctant to show his emotions, cracked in public.[1] It is no coincidence that this emotional earthquake took place following a screening of *Casualties of War*, a film that occupies a special place in De Palma's filmmaking career. A few years earlier, he had confided to Laurent Vachaud and Samuel Blumenfeld, in an essential book of interviews: "I'm especially fond of it, for all sorts of personal reasons. I find the story – which I wanted to tell for many years – very moving, and was overjoyed when I finally managed to convince a studio to finance it. I think the acting is great, even though it's a film I still have a hard time watching because it's so disturbing. It's one of the most horrific stories you can imagine."[2]

Yet *Casualties of War* is not generally considered to be one of the highlights of De Palma's filmography, which includes *Phantom of the Paradise*, *Carrie*, *Blow Out*, *Scarface*, *Carlito's Way* and *Mission: Impossible*. Among the reasons for this underestimation, the most obvious is the subject matter of the film. It is, as De Palma says, a profoundly disturbing work that puts the viewer very much to the test. Based on a real event that occurred during the Vietnam War in 1966, *Casualties of War* recounts the abduction, rape and murder of a young peasant girl named Oanh (played by Thuy Thu Le) by a patrol of American soldiers led by Sergeant Tony Meserve (Sean Penn). Of the five soldiers, only one – Private First Class Sven Eriksson (Michael J. Fox) – refuses to take part in the crime. Wracked by guilt at not having intervened, Eriksson, after denouncing his comrades, is faced with not only their threats but also the dismissive attitudes of his superiors, who downplay the gravity of the incident. The subsequent investigation and discovery of the body of the young Vietnamese woman leads to the trial of the four soldiers in military court, ending with their conviction and sentencing. Eriksson must grapple with the persistent dread that his former comrades, upon completing their sentences, may seek retribution.

Although the broad subject matter of *Casualties of War* was one De Palma revisited years later with his 2007 feature *Redacted*, his 1989 Vietnam drama isn't often immediately identified as being a quintessential De Palma film. While it contains some of his signature motifs (slow motion, split diopter effects, high and low-angle shots), such visual elements are more subdued here, as if he were aiming to simplify his mise-en-scène and place it in the service of a subject that, because of its seriousness, cannot be reduced to an exercise in style, however virtuosic. Perhaps this explains why, with a few exceptions, *Casualties of War* has received less attention than De Palma's other films.[3]

Nevertheless, one might expect the film to take its rightful place in books devoted to cinematic representations of the Vietnam War. Not so. *Casualties of War* is more often than not overshadowed by other feature films in the pantheon of the best-known – and most discussed – works on the subject: Michael Cimino's *The Deer Hunter* (1978), Francis Coppola's *Apocalypse Now* (1979), Oliver Stone's *Platoon* (1986) and Stanley Kubrick's *Full Metal Jacket* (1987).[4] It has also been attacked by historians and theorists, whose criticisms are reminiscent of those the film received on its release in American cinemas.[5] In France, despite the esteem in which some authors hold *Casualties of War*, the film remains generally undervalued. Its contextualization is often imprecise and marred by factual errors, hindering a true appreciation of its distinctiveness.[6]

Methods of writing history:
The archive and the dictaphone

As readers may have already gathered, the writing of this book was initially driven by a fervent desire to illuminate an exceptional film, one largely overlooked by historians but which, on a personal level, has haunted me since my adolescence. Over time, however, this project has evolved, expanding beyond De Palma's film. *Casualties of War* is an adaptation of an investigation by American journalist Daniel Lang, first published in 1969 as an article and then a book.[7] Lang's work, extensively covered by the media and translated into several languages, inspired two independent films in the early 1970s: *o.k.* (1970) by German filmmaker Michael Verhoeven and *The Visitors* (1972) by Elia Kazan in the United States. In Hollywood, though, all attempts to adapt the story for both cinema and television failed, until De Palma – who described Lang's book as a "story that already had 'screenplay' written all over it"[8] – made his film.

Although Kazan's film has been written about, the same cannot be said of Verhoeven's, which was unseen for decades and still unavailable in France when I wrote the initial version of this book.[9] As for those failed attempts, the information I was able to glean was limited to a handful of (generally secondhand) comments I read or heard about here and there, suggesting that filmmakers Jack Clayton and John Schlesinger had at one time been approached to direct an adaptation. I didn't have much more information than that, and there was nothing to indicate that these details – mentioned in passing by Pauline Kael[10] – were anything more than rumor. Verification was necessary, but at the beginning of my research the clues I had collected together were scant.

Little by little, the architecture of a book took shape in my mind. Without fully knowing what final form it might have, I thought it wise to devote an opening chapter to all the projects (completed or abandoned) linked to *Casualties of War* throughout the 1970s, before tracing the history of De Palma's film from the writing of its screenplay to its release in American and French cinemas.

Such an approach raises a preliminary methodological question: how to trace the history of a production more than thirty years after the fact? Unlike Julie Salamon or Jacques

Mandelbaum, who tracked a specific film project from its origins to completion,[11] I wasn't witness to the film being made, so my approach necessarily differs from the usual journalistic investigation.[12] The initial challenge was to identify the various available sources and reconstruct the making of *Casualties of War*. I proceeded by elimination, which was less a conscious calculation than one imposed by certain constraints. A first disappointment: Brian De Palma was unable to give me access to paperwork apparently in his possession, stating that "he was in the process of creating an archive" and, consequently, "all materials relevant to *Casualties of War* [were] unavailable at this time."[13] A subsequent disappointment: the similar request I made (on the suggestion of producer Art Linson) to Columbia Pictures, now a subsidiary of Sony Pictures, also ended with a refusal. By way of explanation, one of the company's executive directors mentioned "commercial and legal reasons,"[14] without deigning to provide further details.

Some production archives, notably the annotated shooting script and daily call sheets (which contain details of that day's shooting, including which actors are required for what shots), were therefore inaccessible, thus complicating my task, especially when trying to reconstruct the day-to-day chronology of filming. Hoping that there must be relevant material scattered here and there, in both Asia and the United States, perhaps in boxes or on dusty shelves in public or private archives, I was determined not to give up. In the end, *Casualties of War*'s screenwriter David Rabe sent me two versions of his screenplay and I discovered other drafts. I was also able to obtain documents that shed significant light on the production of De Palma's film, along with numerous unpublished on-set photographs. Fortunately, one of *Casualties of War*'s crew members still had his call sheets, which meant I was able to reconstruct the shooting schedule.

This work could not have been accomplished without having recorded a number of new interviews. Perhaps more than any other book I have written, it is a story of encounters that buoyed and, in fact, profoundly transformed me. By the time I finished writing, it was as if I had undergone a long initiatory journey – though not without pitfalls.

My correspondence with Rabe, between August 2018 and June 2020, offered stimulating leads from the start and was enriched by a fascinating discussion with Art Linson. De Palma, on the other hand, remained silent after our initial exchange, despite my repeated attempts to schedule a meeting. As the weeks passed, my doubts grew about his willingness to engage with me, and my hopes of a meeting dwindled. The portrait Blumenfeld and Vachaud paint of him in the preface to the first edition of their interview book, of an elusive and taciturn man, is difficult to forget. Blumenfeld and Vachaud deployed great efforts of imagination to convince De Palma to agree to participate, including pretending to be a Swiss admirer disappointed that there were no interview books with him.[15]

In the end, I needn't have gone to such great lengths, as the united efforts of Rabe and Linson ultimately swayed De Palma, who reached out to me. His terse message was a mere two sentences: "I'm coming to Paris in two weeks. I'll email you when I get there and set up a meeting."[16] Eighteen days later, the date, time and place of the meeting were confirmed.

But euphoria quickly gave way to a form of perplexity. I felt ready to put my numerous questions to De Palma, but what could I hope to add to interviews conducted by Blumenfeld and Vachaud, those filmed by Laurent Bouzereau (for the documentary on the DVD of *Casualties of War*), conversations recorded by Noah Baumbach and Jake Paltrow for their 2015 documentary, and the meeting with Bernard Benoliel at the Cinémathèque? In each, De Palma basically said the same things and recounted the same anecdotes. I hoped my questions might push him to say something new. They focused mostly on details, since I knew all too well that broad questions often yield "meager responses."[17] I also suspected that some thirty years after the fact, there would likely be gaps in De Palma's memory.

At the end of my short hour spent with him, disappointment prevailed. Many of De Palma's responses were limited to one or two sentences, punctuated by long questioning silences. Any material I gathered that day was barely usable, especially as our discussion had taken place in the lobby of a hotel with frequent comings and goings, where music occasionally drowned out his responses altogether. As I left,

I asked De Palma if he would be willing to answer more questions at a later date, over the phone, a request he agreed to with a simple nod. But after a brief exchange of emails in the days following the interview, communication was broken off for a long period of time.

No doubt De Palma felt he had said all that was necessary. His silence was, in itself, a response, and I took it as such. At the very least, our meeting had the merit of reinforcing my growing certainty, over the previous months, that I couldn't rely solely on De Palma's words. Along with the film's producer, he was the only person involved from start to finish, so that his testimony is obviously essential for anyone wishing to understand the creative process behind *Casualties of War*. And yet for someone like myself, hoping to record as many details as possible about the making of a film, a focus on the director has the tendency to overwhelm the voices of other crew members, numerous and important as they are. My discussions with Rabe and Linson convinced me of the benefits of cross-referencing testimonies, and at the end of my interview with De Palma I asked him for the contact details of Eric Schwab and Bill Pankow, two of his most loyal lieutenants. He handed me his phone and I simply copied down their numbers and emails. Contact was made the next day. Second unit director Schwab, in particular, showed unwavering availability, even taking time between takes, on the set of *Top Gun: Maverick*, to speak with me from the Californian desert.

I quickly realized that my project would make sense only if my research was as broad as possible. Without aiming for completeness – which is ultimately illusory – I decided I would embark on a quest to pull together the recollections of *Casualties of War*'s crew, and, in doing so, assemble a new archive.[18] In total, including the filmmaker, producer and screenwriter, I interviewed thirty-three people. I spoke with the production manager (Fred Caruso), the production coordinator (Sallie Beechinor), the director of photography (Stephen H. Burum), the Steadicam operator (Larry McConkey), the on-set photographer (Roland Neveu), the second unit director (Eric Schwab), two assistant directors (Brian W. Cook, Carl Goldstein), the production designer (Wolf Kroeger), the chief makeup artist (Paul Engelen), De Palma's personal assistant (Monica Goldstein[19]), the props master (Mickey Pugh), a special effects technician (Yves De Bono), a historical advisor (Deborah Ricketts), two military advisors (Mike Stokey and Art Smith), a costume designer and Thai stand-in (Pasiree Panya), a Thai assistant (Charlie Sungkawess), seven actors (Sean Penn, Don Harvey, John C. Reilly, John Leguizamo, Thuy Thu Le, Erik King, Holt McCallany, Dale Dye), the San Francisco extras casting director (Nancy Hayes), the editor (Bill Pankow), the head of the sound department (Maurice Schell) and one of the sound designers (Marko A. Costanzo).

I opted for semi-structured interviews, most of which took place by phone, though videoconferencing applications were also employed. Whenever possible I met with my interviewees in person. In a few cases, only written correspondence was exchanged. Our discussions, which ranged from half an hour to over two and a half hours, often led to additional exchanges via email or phone so I could clarify details or ask new questions. I transcribed each conversation in its entirety and sent the result to the interviewee for review. I extracted the essence of these conversations, which are spread throughout the second half of this book. Contacting several of these individuals meant trading the methods of an art historian for those of a detective, and sometimes – as was the case with Sean Penn – great patience was needed.

In late January 2019, Penn's assistant, Sato Masuzawa, informed me that he had agreed to answer my questions, provided he had a right to review the manuscript before publication. After confirming his conditions, a phone appointment was set, which Penn – busy with preparations for his film *Flag Day*, in Winnipeg, Canada – canceled with only two hours' notice. Unable to schedule a new date for a phone conversation, I suggested to Masuzawa that I send a series of questions via email, which she agreed to. Weeks passed and I received no response. In early October, I opted for a new strategy of sending a shortened version of my questions, half the length, in the hope of convincing Penn to spend an hour or two on them. After yet another follow-up in February 2020, Masuzawa assured me that Penn promised to "get to it within the week," then asked for an additional few days. The health crisis related to the Covid-19 epidemic seemed to deliver the final blow to my hope. Once again, my messages went unanswered. In early April, I learned that Penn was assisting at a drive-through Covid testing center in Los Angeles. I was about to give up on his participation when, in early June, I sent – out of obligation and, in truth, without much hope – one last message to Masuzawa. Three minutes later she replied that she was, at that very moment, sitting beside Penn, and they were working together on my questions. Penn's contribution reached me the following day.

A few witnesses are still missing, including Ennio Morricone. I contacted the composer through Alessandro De Rosa, who informed me that, despite his advanced age, he was currently on tour. Intrigued by my book project, De Rosa, a composer himself, suggested that he put my questions directly to the maestro upon his return to Rome. It seemed the best approach since I don't speak Italian and Morricone didn't speak English. De Rosa seemed to be the ideal intermediary because, in addition to his expertise, he had earned Morricone's trust and had published a masterful book of interviews with him.[20] After four months of waiting, De Rosa wrote to me that Morricone, inundated with requests, ultimately did not wish to participate in my project.

I should also note here the reason for the absence in this book of one of *Casualties of War*'s lead actors: Michael J. Fox. After I wrote to his agents and sent a letter to his foundation, The Michael J. Fox Foundation for Parkinson's Research, a spokesperson responded briefly, promising to speak to him only if Sean Penn had already granted me an interview. Was this Fox's demand or (as I suspected) an arbitrary request from his representative who was reluctant to have the actor waste time relaying to an interviewer tales from decades ago? As time passed, I feared that Penn's delayed responses might jeopardize my potential meeting with Fox. I decided, after two months, to write again to his spokesperson and update her on the progress of my efforts, but she claimed not to know who I was or what I was asking about. Refreshing her memory accomplished little, and she again insisted that only a response from Penn could resolve the situation. When that response finally arrived in early June 2020, I hurried to contact her again – but in vain. Her "conditions" were actually just an excuse, perhaps related to the actor's health. And so I would also have to do without Michael J. Fox as well.

I set out to compile all the testimonies from Morricone and Fox about the film, including their autobiographies and (at least for Fox) interviews given to the press at the time of the film's release. The significant number of articles found in the National Library of France and through online American databases, along with filmed interviews, enriched a pool of anecdotes from which I could draw.

The ability to augment present-day memories – distant and perhaps imprecise – with those gathered soon after filming, and so presumably more trustworthy, offers a number of advantages, not least that of testing the reliability of newer testimonies. As we all know, "Not all witnesses are sincere, nor is their memory always faithful, so much so that their testimony should not be accepted unchecked."[21] Through my exchanges with interviewees, I was able to identify two main witness profiles. First, there was the Cautious Witness, economical with words, always aware of their own limitations, careful not to rush too quickly into the fog of memory. These witnesses openly confessed their inability to answer when my questions were too specific and generally warned me at the beginning of the interview, "Don't forget that the events we are going to discuss took place *thirty years ago.*" The second witness type, whom I will call the Reckless Witness, was much more talkative and able to bring the past vividly to life. Images of the film's production flashed before my eyes as they were speaking. And yet, recreating the past doesn't always equate to absolute truth. As Marc Bloch puts it, "We only pay attention to things that strike us. Almost all of us move around half-blind and half-deaf in an external world that we only see and hear through a kind of fog."[22] It is certainly true that a witness, however confident, might conceal a tendency to embellish facts, deliberately omit negative aspects, or even fabricate details.

However, "it is up to the historian to conduct panoramic research, to cross viewpoints, to critically doubt, to distance oneself, and to objectify."[23] As part of my attempt at comprehensiveness, I took care to verify oral sources by cross-referencing them with textual and photographic ones. More than just a methodological positioning, this process was an important antidote to the emotion that sometimes overwhelmed me and risked skewing my reading of the past.

Gathering oral testimony implies a certain empathy with the individual being interviewed, and presupposes a genuine ethical commitment to record and document with complete honesty. At the same time, I had to ensure that emotion – an essential driver in conducting research – did not diminish my critical distance. Finding the balance, akin to walking a tightrope, involved constant adjustments and an inner struggle not to succumb to the temptation of glorification. I was careful to "sterilize the analytical instruments,"[24] as Carlo Ginzburg so aptly recommends, by maintaining a distance from my sources – not to empty them of all emotion but to prevent emotion from diluting their rough edges, which might lead to an uncontested historical narrative. I leave it to the reader to judge, but I believe that this concern allowed me to avoid the trap of hagiography.

Bifurcations

While conducting the various steps I have outlined here, I simultaneously undertook a series of investigations into Verhoeven's *o.k.* and the various unsuccessful attempts to film Lang's story. Once again, my method led me to combine oral interviews with archival research. It took a year for me to finally get my hands on a copy of Verhoeven's film, after which I interviewed him and the film's producer, Rob Houwer.

In my search for information about Daniel Lang, who passed away in 1981, I made contact with one of his daughters, Cecily. Our frequent correspondence, between May 2019 and June 2020, led to a radical shift in my work. De Palma, who until then had been the central figure in my book, around whom all others revolved, gave way to Lang, who besides being the author of the text that served as the basis for Rabe's screenplay, was for twelve years the key figure through whom all adaptation projects passed. This redistribution of roles, as summarized in this book, was gradual and contingent upon the vagaries of research. The recollections of Cecily Lang, and later those of her two older sisters, Frances and Helen, proved immensely helpful, but I took a giant step forward when I consulted their father's archives at the Howard Gotlieb Archival Research Center at Boston University, which contains a remarkable quantity of documentation which, wherever possible, was supplemented with interviews with people who had known Daniel Lang.

As is often the case, research is also a matter of fortunate coincidences. A few weeks earlier, while perusing the only monograph dedicated to Jack Clayton,[25] I noted details about his numerous unfinished projects, including *Casualties of War*. I wrote to the author of that book, Neil Sinyard, who had read the original screenplay, hoping he could point me to where I might find a copy. Sinyard responded that it was part of Clayton's archives, housed at the British Film Institute in London. Imagine my surprise when I discovered that in addition to the screenplay, the BFI archive contains hundreds of pages of material related to *Casualties of War*. I spent two days at the BFI dissecting production notes, letters, telegrams and manuscripts annotated by Clayton and his collaborators, most of which didn't overlap with the Lang collection in Boston. This endeavor sometimes required me to play the role of a graphologist, attempting to identify unsigned documents or those with barely legible signatures.

Besides these two primary sources in Boston and London, I mobilized a third and final, equally essential source: the military archives that had served as the basis for Lang's article. This marked the beginning of a long and stimulating process of reshaping and untangling the web of notes I had accumulated during my research. This book is the result. Its diptych structure, I believe, aptly reflects the metamorphosis of my initial project, which evolved from a book about De Palma's *Casualties of War* into a book about Lang's *Casualties of War* and its various adaptations – realized or unrealized – by filmmakers and screenwriters, leading up to De Palma's final work.

The first section covers a period from 1966, the date of the actual historical event, to 1981, the year of Lang's death and his last adaptation project. The first chapter, approached exclusively from a historical perspective, dissects the micro-events that served as the starting point for Lang's text, as well as the investigative work (a cross between oral interviews and archival research) he conducted, leading to the publi-cation of his text in *The New Yorker* and its international reception. The second chapter focuses on the first two films inspired by Lang's work: Verhoeven's *o.k.* and Kazan's *The Visitors*. The third chapter lifts the veil on the various adaptation projects that succeeded each other in Hollywood from the late 1960s to the early 1980s, and the reasons for their failure.

The second part of the book explores the making of De Palma's film. It is divided into four chapters, which deal successively with the screenplay written by Rabe (from May 1987 onwards), the pre-production of the feature film (from August 1987 to March 1988), its filming (from April to July 1988), and finally post-production (from August 1988 to August 1989), culminating in its controversial reception. This second part employs several methods drawn from the historian's toolkit, methods already used in the first half of the book: oral history, micro-history, prosopography. It shifts from an overarching view of the film's preparation and shooting, down to individual destinies, the "parallel lives"[26] of the crew members, from the most illustrious to the most anonymous.

The book aims to shed light on political history through the lens of representation. Its purpose is to demonstrate how the Vietnam War heavily influenced the creation and reception of certain artistic works, as much as to understand what these works – at the confluence of journalism and cinema – tell us about that military conflict and, more broadly, about modern barbarism, male dominance, and violence against women. It also seeks to illuminate, using the unique case of *Casualties of War*, the operations of the major American film studios at a pivotal moment in their history, from the emergence of New Hollywood to the beginnings of a new technological era that signaled, by the late 1980s, the end of a paradigm. Finally, the book aims to question the creative act, its independence, from both a historical and formalist perspective, while avoiding perpetuation of the "myth" or "legend" of the artist.[27] As this chronicle progresses, it becomes evident that the success of *Casualties of War* owes less to the apparent genius of an individual (Brian De Palma, to whom one might readily attribute the traits of a demiurge) than to the conjunction of various factors, some of them circumstantial, which made possible, at the twilight of the 1980s, the realization of a film deemed impossible, even undesirable, at the dawn of the 1970s.

Prologue

Paris. Friday, March 22, 2019, 9:50 a.m.

I have just arrived at the hotel in the 6th arrondissement where Brian De Palma has arranged to meet me. I'm a little early, so I settle down in the small lounge next to the entrance, check my tape recorder, and briefly review the outline of questions I have for him.

10:02 a.m. De Palma, punctual, appears in the lobby. With drawn features and a stooped gait, he sizes me up with his piercing gaze, extends a firm hand, and, without a word, gestures for me to sit. While I explain my approach and the research I've been doing for nearly a year, he listens attentively, arms crossed, occasionally nodding in agreement. I talk about his masterclass at the Cinémathèque française and about the emotion that overwhelmed him at the mention of *Casualties of War*. I venture an initial question.

"Is it a film you sometimes revisit?"

"No. It's a very difficult film to watch. It's too emotional, which is why it wasn't a success. I mean commercially. It's just unbearable to watch."

When I steer the conversation toward his early films, those heavily marked by the specter of the Vietnam War, I sense that De Palma feels more comfortable. He speaks of his personal experiences, his fear of being drafted, the "era of pointless wars" he grew up in, his initial reaction to reading Daniel Lang's text in *The New Yorker*.

"By the way," says De Palma, absentmindedly stroking his beard, "this morning while preparing for this interview I read on the internet that someone has found the archives of the trials. Are you aware of this?"

"No."

"Well, I don't know if it's true or not, but the trial transcripts completely contradict what is reported in

Casualties of War. The guy who unearthed the archives claims there was never a kidnapping and that the girl was never taken into the mountains. A prostitute supposedly came to the camp, the four soldiers raped her, then dumped her body outside the camp, and the Eriksson character turned the guys in. Are we supposed to believe all that? This is what is in the army archives. And my question is: why should we believe what the army tells us?"

"I find it hard to believe."

"Check it out for yourself."

"Don't forget that *Casualties of War* is, above all, a movie," a retired US Army officer told me off the record a few weeks later, assuring me that he had tried to locate the trial archives, but in vain. "JAG [Judge Advocate General's Corps] officers looked for them.[1] They found similar cases for the Second World War, but nothing for Vietnam."

"Nothing." That word echoed in my mind for a long time, reminding me that the "age of witness" is also the "age of denial."[2] I had encountered such talk in my previous work, and found myself grappling once again with a skepticism that, while it sometimes takes on the appearance of "intentional falsehood," more often resembles a form of "involuntary erasure."[3]

I never dug up the internet article that De Palma had mentioned, though to be honest I didn't search very hard. What was the use of venturing into the depths of the dark web when you already knew the traps it contained? I did, however, become convinced of the importance of obtaining the trial archives that Daniel Lang himself had consulted as part of his investigation – not because I ever doubted the accuracy of his reporting in *Casualties of War*, but rather to shed light on the methods of a journalist whom, at that point, I knew very little about. Certainly, I had read *Casualties of War*, but I wanted to understand Lang's motivations for writing it.

I had no difficulty finding details of the trials, in no small part because of the work of Frederic L. Borch on judge advocates in Vietnam. In two paragraphs, Borch deals with the case as reported by Lang.[4] If, for reasons I will explain later, Lang chose to protect the identity of the various protagonists by using pseudonyms, Borch reveals their real names[5] and mentions the file numbers relating to their trials in the military archives. With this information in hand, I initiated a procedure to access the trial minutes, a process made possible by the Freedom of Information Act (FOIA).[6] Less than a fortnight later, a letter from the director of the U.S. Army Crime Records Center in Quantico informed me that the transcripts of said trials were not in their possession, specifying that my request had been transferred to the Clerk of Court's office attached to the legal department of the U.S. Army at Fort Belvoir, Virginia. Barely eight days later, I received a definitive negative response: no trace of files relating to the trials had been found. The letter specified, however, that all cases dealt with between 1917 and 1976 had been transferred to the National Archives in St. Louis after their declassification. I rushed to contact archivists in St. Louis, who went to work searching for the files.

A month and a half later, I received an email. The trial transcripts had been located.[7] It took an additional month for me to receive a complete copy. In the meantime, Lang's daughters informed me that almost the entirety of their father's archives had been deposited in the Howard Gotlieb Archival Research Center. Exploring the collection, coupled with reading approximately three thousand pages of military archives,[8] would give me a close-up view of Lang's work and help me better understand the making of *Casualties of War*.

Part 1

From Headlines to the Screen

A Test of Conscience
1966 – 69

My intention with this book is not to offer a revised or improved version of the investigations undertaken more than five decades ago by Daniel Lang, but to provide the reader with a concise overview of the archives he worked through, and so shed light on the choices that guided his writing process. I have opted for a linear, chronological narrative of events by drawing on intersecting sources from various trials. My hope is that this chapter, presented in the manner of a historical-judicial chronicle, will help readers better understand the approach Lang took when *Casualties of War* was still just an idea, when he was a journalist confronted with a bewildering quantity of documentary material, the exploration of which raises significant ethical and methodological questions.

The planning of the crime (November 17, 1966)

Sergeant David Edward Gervase assembles four soldiers who, under his command, become part of a "pony patrol"[1] scheduled to depart at 6 a.m. the following morning. Present are four Privates First Class (PFC): Steven Cabot Thomas, Robert Marshall Storeby, and cousins Joseph "Joe" Charles Garcia and Cipriano "Chip" Schulz Garcia. The protagonists have diverse backgrounds.

Born on August 27, 1945 in Brooklyn, New York, Steven Thomas, a short, muscular soldier of above-average intelligence, was the first of the five men to set foot in Vietnam. The eldest of seven children, Thomas was raised in a challenging environment. He was fifteen when his father was forcibly removed from the family home due to mistreatment of his wife and children, after which Thomas was forced to rely on public assistance. Little is known of the boy's adolescence. After dropping out of high school during his senior year, he took on multiple odd jobs to assist his mother before enlisting in the army on January 28, 1965 for three years.

At Fort Dix in New Jersey, where he underwent training, Thomas stood out for his dedication and good conduct, and was among the top ten in his class. Following advanced individual training at Fort Jackson, South Carolina and airborne training at Fort Benning, Georgia, Thomas arrived in Vietnam on August 20, 1965 with initial units of the 1st Cavalry Division. He participated in several challenging operations and was cited for the Bronze Star after stepping in at short notice to replace his superior, who had died in combat during a night ambush.

There are, however, troubling aspects to Thomas' personality. After deserting for about fifteen days and receiving his first court-martial on March 23, 1966, he was demoted to the rank of private second class.[2] On May 12, he was tried again, this time for falling asleep on guard duty. The result was six months of hard labor, another salary deduction, and demotion to the rank of private. His exemplary conduct in the months that followed quickly earned him back his rank of private second class.[3]

David Gervase arrived in Vietnam a few months after Thomas. Born on April 23, 1946 in Silver Creek, New York, Gervase was the eldest of three children. He grew up in the small town of Angola, near Lake Erie. While completing his final year of high school, frequent disputes between his parents resulted in his father leaving, and young David was forced to break off his education and financially support his mother, during which time he fell into delinquency. Documents in his trial records report no fewer than three offenses committed between 1960 and 1961. He was arrested for burglary, trespassing on private property, and illegal possession of a BB gun. For these last two incidents he received suspended prison sentences of three and six months.[4]

At the age of seventeen, Gervase found work in a cannery, which he abandoned after enlisting in the army on January 31, 1964. He served in Alaska for eleven months and was picked to take part in the parade in honor of President Johnson's inauguration in January 1965. He then volunteered for Vietnam, where he arrived on March 19, 1966. Gervase swiftly ascended the ranks, attaining the title of sergeant, and garnered a reputation as one who never faltered in completing his assigned missions. But he also displayed a certain cruelty toward the Vietnamese. "He seemed to enjoy shooting and killing people," stated one member of his unit.[5] A soldier named Prince confided that he "treated prisoners like dirt,"[6] noting that Gervase "eliminated" those he suspected of being North Vietnamese communists, telling them to run and then coldly shooting them in the back, claiming they had tried to escape.[7]

The Garcia cousins, on the other hand, were well liked by their comrades. Cipriano (nicknamed Chip), born on September 17, 1945 in San Antonio, Texas, grew up on a farm with three brothers and a sister, all older than him. Their parents evidently died in the early 1960s. Chip married at seventeen and his wife gave birth to a son, but three months later the couple divorced. A year later, on April 7, 1966, he volunteered for deployment. Chip underwent training at Fort Polk in Louisiana and arrived in Vietnam on September 28, 1966 as part of Company C (2nd Battalion, 8th Cavalry, 1st Air Cavalry Division). He was regarded by some of his officers as one of the best soldiers in his regiment.[8]

Chip's cousin Joe was born on March 12, 1947 in Albuquerque, New Mexico. He was raised by his grandparents and at the age of nine or ten went to live with his mother and stepfather. After his high school graduation, Joe worked as a lab technician. He married and had a child before volunteering for Vietnam. Following his training at Fort Bliss in Texas, then Fort Polk, he arrived in Vietnam on September 29, 1966 as part of the same company as his cousin. It wasn't long before Joe was awarded numerous medals for bravery. People liked his sense of humor, and he had a reputation for boosting troop morale when it was at its lowest.[9]

The trial records contain the fewest details about the fifth and final protagonist, Robert Storeby. Raised on a farm in Minnesota, Storeby arrived in Vietnam around October 1966, making him, in the eyes of his comrades, the least experienced of the group. Lieutenant Chester A. Collins suggested that Storeby be part of the mission under Gervase's command because it was necessary to assess his abilities, particularly his adaptability within a reconnaissance patrol.

On the evening of November 17, 1966, Sergeant Gervase gathers his men[10] to prepare for operations the following day. He unfurls a map and indicates the path they will be taking to reach Hill 192, near Bong Son. Their objective: to identify the presence of potential communist hideouts. Their orders are not to intervene under any circumstances. This is *not* a search-and-destroy mission[11] – it is an especially perilous reconnaissance mission. At the end of the briefing, Gervase informs the soldiers that they will be leaving an hour earlier so they can find a girl and bring her along with them.[12] His plan, to which Thomas immediately and enthusiastically agrees, involves kidnapping, assaulting and killing the victim before their return to base.[13] Accustomed to dubious jokes about Vietnamese women, the Garcia cousins laugh. Storeby shows no immediate reaction but is disturbed by what he has heard, and that evening mentions Gervase's plan to Private First Class Randy Pearson, who describes it as nothing more than tasteless fun. "He didn't think even Sergeant Gervase was dumb enough to pull something like this," Storeby later stated at his trial. "So I just let it go as a joke."[14]

The abduction and rape of Phan Thi Mao (November 18, 1966)

Early in the morning of November 18, the patrol departs the base between 4:30 and 5 a.m. While on their way to Hill 192, the soldiers are ordered by Gervase to turn toward the hamlet of Cat Tuong, about a quarter of a mile off the trail they are supposed to be following.[15] Once they arrive in the village, Storeby and Chip are tasked with standing guard and looking after the soldiers' gear while Gervase, Thomas and Joe inspect the houses in search of a girl ("They were trying to find a pretty one," Storeby testified during Gervase's trial[16]). They come back empty-handed.

Chip then points out a bamboo hut where a few days earlier he remembers seeing a girl who might be suitable. While Storeby and the Garcia cousins secure the area, Gervase and Thomas, carrying flashlights, enter the hut. Inside, they find Phan Thi Mao, in her twenties, her younger sister Phan Thi Loc, their mother and several children. Their attention is immediately focused on the older girl. Slim and pretty, she is about five foot three, dressed in black, wearing earrings and a ring. As Chip later tells it, she also has a gold tooth. After tying her up, Gervase and Thomas quickly leave with Mao and the rest of the patrol. The girl's desperate mother catches up to them as they depart the village and hands her daughter a scarf, which Thomas promptly uses to gag her.

The patrol continues on its way and begins the ascent of Hill 192. At the halfway point, the soldiers untie Mao and force her to carry Joe's gear (aside from his weapons, he is also carrying the radio). Around 8 a.m., the group stops to rest and eat. It is during this break that Chip thinks he spots an enemy soldier hidden in the vegetation, and begins shooting. It quickly becomes clear that the supposed communist is actually a water buffalo. The soldiers explore the surroundings and at around 9.30 a.m. discover an abandoned hut, its floor littered with metal, empty cans and other debris. Deciding to make it their headquarters, Gervase orders Chip and Storeby to clean up the place and watch the prisoner while the others scout the area. When she sees the soldiers tidying up, Mao instinctively begins helping, not realizing she is aiding in the preparation of her own torture chamber.

Gervase, Thomas and Joe return an hour later. After a snack, a pumped-up Gervase announces, "It's time now for some fun!"[17] He grabs Mao and heads into the hut. The other members of the patrol stay outside, but for a period estimated to be fifteen to thirty minutes they hear the victim's screams. Storeby stands near the entrance to the small bamboo construction, keeping watch, and notices that Gervase throws a prophylactic through a hole in the wall of the hut.[18] Looking satisfied, Gervase, after exiting the hut, tells his men, "It was real good. It was tight. She was pretty clean."[19] "Who's next?" he asks, looking around at the other four. Thomas points to Chip, who goes into the hut, at which point Mao's cries and sobs start up again. Thomas seems barely able to contain his impatience, and when his turn finally comes and he goes into the hut, Mao's shrieks and moans once again break the jungle silence. He emerges declaring triumphantly, "That's the best I've had in a long time,"[20] proudly explaining that he held a knife to Mao's throat while raping her.[21] Joe is the last to enter the hut. For the fourth time, Mao screams in pain. Storeby is the only one who refuses to participate, despite encouragement, then threats, from his comrades.

After the gang rape, Gervase gathers his men inside the hut to share some food. Storeby listens to them talking about Mao and their sexual exploits of the day, comparing them to those of previous conquests. The victim is present, but she doesn't grasp the nature of the exchanges. Now dressed, there is heavy bleeding around her crotch.[22] Instead of being concerned, Gervase and Thomas joke about it, suggesting that she was probably pregnant and must have had a miscarriage.[23] At the end of the conversation, Gervase takes Mao's earrings[24] as a souvenir, and Chip eagerly mentions that he would like to keep her gold tooth once they are done with her. Of Thomas, Storeby recounted at the trial: "He told me that I'd have intercourse with the girl before the five days were up, that on the fifth day I'd have to kill the girl and use a knife, otherwise they'd probably have to call me in as a friendly casualty."[25] Although he takes these threats seriously, Storeby refuses to yield to intimidation.

That afternoon, Gervase takes Storeby and the Garcia cousins on another reconnaissance mission on the hill. Thomas is tasked with guarding Mao in the hut. After a while, Storeby and Chip return to retrieve some smoke grenades. Bored and hoping to participate in the military operations, Thomas orders Storeby to take his place. Storeby, seeing an opportunity to perhaps save Mao, agrees. He asks Thomas to exchange weapons, handing him an M-79 grenade launcher and taking hold of an M-16 assault rifle, a weapon he is more comfortable with.[26] Once the men are gone, Storeby gives Mao some food, as she has eaten nothing since her abduction. Storeby must make a decision: escape with Mao through the mountains or stay put and try, as best he can, to protect her. He hesitates. What if his comrades pursue and catch him? Will they carry out Thomas' threats? And if somehow he does manage to escape, won't he be risking a court-martial for insubordination and desertion? If he abandons the weapons, might they fall into the hands of the enemy, thereby endangering the lives of his comrades? Storeby deliberates as minutes and hours slip away. It is nearly dusk when the four soldiers return to the hut, and by now too late for Storeby to act.

The murder of Phan Thi Mao (November 19, 1966)

Through the night of November 18, Mao suffers from frequent coughing fits. Thomas, fearing she might disclose their position to the enemy, leads her outside the hut with the intention of killing her. Gervase pushes back, saying he wants to have sex with her the following day.

In the morning, after breakfast, Gervase sends Storeby and the Garcia cousins to fetch water from a stream. When they return, Gervase coldly announces his decision to execute Mao. "The girl is still bleeding and she's no further use to me,"[27] he explains, before ordering Storeby to kill the prisoner. Storeby refuses, as do the Garcia cousins. Thomas volunteers to execute her and discusses with Gervase how best to get the job done. They agree that they will both stab Mao, one from the front, the other from behind.

At 8:30 a.m., Gervase and his men leave the hut and move toward a hill about a thousand feet higher up, which gives them an open view of the valley. They observe the landscape through binoculars. At one point, Chip spots a group of enemy forces below, at a riverbed. Busy making radio calls to set up an ambush, Gervase and the patrol momentarily forget about Mao. In order not to lose track of the North Vietnamese, Gervase, Thomas and Joe move along the ridge, leaving some of their equipment, as well as the prisoner, with Chip and Storeby. After a few minutes, Joe hurries back, ordering them to take the woman and their belongings and join Gervase, who is worried that the helicopters called in for reinforcement will notice her presence.

As soon as they arrive, Thomas grabs his knife[28] and informs Gervase of his intention to kill Mao. The sergeant approves. Storeby, about thirty feet away, is unable to see exactly what is happening, but hears Thomas stabbing Mao – who nonetheless manages to escape. "Well, that sonofabitch," said Thomas. "I stabbed her more than twice!"[29] Ordered by Gervase to shoot at her, Storeby fires in the opposite direction to create a diversion. Thomas then grabs his rifle and runs after Mao. Chip, who has descended fifty feet with Storeby, also fires several times, but it is Thomas, after spotting Mao, who reaches her and finishes her off with two close-range shots to the head.[30] From afar, he shouts to his comrades that he "got her" and asks Chip if he still wants the gold tooth. Doubts linger about the latter's response.

Gervase gives himself an alibi by putting in a radio call to Lieutenant Douglas Duckett, who in the absence of Captain Spigelmire is leading military operations. Gervase informs Duckett that while fighting the North Vietnamese, his men have spotted a woman on the hill, implying that she is an enemy combatant. Duckett asks him to intercept her, but moments later Gervase makes a second radio call to report that they were unable to stop the woman and so had to shoot her. Gervase also contacts Lieutenant Collins and gives him the same story: a woman, whom he claims was a communist sympathizer, was seen in their vicinity. They fired warning shots to make her stop, but when she refused, they were forced to kill her. The matter is considered closed.

Throughout the day, Gervase and his men battle enemy forces. Chip, injured after falling from a rock, is evacuated. During the fight, Gervase saves a severely wounded soldier who has fallen into a tunnel, earning a Bronze Star citation. That evening, Lieutenant Collins orders his men to regroup for operations the following day. Several prisoners are taken, including a highly agitated woman who won't stop screaming. Thomas arrives and is heard to boast of stabbing a North Vietnamese earlier in the day, implying that he could just as easily take care of this prisoner if she doesn't quiet down.[31]

Upon returning to base camp, Storeby informs Pearson about the crime committed by his fellow soldiers, but their conversation is interrupted by Thomas, concerned about what Storeby might be saying. Pearson suggests discussing the matter with Sergeant Stewart, who informs Lieutenant Collins. Initially skeptical, Collins later admits that he didn't believe Storeby's allegations, as they implicated some of his best men.[32] Moreover, Gervase had recently requested that Storeby be replaced, claiming he has displayed extreme fear at the thought of embarking on a new mission. Collins reports the matter to his superior, Captain Spigelmire.

Storeby, fearing for his life, meets with Collins and requests reassignment to another unit as a door gunner on a helicopter, something he reiterates to Spigelmire, who begins processing the paperwork and tries to dissuade Storeby from testifying against the killers. After Storeby expresses his desire to pursue legal action against Gervase, Thomas and the Garcia cousins, Spigelmire warns him that he knows how a court-martial works, implying that the four accused men will likely get away with a mild rebuke or might even be exonerated, and that Storeby and his family would then "really have something to worry about." Thinly veiled threats are issued.[33] Hoping to put an end to the situation before it escalates, Spigelmire is nonetheless furious at the four perpetrators and summons Gervase, Thomas and Joe to discuss Storeby's accusations (Chip is still in the hospital). He hands Gervase a piece of paper on which are written three words: "KIDNAPPING – RAPE – MURDER." "Do you know anything about this?" he asks Gervase, who responds calmly, "Captain, I have no idea what you're talking about." Spigelmire questions Thomas and Joe, who don't display the same assurance as their sergeant. Spigelmire explodes: "You people acted like animals up there, and [don't] deserve to live! I would have never learned about this, but one man had the balls to inform me."[34] He then disbands the patrol, reassigns each of its members to other units, and warns them that if anything happens to Storeby, they will bear the consequences.

Storeby, meanwhile, determined not to leave the matter solely in Spigelmire's hands, asks one of his comrades, David Lillywhite, to introduce him to Newby, the military chaplain. A meeting takes place on December 8, during which Storeby gives Newby a detailed account of the events he witnessed. The chaplain, taking the matter extremely seriously, immediately alerts the Criminal Investigation Division (CID) and Storeby is interviewed that very same day by Jimmie McClendon, a member of the military police.

The next day, Storeby leads a group consisting of McClendon, Colonel Oliver (the provost), Major Herrera (his assistant), Sergeant Hung (a Vietnamese interpreter) and Spigelmire, along with a small patrol assigned to protect the main witness. They head to Hill 192 to find Mao's body. After identifying the rocky ridge where Gervase and his men were on the day of her murder, Storeby takes "five to ten minutes"[35] to locate the spot where the victim's body lies, a period of time explained by there being two areas relatively similar in terms of topography, with tall, dense vegetation. Storeby moves alone toward the first of the two locations, and after confirming that he sees nothing there, confidently leads the group to the second one, where they find Mao's corpse.

Experts place the remains (bones, hair, clothing) in a body bag, the kind used for soldiers killed in combat. They attach a label indicating "Official Murder Investigation" and, in capital letters, the victim's first name, "MAO." She has been identified thanks to Sergeant Hung's investigations in the nearby village. The victim's remains are transferred to the military hospital and received by Captain Putnam P. Breed, who, after a quick examination, prepares documents for their transfer to the U.S. Army mortuary in Saigon, where they will ultimately be received by Major Long. Not all military personnel view these steps favorably. The sergeant in charge of recording deaths protests to Breed about Mao's remains being in the cold room, arguing that it should be reserved only for American soldiers and their allies killed in combat.

On December 12, and again five days later, Storeby visits the hill with CID agent Frank J. Scott, who collects additional evidence – about thirty bone fragments, twenty teeth, and two metal fragments – that is necessary for reconstruction of the body and to determine the cause of death. These items are subsequently transferred to a medical laboratory in Qui Nhon, where on December 11 Mao's remains have already undergone an initial autopsy.

From January 7 to 11, Dr. Tadao Furue, an anthropologist at the University of Tokyo, conducts a skeletal reconstruction of Mao at Tan Son Nhut Air Base. He is assisted by Lieutenant Colonel Pierre Finck, commander of the 9th U.S. Army Medical Laboratory and a specialist in ballistic injuries, who, a few weeks earlier had X-rayed Mao's bones. A renowned expert, Finck was a member of the team that performed the autopsy on President John F. Kennedy after his assassination in 1963.

The reconstruction reveals that the teeth and subsequent bone fragments collected by Scott at the crime scene match the bones collected on December 9, and Furue concludes that they belong to the same body. The victim's dental structure is almost entirely reconstructed, except for three missing teeth (possibly extracted by Thomas to retrieve the gold tooth or shattered by the bullet that pierced the jaw). Based on examination of the skull, ribs and vertebrae, the victim's age is estimated to be between 18 and 20 old (Furue leans toward 19). The pelvic and cranial bones confirm with certainty that it is the body of a well-developed and proportionate South Asian woman. Her height is estimated at 65 inches, with a margin of error of plus or minus one inch, matching the description of Mao given by Storeby and Chip Garcia.

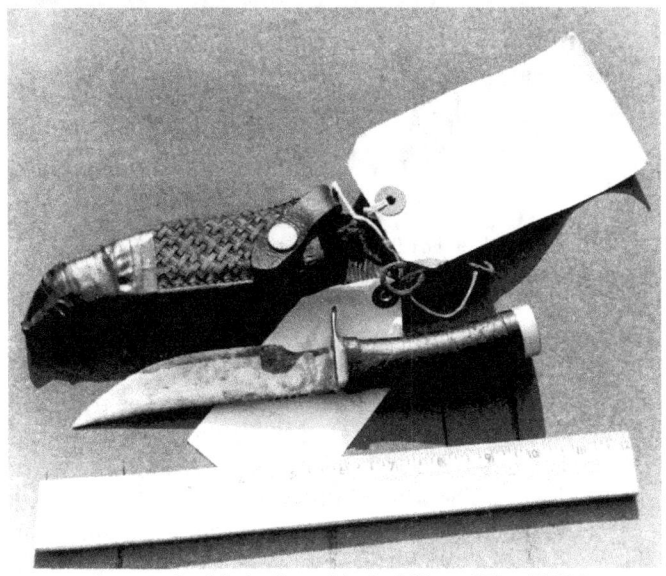

A photograph of the knife used in the killing of Phan Thi Mao that was presented during the courts-martial, March 1967

The examination reveals the presence of a piece of metal embedded in the cranial base which, after chemical laboratory checks, is found to be composed of lead. Having observed multiple fractures, Finck concludes that a projectile entered the back of the skull at high speed. Three cervical vertebrae were shattered and a second projectile passed through the back of the neck, exiting at the level of the lower jaw. Besides the fatal gunshot wounds, other injuries are identified, caused by a sharp instrument on the left side of the skeleton, at chest level, as well as to the eighth rib and sixth and seventh thoracic vertebrae. Finck's conclusions corroborate Storeby's account that Mao was initially stabbed by Thomas, then shot at close range with an M-16.

A photograph of the rifle used in the killing of Phan Thi Mao that was presented during the courts-martial, March 1967

The trial of Cipriano "Chip" Garcia
(Camp Radcliff, Vietnam, March 15-16, 1967)

Chip Garcia is the first of the four soldiers to be tried in a military court for the charges of premeditated murder and rape, violating Articles 118 and 120 of the Uniform Code of Military Justice. The accused pleads not guilty.

After Lieutenant Collins' brief interrogation, Phan Thi Loc, the sister of Phan Thi Mao, is called to the stand, accompanied by her interpreter, Sergeant Le Van But, whose presence is contested by the defense attorney, James P. Mercurio. Mercurio claims that the Vietnamese sergeant is familiar with the case and knows the victim and her family personally, which the sergeant acknowledges before the court. Le Van But had encountered the two sisters on the road to Phu My a few months earlier and had briefly conversed with their mother about the presence of North Vietnamese forces in the area. Shortly after the abduction of her eldest daughter, it was Le Van But to whom she turned in panic and described what had happened, asking him to interpret for her when she spoke to Captain Spigelmire – which he did. After checking, Spigelmire informed Mao's mother that the location of the abduction was not within his jurisdiction, and that therefore the men under his command were not the perpetrators. The woman was forced to investigate her daughter's disappearance on her own, eventually turning to the South Vietnamese military. In light of this information, Mercurio requests that Le Van But be replaced with another interpreter, arguing that the sergeant would not be "neutral" and might have a "bias" in the case.[36] Sergeant Hung is designated to translate Phan Thi Loc's testimony instead of Le Van But.

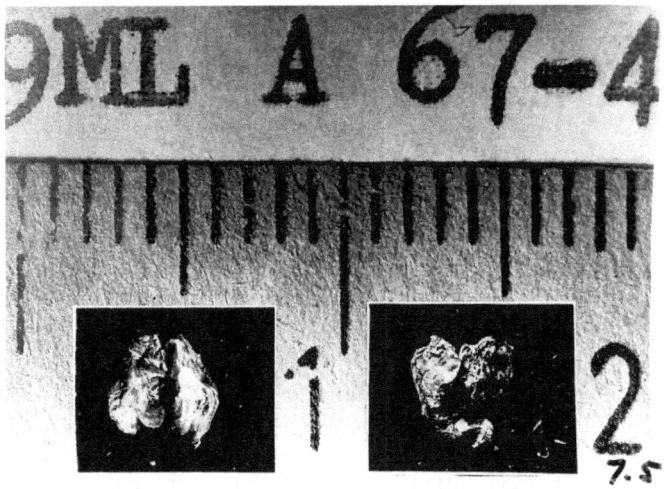

7.5. Composite gross photograph of both sides of metallic fragment removed from sphenoid bone at Crime Laboratory, Camp Zama, by LTC P.A. Finck and examined by Firearms expert, WO1 C.E. Shomber, 27 Feb 67. Fragment is probably lead.

Metal fragments removed from the sphenoid bone
of Phan Thi Mao

Phan Thi Loc tells the court about the soldiers' entry into the house where she was sleeping with her sister, followed by her sister's abduction. She specifies having seen, the day before, one of the soldiers who was part of the patrol. When the prosecutor asks her if that man is in the room, Phan, evidently petrified at the thought of catching the eye of one of her sister's assailants, responds negatively. She is also unable to do so at the start of the afternoon session. Asked if she wants to move around the room to identify one of the soldiers, she remains seated and merely repeats what she said earlier.

The transcript of these exchanges provides no indication of the tone of the young woman's voice, but one can infer, from the prosecutor's remarks, the agitation and profound distress she is experiencing. She indicates that the day before she went up into the mountains to search for her sister, she and her mother had the same dream, in which Mao came to warn them that she was at the top of the hill, in great agony.[37] The premonition came true the following day when, after searching several abandoned huts with South Vietnamese soldiers, they discovered her bra near a pool of blood. That same evening, Mao's mother was kidnapped by North Vietnamese forces, accused of leading South Vietnamese soldiers to one of their hideouts and compromising their food supply.

Storeby's testimony is another key moment in the trial.[38] He confirms in detail the account he had given to the CID agent. The transcript of his exchanges with the defense attorney gives the impression of a reserved man. He speaks sparingly in response to questions, often with short answers: "Yes, sir," "Correct," "No, sir." Several times he is asked to speak louder so that everyone in the room can hear him, and is also asked to repeat himself. Regarding Garcia, Storeby paints a picture of a soldier who initially resists committing rape but eventually succumbs to peer pressure. While he did fire in Mao's direction as she tried to escape after being injured by Thomas, Garcia initially refused to shoot her when ordered by Gervase. He even allegedly confessed to Storeby, "The whole thing makes me sick."[39]

Chip Garcia is portrayed in a favorable light by his officers. Lieutenant Collins describes him as one of the best soldiers he has yet encountered. "He's extremely calm when things really get tough and never seems to break."[40] At this stage of the trial, acquittal of murder seems likely. Garcia's lawyer expresses his dismay that the forensic pathologists' photographs are presented in court when it had already been proved that Mao's death was caused by two close-range bullets fired by Thomas. However, Chip's involvement in the rape remains a lingering question, and the time he spent in the hut alone with Mao becomes the focus of much debate.

Not surprisingly, he vehemently denies the rape but admits to entering the hut to escape the insults directed at Storeby by Gervase and Thomas. Once inside, according to his account, he found Mao lying on the table, naked, hands tied behind her back, bleeding from her genitals, which is why he wouldn't have sex with her. "A little blood won't hurt,"[41] Thomas allegedly told him. Chip employs a similar line of defense when questioned about his request to Gervase for Mao's tooth after her death. He claims it was a strategy to maintain the sergeant's trust in him.

As the trial nears its end, the defense presents arguments in favor of Garcia's acquittal. Phan Thi Loc couldn't identify him as one of the kidnappers of her sister; Storeby didn't physically witness what he did inside the hut; and Chip refused to kill Mao when ordered by Gervase. But prosecutor Yelton is relentless, attacking Garcia, recalling that he was the one who pointed out the hut where Mao lived – and certainly not by chance. He had seen the young girl – who was very pretty – two or three days earlier. In his eyes, this implicates Garcia in the crime of premeditated rape and murder. He dismantles the argument that Chip stayed in the hut for "one or two minutes." The continuous screams heard by Storeby while he was inside are deemed to be incriminating evidence.

Ultimately, the court sides with the prosecution and Garcia is found guilty of non-premeditated rape and murder. He is sentenced to eight years of hard labor, demoted to a regular soldier, discharged from the army, and ordered to pay a fine of $50 a month for ninety-six months.

The trial of Joseph Garcia
(Camp Radcliff, March 16-17, 1967)

Following Chip Garcia's conviction, the court reconvenes to judge the second presumed culprit in the case: Joseph Garcia. Like his cousin, the accused pleads not guilty, both to rape and murder. The same witnesses take the stand and the exchanges seem almost identical to those of the previous day. Phan Thi Loc, once again unable to identify the accused in court, states that "all people in the court" look the same.[42] Storeby's testimony, however, leaves no doubt about Joe's involvement in Mao's rape. Garcia reports that when he exited the hut, his comrades made lewd jokes about him, suggesting that the victim's bleeding had been caused by his supposedly advantageous anatomy. Unlike Chip, Joseph Garcia allegedly voiced no opposition to Mao's rape. But Storeby can only attest to the screams and moans he heard when Garcia entered the hut afterwards. He can't affirmatively answer the defense attorney, Eugene W. Murphy, when asked – insistently – whether he had actually seen Joe rape Mao. Garcia subsequently refused to kill the prisoner, which Storeby confirms: the soldier fired no shots when Thomas and Chip Garcia pursued her.

Confident because of the verdict in Chip Garcia's trial, Storeby is more inclined to discuss his fear of Gervase, and makes troubling revelations to the court. "I was on one patrol with Sergeant Gervase where there was a Vietnamese man standing on the road, on the trail, and he shot the man down for no reason at all. He said later there was no reason to kill the man, but he just felt like it. Also, I went on patrol with him where he has beaten up women. I was also on a patrol with him where he had a couple of prisoners which he killed."[43] Later, when questioned again by Murphy, Storeby adds, "Well, Sergeant Gervase is the kind of man you don't argue with. He doesn't have any value of anybody's human life and if you went against him, you knew for a fact that he wouldn't hesitate to shoot anybody."[44]

With little evidence to contradict Garcia's rape accusation, the defense relies on the testimony of Captain Spigelmire, who expresses his doubts – which he seems to have not yet dispelled – about "the incident."[45] But Spigelmire is unable to substantiate his "intuition" with concrete evidence. Murphy then tries to disprove Joe's deposition recorded by the CID, arguing that it was tainted by several irregularities. Suffering from a migraine and on an empty stomach, Joe confessed to the rape after a night operation and not having slept for two days. Murphy argues that he was not in his "normal state" and was coerced into a confession by the investigators, who also threatened to reveal the details to his wife if he didn't cooperate. This seems implausible, since, as lawyer for the prosecution Captain Blevins points out, fatigue and hunger don't make a man confess to a heinous crime he didn't commit.[46] Feeling cornered, Joe vaguely insinuates that his statement was partly falsified by his interrogators. Murphy also argues that the CID agents didn't inform Garcia of his rights, as per procedure. He finally contests Joe's involvement in the planning of Mao's murder, stating that he didn't join the patrol "of his own free will," didn't take Gervase's plan seriously, and wasn't involved in the young woman's murder.

As with that of his cousin Chip, the pivotal moment of Joseph Garcia's trial is the time he spent alone with Mao in the hut. For the defense, the challenge lies in portraying Joe as an exemplary and loyal soldier. Lieutenant Duckett, testifying for the defense, says of him: "When you went on patrol with him and you had a mission, normally he would be the number one man to assist you in the mission you had to perform. He was not what you would classify as an average soldier. He was an outstanding PFC."[47] Asked about Garcia's personality, a soldier named Prince asserts that he is "one of the best" in his unit and that he "respects life."[48]

But evidence is presented that undermines Joe's sincerity. Contrary to his statements made during the trial, during his detention he wrote vehement letters in which he railed against the government (including to a Senator he knew personally, insisting that he is "wrongly being brought to trial"), and since he deceived the court on this point, Yelton concludes that Garcia likely lied about other things. Flustered, the accused gives way under relentless pressure from the prosecutor. When questioned about why he entered the hut, Garcia asserts that the only reason he did so was to escape Thomas and Gervase's verbal harassment. "You would rather that the platoon think you were a rapist than a man of good moral character?" asks Yelton. "Yes," responds Garcia without hesitation.[49] "Did you consider the rape and murder serious offenses?" asks another member of the court. "Yes, sir, the rape, yes sir. I couldn't see anything [wrong] about the murder. People get killed all the time in the field: VC, Vietnamese nationals. Our men get killed out in the field. I don't see how you can call it murder. I just don't."[50]

Garcia's clumsy and ambiguous responses apparently prompt the court to impose a heavy sentence. Unlike his cousin, he is cleared of murder and found guilty solely of rape, yet receives nearly double the punishment: fifteen years of hard labor. He is also demoted to the lowest rank in the military hierarchy.

The trial of Steven Thomas
(Camp Radcliff, Vietnam, March 18, 20 and 21, 1967)

Thomas' trial, lasting three days, is the longest of the four. Like his two fellow soldiers, he pleads not guilty to charges of premeditated rape and murder, and exercises his right to silence. His lawyer, Lee R. Ratliff, pushes back with some ferocity against every piece of evidence presented by the prosecution.

Storeby's testimony constitutes a crucial moment in Thomas' trial. Questioning by prosecutor Yelton and cross-examination by the defense attorney take up a good part of the morning of March 18.[51] In line with his initial deposition, Storeby asserts that when Gervase shared his plan to kidnap, rape and kill a Vietnamese woman, Thomas "was more than interested"[52] in participating. He then provides damning details about Thomas' attitude during the rape and accuses Thomas of threatening to kill him if he didn't rape the girl before the end of the mission. It also emerges from his testimony that Thomas is the one who killed the young woman, corroborating the findings of forensic experts. But the tenacious Ratliff doesn't give up, and raises numerous objections during Yelton's interrogation. Hoping to unearth contradictions on minor points, he accuses Storeby of inaction in saving the victim and even insinuates that Storeby valued his "personal well-being"[53] over the victim's life. Finally, he tries to prove that Thomas wanted to avoid combat.

Still silent, hiding behind his lawyer's defense, Thomas listens to the incriminating testimony of Chip Garcia, fresh from his own trial, which confirms Storeby's version. Ratliff then plays his trump card: he challenges Chip's presence in the courtroom and exposes his true motivations, suggesting that Chip agreed to testify against Thomas only after encouragement from his Catholic chaplain, who allegedly promised him a substantial reduction in his sentence. According to the defense attorney, such a promise completely undermines the witness' account. The court agrees to hear it nonetheless.

Ratliff, running out of arguments, opts for a surprising strategy: questioning the reliability of the physical evidence that implicates Thomas in the murder. For hours, the debate revolves around photographs of Mao's remains which are presented to various experts summoned to the court (Scott,

Finck, Furue, McClendon) to confirm they match the bones each had autopsied. Details appear that seem to sow doubt in Ratliff's mind. After much discussion, he persuades the officer of the court to bring the victim's bones into the courtroom. He wants each expert to formally identify them

---

DC: I have no questions.

LO: Any questions by any member of the court?

(There was no response from any member of the court)

LO: This witness is excused.

(The witness withdrew from the courtroom)

TC: The prosecution calls as its next witness PFC Storeby.

(PFC Robert M. Storeby was called as a witness for the prosecution, was sworn, and testified as follows)

DIRECT EXAMINATION

Questions by the prosecution:

Q. Would you state your full name, grade, organization and armed force?
A. PFC Robert M. Storeby, Company C, 2nd of the 8th, U.S. Army.

Q. Do you know the accused in this case?
A. Yes, sir.

Q. If he is present in the court would you point to him?
A. Steven Thomas (pointing in the direction of the accused).

Q. Now Storeby, on 17 November 1966 were you selected to be a member of a certain pony patrol?
A. Yes, sir.

Q. In addition to yourself who was selected to be members of this patrol?
A. Sergeant Gervase, Thomas, the two Garcias, and myself.

Q. Were you briefed on 17 November in reference to this patrol and the route it would take?
A. Yes, sir.

Q. At the briefing, after the conclusion of the briefing what was discussed?
A. Sergeant Gervase suggested that we take along a Vietnamese girl. Right away Thomas was more than interested in this.

DC: Objection to that. That is a conclusion. He might testify to something that Thomas had said or something to that effect.

PRES: I'm sorry, sir, I cannot hear the defense counsel.

LO: Well, there was an objection made to part of the witness' testimony and the objection, of course, is addressed to the law officer. Ask the witness to state the basis for any remarks he might make. You can state what the parties there said or did.

Q. What was the discussion that went on between Sergeant Gervase and Thomas in reference to this Vietnamese girl?
A. He discussed that they would kidnap a girl, keep the girl five days on this mission, and during this time they would have intercourse with the girl. On the fifth day they would kill the girl.

Transcript of the interrogation of Robert M. Storeby by prosecutor Yelton in the trial of Steven Thomas

and compare them with the photographs.[54] During his interrogation, Finck does indeed notice a difference in one rib where a portion of bone is missing, but immediately explains that the bone was damaged, suggesting that "somebody may have introduced an instrument into this and that a portion of bone fell [off]."[55]

Ratliff then plays his final card, arguing about the court's inability to clearly define the purpose of Thomas' trial. Is he the instigator or merely the perpetrator of the crime? The last two defense witnesses hope to show that Gervase and his men were indeed in communist territory and that there were female combatants in the enemy's ranks – hinting, vaguely, that Mao could have been one of these combatants. Lieutenant Collins, who speaks highly of the accused, also claims that a woman might have been involved in the attack of November 19, a belief he acquired only through hearsay. Spigelmire asserts that the region where the patrol was operating had experienced several "Viet Cong infiltrations" and that the soldiers were "continually" searching huts to track enemy presence.[56] But when the prosecutor asks if it is normal to take someone prisoner throughout an entire mission, the captain is reluctantly forced to respond in the negative.

Ratliff's efforts to exonerate Thomas ultimately prove fruitless as the court finds him guilty of rape and premeditated murder. He is sentenced to hard labor for life.

The trial of David Gervase
(Camp Radcliff, Vietnam, March 22, 1967)

In comparison to the other three trials, Gervase's day-long trial is relatively quick. Like his comrades, the sergeant pleads not guilty to charges of rape and murder.

After several testimonies, including those from Storeby and the experts who performed the autopsy on Mao's body, Gervase is given the opportunity to speak. The transcription of the interrogation conducted by his lawyer, Captain Eckhardt, initially gives the impression of a confident and talkative man. Gervase provides long and detailed explanations about the events of November 17 and 18, 1966, and seems to have an answer for everything. However, his continuous speech belies a nervousness, to the point that his lawyer urges him to "relax a little bit."[57] According to

Gervase, the kidnapping plan was just a tasteless joke. He claims he suggested to his comrades that they take "five girls" for an "orgy," so as to break the monotony of their mission. While the sergeant admits that he and his men did search huts on the morning of November 18, it was, he asserts, with the intent of finding weapons, as he had personally spotted North Vietnamese in the area three days earlier. He has little difficulty explaining his decision to capture Mao and tie her up: "I decided to take her along because she was acting too suspicious because less than a week before this, a woman led an ambush against one of my squads in my platoon and wounded five of my men and sent four of them to the States because their wounds were so serious. I didn't want to have the possibility to let this woman go because she might be that leader or another leader, which could do the same damage to another patrol that went out."[58]

Later, when his lawyer asks what he did when he locked himself in the hut with the prisoner, Gervase provides a detailed account of his every action. He says he first sat her on the table, still tied up, to prevent her from reaching the grenades stored in a corner of the room, and then, because it was lunchtime, he looked around for his rations. While he was stooping down, he spotted "a prophylactic under the table which was half covered by dirt."[59] He supposedly picked it up with the tip of his bayonet and threw it out of the hut. Eckhardt twice asks him if he had sexual relations with the captive, to which Gervase responds with a vehement "no." For the remainder of his interrogation, the sergeant indicates that Mao attempted to escape, Thomas stabbed her, and Storeby allegedly caused the fugitive's death by firing in her direction with his M-79. This is followed by a lengthy monologue in which Gervase describes, in great detail, the fights against North Vietnamese and how he saved Polk, the soldier who fell into a tunnel after being injured.

Gervase's bravery is confirmed throughout the trial by witnesses who take the stand. Lieutenant Collins stresses that Gervase's military achievements are "outstanding"[60] and paints a somewhat nuanced picture of Storeby. Following an ambush that allegedly took place on November 13 (five days before Mao's abduction), Collins claims to have seen Storeby "extremely scared and extremely jumpy," to the point where he and his men had to support him and help him regain his composure. "I don't think he ever came out of it. I think it affected him,"[61] he ventures further, offering up the image of Storeby as a solider who had lost his grip and wasn't in his normal state when departing on a mission five days later under Gervase's command.[62]

In light of these testimonies, the trial seems to favor Gervase, especially as Chip Garcia's testimony, which incriminates the accused, is discredited by Eckhardt. Eckhardt reiterates the same arguments as Ratliff during Thomas' trial: Chip was supposedly promised a reduced sentence if he testified against Gervase, a fact confirmed by Yelton in an off-the-record hearing.[63] Another testimony supports Gervase's defense: Lieutenant Douglas Duckett[64] affirms, in response to one of Eckhardt's questions, that the area where Mao's body was found was under communist control, and that "the Vietnamese people in the area no doubt… were sympathetic to the Viet Cong."[65] However, prosecutor Yelton tries to defuse the argument with skillful questions, leading Duckett to admit that the villagers, for the most part, had to pledge allegiance to the North Vietnamese for their own survival.

Yelton is particularly aggressive during Gervase's cross-examination, starting with a direct question: "How many times would you say you have told this story you have just told on the witness stand?" "Numerous times, sir. Mostly to my lawyer, sir," responds the accused with a quick-witted rejoinder.[66] But Gervase's insolence gradually gives way to hesitation. Less talkative than he was with his lawyer and now on the defensive, Gervase is repeatedly challenged by Yelton, as when the prosecutor asks why he didn't communicate via radio with Spigelmire to warn him that he had captured a supposed suspect, or when questioned about the type of injuries caused by a grenade launcher – which are incompatible with the bullet wounds found on the victim's neck.

At 5:52 p.m., the court retires to deliberate. Just under an hour later, the verdict is announced: Gervase is acquitted of Mao's rape but found guilty of unpremeditated murder. It is a mixed verdict, a consequence of the prosecution's various errors and the sympathy that most of the military witnesses who took the stand have for Gervase, and who, in contrast, find Storeby less convincing. Before the court deliberates and pronounces the sentence, Gervase is briefly heard one last time. He openly declares that he is not the bloodthirsty rapist some have portrayed him to be, mentioning the time he saved a group of Vietnamese children from a fire and brought them back to life using cardiopulmonary resuscitation. Irritated

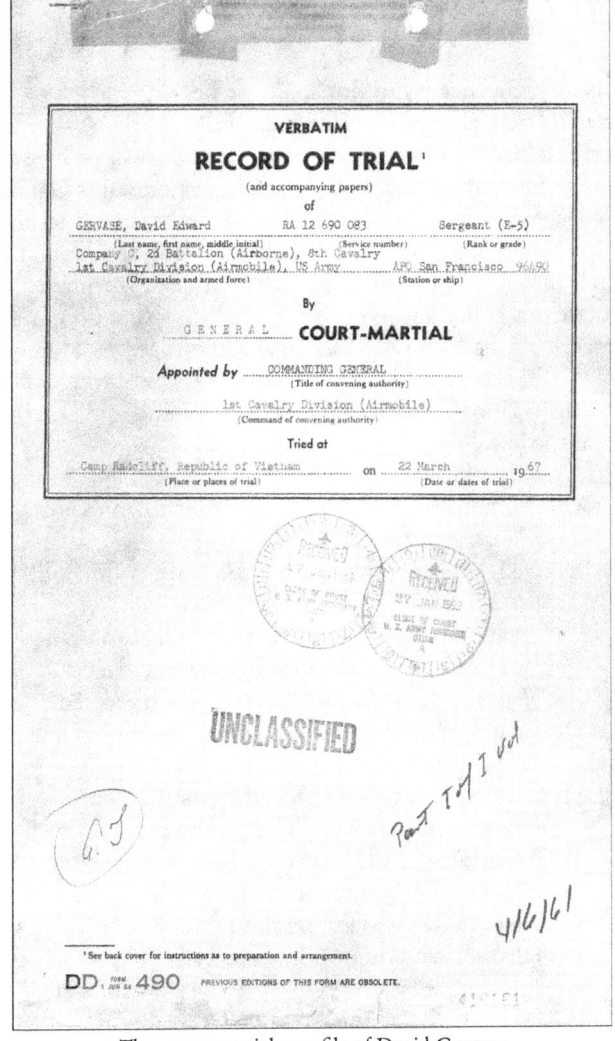

The court-martial case file of David Gervase

by the speech, and that the accused is presenting himself as a hero, an angry Yelton addresses the court: "I have no daughters, and I'm glad of it. If any of you do have daughters, I simply ask that you put your daughter on Hill 192, and impose a sentence on Sergeant Gervase for it."[67]

At 7:46 p.m., Gervase is sentenced to ten years of hard labor. Discharged for dishonorable conduct, he is demoted to the lowest military rank possible.

Appeals, sentence reductions, parole hearings

Joseph Garcia's lawyer appeals, and a little less than two years later, in February 1968, Garcia is retried at Fort Leavenworth, Kansas. Storeby, called to testify, is questioned by Garcia's new lawyer, Captain Robert M. Frazee, who accuses Storeby of doing nothing to save Mao, and asks: "You are attempting to tell the court [that] Joe Garcia is guilty of a crime... but you are not guilty and you were in the same situation, is this correct?" "I had nothing to do with the rape," is Storeby's reply.[68] Frazee asks him about what he saw during Mao's rape, insinuating that he didn't actually see the soldiers come out of the hut.

> A: Did you see them come out? How do you know when they came out?
> B: Well, sir, if you were there, I'm sure you would also know.
> A: I wasn't there so I'm asking you to explain to the court why you know so they can decide.
> B: Well, sir, the girl's cries and moans increased at the time they were probably having intercourse with the girl.
> A: But you don't know that, do you, you have no idea whether anybody was in the hootch [hut] at that time at all? She could have been moaning for a lot of reasons, correct?
> B: I believe this was the reason for it, sir.
> A: This is your assumption, correct?
> B: Yes, sir.[69]

Garcia seems to have regained his memory since his last trial. He claims, for example, that on the day of Mao's abduction, Gervase found a kitten in the Cat Tuong hamlet and stabbed it with his bayonet. Is this anecdote – absent from any of the other trials – true, or has Garcia fabricated it to amplify Gervase's cruelty?

As he did in his first trial, Joe also attempts to paint Storeby in a negative light. He explains that when Gervase asked Storeby to take his turn in the hut, Storeby allegedly responded, "No, I have a pretty wife. I haven't been in Vietnam that long." When Gervase then asked Storeby if he would be going into the hut the following day, Storeby responded with, "Yeah, maybe."[70] Garcia also insinuates that Storeby made his accusations of rape and murder more to avoid the frontlines than out of a sense of morality. Garcia claims that while he and Storeby were battling the communists after Mao's killing, a shaken Storeby said that he would rather be subjected to a court-martial "than go up the hill again."[71]

Prosecutor John E. Kirchner tries to untangle the truth from Garcia's allegations, notably highlighting the contrast between the picture that Garcia paints of Storeby, as a coward trying to avoid combat zones, and the facts. "If he was so scared, how come he wasn't afraid of telling Gervase no and yet you were?" he asks. "Storeby is different, sir," replies Garcia. "He was just brand new. I had been there [for] a month or three weeks before he was. He had just come into the field." Later, while Garcia struggles to explain that a grunt must obey orders from a superior, Kirchner adds, "In other words, you don't believe the military gives you any choice between rules, your orders and your conscience?"

"Well, sir, the army expects you to do it the army way and that's follow orders, sir… You're not an individual in the army, sir, you are part of an organization," replies Garcia.

Kirchner deftly employs all these elements, weaving them together to substantiate the accused's guilt. Frazee, however, exploits every weakness in the prosecution's case to skillfully plant doubt in the court's mind, considering that Storeby – like the accused – did nothing to save Mao. Worse, he suggests that Storeby might be suffering from psychological problems. "Gentlemen, I'm not saying Specialist Storeby is lying," he asserts. "I do not believe this at all. I am sure he is convinced, but the point is why is he convinced? The human mind is strange. You can be convinced of things without actually having experienced them."[72] Doubting Mao's rape prompts a reaction from Kirchner, who recalls that according to Storeby's testimony, the victim's moans intensified when Joe entered the hut, and he remained in there not one or two minutes but between ten and fifteen. The court eventually decides that any doubt should benefit the accused, and at the end of his retrial, Garcia is acquitted. It is stipulated that "all rights, privileges, and property of which the accused has been deprived by virtue of the execution of the sentence adjudged at the former trial… will be restored."[73] In other words, Joseph Garcia has the right to rejoin the army.

While none of the other three guilty parties are exonerated, they all benefit from substantial sentence reductions. Between December 27, 1967 and August 15, 1968, Chip Garcia's request for clemency and reinstatement in the army is denied three times. He appeals to President Nixon and asks Henry B. González, a Mexican-American Democrat in the House of Representatives, for help.[74] González writes several letters supporting Chip's appeal, which takes place on June 6, 1969. Chip's new lawyer, Sheppard F. Miers Jr., notes the harm done to his client due to an unusually lengthy delay in his second trial. Nevertheless, Chip now pleads guilty to the unplanned murder of Mao, but not her rape.[75] Therefore, logically, the court finds him guilty and sentences him to four years of hard labor, quickly commuted to 22 months. By the end of the summer of 1971, he is a free man.

During the weeks and months following his trial, David Gervase, aided by his lawyers, also seeks a sentence reduction, pointing out alleged flaws in his case and irregularities in his trial. On August 17, 1967, he sends a letter to the secretary of the United States Army, arguing that he was a good soldier, having been both decorated and injured, and expressing his desire to rejoin the army. The experts' opinion is positive. They note that Gervase is "very cooperative" and "strongly asserts his innocence." Gervase admits that the military operations he participated in affected him, but claims he "feels he can 'turn off' [his] aggressiveness very much like a professional prize fighter can."[76] On December 11, 1968, his case is eventually reopened. Reinstatement in the army is denied, but his sentence is reduced to seven years. Less than a year later, in July 1969, Gervase is granted parole. Everything indicates that he resumed his civilian life until his death on March 28, 1981, at the age of 34.[77]

Steven Thomas makes similar attempts to overturn his conviction. His request for reinstatement in the army is rejected on December 27, 1967, but on July 25, 1968, on appeal, his sentence is reduced to eight years. His November 5, 1969 request for parole and clemency is denied. A few months later, in the spring of 1970, Thomas is notified of his parole.

Twenty years after returning to the anonymity of civilian life, in the summer of 1992, Thomas, now 46 years old, is involved in a new legal case. He testifies in the trial of one George Loeb, on trial for the murder of a black sailor, Harold Mansfield, a crime committed a year earlier in the parking lot of a supermarket in Jacksonville, Florida. Thomas allegedly helped the perpetrator and his wife leave the city and escape law enforcement. Journalists made the connection between this man and the character of Corporal Clark in *Casualties of War*, released three years earlier, which encourages them to dig up details of the man's troubled past. Since his return from Vietnam, Thomas had become the leader of a white supremacist church.[78] Even though Loeb pleaded self-defense, it was proven that the motive behind the crime was primarily racist, leading to his conviction and a life sentence.

The media coverage of the Loeb trial and revelations about Thomas may actually have prevented another crime. A note found in military archives reveals that less than a month later, in August 1992, an investigator from the Canadian Immigration Department requested a search warrant for Thomas' home. The reason? He was suspected of making homemade explosives with the intent of carrying out an attack on a synagogue. The army archives provide no further details, and many questions are unanswered. Was Thomas arrested? Was he imprisoned? Or did he evade justice and slip back into society?

In late March 1967, the American press reported on the trials of Thomas, Gervase and the Garcia cousins. Several newspapers published details of the verdicts and convictions, later confirmed by military authorities in June of that year.[79] It was while reading one of these reports that Daniel Lang, an investigative journalist at *The New Yorker*, first learned about the case.[80]

The investigations of Daniel Lang

Born in 1913 on New York's Lower East Side into a family of Hungarian Jewish immigrants, Lang worked at the *New York Post* before joining the editorial team of *The New Yorker* at the age of 28. When his editor, William Shawn, saw him wandering through the corridors of the magazine for the first time, he noted: "He arrived in our offices one day in 1941, shortly before the United States entered the Second World War, with an impressive sheaf of clippings of articles he had written for the *New York Post*. He was immediately taken onto the staff and soon wrote his first Reporter-at-Large piece – on the British-American Ambulance Corps."[81]

After traversing various combat zones (North Africa, France, Italy) as a senior reporter, Lang continued at *The New Yorker*, writing on various subjects – particularly the atomic bomb, the theme of his first book, published in 1948.[82] Three more books on the same subject followed, all based on articles previously published in the magazine. "He was aware from the beginning that human survival was threatened by the bomb and he kept after the subject bravely and persistently through the years in a series of Reporter-at-Large pieces and profiles," said Shawn. "He did much to educate people about the nuclear peril. He was one of the most steadfast and talented of our reportorial writers; he never wrote a careless or superficial line; he was artful, self-effacing, deeply responsible – a writer of moral purpose and extraordinary literary powers."[83]

In the 1960s, Lang began to take an interest in the political and moral questions raised by America's involvement in Vietnam, questions that inevitably touched on issues he had explored during the Second World War. Unlike many of his colleagues, Lang was not sent to Vietnam, but that didn't stop him from taking a strong interest in what was happening there. One day, while reading a newspaper during breakfast, he came across a brief mention of the court-martial proceedings of four soldiers for the abduction, rape and murder of a young Vietnamese woman.[84] Lang was particularly intrigued by the attitude of the fifth soldier, who had refused to participate in the crime. "My immediate reaction was to wonder why one man had behaved differently than the others. This was the impulse that caused me to decide to investigate and to write about this incident."[85]

Lang hoped to write a piece that wouldn't be just "a simple newspaper account of the war in Vietnam," but rather a deeper reflection on "the corrupting effect of any war and any man and any country engaged in it."[86] During his travels in various theaters of war, he had witnessed how "perfectly decent individuals take on cruel and callous ways... I also recalled that I had heard years ago – I don't know where or when – that in the Nazi army, a couple of soldiers had been ordered to shoot two civilians; they could not carry out this order in good conscience, and were themselves shot by SS men. So this question of what comes over a man in times of war has been on my mind for many years."[87] A friend of Lang's later confided that "he reflected on the many bystanders who watched the trains carry friends and neighbors to death camps without making an effort to stop them. He wondered why some people are willing to take a stand even when the cost is beyond what can be paid."[88]

Hoping to verify the reliability of the information in the article he had read, Lang set about trying to obtain the trial transcripts, and, after locating the records, requested permission from the Department of Defense to read them. On a visit to the Pentagon, he was informed that all such material was inaccessible until legal procedures and appeals were exhausted. Every few weeks, for a year and a half, Lang called "one of the Pentagon's public officers" who, with some indifference, informed him that the records were still restricted. One day, tired of fielding his calls, the official put him in touch with Katherine Minogue, deputy clerk at the Army's Department of Judicial Affairs in Falls Church, Virginia, who finally gave him the access he needed. "In October 1968, I had my chance at the records, and I pored over them for days at an unoccupied desk that Miss Minogue had found for me. I read the court-martial records at least twice carefully, wondering as I did how I could possibly shape these records into a piece of writing that could have meaning for the public as well as satisfying my own interest in my basic question why four men behaved one way and one man behaved another way."[89]

"But reading the record was not enough," says Lang. "I felt I could not know the answer to my question until I had spoken to the member of the patrol who had refused to take part in the rape and murder of Phan Thi Mao."⁹⁰ Thanks to information gathered from the Department of Defense, Lang tracked down Storeby's mother – a widow working as a school nurse – in a village in northwest Minnesota, not far from the Canadian border. He called her from New York but caught her at a bad time, "in the throes of preparing lunch for the children." "I'm trying to reach your son, Robert Storeby," he ventured. Her response was curt: "I never hear from my son. Write him care of me and I'll give him your letter, if I ever hear from him, which I won't."⁹¹ Lang had no chance to respond before the woman hung up on him.

Daniel Lang

A disappointed Lang made several more phone calls, and a week later met with a friend of Storeby's at Fort Carson, Colorado, who gave him Storeby's address. A remark made by Lang to Storeby at their first meeting – "Too bad you don't get along with your mother" – prompted an unexpected reaction from Storeby, who laughed, then assured Lang that his relationship with his mother was excellent. "Next time," advised Storeby, "call me by my middle name. All my friends do. My mother thought you were one of the patrols on my trail."[92]

This proved to be an ice-breaker, and Lang was invited by Storeby and his wife to join them in their small apartment in Minnesota, where they all enjoyed a cup of tea and slice of cake. As their discussion unfolded, a portrait emerged of an ordinary man who hadn't had an easy life. Raised in "a small farming community in northwestern Minnesota,"[93] Storeby started work on the farm at the age of seven, driving his father's tractor. Three years later, after his father's sudden death, the boy left the farm to train as a carpenter. He married a childhood friend slightly younger than him who worked as a receptionist at an insurance firm and painted in her spare time.

Before the interview, Storeby requested that Lang not disclose his true identity. Anticipating this, Lang explained that he planned to replace the names of the real protagonists in the story he was thinking of writing with pseudonyms – except for the victim, Phan Thi Mao, as "no more harm could come to her."[94] Storeby feared reprisals from the convicted soldiers when they were released from prison, and perhaps also from their cellmates. As implausible as it may seem, in March 1967 the local press had printed not only Storeby's identity but also his home address. It is likely he faced insults and even threats, as he would have been viewed by staunch supporters of the American military in Vietnam as a traitor. It seems that Storeby and his wife didn't feel the need to move after the publication of this information (perhaps they couldn't afford to), but they did exercise a certain caution. Lang didn't hesitate to provide him with the necessary assurances.

Lang spent two afternoons with Storeby documenting his testimony, noting that his subject was neither "articulate nor too well-educated. Writing or speaking are not easy or natural for him."[95] Lang had to be patient, rephrasing his questions and articulating the thoughts that Storeby – frustrated with himself for not being more helpful – only hinted at. There was tension in the air, and it wasn't uncommon during their conversations that one of Storeby's feet trembled nervously. Lang, however, gradually managed to gain the trust of his interlocutor. "I had to win the confidence of [his wife] as well," he explained. "She was even more anxious than her husband about the danger attached to the project in which we were collaborating."[96]

Lang's knowledge of the trials allowed him to steer the conversations with great skill. He asked the right questions and, whenever necessary, provided details that Storeby was unable to recall. Lang didn't record the conversation, which suggested he was extremely focused. "My father took lots of notes," says his youngest daughter, Cecily. "I don't remember him using a tape recorder, and he didn't use an electric typewriter. He was a real purist. Just from what I remember of how he wrote, there would be pads of yellow paper, notes in margins and a lot of detailed notes."[97]

Lang was discreet about the relationship he developed with Storeby, one that evidently lasted until his death. "My father was very private about what he would be working on, which is sort of a superstitious thing," suggests Cecily Lang. She recalls briefly meeting Storeby "for about half an hour" during a trip with her father, but at that time she didn't even know his name. "It was important for Storeby's safety," she explains. "He continued to receive threats quite a long time after he reported the incident. I can remember that during this time, our telephone at home was tapped. I would hear these clicking noises on the line."[98] It is likely that the Pentagon was concerned about the impact Lang's investigations might have on American public opinion, which was shaken with the revelation of the My Lai massacre. Nevertheless, there is no evidence to suggest that Lang faced pressure during the writing of *Casualties of War*, much of which was done at his second home on Martha's Vineyard in what resembled a monastic cell: a small cabin with spartan furnishings (a desk, a cot) and no telephone.

At the conclusion of his investigation, Lang had at his disposal two sets of material – court-martial records and interviews he had conducted – which he drew from to craft his text. Apart from Storeby, Lang spoke with prosecutor Yelton, who provided useful details about Camp Radcliff. Yelton mentioned that the courtroom had the appearance of a "frame structure measuring thirty feet by thirty and roofed with tin," suggesting a stiflingly hot and cramped space.[99] There were regular disturbances, notably the noise of electric fans. Yelton noted that "a diesel generator, the base camp's source of electricity, made a constant racket, causing the law officers frequently to request witnesses to raise their voices."[100] This detail is significant as it partly explains why, in trial transcripts, Storeby is often asked to repeat his statements.

Lang also interviewed the Mormon chaplain who took Storeby's confession. Finding nothing about Storeby in the trial archives, Lang searched for him with Storeby's help and met him twice in Utah before he returned to Vietnam. His valuable testimony sheds light on Storeby's state of mind after reporting Mao's rape and murder: "I can assure you he wasn't being paranoid in thinking he might be shot in the back for seeing me. In war – at least, the war we were in – it was nothing unusual to hear shots that were unexplained, to find a body that might or might not have been shot in combat. Where we were, it was a time and place for thousands of men to play for keeps, and that certainly included [Gervase] and the others in the patrol, because if they wanted to eliminate [Storeby] as a potential witness, they had the M-16s to do it with."[101]

At the crossroads of journalism and literature

The writing of *Casualties of War* took nine months and wasn't without its difficulties. Unable to obtain copies of trial transcripts, Lang twice had to revisit the records office. He also found it necessary to conduct additional interviews with the Storebys in Minnesota. For these reasons, Lang found the writing exhausting, particularly because he also struggled to find a definitive structure for the story. After drafting an initial version that narrated the events chronologically, Lang cross-referenced military archives and discussed things anew with Storeby, after which he embarked on a second draft, which underwent several revisions before culminating in the version published by *The New Yorker*.

"The writing process involves not only an arrangement but selection and exclusion,"[102] posits Lang, who crafted his text with these three factors in mind. The "rearrangements" in *Casualties of War* take various forms. First, there is the use of pseudonyms: Robert Storeby, David Gervase, Steven Thomas, and Joseph and Chip Garcia are renamed, respectively, Sven Eriksson,[103] Tony Meserve, Ralph Clark, and Manuel and Rafe Diaz. The names of secondary characters in the story are also changed, with a few exceptions: Pearson, Spigelmire and Collins are now Rowan, Vorst and Reilly. Only Professor Furue and Colonel Finck retain their real names. While Lang respected the diverse backgrounds of the five primary protagonists, he altered their physical appearance, "to avoid the anger these men might feel toward [Storeby] if there were photographic, typed descriptions of them." He also allowed himself, as the narrative required, to invent pieces of dialogue.

In reviewing thousands of pages from the military archives and selecting what he felt was important for the story he wanted to tell, Lang was never aiming for absolute comprehensiveness. Space constraints clearly played a part. But more importantly, the purely legal aspects of Mao's murder interested him only tangentially. He intentionally removed much legal jargon from his text to ensure that Storeby's story remained clear and relatable for readers, most of whom would be unfamiliar with the intricacies of a military court. Importantly, Lang chose to narrate the case from the perspective of the main prosecution witness. He wanted to understand the motivations of one man, alone in a warzone, who refused to participate in a heinous sexual crime and murder – a narrative decision that reflected a particular ethical stance. Lang never sided with the perpetrators. In this regard, insights from conversations with Storeby are crucial. It is his character, emphasized Lang, "that is the engine of the story. This engine would have been lacking had I not interviewed him." During the hearings, Storeby seemed a taciturn, fierce, almost unsympathetic witness, but Lang paints him as a man attentive to the beauties of nature, sensitive to the pain of others, concerned with moral questions and burdened by a profound sense of guilt for not having been able to save Mao.

The structure of *Casualties of War* intertwines timelines, frequently shifting from the present to the past as Eriksson recalls his memories. In a prologue, Lang introduces his primary character, broadly sketches his story, reveals his feelings about the trials, which are still fresh in mind, and gives a detailed account of the events of November 1966. Where necessary, Lang subtly refers to the trials or offers insights into Eriksson's mood and demeanor. Lang tends toward a general simplification of the story, omitting anything that might overshadow the main narrative. He extracts a few striking images from trial archives (Mao's gold tooth, the scarf that was used as a gag, Thomas' hunting knife) and retains some anecdotes, for example Chip Garcia mistaking "the rump of a wallowing water buffalo"[104] for a North Vietnamese soldier. But certain details and even secondary characters are trimmed down or removed entirely, without compromising the integrity of the facts.

Had Lang been a painter, *Casualties of War* might have resembled not a meticulously detailed historical tableau but a ruggedly sketched landscape, animated by vividly expressive figures reminiscent of Goya. The reference to the Spanish painter isn't arbitrary. More than once *Casualties of War* evokes *The Disasters of War* – particularly those plates in which Goya depicts the barbaric acts committed by Napoleonic soldiers against Spanish women, who were either raped or killed. Contained within these visionary engravings lies the essence of *Casualties of War*. As its title implies, Lang's narrative transcends the specifics of the Vietnam War to explore war in a universal context: how it reshapes the morality of men and desecrates the dignity of women.

But unlike Goya, who spares no detail in showing us the cruelty of the executioners, Lang chose not to include the most macabre details as revealed in court-martial records. He barely elaborates on Mao's physical description after her rape, for example, refraining from stating that she bled after the sexual encounters forced upon her by the soldiers. Likely avoiding sensationalism, Lang also chose not to include testimony that depicts Gervase as a bloodthirsty brute, opting instead for an anecdote from Pearson that Gervase inexplicably shot at and injured a Vietnamese man shortly before Mao's abduction, so as to illustrate his gradual psychological deterioration.

Lang's writing is fluid, sensitive, restrained, subtle and relentless. Unlike the clinical aspect of trial transcripts, where Storeby's testimony is fragmented by legal inquiries, Lang presents his story uninterrupted, allowing it to make its full impact. And yet, Lang doesn't shy away from Storeby's/Eriksson's inner violence, showing time and again that his is not a straightforward testimony. Lang never ignores the moments of silence that precede some of the most harrowing parts of the story. One of the most powerful passages describes Eriksson's interaction with Mao in the hut.

> When Mao saw me come into the hootch, she thought I was there to rape her. She began to weep, and backed away, cringing. She looked weary and ill, and she seemed to be getting more so by the minute. I had the feeling she had been injured in some way – not that I could tell. She had her black pajamas on. I gave her crackers and beef stew and water. It was her first food since she'd been taken away from her hamlet – it had been still dark then, and here it was the middle of the afternoon. She ate, standing, and it was whimper, then eat, whimper, then eat. She kept looking at me, as though she was trying to guess what my game could be. When she finished eating, she mumbled something in Vietnamese; maybe it was 'Thank you' – I wouldn't know. And I told her, in English: 'I can't understand you.' I wanted to tell her other things. I wanted to say: 'I apologize to you for what's happened, but don't ever accept my apology or anyone else's for that. Please don't ask me to explain why they did it. I'll never know. You're hurt, I can see, but how are you? I mean, if I let you go, do you think you can make it home?' I wish Mao and I could have talked.[105]

After Mao's murder, which is described only from Storeby's perspective, Lang emphasizes "the intense feeling of frustration" that now plagues the soldier.[106] He is looked upon unfavorably by his comrades, who are aware of his efforts to expose the rape and murder of the young Vietnamese woman. Lang also reveals the subsequent conversations Storeby had with Lieutenant Collins (Reilly) and Captain Spigelmire (Vorst). Collins attempts to dissuade him from making trouble by recounting a personal anecdote. Three years earlier, his wife, about to give birth, was denied entry to an Alabama hospital for reasons of race. Like her husband, she was black. After increasingly strong contractions, she gave birth to the child on the floor of the hospital's lobby, and her enraged husband wreaked havoc on the place. After the police intervened and arrested him, the young father contemplated some form of revenge, but in the end never followed through. Collins' lesson to Storeby is clear: "What's happened is the way things are, so why try to buck the system? And take it from me… it's even more hopeless to try to buck it in the middle of a war – there's more of a system then than ever. Better relax about that Vietnamese girl… The kind of thing that happened to her – what else can you expect in a combat zone?"[107]

Lang notes that Collins quickly tells his superior, Captain Spigelmire, to whom Storeby initially confided during a field mission, about the rape and murder. Storeby later met with Spigelmire twice, in his office, where the officer assured him that he was taking control of the situation and that he would "handle everything," while emphasizing – albeit ambiguously – the dangers Storeby faced by moving forward with his allegations.[108] That Storeby's life was indeed under threat was evidenced by an event that occurred at the end of November 1966, before the military-judicial machinery had been set in motion. During the pursuit of two or three North Vietnamese, Storeby's patrol came under fire from its flank. It quickly became apparent, after a few seconds of confusion, that the shots were coming from another group of G.I.s. While the two patrol leaders were in conversation, Storeby noticed "a familiar face" among the ranks of the other unit: Joseph Garcia. "We just looked at each other, without saying hello," Storeby reported to Lang. "Seeing him made me think at once of two questions I would have liked to ask him or his sergeant. Just who, I wanted to ask, was the man in Manuel's patrol who started the shooting? And who was the man who fired the last shot? I couldn't even guess at the answers –

not without knowing what kind of jam Manuel thought he was in."[109] Lang doesn't dwell much on this incident, which was perhaps an attempt to permanently silence Storeby. The next day, Spigelmire arranged for Storeby to be transferred to Camp Radcliff, about sixty miles from his section headquarters, and reassigned to the 545th Military Police Company.

Lang then details the investigation to find Mao's body, Storeby's "confession" to the chaplain, his treatment by CID agents, the investigations on Hill 192, and the autopsy. The trials feature only in the final part of *Casualties of War*. Lang cites the archives, but also, crucially, sheds light on Storeby's feelings before, during and after the trials, revealing that "despite his status as the Army's chief witness… [he] took the stand practically cold," that the prosecutor "did warn him […] of the possible consequences for him and his wife of his testifying for the government." Storeby was also advised "to see a psychiatrist before the trials started" and obtain a document attesting to his mental health to counter potential defenses.[110]

More surprising is the distance maintained by Storeby from the legal machinery, the fact that he shares with Lang a belief that the trials "seemed related to Mao's murder in only a surface sense" – almost as if they were a mockery of justice.[111] "As early as the opening day of [Chip's] trial, which was the first one held, he realized that it was idle to consider whether the G.I.s' punishment would, or could, fit the crime. Throughout […] the belief that sustained him was that in serving as the defendants' principal accuser he was carrying out the resolve he had made as he trained his grenade launcher on the cave complex; namely, to let the world know of Mao's fate."[112] Lang effectively contrasts the effusive testimonies of the military toward Storeby with the attacks he has to endure – being alternatively depicted as a soldier lacking any humor or even a coward excessively concerned about his own well-being. These slanders appear to have had little effect on him. He is more concerned with the memory of Mao, who has never left his thoughts since that fateful day in November 1966.

The final pages of *Casualties of War* describe Storeby's return to Minnesota, his reunion with his wife, and how Mao's story has transformed him. Lang presents Storeby not merely as a demobilized soldier but as a man striving to rebuild his life while grappling with the weight of his past, aware that he can never fully leave behind his Vietnam experiences. His wife hints at this: "The girl was very much with us when Sven came home that day, and maybe she always will be."[113] Storeby seems to have found some solace in religion, engaging in parish activities. As a Lutheran, before his deployment he was somewhat interested in spiritual matters, feelings that intensify thanks to time spent in Vietnam. "We all figured we might be dead in the next minute," he reflects, "so what difference did it make what we did? But the longer I was over there, the more I became convinced that it was the other way around that counted – that because we might not be around much longer, we had to take extra care how we behaved. Anyway, that's what made me believe I was interested in religion. Another man might have called it something else, but the idea was simply that we had to answer for what we did. We had to answer to something, to someone – maybe just to ourselves."[114]

But the refuge provided by his faith doesn't spare him from anxiety in the aftermath of the case. Lang reports – without knowing all the details – the steps taken by the accused and their lawyers to reduce the sentences. Following Joseph Garcia's appeal, Storeby confesses that he feels a certain despondency and weariness, especially as the acquittal seemed predetermined. The threat looms of similar re-evaluations of other verdicts.

Lang concludes *Casualties of War* on an ambivalent, almost fatalistic note, with Eriksson observing that his comrades "were among the ones – among the few – who did what everyone around them wanted to do."[115] Clear-eyed about his own actions and not seeing himself above reproach, Eriksson must now learn to live with the weight of guilt, the feeling that he has somehow failed. "He had yet to exonerate himself from the self-imposed charge of having failed to save Mao's life. He had no idea how long this feeling would continue, but for the present, he knew, he lived with the charge daily, often wondering how Mao might have fared in a time of peace."[116]

Once a version satisfactory to all concerned was completed, Lang gave a copy of the manuscript to his wife Margaret[117] and another to William Shawn, to whom he later dedicated the book. He read parts of it to Storeby and his wife to ensure he wasn't misrepresenting anything. And so began the editing process. "They checked what they could and made some editorial suggestions, several of which I accepted," says Lang.[118]

The publication and reception of *Casualties of War*

It took two and a half years from the time Lang became aware of the events in the Vietnamese jungle in November 1966 to the publication of his article in *The New Yorker*. He completed his work, begun during the presidency of Lyndon Johnson, a few months after the election of Richard Nixon – a period when American public opinion was increasingly hostile to the war in Vietnam, not least because the press was reporting on missteps by the American military.[119]

In August 1969, a few weeks before the release of *Casualties of War*, *Esquire* published an article by Normand Poirier with the striking title "An American Atrocity," about horrors committed by Marines in the village of Xuan Ngoc in 1966, including the rape of an 18-old-woman and mother of a three-year-old child, Bui Thi Hong, by five soldiers, in front of her husband, who was later executed. Poirier's article, though more traditionally structured than Lang's, follows a similar progression, recounting first the crimes in Xuan Ngoc, then the investigation conducted by the Marine Corps, and finally the military trials of the ten soldiers involved.

The incidents Poirier wrote about were part of a broader pattern. Nick Turse reports that, during the same period, the American army engaged in acts of torture against peasants suspected of collusion with the North Vietnamese.[120] He cites the murder of one Do Van Man, humiliated and tortured in front of his wife and children, then shot seven times in a forest. This murder was denounced by a 21-year-old soldier, George Chunko, in a letter sent to his parents, the day before his death. The official account is that Chunko was ambushed by the enemy, though everything suggests that he was assassinated by his comrades, who had every interest in keeping him silent, much like the fate narrowly avoided by Storeby. The case eventually led to an investigation that resulted in the indictment of a lieutenant who was found guilty of premeditated murder, before the jury reversed its decision and sentenced him to only six months in prison.

In mid-November 1969, journalist Seymour Hersh revealed the atrocities committed by Lieutenant William Calley and his men at My Lai on March 16, 1968, where members of Charlie Company massacred more than five hundred South Vietnamese civilians, including women and children. After Ron Ridenhour's unsuccessful attempts to bring the truth to light, Hersh succeeded in getting his article circulated through a press agency and distributed to 35 newspapers. A stunned America discovered that the My Lai killers were "the boys next door": sons, brothers, husbands and fathers, all thought to be beyond reproach. It was particularly challenging for the general public to accept that the perpetrators were also rapists. Before the massacre, many female villagers – some young teenagers – were sexually abused and tortured, but the press never dwelt on these facts, nor were any of the perpetrators ever brought to trial. Rape in Vietnam, it turns out, was an "everyday affair," a "standard operating procedure, and it was a rare GI who possessed the individual courage or morality to go against his buddies and report, let alone stop, the offense."[121]

Such was the backdrop to the publication of *Casualties of War*. Daniel Lang, aiming to imbue his work with a universal dimension, deliberately avoided crafting a diatribe against government policy, but this didn't stop his publisher from capitalizing on current events. The release of Lang's reporting as a book, after its initial publication in *The New Yorker*, coincided with the Moratorium to End the War in Vietnam on November 15, 1969, when nearly half a million people gathered in Washington D.C. *Casualties of War* had all the potential to become a focal point for feminist artists like Nancy Spero, Yoko Ono and Judy Chicago, who at the time, with remarkable freedom of expression, were reflecting on the relationships between the female body and war. But that never happened, maybe because Phan Thi Mao's ordeal was seen entirely through a male perspective, reducing the victim, by necessity, to a silent figure – albeit not an insignificant one.

Another reason for the missed connections between *Casualties of War* and the outpouring of the era's visual artists is that Lang narrates an event without images, which makes it a very different affair from My Lai. When the press exposed that crime, they immediately released a series of horrific photographs taken by Sergeant Ronald Haeberle, images that provide a glimpse of the extent of the massacre and that were used by numerous artists for purposes of condemnation. And the crimes committed against Mao were primarily of a sexual nature. Before Susan Brownmiller's seminal 1975 book on rape,[122] this crime was widely perceived as an "inescapable dimension of wars,"[123] and as historian J. Robert Lilly points out, it was difficult at the time to obtain court-martial statistics on rapes committed by the U.S. Army in Vietnam.[124] The specificity of Lang's book – which was ahead of its time – wasn't fully recognized. Commentators focused instead on other aspects of the work, during a period marked by Hannah Arendt's philosophical concept of the "banality of evil."

Critics unanimously praised the literary qualities of *Casualties of War*. Ward Just deemed it an instant classic, praising Lang's "fine sense of morality, intelligence, and literary skill" and his ability to avoid the pitfalls inherent in such an endeavor, notably "sentimentality and preaching."[125] Richard Christiansen noted Lang's "beautifully understated style,"[126] while Christopher Lehmann-Haupt of *The New York Times* considered it an example of "reporting at its best."[127] In terms of substance, critics agreed that *Casualties of War* was "a powerful metaphor for American involvement in Vietnam,"[128] an idea embraced by Brian De Palma twenty years later, even though that was never Lang's intention as a writer. For him, Vietnam serves as a backdrop to his narrative. In his review of Lang's book, John Raymond notes: "Lang's 'casualties' are the girl who loses her life, the soldiers who lose their humanity and the system that loses a sense of justice. War is hell – we all know that, Sherman knew it, Caesar knew it. Lang simply says it again. But this little book is disturbing not because of what it says about war. It is disturbing because of what it says about humankind whether in war or peace. For if most of us can change into killers so easily – and remember a 'civilized' nation did that only a few decades ago – if our humanity is such a fragile thing, then it's only a matter of time."[129]

Raymond's observation prompts a moment's reflection on the title selected by Lang for his article and book – a universal choice that veils the particulars.[130] The use of the plural suggests that there might be other victims besides Mao: Eriksson, certainly, but also his comrades, those deemed to have acted, as Gervase's lawyer described it, "outside of civilization." According to this interpretation, they might all be considered victims of war. Does this then imply that the line between victim and perpetrator is a thin one? Definitely not. In this regard, Raymond misinterprets by suggesting that anyone could become a killer, implying a reversible role that inherently disregards questions of free will and moral conscience.

Furthermore, Lang demonstrates in his book no sense of the "banality of evil." On the contrary, he poses the vital question of individual responsibility. What drives a man to step outside the bounds imposed by a military infrastructure? Ultimately, Lang interrogates the capacity for disobedience through the unique example of Storeby. But Storeby only partially disobeys. He refuses to contravene Articles 118 and 120 of the military code and compromise his own morality, but doesn't go as far as desertion, aware as he is that it could lead to a court-martial, even though such a move might have saved Mao's life. This is why Lang's Eriksson emerges as a tragic hero, defined by his powerlessness and a deep sense of failure, and why *Casualties of War*, far from offering comforting clichés, poses a question to every reader, one that only they, deep within themselves, can answer: "And you – what would you have done in Eriksson's place?"

Casualties of War was quickly and widely disseminated. Republished by the British newspaper *The Observer*,[131] the article was translated into other languages, in book form, across Europe and even Asia. Lang collected several awards,[132] and just days after its publication in *The New Yorker*, film producers of various nationalities rushed to acquire the rights. Thus begins the second chapter of the complex and captivating story of *Casualties of War*: its cinematic evocations.

From the Forests of Bavaria to the Snows of Connecticut: Variations and Extensions
1970 – 1972

Attempts to adapt *Casualties of War* for both the big and small screen played out in Hollywood for nearly two decades. Each one failed in turn. Before tracing these histories, it is important to explore two films that, within a short period, were inspired by Daniel Lang's text without constituting literal adaptations: *o.k.* by Michael Verhoeven and *The Visitors* by Elia Kazan. Both were released at a time when the Vietnam War had not yet become a significant subject for American film. Both, in their own way, are important, if overlooked or forgotten, milestones in cinematic representation of the conflict.

André Muraire speaks of "avoidance strategies" regarding the partly "unspeakable" subject of the war in Vietnam, correctly observing that films using the conflict as a backdrop are, for the most part, "minor works" that often present "political-diplomatic intrigues and espionage."[1] The only Hollywood film of the 1960s that centered on Vietnam, *The Green Berets*, made no attempt to conceal its objective: to legitimize the fight of the American military against communism. The Pentagon actually supported the production of the film by providing nearly a million dollars' worth of material aid.[2]

Hollywood's attempts to denounce the war in Vietnam were initially implicit and camouflaged.[3] Consider in this context Robert Wise's *The Sand Pebbles* (1966). Although set in 1920s China, its action serves to underscore a decidedly critical line against American interventionist policy.[4] Toward the end of the film, gunboat commander Captain Collins

(Richard Crenna) tries to persuade missionary Jameson (Larry Gates) and Miss Eckert (Candice Bergen) to evacuate from the monastery where they are staying. When he asserts that Eckert will be raped by the Chinese, Jameson responds with: "What have you ever cared of Chinese women raped and butchered by the warlord troops you favor with your unequal treaties?" – a critique squarely targeting the American army in Vietnam. When the film premiered in American cinemas, barely a month after the rape and murder of Phan Thi Mao, reality had caught up with fiction.

The late 1960s to the mid-1970s brought a wave of protest films. Alongside well-known titles like *Alice's Restaurant*, *Zabriskie Point* and *Punishment Park* are a number of lesser-known works that merit recognition, including *Hail, Hero!*, *Summertree* and Brian De Palma's early films *Greetings* (1968) and *Hi, Mom!* (1970). Documentary cinema – notably *In the Year of the Pig*, which sparked intense reactions upon its release, and *Winter Soldier*, filmed during the winter of 1971 at a meeting organized by the Vietnam Veterans Against the War – is part of this framework.[5]

In this context, Verhoeven's and Kazan's films are important not just because they explicitly tackle the Vietnam War but because they both take Lang's *Casualties of War* as a starting point and yet employ narrative and aesthetic strategies that are poles apart.

o.k.: the story of a long-invisible film

Most historiographers fail to recall that the very first film-related mention of *Casualties of War* came about in Germany in 1970. Seldom referenced by film historians, Verhoeven's *o.k.* is notably absent from the comprehensive encyclopedia of films on the Vietnam War edited by Jean-Jacques Malo and Tony Williams in 1994, which catalogues six hundred films from various countries. While there are some allusions to *o.k.* here and there, including on the internet, they mostly revolve around the historical scandal that the film sparked during its 1970 premiere at the Berlin Film Festival. The story of *o.k.* is certainly bound up in its own tumultuous reception, but we should not ignore the fact that it is an extraordinary, radical and uncompromising work, among the most astonishing anti-war statements in film history.

In defense of the historiographers, Verhoeven's work was almost unseen for nearly fifty years. Viewing *o.k.* had long been a challenge, especially for non-German-speaking researchers. The film received its first broadcast on German television in February 2002, in a late-night spot on the private channel VOX. Accessible at the Bundesarchiv, which has a copy with no subtitles, the film was digitized by the Munich Film Museum in 2016 using the original camera negative,[6] but for legal reasons wasn't seen until 28 February 2020, when it was screened to mark the fiftieth anniversary of its premiere at the Berlin Film Festival. This was followed by a remastered DVD release by the Munich Film Museum. Once a *film maudit*, *o.k.* is now on the brink of rediscovery and celebrated as a significant work of German cinema. Although unquestionably deserving of its re-emergence from obscurity, it also raises delicate questions about the appropriation of Lang's text, necessitating an extended analysis of the film and its reception.

The genesis of *o.k.* is fascinating, on several counts. In late 1969, Michael Verhoeven, a young filmmaker who until recently had worked in the theater, read an article in *Der Spiegel* recounting events similar to those detailed by Lang in *The New Yorker*. The soldiers mentioned in the article had German names instead of Lang's American pseudonyms.[7] Verhoeven was immediately drawn in and decided to adapt the article into a play entitled *Alles o.k.* [*Everything's o.k.*]. A small Munich theater expressed interest.

Verhoeven, meanwhile, wasn't happy with the contract he had with his producer, Rob Houwer, for whom he had directed two comedies, *Hoppe Hoppe Reiter* (1968) and *Der Bettenstudent* (1969). Contractually obliged to make a third film, Verhoeven was offered a new comedy by Houwer, which he found uninteresting and so turned it down. Instead, he presented Houwer with his newly written play, suggesting he adapt it into a film. Houwer agreed. "Michael pleasantly surprised me with the quality of his script," recalls Houwer. "He said it was based on a real incident during the Vietnam War but never mentioned its source. I acquired the rights to the screenplay for production."[8] Verhoeven, meanwhile, discovered that the story he had read in the German press had been originally published in *The New Yorker*, prompting him to modify the names in his script, mistakenly believing them to be the actual identities of the individuals involved. He never thought it necessary to inquire into the adaptation rights of *Casualties of War*.

Houwer and Verhoeven signed a new contract, and pre-production on *o.k.* began. It was a low-budget production. The actors, for example, brought their own props. As with his theater work, realism wasn't Verhoeven's primary concern. Instead, he wanted *o.k.* to serve as a discussion on how Germans perceived – and accepted – the Vietnam War. "Every evening, when people sat down for dinner, the Vietnam War was like a *divertimento*. People watched it on their TVs. There was nothing hidden, as was the case with later wars. I wanted to tell this story to Germans and make Americans seem more relatable to them, for instance by having them speak Bavarian, so the audience would feel closer to the conflict. The younger German generation was against the war, just like young Americans in the United States, while older people supported it. They had no idea where it was happening – Vietnam was very far away – but they thought it was necessary because Americans were supposedly fighting for our freedom."[9]

A few months prior to *o.k.*, Verhoeven had made a ten-minute film entitled *Tables*, which serves as a kind of first draft of his feature. It deals with the absurd quarrel that erupted in Paris in early 1969, during the peace negotiations, over the shape of the table around which Americans and North and South Vietnamese were to debate. Dialogue-free, *Tables* combines brief images of tables, both archival and newly filmed, with those of the ravages of war in Vietnam (bombs dropped, scenes of atrocities, portraits of grieving or mutilated children), all to the sound of melancholy music. The forcefulness of the editing is enhanced by the sounds of bombs and machine-gun bursts grafted onto sequences showing the construction of wooden tables. Operating and autopsy tables are filmed, as well as forensic instruments in morgues and medical faculties, signifying that while negotiations have bogged down, corpses are piling up.

With his discovery of Mao's story, Verhoeven believed he had found a way to extend and even intensify his critique of the Vietnam war. His project was reminiscent, in its intention, of the series of fifteen photomontages by the American artist Martha Rosler, "Bringing the War Home" (1967-72), a scathing critique of American intervention in Vietnam and how it was presented to the public, comprised of *Life* magazine photographs of current events juxtaposed with shots from interior design magazines. Nicole Schweizer notes that "this intervention into the space of representation shaped by the media is to be read in the broader context of image production and circulation during the Vietnam War – the first war broadcasted into private spaces via the small screen."[10]

The most famous of these photomontages, "Tron (Amputee)," was created from a photograph by Larry Burrows that appeared on the cover of *Life* magazine. It shows a twelve-year-old girl, Nguyen Thi Tron, injured by a bomb dropped by an American helicopter in a "free-fire zone," waiting for a prosthetic that is being made for her. In Rosler's version, the girl appears in the foreground, in front of an elegant living room replete with sofa, coffee table and television. According to Mignon Nixon, Rosler "de-domesticates the war image" by choosing to shift the figure of the mutilated girl to the edge of the frame, thus distancing her from the place she occupies "in the genre of popular war reportage."[11] The television screen in the background also takes on an accusatory function that surpasses the strict framework of the Vietnam War, echoing Susan Sontag's critique: "The war America waged against Vietnam, the first to be witnessed day after day by television cameras, introduced the home front to a new tele-intimacy with death and destruction. Ever since, battles and massacres filmed as they unfold have been a routine ingredient of the ceaseless flow of domestic, small-screen entertainment."[12]

The way in which war is made visible – turned into a spectacle through television coverage – is also targeted by Verhoeven. He aims to show the other side of the coin: not the suffering endured by American soldiers but the atrocities they commit, far from the cameras, in the name of their supposed values. Verhoeven rejects the notion of Mao as mere collateral damage of the war the Americans are waging against the communists. Her ordeal becomes a testament to another form of violence, less about the war itself than about underlying fascism and entrenched misogyny – a topic of heated contention in post-war Germany. Verhoeven's strategy isn't about reconstructing the war but bringing it home.

Most of *o.k.* was shot in the forest adjoining the small town of Grünwald in Upper Bavaria, the village school of Oberhaching, several miles from Grünwald, and on the banks of the Isar, the river that runs through Munich. Because of time and budget constraints, Verhoeven didn't hold auditions and chose to play Eriksson himself, a role he "personally identified" with. The other four male leads, all relatively unknown in 1970, are Friedrich von Thun (Meserve), Hartmut Becker (Clark), Wolfgang Fischer (Rafe) and Ewald Precht (Diaz). The actors playing Lieutenant Reilly and Captain Vorst, Rolf Castell and Gustl Bayrhammer, were experienced German television actors. Eva Mattes, in the role of Mao, spotted by Rob Houwer when he was casting another of his films, was only 16 years old. (In addition to her well-known collaborations with Werner Herzog and Rainer Fassbinder, Eva Mattes later played the heroine of Helma Sanders-Brahms' *Germany, Pale Mother* [1980], who is raped by American soldiers at the end of the Second World War.)

After three weeks of rehearsals, the 11-day shoot began with black-and-white film stock. Verhoeven felt that color imagery would have "nullified the harsh reality" of the story (an arguable point given that many images from Vietnam are in color).[13] This aesthetic choice gives the film a cold, rough look. Post-production of *o.k.* was completed in time for the film to be included for selection in the Berlin Film Festival, which began on June 26, 1970. But before delving into the film's reception, it is important to examine in more detail its singular nature and to consider its relationship with Daniel Lang's text.

The main narrative of *o.k.* is situated between a prologue and epilogue, inviting the viewer behind the scenes of the film. The seven-minute opening sequence shows Michael Verhoeven and his actors walking into a building, one room of which is filled with costumes, lights, camera equipment and a film crew. A clapperboard marked "HOUWER FILM" appears in front of the camera, and then, while standing in front of a window, the five main actors take turns identifying themselves and stating the name of the character they will be playing in the film.

From the Forests of Bavaria to the Snows of Connecticut

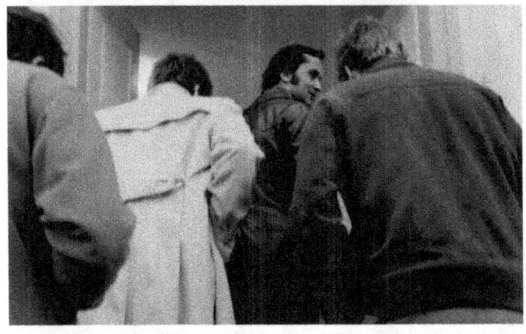

From the Forests of Bavaria to the Snows of Connecticut 71

The camera cuts and tracks across the room to frame Eva Mattes, standing alone, also in front of a window. In an extreme close-up, she identifies herself and says that she will be playing the role of Mao. Verhoeven explains: "It was a kind of rendezvous between the creators of the film and the audience. 'We're going to tell you a story that might interest you. But this isn't reality. Reality is different. We will show you how we think things could have happened.'" Verhoeven's hope is to "demystify the artistic process" so that that the viewer feels the gap between reality and its representation. As Bertolt Brecht wrote: "Just as the actor no longer has to persuade the audience that it is the author's character and not himself that is standing on the stage, so also he need not pretend that the events taking place on the stage have never been rehearsed, and are now happening for the first and only time."[14]

Seven years earlier, Jean-Luc Godard referenced Brecht in *Les Carabiniers*, his war satire with intentionally grimy aesthetics, filmed with a handheld Cameflex camera on shabby sets near Paris.[15] The film tells the story of two uneducated brothers, Ulysses and Michelangelo, conscripted by order of the "king" to participate in a conflict that, it is hinted, may yet become global. Hoping for riches, they head to the front and commit the worst kinds of atrocities (looting, murders, rapes). Raw and impure, *Les Carabiniers* contains numerous allusions to rape without showing it on screen. The two soldiers who visit Ulysses and Michelangelo at the beginning of the film promise that, upon enlisting, they will have the right during wartime to take anything they want, including "women of the world" and "women who undress." Gesturing as they speak, one of the soldiers pulls out pin-up photos from his jacket, arousing the brothers' interest. Once on the road, they eagerly fulfill their fantasies: the younger brother delights in lifting women's skirts with the barrel of his machine gun to see "what's hidden there," and even asks one of his captives, after chasing away her child, to undress and get on all fours so he can mount her like a horse. They later stop a car, force the driver out, and continue the journey with his wife (subsequent events are easily imagined). In the final part of the film, as defeat approaches, the victors turn into executioners, suggesting that all armies regress "toward the zero degree of humanity."¹⁶ This is also the essence of Verhoeven's film, which like *Les Carabiniers* unfolds in a kind of timeless realm where barbarity has found a home.

o.k. is divided into 16 segments, each introduced by an intertitle and the same slightly deranged refrain from *krautrock* group Improved Sound Limited. The film is more or less inspired by the tableaux of the Bavarian Passion (*Passionspiele*), as re-enacted every ten years by the villagers of Oberammergau, depicting the sufferings, death and resurrection of Christ. In *o.k.*, however, instead of Christ, there is a fifteen-year-old virgin whose rape constitutes the Way of the Cross.

The first seven segments show the soldiers doing military exercises under Sergeant Meserve's command in a clearing where dozens of trees have been cut down. The men are seen carving stakes, setting up barbed wire, digging foxholes and traversing the forest at a quick pace with their faces hidden behind gas masks. But this preparation doesn't lead to any scenes of combat, and the enemy remains mysteriously unseen. At most, its presence is suggested by the sudden

appearance of an artillery shell that lands in front of the men, seemingly out of nowhere, during a card game. Even this elicits no response from the soldiers, who, once the smoke clears, opt to continue their game as if nothing has happened. This sequence typifies the film's offbeat tone, one that aims primarily to satirize war itself and, by extension, how war is generally represented on film. Two decades earlier, Stanley Kubrick had set his first feature, *Fear and Desire*, in a forest where a war is taking place at a moment in time that is "neither past nor future," where the enemy is invisible and "everything that happens is 'outside History.'"[17]

The first half of *o.k.*, filled with Rafe's antics, is a knockabout army comedy that flirts occasionally with the mundane (close-ups of soldiers' mouths as they eat rations and chew gum). Stylistically, the film, which is far from conventional, leans toward the experimental. The wide range of shots (high- and low-angle, close-ups) and camera movements (lateral or circular tracking shots, panoramic views, zooms, handheld) all help to disrupt the film's visual unity and (at least in the first half) potentially obscure any political message it might have. The complexity of some shots betrays an aestheticism that a purer, less ostentatious style might have mitigated. But it is precisely this varied aesthetic that gives the film much of its originality, strangeness and intensity.

Mao makes only a brief appearance in the first half, in the fourth segment entitled "Mensch und Natur" ("Men and Nature"). While the soldiers chat in their foxholes, their conversation is abruptly interrupted by a metallic noise off-screen: the sound of a milk can attached to the handlebars of Mao's bicycle. It is later revealed that she is going to the city to fetch supplies for her younger brother, who is sick. The camera follows her journey through the foliage from the perspective of the soldiers. With his comrades watching, Rafe pretends to shoot at her, mimicking the sound of bullets fired from an imaginary automatic weapon.

Mao reappears about 20 minutes later, in the eighth segment, as she makes her way back to her village. This time Diaz stops her and takes her to Meserve, who begins his interrogation under Rafe and Clark's amused gaze. We learn that she is 15,[18] Catholic, training to be a seamstress, and that her father "collects scrap paper for the Red Cross." Accused of being a communist spy, Mao defends herself. At this point Eriksson, who until now has been sitting apart from the soldiers and Mao, observing, decides to intervene. He walks over, picks up the bicycle, and to everyone's bewilderment hands it to Mao, telling her to go home. An unyielding Meserve grabs the bike, pushes it to the ground, grabs the young girl by the wrist, and tells Eriksson to stand down.

His interrogation of Mao takes a turn when the soldiers force her to make a mock religious confession, on the pretext that she can leave if she confesses to masturbating. "Since fourth grade," she answers shamefully. As she tries to escape, Diaz, holding her milk can, pours its contents onto the ground. Mao's fate is sealed. It is now clear that she will not escape unscathed.

The satirical, offbeat tone of the first part has given way to a cold representation of Mao's ordeal as Diaz, Rafe, Clark and Meserve rape the girl in turn. Each assault is the subject of a segment, for a total duration of almost ten minutes. Never before had rape been shown in cinema with such brutal realism.[19] Diaz is first, with the help of Clark, who slaps her twice before holding a knife to her throat. Meserve then throws her underwear in her face. He is ready to let her go, but Rafe voices his disapproval, claiming he should "have the same rights as Diaz." Attempting to escape again, Mao struggles as Clark and Diaz overpower her. Eriksson tries to seize the moment and grab a weapon, but Rafe stops him. To muffle Mao's screams, Clark fills her mouth with earth and Rafe rapes her.

Eriksson remains stoic throughout, and theatrically proclaims: "Don't worry, Mao. I'll report them all. I'll tell the company commander tonight." "No one will believe you," says Meserve. Eriksson starts to run, only to be caught by Meserve, Clark and Diaz, who beat him. Mao again tries to escape from the clutches of her captors but is stopped short by barbed wire. She cries out "Mama, mama!" as she falls and is scratched in several places. Rafe, Diaz and Clark grab her and Clark rapes her, followed by Meserve. Eriksson's comrades try to force him to take his turn, undressing him and holding him over the victim. He struggles, resisting and spitting on Meserve.

Rafe eventually frees Mao from her restraints, but her body is limp. Anguished, Eriksson tries to drag her away. Clark – either to confirm her death or out of sheer cruelty – stabs her in the stomach with a knife. Mao suddenly rises (she was only unconscious) and begins to crawl on all fours, like a wounded animal, to escape her assailants. Meserve fires a shot, followed by Clark, who unleashes a burst from a machine gun. Even though she is already dead, they are merciless in their assault on her body. The images cut between close-ups of various faces: Meserve, Clark and Mao, her eyes frozen.

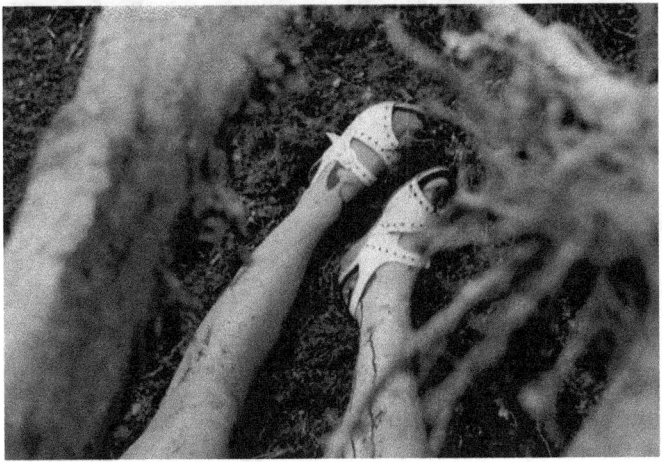

A breathless chase ensues between Eriksson, who has managed to flee on the victim's bicycle, and the trio of Clark, Diaz and Rafe. Having partially outpaced his pursuers, Eriksson is slowed by a hill and forced to dismount his bike. The other three soldiers catch up, and when Eriksson is finally in sight, Clark pulls out his pistol, fires several times, and eventually hits the bike's rear wheel. Eriksson abandons the bike and runs for his life.

Meserve and his men dispose of Mao's body by tossing it into the Isar River. (The scene was filmed in the middle of March. Eva Mattes was instructed to remain still in the icy water, which she did – admirably). Eriksson reports his comrades to Lieutenant Reilly and Captain Vorst, who listen disdainfully and argue on behalf of Meserve and his men. When Eriksson suggests that the officers are duty bound to do something about the crimes that have been committed, Vorst responds with: "I don't have to do anything, my friend. You remember that. I understand you. You're a bright young guy and atrocities like this don't sit well with you. That's perfectly okay. But you're forgetting one thing: we're defending the freedom of this country and the human rights of Western liberal democracy in their entirety. And we make the greatest sacrifices on behalf of this defense. Consider the untold suffering American soldiers have undergone on behalf of the Vietnamese. You'll realize on your own that a story like that one, as sad as it may be in this particular case, cannot be blown out of proportion."

Encouraged by Vorst to talk about Meserve, Reilly declares that the sergeant's "character and courage are among the finest" he knows, that he is "a first-rate soldier who never makes mistakes and executes every order without opposition." "He's a cruel bastard," replies Eriksson. "Shut up, you stupid kid," says Vorst, implying that the highest form of justice will be the inability of Meserve and his men to absolve themselves of their guilt. "The matter will remain between us and is settled," concludes Vorst firmly, insisting, as Eriksson leaves the room, that this crime was committed "outside civilization." A disgusted Eriksson has no choice but to rejoin his comrades in the forest, where they pass the time playing cards and where he now faces their mockery.

The film ends as it began: the actors take off their costumes, while a voiceover announces that the culprits, tried and convicted, have all had their sentences commuted, and that one of them has even been reinstated in the army. Verhoeven and his crew, dressed casually, exit the building, with Eva Mattes embracing the director. They depart, laughing.

o.k. is clearly not a literal adaptation of Lang's text. Verhoeven used only a general outline, and the first half of the film has little to do with the actual events. Moreover, Mao's rape and murder, unplanned by Meserve, appear to be the result of a jest gone wrong.

The heroic nature of Verhoeven's Eriksson contrasts with the more complex portrait that Lang paints of the soldier in *Casualties of War*. In *o.k.* he intervenes, tries to save Mao, puts his own life in danger, and eventually flees after the murder to report the crime to officers who ignore it. The tragedy and ambiguity of the character has been stripped away. But Verhoeven isn't interested in historical reconstruction. The Bavarian forest replaces the tropical jungle; the soldiers, despite the American names on their uniforms, speak Bavarian; except for her name, the victim isn't Vietnamese; and while the Vietnam War serves as a backdrop to the story, it is more than anything a pretext for a universal discourse on the barbarity perpetrated by the so-called champions of freedom.

The quote that opens the film – "The bullet went in one of humanity's ears and out the other" – is from Karl Kraus' play *The Last Days of Mankind*, published in 1922, from which Verhoeven draws much of his inspiration (a satirical tone, the story's fragmented structure, its critique of the media). In scene 54 of Kraus' play, the character of the Complainer launches into a long monologue, which concludes with: "I have done no more than condense the scale of mass murder, taking the measure of the amorphous alliance between the age of journalism and the journalism of the age. Its blood was merely ink – now the writing will be in blood! This is the World War. This is my manifesto. I have weighed everything in the balance. The tragedy, fractured into scenes reflecting mankind's fallen state, I have taken upon myself, so that it may be heard by a spirit that takes pity on the victims, even if it had renounced forever all connection to a human ear. Let it hear the keynote of these times, the echo of my bloodthirsty obsession, which makes me complicit with these cries. Let it be an act of redemption!"[20]

This searing tirade from Kraus resonates powerfully with *o.k.* and its unwaveringly anti-military stance. In the midst of a tense and combustible international climate, the film's unflinching message proved too incendiary to escape the grip of censorship. The clash reached its explosive climax in June 1970, on the world stage of the Berlin International Film Festival.

Established in 1951 under the impetus of Oscar Martay, an officer in the American army, the Berlin Film Festival (Berlinale) was designed to be a strategic political act, intended to play "a key role both in the construction of West Germany's national identity and in the cultural policies of the Cold War." Thus, "festival organizers made special efforts before 1961 to entice visitors from East Berlin, offering reduced ticket prices and screenings in the Soviet sector to ensure the broadest exposure in the East."[21]

The status that the Berlinale has in Germany is best understood by recalling tensions between West German cinema, heavily influenced by American film, and that of the East, guided by the Soviet Union in a "democratic and humanistic" direction.[22] As highlighted by Bernard Eisenschitz, the startling contradiction within East German cinema was that for two decades its films were notably superior to those of the West, even while they were forced to toe the Soviet line, specifically "ritual formulas of adherence to socialism."[23] In the West, the film industry – initially marked by a form of amnesia regarding its Nazi past, one that the American model more or less obscured – saw the emergence in the mid-1960s of a new generation of filmmakers, including Wim Wenders, Volker Schlöndorff, Rainer Werner Fassbinder and Werner Herzog. These filmmakers, however talented, operated within a "network of parallel cinemas" mainly frequented by a student audience.[24]

As Marijke de Valck notes: "While events of 1968 became the turning point for both Cannes and Venice, the Berlinale had to wait two more years before a conflict stimulated dissatisfaction to the point where significant changes were made to the festival's format."[25] As the Berlinale's twentieth edition began, however, there were no signs of any such upheaval. The selection that year was impressive. Among the notable films playing were Satyajit Ray's *Days and Nights in the Forest*, Ruy Guerra's *The Gods and the Dead*, Kei Kumai's *Sandakan 8*, Fassbinder's *Why Does Herr R. Run Amok?* (co-directed with Michael Fengler) and Bernardo Bertolucci's *The Conformist*. Also present in the official selection was none other than Brian De Palma. At the start of his career, De Palma was by no means a complete unknown to festivalgoers, as he had won the Silver Bear the previous year for his satire on Lyndon Johnson's America, *Greetings*.

Shortly before the Berlinale screening of *o.k.*, rumors were circulating regarding the supposed anti-Americanism of Verhoeven's film. On the day of its unveiling – June 30, at Zoo Palast – a frenzy of young, excited spectators jostled to get into the crowded room. The audience was largely appreciative, and at the end of the screening Verhoeven and his crew received a standing ovation.[26] But behind the scenes, the jury president, George Stevens, threatened to walk out if the film was included in the official selection. For him, *o.k.* was akin to radicals defiling the American flag.

Stevens, one of the most significant Hollywood filmmakers of 1950s, had been profoundly marked by the Second World War, the final stages of which he filmed alongside a small group of soldiers he traveled with through France and Germany. On May 1, 1945, he reached the Dachau concentration camp, liberated two days earlier with the arrival of Allied forces, and filmed the emaciated survivors, the mountains of corpses and the remains of bodies burned in the crematoria. When he returned to the United States, Stevens was "no longer the same man."[27] His experience in Germany, besides "altering his vision of cinema," pushed him to engage in a "movement of testimony and expiatory catharsis" with *The Diary of Anne Frank* (1959), followed by *The Greatest Story Ever Told* (1965), "a kind of historical allegory about war and America" haunted by the specter of the camps.[28] For Stevens, who ended the war as a lieutenant colonel, the American army was a force for good, one that had rid Germany of the Nazis, and he felt it wholly inappropriate, if not downright unacceptable, that a country which only a few years earlier had exterminated millions of Jews in gas chambers was now denouncing war crimes committed in Vietnam by American G.I.s.

Stevens' stance seems to have been a matter of principle rather than a political maneuver. Some twenty years earlier, amidst the Red Scare, he resigned from his position at the Screen Directors Guild after Cecil B. DeMille, plotting against Guild president Joseph L. Mankiewicz, demanded that members sign a loyalty oath stating they had never been members of the Communist Party. Stevens reproached the anti-communists for trying to foment divisions under the guise of patriotism and for being "more concerned with communism than with defending the rights of directors"[29] – a remarkable position given that DeMille's motion was "adopted by an overwhelming majority."[30] But in Berlin, in 1970, Stevens harbored no such scruples.

George Stevens at the Berlin Film Festival, 1970

Although he had not dealt directly with Stevens, Verhoeven realized there was a plot brewing against his film. In the euphoria that followed the screening, he and his crew went to a bar on Tauentzienstraße, only to be denied entry. Surprised, Verhoeven signaled to a friend, an editor whom he recognized among the customers. She pretended not to see him, but a few moments later, as she exited the bar, she whispered, "I can't talk to you here."[31] Verhoeven learned that the owner of the bar was film producer and Berlinale jury member Manfred Durniok.

On the jury, Stevens' attitude divided opinion. While Durniok and German filmmaker Klaus Hebecker were aligned with his cause, others – including Serbian director Dušan Makavejev, a leading figure of the Yugoslav Black Wave[32] – were unhappy about their jury president clearly overreaching. Two years earlier, Makavejev's film *Innocence Unprotected* had gained attention and an award in Berlin.

In 1970, he hadn't yet fled his country (he would be compelled to do so the following year, after the release of his film *W.R.: Mysteries of the Organism*), but his deep resistance to any form of censorship was evident. As Verhoeven recalls, an outraged Makavejev alerted producer Rob Houwer after the two men crossed paths in a corridor of the hotel where they were both staying. "There are plots against your film," he explained. "I can't tell you more because as a jury member I'm not allowed to talk to you. But let me give you a hint: try to talk to Dr. Bauer and find out what's going on."

Alfred Bauer, director of the Berlinale since its inception, had been credited for intervening in favor of Alain Resnais' concentration camp documentary *Night and Fog*, which was presented in a special Berlinale session in 1956.[33] What was perceived at the time to be a courageous stance was, in fact, a calculated strategy to camouflage an unmentionable past. Bauer had been a member of the Nazi party and fervent SA member before the war, and a high-ranking operative of the Third Reich's film production unit. After the war, he rebuilt his reputation at the helm of the Berlinale, vehemently opposing any kind of censorship so as to avoid raising suspicion about his wartime years. His true identity resurfaced only after his death in 1986.[34] What is now known publicly was, in 1970, a well-kept secret.

Immediately after being informed by Houwer about his discussion with Makavejev, Verhoeven – convinced that Bauer wasn't one to yield to political intimidation – sought a meeting with him, which took place the following day. His hopes, however, quickly faded. Bauer denied any clandestine maneuvering by the jury and tried to buy time. He knew that if the press got wind of Stevens' scheming, the scandal might compromise the smooth running of the festival. Bauer's strategy? Play dead, hoping that the final eight days of the Berlinale would pass without any leaks to the media.

The opposite happened. As the controversy swelled, press releases and crisis meetings followed, culminating in a press conference that sealed *o.k.*'s fate. In a packed hall, Walther Schmieding, director of the Berliner Festspiele, initially blamed Verhoeven for the controversy surrounding the film. Verhoeven and Houwer then played their trump card: an informant on the jury had accused George Stevens of censorship. In a rather surreal moment, a voice was heard from the back of the room and a postman announced that he had a telegram for Dr. Bauer. Making his way through the crowd, the postman delivered the message to the festival director who, taken aback, had no choice but to read it in front of the cameras and microphones of the international press.

> Dear Dr. Bauer,
>
> Instead of discussing the quality of the films, the jury has assumed the role of censor toward the program and the policy of the festival leadership. In this the jury has exceeded both its remit and authority. Through yesterday evening's letter to the selection committee, a carbon of which was sent to the Senate, the jury is attempting to involve political organs. I personally am consistently opposed to taking such a position and against the conduct of the jury. I do not agree with the majority of the jury concerning the film *o.k.*, as I believe the film does not insult any nation, including the people of the United States.
>
> Dušan Makavejev[35]

A voiceless Bauer was devastated. He knew that the missive from the Serbian filmmaker was the death knell for the festival. Carried by the thunderous applause that filled the entire hall, an exulted Verhoeven rose, brandishing a furious fist as a victory sign. Every filmmaker in competition withdrew in solidarity and the entire festival eventually shut down. No prizes were awarded that year.

Despite significant restructuring, the festival resumed the following year, and in the official selection was a new film by Michael Verhoeven, *Wer im Glashaus liebt...* (1970). In the meantime, Verhoeven went on to present *o.k.* at the San Francisco Film Festival, where it was a great success. "That surprised me," he admits. "I wasn't sure if American audiences were ready for the film." Proud to have emerged victorious from the Berlinale battle, Verhoeven never suspected that at

Michael Verhoeven (second from left)
and Alfred Bauer (second from right)

Alfred Bauer

that very moment, his film was in the sights of one of Hollywood's biggest studios, and that an intense legal battle awaited.

During the summer of 1970, echoes of the Berlinale scandal reverberated all the way to East Germany, where Phan Thi Mao's story found deep political and ideological resonances. She became the emblem of America's brutality against Vietnam, and more broadly its communist supporters. The impact of Verhoeven's film was such that DEFA, East Germany's main film production base, co-produced a nine-minute short entitled *US-Soldat Erikson gibt zu Protokoll* (*US Soldier Erikson Gives Testimony*, 1970).[36] A montage film, it is crafted from composite visual material and a commentary that closely follows the story of *Casualties of War*. The factual narrative, which lays out the sequence of events as shaped by Daniel Lang, allows for occasional literary digressions, where the narrator directly addresses Mao informally, thus creating a strong empathic link between viewer and victim.

How do you tell the story of an event without using pictures but still employing documentary techniques? The voiceover narration underscores this dilemma: "We don't know how she lived, we only know how she died," notes the narrator of Mao. Due to the absence of images of the young Vietnamese woman and the soldiers involved in the incident, the filmmakers mobilize different visual sources, ranging from sequences of Marines in training to filmed/photographed images of Vietnam, as captured by army operators and journalists. Much of this imagery depicts atrocities committed by the military: intense interrogations, torture, executions, village destruction.

Among this archival material is a photograph taken by John Schneider in November 1967 of an elderly Vietnamese woman, suspected of collusion with North Vietnamese communists, being held at gunpoint by an American soldier, who aims the barrel of his rifle at her temple. Detached from the usual journalistic implementation, the photograph has been recycled, like those from My Lai, by various artists, among them Liliana Porter, who took the image from *The New York Times*, reprinted it, and added the following text:

> This woman is
> northvietnamese
> southafrican,
> puertorican,
> colombian,
> black,
> argentinian,
> my mother,
> my sister,
> you, I.

The text/image montage hopes to elicit from viewers their identification with this anonymous victim who, beyond her own identity, becomes a Universal Victim of War, regardless of the political convictions of whomever is looking.[37] In *US-Soldat Erikson gibt zu Protokoll*, the use of Schneider's photograph serves the same purpose. Placed in the flow of the montage, as an introduction to a series of images of atrocities, it becomes a substitute for Mao's absent image, thus embodying her tragic fate.

Ironically, following a caption mentioning the trials and the reduction of the four killers' sentences, the film concludes with footage of President Lyndon Johnson's visit to Vietnam on October 26, 1966, where he reviewed troops at Cam Ranh Bay. When the head of state is seen awarding medals to soldiers, the image freezes, suggesting that he is decorating criminals. This emphasized synecdochic effect is achieved by the filmmakers at the cost of a temporal shortcut, as the archival imagery was shot slightly earlier than the events denounced in the film. Nevertheless, it takes on undeniable suggestive power insofar as the four rapists whose story is told in *Casualties of War* were decorated for their bravery in combat before committing their abhorrent crimes.

Questions linger about the exploitation, for anti-American propaganda purposes, of Phan Thi Mao's tragedy. The film overlooks the fact that after suffering at the hands of American soldiers, Mao's family also faced the cruelty of the North Vietnamese, who kidnapped – and probably executed – her mother, who was accused of endangering communist interests. Daniel Lang took care not to dilute the complexity of Eriksson's story into a one-dimensional diatribe against the

American military. With *US-Soldat Erikson gibt zu Protokoll*, however, the narrative is skewed, repurposed to cast Mao as a symbolic victim of American imperialism.

Elia Kazan's *The Visitors*

Across the Atlantic, as echoes of the Berlinale scandal reached the United States, Elia Kazan, legendary film and Broadway director and co-founder of the iconic Actors Studio, turned his attention to Lang's text and, with the help of his son, imagined what an adaptation might look like. What eventually emerged was Kazan's penultimate film, *The Visitors*, released in American cinemas in February 1972 and screened three months later in the official selection at the Cannes Film Festival.

At the beginning of 1970s, Elia Kazan was experiencing a profound crisis. In 1969, he had written, produced and directed *The Arrangement*, an adaptation of his own novel. Besides the many difficulties encountered during the film's production, *The Arrangement* had been both a critical and commercial failure, which left Kazan emotionally drained and fueled his deep resentment of Hollywood. His assessment, that he was entangled "in the film industry" and not able to make genuinely expressive cinema, is clear-eyed and tinged with bitterness. "Things were topsy-turvy," he explained at Wesleyan University in May 1971.[38]

Despite some good reviews in Europe, the failure of *The Arrangement* convinced Kazan that he never wanted to work in Hollywood again.[39] However, rather than abandoning filmmaking entirely, he began exploring alternative strategies to challenge the studio system. "I would show myself and the men who controlled the industry that films could be made inexpensively, that the process was essentially simple and didn't need the pumped-up costs, the services of coddled stars, and the pressure by the men who bring the money."[40] Kazan's first project within this new framework was *Wanda*, produced with a stripped-down crew and budget, which his wife, Barbara Loden, who played the lead role, ended up directing. Screened at the Venice Film Festival in August 1970, *Wanda* was received positively by critics, but despite costing only $135,000 was a commercial failure. An undaunted Kazan

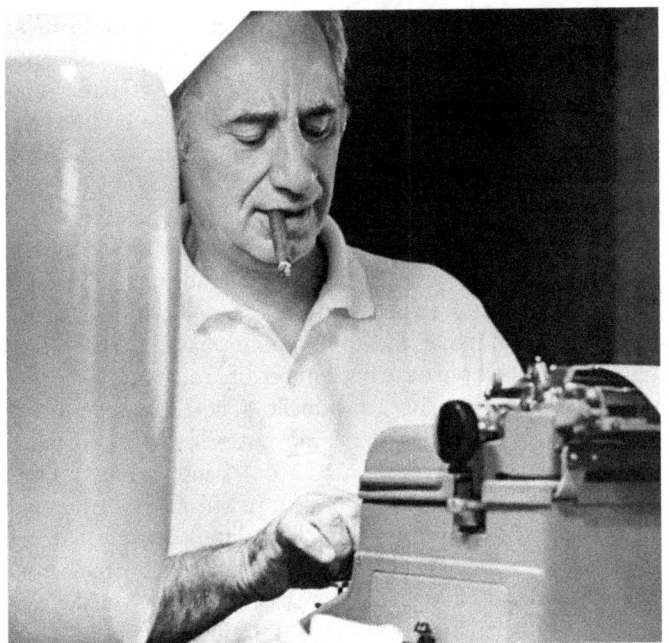

Elia Kazan

was now convinced that "commercial criteria – especially those determined on a scale of operation that is no longer realistic – should not determine what films are NOT made or even, to judge from the recent past, what films ARE made."[41] A small budget and crew, and a short shooting schedule on location: this was Kazan's strategy for his next feature.

Around the same time, Kazan was discussing with his son Chris "the effect of the war in Vietnam on the United States' civilian population," especially after the events of My Lai.[42] Their reflections quickly crystalized around an article that Kazan had read. In his memoirs, he writes of handing his son a press clipping, "the story of an ex-GI who'd brought evidence of a war crime – the rape and murder of a Vietnamese girl – against two former buddies, and how these two men came looking for him at the end of the war to hold him to account."[43] This turns out to have been Daniel Lang's *New Yorker* article.[44] Kazan was aware of the military trials and the sentences imposed, leading him to speculate: what would happen if after serving their sentences, the ex-convicts visited the soldier who had reported their crimes to the authorities? Intrigued by the idea, Chris wrote a script provisionally entitled *Home Free*, which he presented to his father and asked him to direct. For two weeks father and son refined the screenplay, then set about to find funding, but soon realized that raising finance for a project of this kind, even one with such a minimal production budget, would not be easy.

The idea of imagining a sequel to *Casualties of War*, rather than adapting it, presented considerable advantages from a financial standpoint. Expensive historical re-enactments could be avoided, and father and son wouldn't have to pay for the rights – which would have been impossible anyway since they were already owned by a producer. (The Kazans evidently never contacted Lang; there is no letter in the filmmaker's correspondence addressed to or from Lang.[45]) *The Visitors* was conceived with almost complete artistic freedom, beyond all financial and legal constraints. Kazan took out a bank loan, the small crew he assembled was non-union, and the actors weren't under contract. "It was the only way to make this film, and rather than be thwarted, I decided to go the illegal route."[46] (Kazan was later forced to pay a fine to the Directors Guild.)

The Visitors, with a budget not exceeding $175,000,[47] was shot on the Kazan property in Connecticut and produced by Chris Kazan and Nicholas T. Proferes, who wore multiple hats (he was also the cinematographer and editor). The technical crew comprised four other people: a sound recordist, a lighting technician, an assistant cameraman and a handyman. During filming, Chris prepared meals for the entire crew. Kazan assumed multiple roles himself, as director, casting director and props master. He also carried the tripod, moved cars when necessary, and even cleared snow (the film was shot in the dead of winter). Most of the actors were unknown. James Woods and Steve Railsback, who play the two primary male roles (Bill and Nickerson), made their film debuts. Patricia Joyce, in the sole female role, had appeared in a few television shows in the mid-1960s and had recently finished her drama studies at Yale. Chico Martínez (as Tony Rodriguez) was "a Puerto Rican cabdriver who aspired to be an actor."[48]

The completed film closely follows Chris Kazan's script.[49] Elia, who always regarded his son as the real author of *The Visitors*, added only a few details during filming – always with Chris' blessing.[50] There are notable differences between Lang's version of events and how they are portrayed in *The Visitors*, starting with the names of the protagonists, which have been changed, and the character of Bill Schmidt, brilliantly portrayed by Woods, who doesn't quite match Lang's description of Eriksson. Bill lives with Martha, a young woman with modern morals who doesn't believe in marriage, and her father. We know nothing of his past, only that he works in a helicopter factory, the only place he could find a job after returning home from Vietnam.

The film begins one winter Saturday morning in Connecticut. Bill is taken by surprise when Mike Nickerson and Tony Rodriguez, two old army comrades he reported to the military authorities for raping and killing a young Vietnamese woman, show up at his door. The two men have recently been released from imprisonment in Fort Leavenworth. Nickerson is easily recognizable as Sergeant Meserve (his accomplice calls him "Sarge" rather than "Mike," even though they are no longer in active service). Martha and her father are captivated by Nickerson, who exudes a definite charisma. Rodriguez is a blend of three characters: Corporal Clark and the Diaz cousins. Like Clark, he is the sergeant's right-hand man, a reliable enforcer and a formidable marksman.

Martha warmly welcomes the two men while Bill remains on edge, assuming they have come for retribution. Rodriguez only partly eases his fears when he says, "As far as I'm concerned, the past is the past… I forgive you." "As far as *you're* concerned?" responds Bill, eager to know if Nickerson is in the same frame of mind. Railsback captures the dark ambiguity of his character, undressing Martha with his eyes at their first meeting and pretending to go to the bathroom as he inspects the upper floor of the house while Bill is outside. He also hints at a kind of vulnerability, as if he were a victim of warfare. In contrast, Bill appears as a timid character, almost dependent on Martha's father, Harry Wayne, a Second World War veteran and author of Westerns. The couple lives in one of the two houses on the novelist's large property. Bill longs to break free from this life – he scans the real estate ads in the local paper – but is unable to, partly because Martha opposes the idea.

The conflict between the two main characters, so vivid on-screen, was deliberately heightened by Kazan's direction of the performers. "Because I played this isolated character," recalls Woods, "[Kazan] didn't want any of the other actors or anyone else to talk to me. You know, we were having dinner and they'd all ignore me. Finally, I said to Kazan, 'You know, this is fuckin' bullshit. I know how to act. I don't have to sit here after a day's work and have everyone ostracize me!' I refused to put up with it. I didn't care if he directed *On the Waterfront* and *East of Eden* and these other famous films. I didn't give a shit who he was."[51]

Kazan's purpose in isolating Woods during the shoot sprang from the essence of *The Visitors*, a story less about the Vietnam War than about the bonds and betrayals among men. Harry's disdain for Bill arises from Bill's failure to conform to the mold of masculinity. He lacks the raw, rugged traits that Nickerson and Rodriguez possess, men with whom Harry quickly forms a camaraderie. The three share war stories – from the Pacific to Vietnam – and their violent impulses come to a head when Harry executes the neighbor's dog, which has injured his own dog. Rodriguez carries out the deed with a single shot without even having to look through his rifle sight. The next scene is pivotal. The two veterans and their host retrieve the dog's corpse and traverse the snowy landscape to its owner's house. Simultaneously, in a parallel sequence, Bill confides to Martha about the rape and murder he witnessed.

His voice narrates briefly over the snowy expanse, where silhouettes of the three accomplices carrying the dead animal evoke the image of hunters bearing their prey, akin to figures from a Bruegel painting.

MARTHA
Those are the men, aren't they?

BILL
What men?

MARTHA
You have to tell me about it now.

From the Forests of Bavaria to the Snows of Connecticut 93

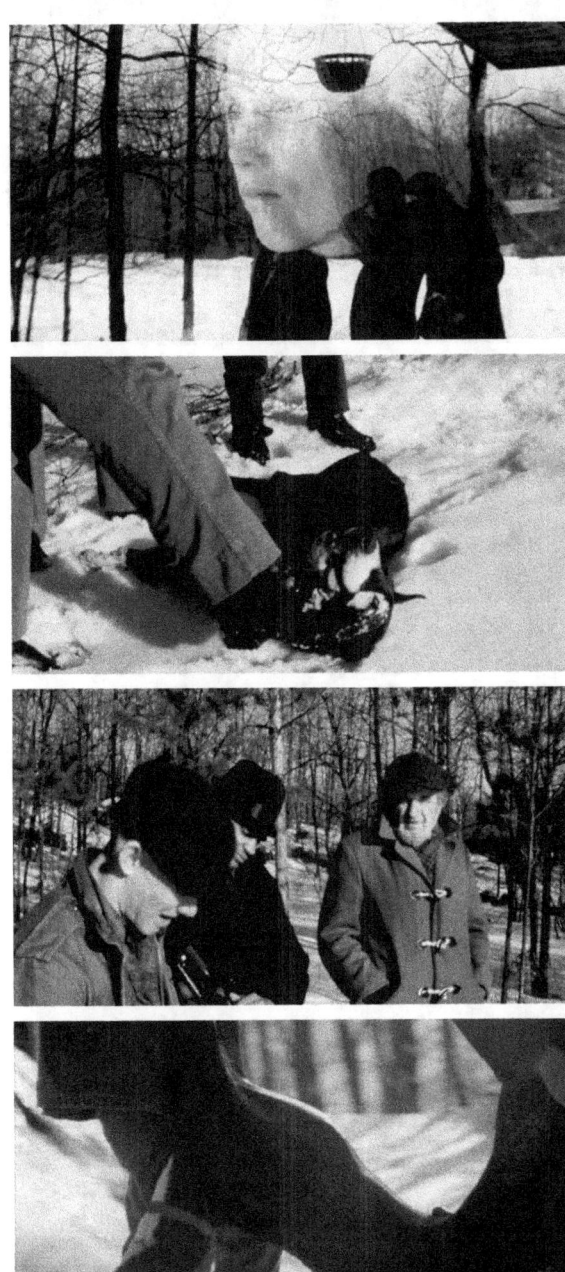

BILL
We were just supposed to look for supplies. By the third day we hadn't found anything, and Nickerson was beginning get edgy. So we get to this village, as marked "friendly" on the map, but Nickerson decided to get everybody out and search the huts for arms. So we line them up while he and Tony looked the place over. They thought we were going to shoot them all, and I think Nickerson almost did. He was so... angry about not finding anything. Well, in the last hut, a girl was hiding. Nickerson pretended he thought she was a VC, and he told one of the old men of the village, "We're going to take her along as a hostage."

MARTHA
What did she look like?

BILL
She was young... fifteen or sixteen. Pretty. I guess that's why she was hiding. That's what her mother said at the court-martial. A couple of miles up the road, Nickerson took her into the tall grass. The sound she made... After a while it was like... It was just whining. And then Reilly went next, and Josephson and Tony. And then they were waiting for me to do it. But I couldn't move. It didn't take any thought, any bravery – I just couldn't walk. Nickerson... he looked at me for a long time. You know the way he does? He looks at you. He had a rifle in his hands. And he handed the rifle to Josephson, he jerked his thumb toward the grass, and...

MARTHA
And you turned them in.

BILL
When we got back to camp.

MARTHA
(*hugging him*)
Why didn't you tell me this before? It was the bravest thing to do.

BILL
No, it was too late. I should have stopped them! What's the point of punishing them afterwards?

MARTHA
Criminals have to be punished.

BILL
The Viet Cong do exactly the same thing. Everybody does, every day, everywhere. Why blame these guys? They were my friends. They were my buddies.

Harry then invites Nickerson and Rodriguez to watch an American football game at Bill and Martha's house. The images cut between the excited expressions of the three spectators who are drinking heavily, and magnified, slow-motion shots of the football players. Once again, we are treated to a male bonding ritual from which Bill feels estranged. Harry, who once remarked that Bill should have been a nurse instead of a soldier, concludes that he "must be half queer" – an opinion presumably shared by Nickerson and Rodriguez.

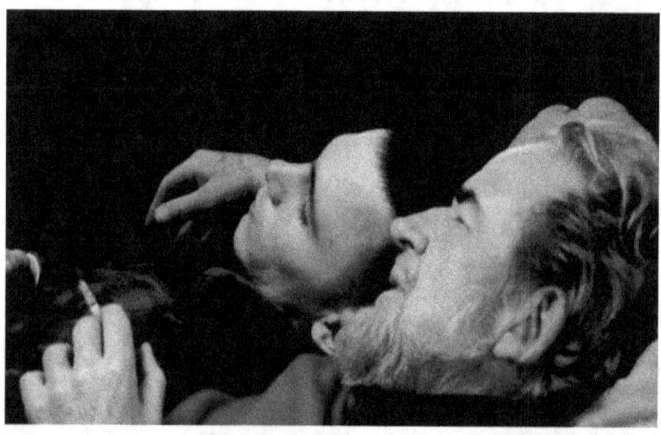

Ultimately, Harry sees in Nickerson the son-in-law he refuses to acknowledge in Bill, as evidenced by the shot of the two men lying on the couch together, the older man's arms wrapped around the former soldier. For Kazan, this scene provides a crucial insight into the unfolding dynamics. "You could say that the rapist was Wayne's son. He created him. He approves of him. The approval is total. One minute, he says to Nickerson, 'Why didn't you cut his [Bill's] throat?' And the next thing Nickerson does is [go and] rape his daughter."[52] The script suggests that Harry abandons Martha to Nickerson. After the dinner scene, where he injures his hand cutting meat, Harry returns home and disappears from the story. He is of no help to the couple when Nickerson and Rodriguez attack Bill, then Martha.

The character of Martha, portrayed with great sensitivity by Patricia Joyce, is in Kazan's eyes a metaphor for America's contradictions regarding the situation in Vietnam. "On one hand," he says, "she lives and sleeps with [Bill], but she doesn't want to marry him. Something is missing; she doesn't see her father in this boy. What she feels lacking in the young man [Nickerson] is exactly what she despises at the same time. She marches in anti-war protests, but she feels the absence of that violence and strength in her lover that would have made him shoot the dog when it threatened her. She scolds him, yet simultaneously wishes he were stronger. And this is very characteristic of this country."[53]

From the outset, Martha harbors a strong attraction to Nickerson, an attraction she seeks to suppress when she learns that he raped and killed a Vietnamese woman. But following an encounter with Nickerson in the living room while Bill and Tony are in the kitchen, she changes her mind. When Nickerson reproaches Martha for not being married, she asks him not to moralize, alluding to his own behavior in Vietnam. Nickerson justifies himself by explaining: "You go into a village, handing out candy bars to the kids. And then you see your best buddy's legs blown off by a mine because the people you gave the candy bars to forgot to tell you Charlie was in town." Martha softens, as if Nickerson's revelations suddenly absolve him of his criminal act.

Martha puts on some romantic music. Nickerson, excited by Martha's opposition to the war, asks if she has attended any peace marches. Martha, lying on the couch, lets her upper thighs show and answers Nickerson only by telling him that Bill once asked her to marry him, but she refused. Nickerson asks her to dance. Martha is hesitant. He places her arm on his shoulder and they dance slowly together. Bill eventually wanders in from the kitchen and watches them together. Angry at them both, he shouts at Martha ("That's enough!") and punches Nickerson. The confrontation continues outside the house, partly obscured by Nickerson and Rodriguez's car. Bill seems to have the upper hand, but it is Nickerson who emerges victorious. The fight serves as a prelude to Martha's rape. Nickerson pursues her into the couple's upstairs bedroom, and after tearing off her nylon stockings attacks her. The rape is filmed elliptically. We see no nudity, just Nickerson's body moving over Martha's helpless, resigned body, which finally lets out a few moans. A low-angle shot then shows Nickerson standing at the door, pulling up his fly. Martha, humiliated and defiled, lies on the floor.

When Nickerson goes downstairs, Rodriquez is ready to leave, but the sergeant signals to his corporal to go up and take his turn. Like a good soldier, Rodriguez complies, and is seen standing over Martha, before slamming the door shut. Martha's second rape occurs off-screen. Kazan prefers to follow Nickerson, who has left the house to breathe in the cold night air. He lies down on the hood of his car, and at that precise moment a brief flashback saturated in green – the jungle – creates a sharp chromatic contrast with the wintry palette that envelops the rest of the feature film. He sees the Vietnamese woman he once raped fleeing, running through the reeds, stumbling, turning back toward her assailant, her gaze filled with terror. The scene is filmed from a subjective point of view, blending Nickerson's point of view with that of the viewer, marking the first instance in the film where the audience enters directly into a character's thoughts. Kazan endeavors to stir empathy for Nickerson, depicting him not solely as an oppressor but as a soulful, melancholic figure adrift in a society that shaped him yet ultimately cast him aside.

"The important thing to me," explains Kazan, "was to try to make the villains, the two visitors, not heavies, not psychos, not criminals, not monsters, but absolutely typical and characteristic young American boys. What so shocked the

From the Forests of Bavaria to the Snows of Connecticut 99

American public about My Lai was that for the first time we saw that butchery and monstrosity committed in war can be done by someone as ordinary and familiar as Lieutenant William Calley."[54] In essence, *The Visitors* suggests that – except for Bill, a figure on the fringes, grappling with his sense of masculinity – evil is, in fact, commonplace, residing within us all, woven into the fabric of every male character in the film. When the opportunity presents itself again, Nickerson and Rodriguez act again, this time not in a wartime context but in civilian life. Martha's rape fuels a deep sense of humiliation in Bill and serves to undermine his masculinity even further.[55]

Kazan's hopes of avoiding a facile good/evil binary in his film is admirable. And yet *The Visitors* ultimately leans toward the notion of shared culpability: Nickerson and Rodriguez are guilty of rape and murder, but Bill and Martha, too, bear responsibility – Bill for failing to prevent the crime he witnessed in Vietnam, Martha for assuming a seductive role from the moment the two ex-soldiers walked into her home. After all, one of the sequences following their arrival shows her in her room, dressing up and putting on makeup, before reappearing in a miniskirt and leather boots, poised to allure.

If we agree that *The Visitors* is a metaphor for the state in which America finds itself after the Vietnam War, then Bill and Martha's tragic fate mirrors that of the entire country, as suggested by the final shot of the film. They sit in the darkness of their home, facing each other, still stunned by what has just happened. Bill, presumably covered in blood, asks Martha if she is all right – a purely rhetorical question that the film addresses to its audience. Will America ever recover from the trauma of Vietnam? Can it ever heal and move forward? Is such a path even desirable?

The message of *The Visitors* is thus an ambivalent one. While it critiques war and exposes its brutal consequences, it also leaves room for a kind of fascination with the allure of the oppressor. It is noteworthy that Kazan inexplicably avoids the reality of the facts. What was a rape and a planned femicide in Daniel Lang's book becomes, in his film, a simple military mistake. According to Bill's account, Nickerson and his men were searching huts for weapons when they accidentally stumbled upon their victim. *The Visitors* also evokes issues of informing, a theme that haunts Kazan's work and life. In 1952, after being summoned to appear before the House Un-American Activities Committee (HUAC), he provided a list of eight names of people who had connections to the Communist Party. Despite his own brief membership in the party (1934 to 1936), Kazan's stance starkly contrasted with that of many of his peers who defied cooperation with HUAC and endured harsh consequences, including imprisonment, exile and blacklisting.

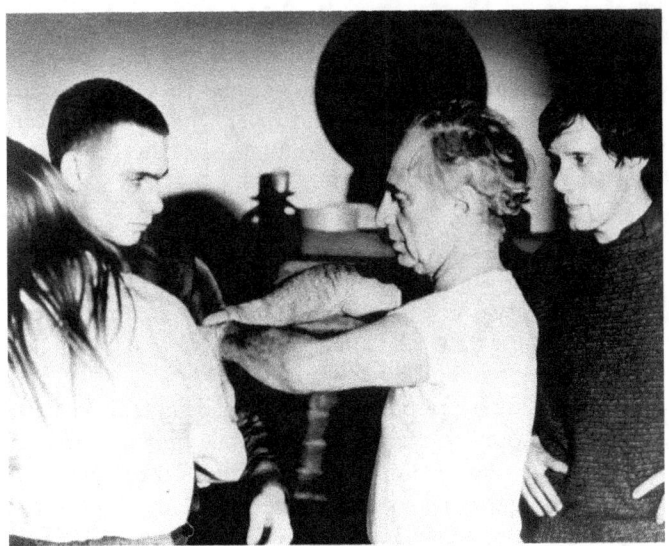
Elia Kazan directing *The Visitors*

Kazan's position impacted the rest of his career and perhaps influenced the character of Bill in *The Visitors*. Here is a man unable to prevent his fellow soldiers from committing atrocities and who later regretted having informed on them. Might this be a veiled confession by Kazan? During filming, James Woods dared question Kazan about his experiences with HUAC, hoping to understand the feelings that the character of Bill might experience after denouncing his comrades, but Kazan never opened up on the subject.

The poor reception of *The Visitors* in the United States was partly due to Kazan's personal history. The openly anti-communist stance he had taken twenty years earlier clashed with his denunciation of the Vietnam War, which, in the eyes of many Americans, was seen as a fight against communism. This is evidenced by a letter from Kazan to his son and Nick Proferes in which he expressed a fear that *The Visitors* would be misunderstood or unfairly judged. He recommended showing it separately to the most influential critics in order to create an environment conducive to reflection. "If there ever was a film to which the public has to be brought by the critics, this is it," asserted Kazan. "The critics have to tell (instruct!) the public that this is an exceptional film, an experience they must not miss, the film of the day. I think they will."[56]

Kazan, however, was mistaken. The film was booed at its premiere in New York, and reviews, with the notable exception of Vincent Canby's in *The New York Times*, were almost all negative.[57] In France, however, where Kazan could always rely on critical favor, *The Visitors* was well received and even selected for the Cannes Film Festival. The jury that year was chaired by Joseph Losey, whose *The Go-Between* had previously won the festival's highest honor, the Palme d'Or. Losey, who had briefly worked with Kazan in the 1940s, was a victim of the HUAC. As a member of the Communist Party and after being blacklisted, in 1952 he exiled himself from Hollywood to Great Britain.

United Artists, responsible for distributing *The Visitors*, feared that Losey might do damage to the film's reputation and that journalists would want to discuss Kazan's personal history during the press conference following the screening.[58] That didn't happen, and in the end both public and critical response to the film at Cannes was positive. Losey seemed to appreciate the film's formal qualities but was troubled by its subject matter. He saw it as "a confused metaphor" and suspected that Kazan, under the guise of addressing the Vietnam War, was covertly referencing his stance during the McCarthy era. In the end, the Cannes jury awarded prizes to a number of political films – including Francesco Rosi's *The Mattei Affair*, Elio Petri's *The Working Class Goes to Heaven* and Revé Vautier's *Avoir vingt ans dans les Aurès* – but not *The Visitors*.

Swedish actress Bibi Andersson, who was a member of the jury, reported to Kazan that she and two other members had voted for his film, but Losey "was violently, persistently, and most absolutely against it and never let up attacking it."[59] His influence undoubtedly carried significant weight in the final vote.

Palimpsest bodies

A forgotten film due to its marginal status in Kazan's filmography and – Kazan himself acknowledged – because it is far from the usual formal standards of Hollywood cinema,[60] *The Visitors* nonetheless remains a captivating and complex work. It is also a film that benefits from comparisons with American exploitation cinema of the early 1970s. *The Visitors* is in the same tradition as the so-called "redneck" film, a subgenre that includes "the Western (with its themes of vengeance and history), horror films (with their atmosphere of claustrophobic terror and explicit violence), [...] and also documentary cinema (with its grainy image, its relationship to reality, and anthropological framework)."[61] Unlike most redneck films, Kazan's *The Visitors* isn't set in the Deep South, and any menace comes not from degenerate country folk living deep in the Bayou but from the countryside, from which it infiltrates into the isolated property where Bill believes he has found a semblance of security and anonymity.

The Visitors, however, does contain the figure of a war-traumatized individual, a standard redneck character trope,[62] as well as rape, a fundamental component of the genre. The aesthetic of the redneck film even gave rise to the rape and revenge movie, a subgenre to which a feature film released the same year as *The Visitors* belongs: *The Last House on the Left* (1972), the low-budget, trashy and visionary debut by an emerging filmmaker from Cleveland named Wes Craven.

The Last House on the Left tells the story of a sordid double femicide: the rape and murder of two teenagers, Mari Collingwood (Sandra Peabody) and her friend Phyllis Stone (Lucy Grantham), by a group of sexual deviants, led by Krug (David A. Hesse), which includes his younger brother Junior (Marc Sheffler), his girlfriend Sadie (Jeramie Rain) and an accomplice, Weasel (Fred Lincoln). In the second part of the story, the killers themselves become victims due to a singular turn of events after inadvertently ending up in Mari's parents' home, which they aren't allowed to leave alive. The brutality of the film lies in its extreme violence, unprecedented for the time, as well as its sudden shifts in tone, as it moves from pure horror to slapstick comedy, following the misadventures of two Laurel and Hardy-like policemen as naïve as they are incapable, who fail miserably to apprehend the killers. Faced with the incompetence of law enforcement, the Collingwoods decide to take justice into their own hands after discovering that their hosts are the murderers of their daughter. The story ends in a bloodbath. Weasel is emasculated with biting force, Sadie's throat is slashed, and Krug is dismembered with a chainsaw.

The Last House on the Left, freely borrowing the narrative framework of Ingmar Bergman's *The Virgin Spring* (1960), is deeply influenced by the violence of the Vietnam War. In a brilliant analysis, Adam Lowenstein detects in the film's publicity poster the imprint of the famous photograph by John Filo, taken on the campus of Kent State University on May 4, 1970, linking the protagonist of the photo, Mary Ann Vecchio – screaming beside the lifeless body of Jeffrey Miller, shot dead by the National Guard – to the character of Mari Collingwood in the film. Two teenage girls, their defiant bodies exposed to violence, symbolize the anxieties of the political and social turmoil engulfing America. In Craven's film, Mari's pacifism is hinted at through the birthday gift from her parents: a necklace bearing the peace and love symbol as a pendant. Yet despite its symbolism, the jewel holds no protective power and offers Mari no help when she falls victim to her tormentors.

Rejecting the usual Hollywood aestheticization of violence, Craven sought to capture the essence of "raw documentary footage from Vietnam that he suspected was being censored in film and on television."[63] Scenes in *The Last House on the Left* were shot handheld with an Auricon camera synchronized to a videotape recorder, in an attempt to mimic the aesthetics of field reports during the war. Surprisingly, Craven admitted seeking to replicate the grainy footage of Nazi concentration camps, images imprinted on his memory since childhood. This collision of memories of the destruction of European Jewry and the Vietnam War aligns with a phenomenon observed by Ophir Levy among filmmakers as diverse as Ingmar Bergman, Jean-Luc Godard, Stan Brakhage and Oliver Stone. Levy notes that "because they revived its core of terror, the repeated eruption of unbearable images from Vietnam had the effect of causing the re-emergence in cinema of archival images of deportation and genocide."[64] In *The Last House on the Left*, their presence transcends mere representation, as seen for example in Bergman's *Persona* (1966), blending seamlessly into the film's texture until they become imperceptible, and serving as an invisible catalyst. Craven aimed to imbue these images with a traumatic intensity by stripping them of context, highlighting that the motives of Krug and his gang appear to stem from nothing other than the sheer, unbridled pleasure of gratuitous violence and sadism.

Mari and Phyllis being kidnapped, tortured, raped and brutally murdered in Craven's film unmistakably recalls the gruesome events detailed in Daniel Lang's *Casualties of War*. Among the killers in Craven's film is a character who, from the beginning, strongly resists any participation in the rape: Junior, Krug's junkie brother, who passively witnesses his older brother's misdeeds. At a certain point, when Phyllis escapes to try to divert attention and save Mari, she finds herself alone with Junior, just as Mao does with Eriksson. Junior doesn't possess Eriksson's morality, but one can sense his nervousness and that he is moved by Mari's pleas. At first feigning affection to manipulate him, Mari convinces Junior that her doctor father can provide the methadone he craves. Initially hesitant, fearing his brother's wrath, Junior reluctantly agrees to escort her home. Yet Mari's hopes are dashed with the return of Krug, Weasel and Sadie, who have just murdered Phyllis.

The depiction of the murders is especially harrowing. Having escaped her tormentors, Phyllis navigates through the forest until she reaches a small clearing where there is a small cemetery. Just beyond lies the road, which offers a glimmer of hope. Phyllis, believing that salvation is within reach, is about to flag down passing motorists for assistance, but Krug, wielding a machete, blocks her way. After Weasel stabs her in the back, Phyllis crawls through the grass before collapsing. The murder turns into a collective execution, with Weasel, then Sadie, delivering violent knife blows. The realistic blood color (a mix of food dye and caramel syrup) contributes to the extreme brutality and impurity of the sequence, leaving the viewer on the verge of nausea. This first crime is a prelude to the second, that of Mari, first tortured by Krug, who chisels the four letters of her name on the top of her chest before raping her. When he is finished, the camera zooms in on the dismayed faces of the three companions, almost ashamed of having succumbed to such acts of barbarism. But this curious moment of introspection doesn't lead to any self-reflection. Mari stands, pulls on her clothes, and heads slowly toward the lake. As she stands in the water, Krug shoots her three times.

108 Casualties of War

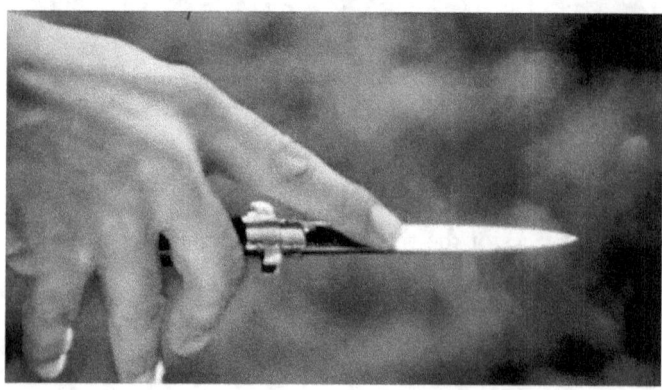

Is Craven intentionally transposing the violence of *Casualties of War* into an American context? Did he read Lang's text and use it as a subtext in *The Last House on the Left*? While the question remains open, the hypothesis gains some weight when we learn that one of Craven's unrealized projects featured a colonel court-martialed for reporting atrocities committed by Americans in Vietnam.[65] *The Last House on the Left* clearly isn't about Vietnam, but the film is certainly haunted by a traumatic backdrop that resurfaces through the very flesh of the characters of Mari and Phyllis, who here embody "palimpsest bodies." As explored by Ophir Levy, this is the idea of a body – entirely or partially naked, appearing in a contemporary cinematic fiction – which "represents, is a substitute for, symbolizes or embodies other bodies," those from another time and place.[66] Thus, Mari Collingwood and Phyllis Stone are unaware that the violence endured by their bodies reflects the violated corpses of My Lai and Phan Thi Mao.

The three films discussed in this chapter – *o.k.*, *The Visitors* and *The Last House on the Left* – each uniquely evoke the trauma of Vietnam. Two of them also serve as stirring harbingers of *Casualties of War*. Beyond any formal and narrative correspondences that can be identified from one film to another, one particular thread connects them: they are all products of the underground, created against the tide of traditional forms, outside of any constraints and with few means, as if their creators sought to assert their aesthetic and political independence from a system where, despite appearances, censorship held sway. Could one seriously hope to see an adaptation of *Casualties of War* in Hollywood while the Vietnam War still intruded daily into American homes and dissent was growing ever louder on college campuses? Yet this is what a handful of producers, filmmakers and screenwriters believed. It is on their hopes, their struggles and disillusionments, that the next chapter is focused.

Casualties of War in Hollywood: On Some Inadaptations 1970 – 1980

Throughout the 1970s and into the early 1980s, Hollywood made several attempts to bring *Casualties of War* to the screen. Despite the involvement of renowned authors, these adaptations rarely advanced beyond the script stage.

Jean-Louis Jeannelle raises a critical question: "The screenplay is not a film. On that, everyone can agree. But does that necessarily mean it isn't a work of art?" Jeannelle has explored the reasons why there is such caution when it comes to granting the screenplay legitimacy as a work of art in its own right – not least because so many stakeholders (the writer, the director, even the producer of a film) have claim to its "authorship."[1] Unlike the theatrical play script, writes Jeannelle, which gains depth through repeated productions, "the screenplay dissolves into the visual and auditory continuum for which it was specifically written." But surely the screenplay can be a complete artistic gesture unto itself, one that should not be assessed solely in terms of its transformation into an audiovisual object, imprinted on celluloid? This is especially true in cases of adaptations, where the screenwriter has appropriated literary material and translated it into sounds and images that are, in effect, a subjective vision of the original text, as informed by the screenwriter's own interests and biases. And what do we make of "(in)adaptations" (the term is Jeannelle's), those screenplay adaptations never produced as films?

Such questions are essential when considering the numerous failed attempts to adapt *Casualties of War*.

Prospects (October – December 1969)

Daniel Lang's article sparked significant interest from American producers and filmmakers, leading to numerous inquiries about adaptation rights. Just three days after its publication in *The New Yorker*, George Willner, of the International Famous Agency, sent a letter to Lang on behalf of one of his clients, whose name he withheld.[2] It is likely that Lang's text interested Willner (who had been targeted during the McCarthy era because of his activities as a member of the Communist Party[3]) and his client for political reasons, and that their hope was that any film adaptation would serve as an indictment of American anti-communist policy in Vietnam. But Willner wasn't the only one eyeing *Casualties of War*. Two days later, two more letters, one from the Kalmus Corporation, the other from a New York law firm, noting that each party would like to discuss a potential film adaptation, for either film or television.[4]

In England, the publication of Lang's *New Yorker* piece in *The Observer* on November 16, 1969 triggered a new wave of requests from agents and producers, most of whose names have not been recorded for posterity. A certain John St. Clair, based in London, sent a lengthy letter to Lang c/o *The New Yorker* that is notable for its detail.[5] St. Clair, clearly knowledgeable about the Vietnam War, had read Normand Poirier's *Esquire* article about horrors committed by Marines in Vietnam and told Lang that he was considering making a film of it. But, he continued, *Casualties of War* had impressed him even more. He noted its "extraordinary cinematic qualities" and the fact that, unlike Poirier's article, Lang's narrative was focused on a single victim. St. Clair was eager to start production but had reservations about the project's feasibility. With the legal status of the accused still pending, was it even possible to tell the story? St. Clair was concerned that government censorship might hinder the project and wondered if the "real Eriksson" would agree to advise on the production.

In early December, Milton Greenstein, vice president of *The New Yorker*'s legal department, received a letter from the London agency Richard Hatton Limited, two of whose clients, a producer and a director, expressed keen interest in acquiring adaptation rights for *Casualties of War*.[6] Three weeks later, one Nicholas de Grunwald stepped forward for the same reasons, convinced that Lang's text would make an "incredibly powerful film."[7] In early 1970, new proposals arrived from other parts of the world. Peter P. Townley, executive director of Premiere Pictures in Sydney, sought a commitment from Lang for a film adaptation that, he promised, "will remain faithful to the book's intentions."[8] The Italian translation of Lang's article caught the eye of executive producer Bruno Todini, known for his collaborations with illustrious compatriots (Roberto Rossellini, Mario Monicelli, Mario Bava) and prominent American directors (King Vidor, John Huston).[9]

But Daniel Lang pursued none of these proposals – for one simple reason. When it came to the person he wanted to bring *Casualties of War* to life, he already had someone in mind: Fred Zinnemann.

Often considered more of a craftsman than a bona fide *auteur*, Zinnemann remains chiefly known among cinephiles for two emblematic films of classical Hollywood: *High Noon* (1952), dubbed an "anti-Western" by André Bazin, and *From Here to Eternity* (1953), with its constellation of stars, eight Academy Awards, and the iconic image of Burt Lancaster and Deborah Kerr's passionate beach kiss. Not content with directing the greatest male and female performers of their generation, Zinnemann fearlessly tackled subjects such as Nazi barbarity in *The Seventh Cross* (1944) and *The Search* (1948), and the absurdity of war in *The Men* (1950), which features Marlon Brando, in his film debut, as a paraplegic soldier.

Before shining in Hollywood, Zinnemann, born in Vienna in 1907, had a relatively atypical journey. After studying cinema in Paris, he traveled to Berlin, where he became an assistant to Edgar Ulmer and Robert Siodmak, before being invited by Robert Flaherty to collaborate on a film in the Soviet Union. That project never materialized, but the experience was significant enough for Zinnemann to acknowledge Flaherty as his mentor. Some years later, photographer and filmmaker Paul Strand hired him to supervise the making of *Redes* (1934-36), about a strike among a small community of exploited Mexican fishermen.

Fred Zinnemann

There were creative differences between Zinnemann and Strand during filming, yet the experience proved crucial for Zinnemann in his apprenticeship as a filmmaker.

Recruited by MGM, he made a few short films before moving onto features, though his continued interest in documentary cinema culminated in what remains his masterpiece, *The Search*, in which Montgomery Clift plays American soldier Ralph Stevenson, who takes a young Czech boy, a survivor of Auschwitz, under his wing. Zinnemann spent almost a year in Europe conducting research for the film, including interviewing children under the care of the United Nations Relief and Rehabilitation Administration, consulting reports provided by the organization and compiling photographic archives, then translating and refining Richard Schweizer's screenplay and shooting the film – largely with young, non-professional actors who were camp survivors – amidst the rubble of postwar Germany. Far from being overtly patriotic, *The Search* reflects a certain skepticism regarding "America's past and present commitments."[10] It also stands as the most personal work of its creator, who, being Jewish, was deeply affected by the Holocaust. His father perished in Belzec in 1941 and his mother the following year in Auschwitz.

Like Zinnemann, Daniel Lang was from a family of Jewish immigrants, and many of his relatives who remained in Europe during the war also perished in Auschwitz. It can be presumed that Lang was familiar with Zinnemann's films and appreciated not only how true to life they were, but also their contemporary relevance. *The Search* is the only film produced in Hollywood immediately after the war that depicts the fate of children cared for by UNRAA, and is one of the few films of the period to address the Holocaust so directly.

"Neutrality was never an option for Zinnemann,"[11] just as it wasn't for Lang. As a college student, Lang developed an affinity for communism, and even leaned toward Marxism. But upon discovering that Jews in the USSR were also persecuted by Stalin, Lang distanced himself from the Communist Party[12] while remaining a leftist throughout his life who "embraced the cause of liberalism."[13] Some of his friends were even interrogated by HUAC and blacklisted for their political beliefs. This context explains why, if Elia Kazan had sought to contact Lang while working on *The Visitors*, Lang "probably would have had nothing to do with him,"[14] as his youngest daughter suggested to me.

Uncompromising toward those who collaborated with the McCarthyite purges, Lang likely appreciated Zinnemann's political stance, evident through the numerous allusions woven into his films. *High Noon* can be seen as an "allegory of Hollywood's cowardice during the HUAC hearings,"[15] and a few years later, *Behold a Pale Horse* (1964) offered Zinnemann subtle opportunities to reflect on the political climate of the United States. That film, adapted from a novel by Emeric Pressburger, draws poignant parallels between the sacrifice of its main character, Manuel Artigue (Gregory Peck), who returns to Spain to meet his end and cast a global spotlight on the brutality of the Franco regime, and the self-immolation of the Buddhist monk Thich Quang Duc in Saigon in 1963, who was protesting President Ngô Dinh Diêm's repressive policies against the Buddhist community.

All these reasons, along with Zinnemann's skill in directing actors and crafting images, his commitment to meaningful stories and an ability to weave visual motifs with poetic and musical sensitivity, likely strengthened Daniel Lang's belief that Zinnemann was the best choice to bring *Casualties of War* to life on-screen. Three days before publication in *The New Yorker*, he sent Zinnemann a copy of his article.[16] His intentions were clear: he supposed that the text would be of interest, possibly encouraging Zinnemann to consider a film adaptation.

But things didn't go as planned. Due to an unusually long delay, Lang's letter took nearly three weeks to reach Zinnemann, who was in London at the time, and it was another two more weeks before Zinnemann had the chance to respond. This lapse in time can be explained by the challenges that Zinnemann was dealing with. Ever since his last film, the Academy Award-winning *A Man for All Seasons* in 1966, he had been working alongside screenwriter Han Suyin on an ambitious adaptation of André Malraux's *Man's Fate*, to be produced by MGM. Jean-Louis Jeannelle, in his detailed history of the various (in)adaptations of Malraux's novel, points out that Zinnemann's ultimately aborted version "unfolds against the backdrop of an anti-communist crusade and constantly risks drawing fraught parallels: the bloody repression ordered by Chiang Kai-shek in 1927 could indeed find a tragic echo in the war against the National Front for the Liberation of Vietnam."[17]

Jeannelle mentions a striking detail: on the back of the title page of Zinnemann's annotated working script, alongside a postcard of Goya's *Saturn Devouring His Son*, is a photograph taken from *The Times* dated October 14,

1969 (one month and ten days before the scheduled start of filming), with the caption: "South Vietnamese soldiers tie up a Viet Cong prisoner captured during fighting on the Cambodian border."[18] The presence of this photograph in the archives indicates that Zinnemann aimed to connect the fate of Shanghai in 1927 to the Vietnam conflict (as Robert Wise had already done in *The Sand Pebbles*), by making the revolutionary Kyo Giors – a central character in Malraux's novel – a sort of prefiguration of Hô Chí Minh. In order to prevent his Hollywood epic from becoming a pro-communist propaganda film, Zinnemann carefully avoided making any historical parallels when negotiating with studio executives and authorities from whom he sought support. And yet, explains Jeannelle, the war in Vietnam haunted the production of *Man's Fate* and contributed to its eventual cancellation.

In his letter to Daniel Lang dated November 18, 1969, Zinnemann revealed that filming on *Man's Fate* was set to begin six days later. He was deeply involved in final preparations at Borehamwood studios, where the interior scenes were to be filmed. And yet, despite being so preoccupied, Zinnemann took time to share his opinion of *Casualties of War* with Lang. His judgment was decisive: "I think it is one of the truly memorable pieces of its kind, one of the best in recent years." But he was more cautious regarding the possibilities of an adaptation, suggesting that the material might be more suited to theater: "I think that it could be made into a very powerful stage play (perhaps a brief one). It is possible that one could transfer it onto film, but I'm not at all certain that a film would carry a shock equal to the shattering impact of your story."[19] Zinnemann took care to soften this somewhat hasty judgment, adding that he would need "to think about it" and would be happy to do so if Lang would kindly give him "a bit of time."

Zinnemann would have more time on his hands than he thought. While in rehearsal with his crew on November 19, the day after his letter was sent to Lang, news arrived of the outright cancellation of *Man's Fate*. The decision was made by MGM's newly installed president James Aubrey, who insisted that the film's budget was too high. The particularity of *Man's Fate*'s cancellation is not that it happened during pre-production but that the decision to halt production was made only a few days before filming was to begin, with nearly half of the budget already spent.[20] The publicly stated reasons concealed deeper, more complex motives, including pressure from the Taiwanese government to abandon the project.[21]

The cancellation of *Man's Fate* might have provided Zinnemann with the opportunity to fall back on *Casualties of War* and explore the possibility of an adaptation. But luck was not on his side. By the time his response reached Lang, a preliminary agreement between Lang and American producer David Susskind had already been made, with John Schlesinger – whose latest film, the controversial *Midnight Cowboy*, had been a huge success – slated to direct.

Lang immediately informed Zinnemann of these developments. On December 23, 1969, a saddened and overwhelmed Zinnemann responded, mentioning the late receipt of the first letter, which had arrived when he was in the midst of the *Man's Fate* debacle and so unable to give Lang's proposal the attention it required. Engaged in a legal battle with MGM that would last several years, Zinnemann expressed deep regret. "I hope that you will understand and forgive my seemingly casual way of dealing with a work of such importance as your story… I would be very glad to speak with the producer if you would like to give me his name, although I presume that, in view of the interest shown by John Schlesinger, it is now too late for any sort of meaningful discussion." Zinnemann further confessed that he hoped to revive *Man's Fate* "under different auspices," emphasizing that his "first loyalty belongs to that film."

The name Zinnemann – omitted by Pauline Kael when she documented attempts to film Lang's book[22] – was destined to remain buried in archives until chance decided otherwise. A serious oversight, to be sure, considering Zinnemann's skills as a filmmaker and the fact that his adaptation would surely have been a notable work. We can only wonder what a collaboration between Lang and Zinnemann would have looked like. In truth, unbeknownst to either man, the unfortunate demise of *Man's Fate* foreshadowed the future awaiting *Casualties of War*.

The Susskind/Clayton collaboration (1970)

An independent television producer, David Susskind co-founded Talent Associates Ltd. in the late 1940s, and later other companies, including Paman Productions.[23] In addition to his reputation as a tenacious producer, he was known for taking strong positions on controversial subjects, including civil rights, homosexuality and the Vietnam War, and the television programs he produced were closely monitored by the FBI. His talk show *Hot Line*, which ran for only one year (1964-65), featured Susskind himself alongside personalities such as author Gore Vidal, Reverend William Sloane Coffin and journalist Dorothy Kilgallen answering questions from viewers, and was openly critical of "the FBI's handling of civil rights cases and bombings in the South [Vietnam]."[24] By the late 1960s, Susskind sought a fresh start for Talent Associates, and in August 1968, he sold the company to Norton Simon Inc. His new strategy was to pitch film projects, asking Norton Simon for "a production fee and a minimum of one-third of a film's profit."[25] Among the ideas Susskind began developing was one close to his heart.

"He liked *Casualties of War* because it fit his brand as an iconoclastic producer, someone who worked on tough themes," explains screenwriter Heywood Gould, who began his collaboration with Susskind in the late 1960s.[26] Susskind's interest in Lang's story stemmed from his staunch opposition to the war in Vietnam and, more broadly, to any form of discrimination and racism. He also sensed that Lang's text, with its exceptional cinematic potential, could become a major film, provided it was made by filmmakers and actors of substance. In January 1970, a 16-page agreement gave Susskind exclusive film adaptation rights to *Casualties of War*.[27] A clause forbade any mention of the real names of anyone involved in the actual case, a measure aimed at protecting Storeby and his wife from potential repercussions, given that it was only three years since the military trials and that two of the guilty soldiers had already been released from prison.

Initially in the running to direct the film, John Schlesinger was ultimately sidelined. The reasons behind this move are obscure. Schlesinger's name doesn't appear in the BFI's Jack Clayton archives and there is no mention of *Casualties of*

David Susskind

War in either Schlesinger's own archives (also at the BFI) or William J. Mann's Schlesinger biography. However, Mann does extensively cover *Sunday Bloody Sunday* (1971), a film Schlesinger began preparing in the fall of 1969 and shot immediately following *Midnight Cowboy*. Everything indicates that his defection from *Casualties of War* was the result of a busy schedule, and that Susskind approached a number of directors to work on the project at Warner Bros.[28] One name eventually emerged: Jack Clayton, a prominent member of the British New Wave movement.

Born in 1921 in Brighton, Clayton transitioned to directing late in his career after working as an assistant director and associate producer for Alexander Korda and John Huston. His first feature film, *Room at the Top* (1959), won the Academy Award for Best Adapted Screenplay and Best Actress for Simone Signoret. Clayton's next film was the sublime *The Innocents* (1961), a ghost story adapted from a Henry James novella, followed by *The Pumpkin Eater* (1964) and *Our Mother's House* (1967). Within a decade Clayton had established a reputation as a demanding filmmaker adept at various genres (social drama, melodrama, fantasy) and capable of directing highly talented actors (Deborah Kerr, James Mason, Dirk Bogarde).[29]

Journalist Pete Hamill was entrusted with writing the initial script version for *Casualties of War*. Some years earlier, Paul Sann, his editor at the *New York Post*, had sent him to cover events in Vietnam. Hamill, who arrived in Da Nang after Christmas in December 1965, briefly recounts his Vietnamese experience in his memoirs: "Every few days I went out to the killing fields, saw boys dying, heard the anguished screams of the wounded. A tourist at the war. Then I came back to Saigon and wrote my pieces in the room at the hotel, and took them down to the post office for shipment to the *Post*."[30] Hamill would have liked to stay longer in Vietnam, but his family situation (he was a father of two) didn't allow it. He drowned his sorrows in Saigon's bars to the rhythms of the Rolling Stones and talked with heady-scented prostitutes. "They were all very young," he recalls, "but their faces were hardening and they had no stories they were proud to tell. The sensuality of the war, its *erotic* demands, urged me toward sex with them; but I was afraid of disease, of having my money stolen, of ending up in some humiliating public mess. I got drunk instead."[31]

By the end of the decade, Hamill was diversifying. He published his first novel, *A Killing for Christ*, and had dabbled in the film industry, including working as a researcher on a documentary produced by David Susskind.[32] In late 1962, during the New York newspaper strike that left him temporarily unemployed, Hamill was hired by George C. Scott – star of the series *East Side/West Side*, produced by

Talent Associates – to conduct research for an episode on nepotism. He wrote a six-page document in which "he listed detailed examples of scandals and investigations involving past New York mayors, the police, the state legislature, gangsters, and Tammany Hall."[33] So dedicated to the job was Hamill that he "pounded the manual typewriter keys with such vigor that the paper used for the memo was riddled with holes."[34]

Talented, daring and with excellent knowledge of the Vietnam War, Hamill was the perfect candidate for the *Casualties of War* script, and in the early days of 1970 sent Clayton a 13-page outline.[35] In his accompanying letter, Hamill wrote of the "three-act structure" he was working with ("Foreplay, Rape, the Remission of Sin"[36]) and urged Clayton to share his thoughts. He asked Clayton for feedback, and made himself completely available, providing the director with phone numbers for his office, his ex-wife, even his current girlfriend. Hamill didn't try to hide his enthusiasm: "Needless to say, I'm really looking forward to working with you, and think this could be a hell of a film."[37]

Hamill's outline, while broadly following Lang's text, introduces several additions or modifications that, as we will later see, posed problems for Clayton. It opens with Eriksson driving a blue van across a wintry landscape in Minnesota, with his wife Kirsten beside him. Gunshots suddenly ring out. A panicked Eriksson slams on the brakes and throws his wife to the floor before grabbing at the glove compartment and retrieving a handgun. Thinking they are being ambushed, he runs to take cover behind the vehicle. The image of Phan Thi Mao, "frozen in fear and pain," flashes before him.[38] Gradually regaining his composure, through the windshield Eriksson sees a frightened deer crossing the road. Voices are heard, and three hunters emerge from the forest, searching for the animal. Eriksson puts the gun back in the glove compartment, and then, without looking at Kirsten, slowly drives away to the sound of "mournful and sad" harmonica music. As the credits roll, the grey and white tones of the snowy countryside fade and are replaced by the warm, lush colors of the Vietnamese jungle. And so begins a flashback that occupies the remainder of the film.

Hamill's powerful opening may have been inspired by a phrase uttered by Storeby during the trial, as reported by

Lang, describing the sound made by the knife that Thomas plunged into Phan Thi Mao's body: "Well, I've shot deer and I've gutted deer. It was just like when you stick a deer with a knife – sort of a thud."[39] If the image of the deer (or stag) subtly references that line, it is also more directly a symbolic image of America, evoking a particular idea of the West – as seen in James Fenimore Cooper's *The Deerslayer* (1841) and much later in Michael Cimino's *The Deer Hunter* and Oliver Stone's *Platoon*, where, in an almost dreamlike moment, a deer appears as the "awe-inspiring symbol of American pastoral lost in a field of corpses in the middle of the Vietnamese jungle."[40] What is so striking about Hamill's prelude to the story, besides its obvious dramatic poetry, is his evocation of Eriksson as a victim, not so much of the war as of the horrendous crime he witnessed. Post-Traumatic Stress Disorder is a central element of the traditional image of the returning veteran, but it is only in later years that we see its full representation on-screen. In this respect, Hamill's version of events is ahead of its time.

The rest of his outline is more conventional, broadly following the chronology of actual events. Reilly sends Meserve, Clark, Eriksson and the Diaz cousins on a reconnaissance mission to flush out a cave where North Vietnamese are said to be hiding. Meserve, in command, announces to his comrades that they are going to find a girl ("a little pussy" in the text) to brighten their days. The description of the kidnapping, rape and murder of Mao relies on elements from Lang's book, down to the smallest details (including the victim's gold tooth). Once the crime is committed, and after a "furious shootout" with North Vietnamese during which Rafe is injured and evacuated, Meserve and his men return to their base and Eriksson goes directly to Lieutenant Reilly to inform on his comrades. Perhaps in an attempt to steer clear of overly verbose scenes, Hamill's outline includes no scenes of the trial. Instead, Chaplain Kirk brings news of the convictions to Eriksson, who confronts the four soldiers as they leave the courtroom. Clark insults him, and Meserve, after promising to find him when he gets out of prison, spits in his face.

Hamill sets the resolution of the story in Vietnam. Waiting for his plane to return home, Eriksson strikes up a conversation with a soldier from Minnesota, who recognizes him as the patrol whistleblower. "You're gonna have to live with that for the rest of your life," he says. A Vietnamese hostess welcomes them, and Eriksson catches a brief glimpse of Mao's face – "with the dull blue earrings, and the pathetic gold tooth, and the hunted look as she crouched in a corner." It is understood that he will be forever unable to erase her from his mind.

Clayton expressed mixed feelings about Hamill's work when the two met in London in January 1970. He had reservations about the opening and the epilogue, the structural imbalance, the fact that the flashback didn't come full circle and return to the opening scene. In accordance with Lang's narrative, Clayton felt that any epilogue should be set in the United States, with Eriksson's return to civilian life. Hamill promised to keep Clayton updated on his progress with the script, but as more phone calls went unanswered, Clayton grew worried.

As a last resort, in early February, he sent a letter to Hamill c/o the *New York Post*'s Brooklyn office.[41] Its tone is polite, but Clayton – unaware that Hamill had gone to Puerto Rico for his newspaper – stressed the importance of discussing script issues during this initial writing phase, fearing it might be too late afterward. He enclosed a four-page document with a series of observations (a copy was also sent to Susskind), most of which they had spoken about at their London meeting.[42] For example, he wasn't entirely convinced by the opening, which he (unfairly) deemed too mannered, despite acknowledging that it "creates a certain tension and mystery." He suggested to Hamill that the film begin with an ambush scene in the jungle, so as to depict "some of the danger, pain and frustration that young American soldiers go through during their sojourn in Vietnam. It may also help to explain their feelings toward the Vietnamese civilians, about whom they can never be sure." Overall, Clayton hoped that a rewrite would bring the script closer to Lang's original. He wasn't too pleased with the liberties Hamill had taken with the original material, notably the complete removal of certain characters from his adaptation, and asked Hamill to reintegrate the "accidental" exchange of gunfire between the two patrols (where Manuel almost kills Eriksson), the search for Mao's body, and the trials. Clayton was also surprised by

Jack Clayton and Deborah Kerr on the set of *The Innocents* (1961)

the removal of Rowan, whom he considered to be a pivotal character. He is, after all, Eriksson's only friend and so is able to act as a confidant, the person Eriksson goes to first, which seems more credible than Eriksson talking to an officer.

Neil Sinyard defends the idea that Clayton's films, as a whole, serve as "models of cinematic adaptations."[43] According to Sinyard, great literary film adaptations rely on three criteria: "They go for the spirit of the original [...], they use the camera to interpret and not simply illustrate the text; and [...] there is some kind of creative empathy between the author of the original text and the director of the film."[44] These were precisely the intentions guiding Clayton's sharp and rigorous assessment of Hamill's outline. The relevance of his remarks demonstrated how deeply he understood Lang's original – perhaps more so than the screenwriter who, despite some masterfully crafted passages, seemed not to have fully exploited its potential or fully grasped the issues.

Most of Clayton's observations were shared by Jeanie Sims, his script editor on *The Innocents* and *The Pumpkin Eater*, who sent him a seven-page memo about Hamill's draft.[45] Her remarks on the opening and epilogue, and on the erasure of Rowan and the trials, align with Clayton's.

She appears sensitive to the coherence of the narrative, particularly from a historical and legal standpoint, and regrets that because the premeditation of the murder isn't clearly expressed during Meserve's briefing, the crime appears little more than a joke gone awry. She notes: "In the outline, the first we hear about killing the girl is when Clark suggests it after she becomes ill. Thus, her illness – and the possible danger that her coughing might reveal their presence to the V.C. – becomes the motive for her death. In fact, as we know, while it hastened her murder, this was always part of the plan. Again, by not making the point that the killing was pre-ordained, we lose one of the most important points of the story, and detract greatly not only from the crime itself, but the subsequent trials, verdicts, and sentences."[46] Sims also found the character of Clark to be insufficiently nuanced, and commented on one of the passages where he gratuitously shoots the dead body of a North Vietnamese: "Although Clark is, to my mind, clearly a psychopath, he obeys orders. At no time does he act on his own initiative: he is Meserve's tool and disciple."[47]

At this point, two different visions of *Casualties of War* emerged. Clayton and Sims advocated for a film closer to the facts of the case (perhaps at the expense of Hamill's creative impulses), one less focused on the murder itself than on Eriksson's struggle to have the criminals brought to justice. Hamill, more concerned with making the obscenity of war felt by audiences, brought to bear his personal feelings. "When I was in Vietnam," he wrote to Clayton, "I was struck by the absolute proliferation of *Playboy* posters, something I suppose that started in the Second World War, when it was Rita Hayworth and Betty Grable. But I think there is a peculiar comment we can make here, and perhaps an important one: the pictures of women in *Playboy* are really rhetoric. They are the rhetoric of fantasy, of perfect orgasms, of the innocent woman who is a whore in bed. They promise everything and give nothing, because of course they are not real; they are plastic fantasies. Then suddenly these young men (Meserve is only 20) find themselves in a situation that is real, where they can act out their fantasies on the body of an anonymous woman [...] but when they are finished, the object of the fantasy is squatting in the corner, coughing. The only way to be rid of the fantasy and get on with the real world again (which in this case is fighting in the war) is to kill the object."[48] Hamill wanted to explore the relationship between war and pornography: "I've tried to indicate that brutal texture of obscenity that all soldiers employ, and which I think we agree should be a major factor in the style of the film," he told Clayton.[49] But neither Clayton nor Jeanie Sims, who expressed discomfort with the recurrent use of obscene language, were willing to follow him in this direction.

The working relationship between Clayton and Hamill was, from the outset, a fragile one, and more creative differences emerged. But there was more at play than mere disagreements over the script. Other factors strained the relationship between the two men, notably the fact that Hamill was grappling with personal issues during this time, including a marital crisis (and ultimately a divorce) partly due to his alcoholism. In need of money, he took on as many articles, columns and scripts as he could handle, and his work on *Casualties of War* likely suffered. He simply wasn't able to dedicate himself fully to the project and give it the focus that Clayton demanded. For his part, Clayton – seemingly aware of these issues (which are indirectly referenced in one of his letters) – might have also lacked tact in conveying his notes, overlooking the fact that Hamill was something of a star journalist and a celebrated luminary of the *New York Post*.[50]

Clayton didn't wait for Hamill's full script before moving forward. In late January, Jeanie Sims sent a series of documents aimed at clarifying various story elements: a brief synopsis, a detailed list of main characters and locations, a summary of trial verdicts and convictions, and an exhaustive timeline, starting with Mao's murder and ending with Storeby's testimony.[51] A list of 37 questions, designed to prevent factual errors, was later written and sent to military advisor Alexander A.C. Gerry.[52] These questions touched on soldiers' daily life, military hierarchy, and also the specifics of the incident as detailed by Lang. One question, for example, was whether Eriksson's reaction – not fleeing with Mao to avoid being seen as a deserter – was plausible, and what sanctions a soldier would face if he abandoned his patrol. By early April,

Gerry provided comprehensive answers, supplemented with explanatory diagrams. Clayton's archive also contains maps of Southeast Asia, presumably because potential filming locations were being considered. Due to the ongoing war, the film couldn't shoot in Vietnam.

It was during this period that Clayton made contact with Lang, probably through Susskind. In a letter dated February 2, 1970, Clayton expressed a desire to meet Lang while visiting New York, where he was scheduled to be in about ten days. One can imagine that the two discussed Hamill's script. Their correspondence suggests that this meeting marked the beginning of a close friendship. The warm tone in Clayton's letters to Lang is in stark contrast with the more distant and strictly professional tone of letters from Clayton to Hamill during the same period.

By late March 1970, Clayton, still awaiting Hamill's script, was growing increasingly frustrated with the situation. Hamill's agent claimed that his client had sent a letter to Clayton and would telephone him within two days. This didn't happen. To allay his fears, Danton J. Rissner, a Warner Bros. executive, sent Clayton a letter at the end of March, anticipating Hamill's potential departure by proposing a list of authors who could replace him.[53] Among the names mentioned were William Goldman, known for writing *Butch Cassidy and the Sundance Kid*; Robert Anderson, author of the adaptation of Richard McKenna's novel *The Sand Pebbles*; John Milius, future writer of *Apocalypse Now*; J.P. Miller, known for his scripts of *The Young Savages* and *The Day of the Outlaw*; and Paddy Chayefsky, primarily a television writer before his work on *Network* a few years later. Clayton had plenty of options, but the list proved unnecessary because in early April, Hamill unexpectedly delivered a 125-page script.[54]

Casualties of War – script #1 (Peter Hamill)

Relieved to finally have a solid foundation to work from, Clayton quickly realized that Hamill had ignored many of his recommendations. On the eve of his New York trip (April 6, 1970), he wrote to Susskind, stating that the script "still requires a considerable amount of work."[55] His concerns extended beyond the details of the story itself. In the same letter, Clayton wrote about how the film could be perceived by the authorities, expressing concern that it might present the American military and judicial system – "for which we both have a high regard" – in a bad light. Moreover, Clayton believed that capitalizing on the current wave of scandal sweeping across America would be a mistake, and was adamant that the film not actively reflect more current events, including the revelation of the My Lai massacre.

Clayton flew to New York on April 7 and drafted a series of questions for Lang.[56] Were place names changed in the book? Have the convicts been released from prison? Would it be possible to meet the real Eriksson? Did Lang have access to trial transcripts? Was there any response from the Pentagon following the publication of his text in *The New Yorker*? Clayton's main concern was to be as faithful as possible to Lang's text and, by extension, the historical truth – perhaps compensating for what he felt were the shortcomings of Hamill's script. During this same trip to New York, Clayton and Hamill had what appears to have been a rather tense meeting, during which Clayton stood his ground and reiterated his suggestions to Hamill. Clayton then traveled from New York to Los Angeles to meet Susskind and Warner Bros. executives. In a note written the day before his departure, he listed a series of points he hoped to address, including asking Susskind to get in touch with *Life* magazine and the Magnum photo agency to try and obtain images of the approximate location of Hill 192.[57] He also checked to see if the production team had made enquiries about Vietnamese communities in the United States, presumably because such information would be useful when it came to casting the role of Mao.

Three days after his return to London on April 12, Clayton drafted a six-page document, evidently intended for Hamill.[58] His overall impression is unequivocal: "The basic story from the book is there, but the human element has vanished." Clayton noted that the character of Eriksson "emerges in the script as rather a bore and a prig. This, of course, is disaster for the film." He suggested modifying this portrayal of the main character, keeping in mind that he grew up in the country and so is theoretically "less gregarious than an urban boy," "infinitely more self-reliant" and instinctively aware of the physical environment around him, for instance, being intrigued by "bird calls he has never heard at home."

Clayton's remark feels out of place, as Hamill's screenplay does indeed include such a reference (as the patrol crosses a field, Eriksson marvels at the beauty of the landscape: "My God, this country can be so beautiful!"). Hamill also made efforts to incorporate some of Clayton's other suggestions, for example abandoning his initial – and very effective – idea of a prologue in Minnesota, setting it in Vietnam instead. The screenplay opens with a shot of lush jungle. A child's voice singing in Vietnamese gradually becomes audible, mixed with sounds of nature (insects, birds, wind). A four-year-old girl, dressed in traditional garb, delicately picks flowers near a road. As she marvels at a butterfly, a muffled sound grows louder. Suddenly, an elderly peasant woman covers the girl's mouth and holds her close. "In both their eyes: deep, primitive fear." A convoy of U.S. Army armored vehicles approaches. Hamill vividly contrasts the poetic imagery of nature with the violence of the military vehicles' abrupt intrusion, a deafening roar that scatters birds from bushes. Their entrance into the scene – "metallic, non-organic, brutal" – is shown from the perspective of the woman and child. Hamill then introduces the main characters of the story as the convoy, constantly under threat, continues its journey. One of the trucks eventually hits a landmine and explodes.

Following Jeanie Sim's comments, Hamill re-wrote Rowan back into the story and added an essential detail. When Eriksson tells his friend Rowan about Meserve's scheme, there is no doubt that the crime is a premeditated one: "Meserve says they will get a girl, any girl, take her with us, screw her for five days, and then kill her. I gotta let someone know."

Despite these revisions, Clayton wasn't convinced. It can be assumed that numerous trivial details punctuating the beginning of the narrative (the appearance of scantily clad prostitutes, an elderly woman defecating), as well as the soldiers' vulgar language, full of sexual allusions, troubled him. Meserve's crudeness is on full display in the scene preceding the rape when, after calling Eriksson a "faggot," he suggests: "Maybe he's got a pussy himself." Manuel, portrayed as a sex maniac, forcefully kisses Eriksson, using his tongue, triggering Eriksson's visceral reaction as he violently pushes him away, draws his gun, and aims it at him. In the rape scene, Hamill alternates perspectives, showing the action through Eriksson's and Rafe's eyes when the latter enters the hut to take his turn. He glimpses Mao's slender body, her small breasts, then lingers on her face, mouth open and closed eyes, noting that she looks "terribly young."

Clayton doesn't elaborate on these passages in his notes, deeming the sequence of the search for Mao's body (absent from the outline) overly erbose. Perhaps inspired by his recent conversation with Lang,[59] and undoubtedly motivated by the desire to return to the original structure of his book, Clayton suggested that the story be told through the eyes of Lang himself, possibly with the use of a voiceover. Even though the character of Rowan had been reintegrated, some characters still seemed underutilized to him, notably Kirsten, Eriksson's wife, whom he suggests should appear at the end of the screenplay. But despite Clayton's requests, Hamill didn't think it necessary to transport Eriksson back to his native Minnesota, and the script ends in the first-class compartment of a plane taking him home. From the window, before the plane takes off and disappears into the sky, he glimpses the old peasant woman and the girl from the beginning of the film. Credits roll. The vision of Mao has mysteriously disappeared.

One can easily imagine Clayton's disappointment in reading this ending, which doesn't match the opening. The epilogue, Clayton insisted in his notes, must take place in the United States, once Eriksson returns from Vietnam. His fear is crystallized, and back home he lives with a sword of Damocles hanging over his head (the retaliation of those he denounced). "There is the possibility of a wonderful scene at the end between Eriksson and his wife – alone, and yet it seems there is a third person present, Mao,"[60] proposed Clayton.

Overall, Clayton's reservations were shared by Warner Bros. executives. In an internal note intended for producer John Calley, Danton Rissner regretted that the screenplay, though closely following Lang's text, falls apart as soon as the patrol leaves Hill 192 to return to base, and recommended a rewrite.[61] When this note reached Clayton, it ignited a firestorm. He wrote a lengthy letter to Hamill in which he expressed numerous problems, emphasizing that the studio executives weren't happy with the screenplay. "Remember, doubt in the film industry is both infectious and self-destructive," he warned, before adding, with a heavy heart: "I have never before been placed in such an absurd and unhappy position."[62] Clayton issued an ultimatum to Hamill: "Now, I would like you to understand the following: my contractual arrangement on this film, as on all the others that I have made, entitles me to work on and *approve* the script that is delivered to the production and distributing companies. From now on, I intend to fully exercise this right. Although there are parts of the script that you have written which I like very much, there is an enormous amount of work to be done before, in my opinion, it could be called a screenplay. If you would like to work on a new draft with me, I should be delighted. But this time it will have to be *with me* and this time it must be your sole preoccupation as it is mine. Let's this time, for a change, keep the agreed appointments."[63]

Clayton concluded his letter by inviting Hamill to meet him the following day at The Terrazza restaurant in Soho.[64] This reconciliation never took place. Hamill sent a terse telegram: "OBVIOUSLY IMPOSSIBLE FOR US TO WORK TOGETHER AFTER THAT LETTER – STOP – SUGGEST YOU GET ANOTHER WRITER."[65] And so the Clayton/Hamill collaboration reached its sad conclusion.

Casualties of War – script #2 (David Giler)

A replacement was sought. The list sent to Clayton at the end of March, in anticipation of Hamill's defection, offered enticing leads, but ultimately none of the names on it were selected. Instead, the job went to David Giler.

Giler, who later became a successful producer (notably with director Walter Hill and on the *Alien* franchise), already had several credits, including a number of Warner Bros. television series.[66] He and Clayton appear to have worked well together, and Giler later described Clayton as "brilliant."[67]

Giler's version starts much like Hamill's, with a sequence where an American army convoy, carrying Clark, Meserve, Rafe and Eriksson, arrives in a village under the passive gaze of locals. They exchange jokes and make obscene gestures toward prostitutes before one of the trucks, leaving the village, explodes after hitting a mine. The soldiers assume the villagers were aware of the dangers and harbor strong resentments against them. Later, during Meserve's briefing before the reconnaissance mission, he jokingly tells the men that because of the length of their mission, they will need to requisition volunteers from the civilian population – mostly females – to boost troop morale. Giler takes care not to emphasize any notion of premeditation when it comes to Mao's treatment. Just before dawn the next day, Meserve follows through on his threat. The woman's abduction and subsequent events remain faithful to Lang's account. Giler seems to want to maintain the rawness of Meserve and Clark's language, even though the obscene jokes from Hamill's script have been omitted. The two soldiers accuse Eriksson of being a "queer," a "faggot" and "chickenshit" when he refuses to participate in the rape of the young woman. "You want to suck my cock, faggot? Huh? You want to suck my cock?" Meserve shouts at him.

Eriksson endures rather than responds. Later, while Mao is being raped, he is described as sitting on the ground, legs up against his chest, his head on his knees, in pain – a posture too demonstrative to be entirely plausible. Eriksson's helplessness is better conveyed by Giler in the long sequence where the soldier tries, without truly succeeding, to communicate with Mao. Realizing that he doesn't intend to harm her but wants to help, she pleads for his assistance. Eriksson hesitates – and ultimately, it is too late. When Meserve and the others return to the hut from their mission, Mao is no longer the sexual object they desire. "She don't look that hot either," says Clark, who later suggests getting rid of her because of her persistent cough, which might give their position away to the enemy.

Giler respected Clayton's wish to stick closer to the book, certainly more than Hamill did, and he sometimes uses Lang's exact words and expressions, such as his remark that the sound of the knife sinking into the victim's stomach is akin to gutting a deer. But Giler didn't always fully grasp Clayton's and Jeanie Sims' comments. Although he made sure to reintroduce Rowan's character, the murder is first reported by Eriksson to Reilly before he discusses it with Rowan.

The second part of Giler's script is characterized by long dialogue scenes between Eriksson and Chaplain Kirk, then between Eriksson and Major Vinson, an investigator probing the truth of his claims. For the sequence when Mao's body is eventually discovered, Giler – following Clayton's advice – partially abandons dialogue and focuses on Eriksson's nervousness. The sequence spans several pages. After the slow ascent of the mountain, Eriksson heads toward a bush where he believes he will find the body, but it isn't there. He searches around, but still nothing. Doubt grips him and he starts to panic. Then something catches his attention, something "glinting in the sun." He leans down and picks up a blue earring, just like the ones Mao wore. Slowly parting the foliage, he discovers a decomposed body.

In Giler's script, the trials span nearly twenty pages. The pathologist, ballistics experts, then Mao's sister, Loc, whose responses are translated by an interpreter, take the stand. Following them are Eriksson – grilled by one of the defense attorneys, Major Ashton – and the four accused: Rafe, Meserve (who claims Mao was North Vietnamese and denies her rape), Clark (who painfully admits to following orders) and Manuel (whose only defense is obeying Meserve's orders). After the court's verdict, the prosecutor warns Eriksson: "For your sake, boy, I hope you've got a nice safe place to hide."

Again following Clayton's notes, Giler sets the epilogue in the United States. He contrasts Eriksson's despair with alternating scenes showing the elation of the four accused after their release from prison. The reunions of the former convicts and their families, across a timespan of three years (1968 to 1971), are joyful and moving. In Mexico, Manuel is welcomed home by his brother, wife and child. Rafe is greeted by his wife, who picks him up from Fort Leavenworth. Clark arrives by bus at his home in South Carolina, where a small group of friends welcomes him and his mother bursts into tears as she hugs him tightly. Last to be freed, Meserve arrives in civilian clothes at Grand Central Station in New York. His father hugs him, tousles his hair, and gives him a pat on the shoulder, as if reuniting with an old comrade. They walk away together, laughing.

Giler poignantly contrasts the euphoria of the four men returning to civilian life with Eriksson's slow descent into hell. His arrival at the Minneapolis bus station is tinged with a deep, inescapable anxiety that only intensifies as the months turn into years. He is seen working listlessly in his carpentry shop, then sitting, despondent, by the window in his living room, under the watchful eye of his worried wife. A sequence shows him walking, troubled, down a street in Minneapolis. He stops in front of a gun store, looks at the display, and goes inside, where he buys a .45 automatic pistol, then leaves with his package and, as night falls, boards the bus. Opposite him, a young Asian woman adjusts her hair, catching her reflection in the window. For a brief moment, Eriksson sees Mao's face instead of hers. After apologizing for staring, he steps off the bus and disappears into the crowd – just another silhouette in the anonymous throng of the city.

The first version of Giler's script is dated August 12, 1970. Lang annotated his copy, crossing out and underlining things that needed revision, proposing changes to a few lines of dialogue and adding factual details. He also made comments on his expectations regarding the filmmaking and imagery. His remarks, likely made in conjunction with Clayton, led to a rather uncomplicated rewriting phase, as the initial draft had already won over the Warner Bros. executives. This is evidenced by John Calley's effusive telegram to Clayton: "I THINK YOUR DRAFT OF CASUALTIES OF WAR IS A SUPERB JOB – STOP – I THINK YOU COULD SHOOT EXACTLY AS IT IS WRITTEN AND HAVE THE BEST ANTIWAR FILM EVER MADE."[68] With the studio's approval, *Casualties of War* entered the pre-production phase.

In mid-July, after trade newspapers reported that the film was in development, and while Giler's script remained unfinished, Clayton received several letters from actors expressing interest in the project and requesting a meeting.[69] The production also began recruiting crew members, searching for locations, and considering location scouting in India.[70] It is possible that the shooting schedule – an undated copy of which is in Clayton's archive – was developed around the same time.[71] Estimated at 53 days, the shoot was to begin with all sequences set in the military base (before and after the murder), followed chronologically by Mao's abduction and murder. The sequence of Eriksson's discovery of her body was slated for a two-day shoot. On the fiftieth day, the crew would return to the United States and spend four days filming the final sequences.

But Clayton likely found this shooting plan too ambitious. A handwritten note, possibly his, advises extending the schedule by 26 days, totaling 79 days (72 abroad), which would have had inevitable budget consequences. Were Clayton's demands too much for the Warner executives to handle? In September 1970, he was informed that the location scouting in India was canceled. Warner Bros. had been told that the Indian government would never allow a film like *Casualties of War* to be shot there. But this official explanation concealed other, undisclosed reasons.

The Munich trial

In July 1970, Lang learned that the film that had halted the Berlinale earlier that year was heavily inspired by *Casualties of War*. A three-page summary of *o.k.*, likely drafted by a Warner Bros. insider who had attended the screening, was sent to studio executives and Lang.[72] The text offered a fairly accurate description of the film's content, with the author identifying similarities and differences between *o.k.* and Lang's text. It noted that the overall plot had been "completely changed," with the film portraying "the contrast between the easy and joking life of the soldier" and the moment they "suddenly and without apparent reason develop into brutal beasts." "Even the murder of the girl is not planned, but happens more or less like an accident," the report stated. However, it listed several elements borrowed from Lang's original text: the soldiers' pseudonyms, the description of the rape, and the dialogue between Eriksson, Vorst and Reilly (noting that this part of the film contained the most obvious borrowings from Lang's work). "We should be able to prove infringement to a considerable degree," concluded the report.[73]

To Lang, Susskind and Warner Bros., *o.k.* quickly appeared as a "pirated version" of *Casualties of War*.[74] In Lang's archives is a copy of *Variety*'s negative review of *o.k.* (which doesn't mention his name).[75] In response, he drafted a ten-page document revisiting the genesis of his text, highlighting various similarities between Verhoeven's film and his *New Yorker* article. He dismantled the argument that Verhoeven had found inspiration from daily newspapers, pointing out that the "episode lay dead or dormant in brief newspaper accounts for more than two years" until he "gave it life." "It is my work, the product of my interviewing, my selection, transposition and arrangement of events, my dialogue, my characterization and my names and description for the characters that *o.k.* has <u>stolen</u> [exploited?]," he explained.[76]

Rob Houwer, *o.k.*'s producer, was taken aback when Warner Bros. sued him for plagiarism. "It was a rough and totally unexpected blow," he says. "Michael Verhoeven never mentioned or gave any indication that the script he sold to me for this film, to be directed by him, was based on an excerpt of Daniel Lang's book that had been published in *The New Yorker*. I learned this only from the accusations made by Warner Bros."[77] What appeared to Warner Bros., Susskind and Lang as clearcut plagiarism could have been the result of Verhoeven's lack of understanding of intellectual property rights. While he initially became aware of the story through an article in the German press before discovering Lang's text published in *The New Yorker*, Lang's book had, in fact, been translated into German and published in Hamburg at the beginning of 1970.[78]

The legal case brought against Houwer played out in Munich during the summer of 1970. Decades later, few documents are accessible. A search in Warner Bros.' archives proved fruitless. Shannon Fifer, manager of Warner Bros. Motion Picture Rights office, explains: "The files we have do not talk about any lawsuit," although she did find "mention of a German movie that may have been made using Daniel Lang's article without his permission."[79] It is likely that the studio handled the case with the utmost confidentiality.

"I had to act alone in court," recounts Houwer. "Michael Verhoeven – responsible for this disaster – sat there silently. To start with, Warner Bros. wanted a million dollars from me, plus legal costs. Their vice president and a group of American lawyers flew on first-class tickets to Munich. They wined and dined in the city's most expensive hotel, convinced of easy victory. In the courtroom, Warner Bros., represented by their prominent German lawyer, proved, page after page, that the script I had acquired from Michael Verhoeven had been plagiarized. My poor lawyer had no valid response. I prayed in despair, pleading for inspiration. Suddenly it hit me! I jumped up from my seat, walked to the judges who were sitting on a raised stage, hit their table with my fist, pointed my finger at the Warner Bros. delegation, and, in a very loud voice, said, 'How is it that here in

Munich, America is now claiming the artistic copyright of the inhumane and horrible war it is waging in Vietnam?!'"[80]

The producer's thunderous declaration had its desired effect, triggering enthusiastic applause from the audience. After half an hour of deliberation, the judges returned and announced that Houwer was not liable. Morality had triumphed over the strict application of the law. There was astonishment and incomprehension amongst the Warner executives. "The American delegation couldn't believe what they were hearing," says Houwer. "*o.k.* continued to play in cinemas. Warner Bros., meanwhile, sued me in Denmark too, where the film was also being screened. I won again in Copenhagen with the same moral argument I had made in Munich. After two losses, Warner Bros. gave up. Victory for me, and a narrow escape for Michael Verhoeven. If I had lost, bankruptcy for me and my company would have been unavoidable – and most probably for Michael too."[81]

Did Lang attend the Munich trial? Among his correspondence is a letter accompanying a refund check from Warner Bros. for a trip taken to Germany around the time of the trial.[82] He might have been there for other reasons – neither Rob Houwer nor Michael Verhoeven can confirm if he was present in court during the hearing. Nonetheless, it is presumed that the verdicts of the Munich and Copenhagen trials dealt a serious blow to Lang. The studio could have appealed. But then, unexpectedly, in early September 1970, Lang received a letter from one of his attorneys informing him that Warner Bros. had decided to drop the case. Studio executives claimed they could have won the appeal but feared that "continuation of the litigation would be more damaging than the German movie," which they apparently no longer saw as a "serious obstacle" to their film version.[83] The letter, however, leaves serious doubts as to Warner Bros.' willingness to see its own adaptation through.

Was *Casualties of War* really the kind of film that Hollywood wanted to be seen making while American troops were still engaged in Vietnam? Warner Bros. appears to have deliberately let the situation deteriorate, pretending not to abandon *Casualties of War* while at the same time not undertaking any significant effort to push it forward. Clayton took the situation badly. In early October, he wrote to Alan Shayne, his casting director, expressing his bitterness.[84] Around the same time, Charles Maguire,[85] the production manager, returned from the Philippines, and new meetings were scheduled regarding possible funding. But any remaining hopes would soon evaporate.

The absence of documents in the Clayton archives relating to *Casualties of War* from mid-October 1970 to mid-March 1971 suggests that the pre-production phase was, indeed, interrupted. During this period, Clayton and Lang met in New York. Their discussions didn't revolve solely around a *Casualties of War* adaptation. Lang spoke of a new project he was working on for *The New Yorker*, which Clayton later wrote to him about: "I have a strong feeling that your new piece – suitably enlarged – would make an exciting and important film."[86]

On March 19, 1971, Clayton was contacted by Lang,[87] who informed him that a certain Shedlo,[88] based in Burbank, California, was considering a theatrical adaptation of *Casualties of War*, in collaboration with Giler. A clause in the agreement Lang signed with Paman Productions guaranteed him the theatrical adaptation rights within four years after the film's release, or six from the signing of the contract.[89] The idea of a play, first suggested by Fred Zinnemann in his letter of November 18, 1969, had finally taken hold in Lang's mind. On September 11, 1970, Lang, after being told that Warner Bros. had distanced itself from Clayton's film, wrote a letter to John Calley asking that this clause about theatrical adaptations be removed from his contract.

A few months later, however, Lang learned from Shedlo that Warner Bros. had reconnected with Clayton, jeopardizing the theatrical adaptation. A concerned Lang contacted Clayton, who confirmed that John Calley was willing to discuss *Casualties of War* with Richard Zanuck, who was newly arrived at the studio. "Whether this will work or not, I don't know, but feel it's the best that can be done for the moment, as I am sure David Susskind has totally 'flogged' the other possible companies,"[90] he concluded, suggesting that relations with the producer were no longer at their best. The Zanuck connection ultimately went nowhere. The chances of a *Casualties of War* adaptation waned with each passing day.

In the midst of June 1971, as the Pentagon Papers affair raged, a new player entered the game: Stanley Chais, a private investment advisor based in Los Angeles who was part of the entourage of swindler Bernie Madoff. His preferred hunting ground was the film industry, a domain he was relatively familiar with, given that his wife Pamela was a screenwriter and daughter of a Broadway dramatist. It is conceivable that Chais learned about *Casualties of War*, and the challenges Clayton was facing in getting the project over the finish line, through word of mouth.

Chais approached Lang to determine the availability of rights to his book. An inconsistency arises in the first letter he sent. Chais initially claims that he first learned about the story by reading Lang's book, which came out after *The New Yorker* article, but then says that he has been contemplating turning the story into a film ever since reading about it in the magazine.[91] Which version is true? Was Stanley Chais sincere? Was he genuinely moved by *Casualties of War* or did he simply sense an opportunity to attract wealthy investors to a potentially lucrative subject?

Whichever is true, Lang took the bait and agreed to speak to Chais. In anticipation of this phone conversation, Chais sent a second letter, expressing his willingness to share more about himself. He introduced himself as "a private investment counselor with absolutely no experience in motion picture producing."[92] However, he continued, "several of my investors are prominent in the picture business, and with some luck, hard work and money I do believe that something can be done about getting your picture produced."[93] After praising Lang's book, Chais sought to reassure: "Since I am not a theatrical entrepreneur I will not […] play the theatrical shell game," he promised bluntly, before mentioning to Lang that his wife was also a screenwriter and that he was all too familiar with "the wringer that agents, lawyers, and producers" can deploy.[94]

Lang informed Chais that the film developed by Warner Bros. was no longer happening, and suggested that Chais contact Clayton for more information. The tone of Chais' letter to Clayton is persuasive yet vague, noting that he works with unnamed "clients who have both the expertise and the money to set things in motion."[95] In other words, Chais presented himself as someone able to revive the project that had been abandoned by Warner Bros. His approach was well honed: "I will confess that after hearing the dreary saga of *Casualties* in Hollywood, my impulse was to run like hell. Obviously an enormous amount of money had been spent (and misspent) – and presumably would expect to be recouped by Warner; and I have little appetite for buying the mistakes of others – particularly those of motion picture moguls with public money. How then can this book be ransomed and its motion picture prospects resurrected? It's a great book and deserves a better fate. If you care to pursue the matter further, please write to me at the above address."[96]

In his mind, however, Clayton had already turned the page on *Casualties of War*, and it is highly likely that Chais, sensing a dead end, pushed it no further. There is no mention of the film in the letter Clayton sent Lang less than three months later, in which he expresses regret for not being able to write earlier and explains how busy he is working on two new projects.[97] After a brief mention of Lang's latest article, which he found "quite brilliant," Clayton inforrms him of his visit to New York the following weekend and makes a promise to call when he arrives. We can only speculate about what the two men might have discussed, but one imagines that Clayton finally announced to his friend that *Casualties of War* was now joining cinema history's long list of unmade films.

The return of David Susskind (1977–79)

Casualties of War disappeared from Hollywood's radar between 1971 and 1976, at which point the reversion clause in the agreement signed by Daniel Lang with Paman Productions took effect. If within five years a film adaptation hadn't been produced, the rights automatically reverted back to him. In January 1975, Lang was released from all legal commitments. But David Susskind hadn't yet given up on *Casualties of War*.

When, in 1974, Talent Associates Ltd. began facing financial difficulties, Norton Simon sought to sell it. Susskind stepped forward as a buyer, and in July 1975, after his offer, a symbolic $1, was accepted, he once again became the owner of the company he had founded. Besides his television work,

Susskind developed projects as feature films and Broadway shows, and it was in this context – eager to overcome the Warner Bros. debacle – that he made a new agreement with Lang for the adaptation rights of *Casualties of War*.[98] Talent Associates took a one-year option on the book, extendable by two consecutive six-month periods. The contract thus bound the two parties for a maximum of two years, after which the option would expire if a film hadn't been made.

But Talent Associates was hardly a stable operation, and only two years later Susskind was again forced to part ways with his company. On August 5, 1977, Time-Life Films, a subsidiary of Time Inc., whose mission was to sell "educational movies, documentaries, and BBC shows to television," bought Talent Associates for $1 million.[99] Susskind lost the independent status he had maintained when the company was owned by Norton Simon. At Time-Life Films, he was now a contract employee, a radical change of circumstances that he struggled to cope with.

The clutch of projects that Susskind was working on through Talent Associates, including *Casualties of War*, found a new home at Time-Life Films. In mid-September 1977, Time-Life Television Productions (a division of Time-Life Films) sent a letter to Sidney Cohn, Lang's lawyer, confirming the commitment made by Talent Associates and offering Lang a fee for his consulting services. *Casualties of War* was now going to become a relatively low-budget TV movie.

The background of the screenwriter hired for the job, Heywood Gould, was strangely similar to Pete Hamill's. The two were actually good friends. Gould started as a copy boy at the *New York Post*, where Pete Hamill also worked. "I brought him his breakfast – light coffee, two sugars, pack of Parliament cigarettes. We came from the same neighborhood in Brooklyn. He had dated the eldest sister of one of my friends. He was friendly, not at all snobbish. I was a fan."[100] Hamill was an inspirational model for Gould because he had dared switch from reporting to screenwriting. Gould would follow suit.

But before finding a place for himself in Hollywood, and as the situation in Vietnam worsened, Gould was promoted and became a reporter at the *Post*. "I covered anti-war activities in New York – demos, meetings, interviews with Spock and Dellinger and prominent pacifists. I saw construction workers manhandle members of the War Resistance League while cops stood by. I saw cops dragging protesters by their hair. I saw Students for a Democratic Society-types spit on sailors and douse them with red paint and covered people burning their draft cards on the steps of City Hall. I asked to be sent to Vietnam, but I was a 21-year-old 'street' reporter and didn't have the gravitas, so they sent Pete Hamill. It made sense, but I was still pissed off."[101]

After being drafted into the army and narrowly escaping combat in Vietnam,[102] Gould left the *Post* in 1966 and, unable to transition to independent journalism, took on various odd jobs. It was around this time that he began writing and published a biography of architect Christopher Wren, a novel (*One Dead Debutante*), numerous articles on cinema, and his first screenplays, including three episodes of the *N.Y.P.D.* series. The first TV show to be officially endorsed by the New York Police Department, it was created by Arnold Perl and… David Susskind. Susskind noticed Gould after reading his emblematic 1973 screenplay *Fort Apache, The Bronx* (filmed by Daniel Petrie in 1981). Shortly before that, two other scripts by Gould were filmed: John Flynn's *Rolling Thunder* (1977), which has Vietnam trauma as a backdrop, and *The Boys from Brazil*, directed in 1978 by Franklin J. Schaffner.

Talent, renown, an excellent understanding of the Vietnam conflict – all reasons why Heywood Gould was the ideal candidate to write a third, completely new adaptation of Lang's text. When hired by Susskind, Gould was unaware of Clayton's aborted project, and the producer carefully avoided informing him of its history or letting him see copies of Pete Hamill and David Giler's screenplays. Gould would only learn years later – as David Rabe's screenplay was about to be filmed by De Palma – that his friend Hamill had written an early draft.

Casualties of War – script #3 (Heywood Gould)
Gould was on the job between late 1978 and early 1979, during which time he met Lang several times. "We had a few friendly lunches," recalls the screenwriter who, like Lang, comes from a family of Jewish immigrants. The pair shared other similarities: "We had both worked for the *New York Post* and knew some people in common. I was interested in how he

had happened upon the story, who were his main sources, if there were aspects he wanted to emphasize. I suspected that there was a little fictionalizing here and there, which is often done in this kind of reportage, but he didn't bring it up."[103]

There are two versions of Gould's script (which he says he wrote solo, without Lang's assistance). The first, dated March 26, 1979, is 116 pages long.[104] The second, undated, is 142 pages.[105] It would make sense that Gould wrote the longer version first, then made cuts based on Lang's feedback, but this hypothesis is contradicted by the rough draft notes made by Lang, including a seven-page document dated May 28, 1979, in which he offers his opinion on the script, referencing the pagination of the longer version.[106] We can therefore conclude that the "extended" version was written after the initial, shorter draft.

Gould's first (shorter) draft begins with a striking scene in "a small clearing amidst dense jungle undergrowth." Eriksson stands next to an old Vietnamese villager at a mass grave, contemplating the bodies of young boys massacred by North Vietnamese, piled up haphazardly in the pit.[107] His comrade, Pierce, barely has time to encourage him to leave the area when there is an explosion and a thick curtain of smoke blows through the scene. Sporadic gunfire and muffled voices are heard. As the smoke clears, Sergeant Meserve – "young, compact, dark-haired and grim-faced" – appears, inquiring about Eriksson's condition. Covered in dust, Eriksson gets up and stumbles upon an inert body, which turns out to be Pierce, and the old villager, who is still alive. The explosions and gunfire intensify, and Meserve yells at Eriksson to leave. When Eriksson replies that the old man is injured, Meserve shouts back, "That's a gook! Are you crazy? A gook!" After giving him a slap on the back of the head, he yells, "Move it! That's an order! NOW!" A clash between two antagonistic personalities. On one side is Eriksson, who refuses to compromise his values, on the other is Meserve, for whom life holds little value unless it belongs to an American soldier.

Gould, perhaps feeling that this opening scene was too brief and that a deeper investigation of his protagonists was required, expanded his initial draft by about 30 pages, exploring the physical and psychological consequences of war on Meserve and his men.

In South Vietnam (Quang Loc province) in 1966, a unit led by Lieutenant Reilly, which includes the main characters of the story, carries out a search-and-destroy mission. The soldiers brave an exploding mine and sniper fire before searching some village huts, where they find no weapons caches or North Vietnamese, but do uncover a pit where the bodies of young villagers lie, murdered a few days earlier by the rebels. Doubting the explanations of an old farmer, Meserve convinces himself that the bodies are those of North Vietnamese killed by Americans, staged to make it seem like the villagers are not collaborating with the enemy.

Later, after Reilly and Captain Crane provide him with details of the mission, Meserve informs his men of his intention to find "five of the nicest chicks." And so what was in reality a planned collective rape becomes in Gould's screenplay a joke among barrack mates who are accustomed to visiting brothels together. Eriksson expresses his disapproval not because he refuses to participate in a crime but because he is married. "I won't tell your old lady, farmer," responds Meserve sarcastically, making mention of Eriksson's background. Because of this, the conversation that appears in other versions of the script between Eriksson and Rowan, in which Eriksson tells Rowan of Meserve's plan to abduct and kill someone, is replaced by a discussion between the cousins and Eriksson, who worries about being caught with girls during their mission. Manuel reassures him about Meserve: "Don't worry about it, farmer. He was just dreamin'."

Gould's emphasis on Eriksson's morality seems heavy-handed. More troubling are the alterations to the original narrative, obscuring the uniqueness of the crime committed by Meserve and his men – an issue, despite Clayton's warnings, present in previous scripts. "I always felt that the incident started innocently and got out of hand, as these things often do," says Gould. "The sudden realization that they are committing a crime that could lead to a court-martial then leads to the cover-up. Things go downhill from there."[108] Gould's personal intuition is, of course, invalidated by trial records, in which there is no mention of an orgy with prostitutes, and when Gervase and his men kidnap Mao, it is clear that they intended to rape a single girl, not engage in sexual relations with several women, whether consensual or not. Gould even repeats the false statement made by Gervase in court: "I said, 'It'd be nice if we could pick up five women for the five days up there and have an orgy,' and everybody had comments, laughed. Then all the joking was set aside and I asked my men again if they had any questions."[109] In his attempt to reshape the story to fit his vision of the story, Gould unwittingly adopts the language of the oppressor. And, thus, the screenplay falters doubly.

By contrast, the soldiers' abduction of Mao closely follows Lang's account. Although there are moments of excessive chatter (the dialogue between Eriksson and Rafe, with the former accusing the latter of pointing out the hut where the girl is hidden, feels somewhat incongruous), Gould is also capable of flashes of brilliance, as when he depicts Mao's mother's desperate attempt to give her daughter a scarf. In Lang's text the scene is brief, but Gould expands it. The sight of the old woman, breathless and tearful, chasing after the soldiers already on the trail to offer them a pitiful talisman – a scarf, the only fragile link now connecting her to her beloved daughter – is rendered deeply poignant.

The patrol resumes its journey, and Mao's ordeal drags on. Gould sticks to the actual chronology of events (Meserve gives Mao an aspirin, Rafe forces her to carry his gear) but takes liberties with the dialogue. Throughout this section, Eriksson appears mostly silent and timid. His demeanor shifts only when the soldiers reach the hut. While Meserve, Clark and Rafe go to fetch water, Eriksson tries to persuade Manuel to let Mao go, even suggesting they escape with her, but Manuel refuses, reminding him that desertion is punishable by court-martial. Then he utters a startling "prophecy": "Look, in six months this chick'll be wearin' an áo dài slit up to her butt and sittin' in a damn bar somewhere hustlin' drinks. It'll be anything you want for three thousand p's, man, anything. She'll be speakin' real good English, then… I mean, it don't matter what we do, that's what's gonna happen." Vietnamese women are nothing but sex objects, says misogynist Manuel. They always end up as prostitutes.

During the rape, Gould depicts a tormented Eriksson, his face "contorted in anguish," covering his ears with his hands to avoid hearing Mao's desperate screams as she falls victim to Meserve's assault in the hut. Storeby reported that the soldiers were inside the hut because of the intense heat outside, to share a meal, and discuss their present and past sexual exploits, during which time Mao found refuge in a corner of the room. Gould, however, places the four rapists outside the hut. While they smoke and discuss their conquests, Eriksson pretends to get a beer, at which point the narrative adopts his point of view. He sees Mao huddled up, motionless, her face against the wall, hands tied behind her back, clothes torn. He approaches her gently and tries to turn her toward him. "It's all right, I'm not gonna hurt you," he murmurs in her ear. She resists at first, then surrenders, and Eriksson sees her face: "Her forehead is scraped, little trails of blood come from her nose and her lower lip. Her face is bruised. There are tiny scratches on her neck." As he attempts to provide her with basic care, the conversation between the men outside, boasting about their sexual performances, is audible off-screen.

"I wanted to focus on Eriksson and Mao," says Gould. "Isolate Eriksson from the others and emphasize his difference from them."[110] The contrast between the soldiers' bragging and Eriksson's uncomfortable, powerless stance is thus reinforced. Undoubtedly one of the strongest scenes in Gould's script, it ends with a close-up of Eriksson, inside the hut, in the dim light, his comrades laughing heartily outside. Once Meserve realizes that Eriksson hasn't reappeared for a few minutes and becomes worried, he calls him. Eriksson appears in the doorway, wordless, his face expressionless, impenetrable.

A cross-fade marks a transition to the next sequence, in which Gould allows himself a few additions to Lang's text. As night falls over the jungle, Eriksson asks Manuel who it was that beat Mao. Manuel swears he didn't do anything to her and issues a warning to his fellow soldier, reminding him of his duty of loyalty to his brothers-in-arms. Later that night, while on watch, Eriksson overhears a discussion between Meserve and Clark, plotting Mao's death. Eriksson points his rifle toward the two men, but Meserve is unimpressed. "Get some sleep, farmer," he says, to which Eriksson responds with, "I'm not tired." He enters the hut, sits near Mao, and places his gun on his lap, the barrel still aimed at Meserve and Clark. Meserve mocks him: "He's afraid something's gonna happen to his girlfriend…"

The next day, Mao's condition worsens, and her cough, amplified by the echo of the hills, threatens to reveal the patrol's position. "If she keeps coughin' like that they'll be able to hear us in Hanoi," grumbles Clark. Faced with successive refusals from Eriksson, Manuel and Rafe to kill her, Meserve and Clark take it upon themselves to do the dirty work. Watching them disappear into the marshy forest, Eriksson addresses the Diaz cousins: "Are we just gonna let them do this?" "Them two are the only ones that's doin' it. Them two are the ones that'll get in trouble," replies Manuel confidently, as if to appease his conscience and absolve himself of the impending crime. But Eriksson warns, "We're all responsible. We'll all be blamed." Eriksson, at the point of Rafe's gun, can do nothing, and falls silent. The crime is shown entirely from the perspective of the three soldiers, who see nothing but hear "a short shriek" interrupt the coughing fits. Then silence. "The [Diaz] cousins look at each other guiltily. Eriksson just stares off into the swamp. There is the sound of voices and footsteps. Laughter. The footsteps grow louder. Meserve and Clark come into view, sloshing jauntily through the mud. Clark has his knife out, and is rubbing it clean against his pants… They are happy, their anger and tension gone. Clark holds up his knife for all the men to see. Something glitters in his other hand. 'Anybody wanna buy a gold tooth?'" he asks, brandishing his trophy.

After a battle with enemy troops, the soldiers return to base and Eriksson confides to a certain Kramer, then Sergeant Long, who informs Reilly and Crane. Long takes the trouble to warn Eriksson of the possible consequences of his denunciation for a crime that has been committed "in every war in history." In successive encounters with Reilly and Crane, Gould's dialogue generally follows Storeby's testimony. The same goes for Crane's summoning of Meserve, Clark and the Diaz cousins, after which Clark suggests eliminating Eriksson by tossing a grenade into his tent. Meserve advises his men to keep a low profile. "If we stay cool we'll get outta this. Everybody's on our side. Understand? Everybody," he asserts confidently.

Clark does indeed carry out his threat, aided by Rafe. While Eriksson, now under Long's command, patrols a rice field, gunfire erupts toward the group, and one bullet narrowly misses Long. It turns out the shots are coming from another squad, in which Eriksson spots his two former comrades. Urged by Reilly, Crane agrees to transfer Eriksson to another company, perhaps thinking he will decide against exposing his former comrades. But a tenacious Eriksson is eventually questioned by the CID. Gould stresses the incredulity of the CID inspectors, who treat Eriksson as a suspect and put him behind bars, until he leads them to the spot where they find a decomposing body. Forensic doctors are sent in and the body is evacuated by helicopter under Eriksson's watchful eye and those of the culprits who, under tight security, are present.

Gould skips through the trial in less than ten pages, perhaps fearing repetition of what the audience already knows. After the testimony of the pathologist, who presents the autopsy results (death caused by multiple stab wounds and strangulation, no gunshot wounds), comes Eriksson's interrogation by his lawyer, then by the lawyer representing the accused, who portray him as a liar and a coward, accusing him of having "traded that girl's life for his own well-being." Meserve is questioned, followed by Manuel, who confesses to the rape and lays blame on Meserve, whose behavior as the trial concludes is surprising: he puts his head in his hands and sobs. Outside the courtroom, as two military police officers place him in a jeep, Meserve "looks and sounds nothing like the tough soldier of previous scenes. Now, he is just a frightened boy." In tears, he addresses Eriksson: "Why didn't you kill me when you had the chance? That's what you wanted to do, wasn't it? Anything would have been better than what I'm gonna get now."

By choosing to crack open Meserve's tough exterior, Gould softens the brutality of the character, reminding us that he is first and foremost a human being as vulnerable as any other. "Meserve had been in the field for nearly a year," explains Gould. "He was worn down and should have been pulled for a long leave. But the U.S. Army had a policy of keeping experienced troops on the line. Meserve is facing disgrace, imprisonment and the end of his life as he has known it. It is no wonder he has a moment of despair."[111] Meserve is humanized and the threat hanging over Eriksson is diminished, as it seems unlikely that such a "frightened boy" would seek revenge once out of prison. Gould's portrayal of Meserve is that of a formidable fighter whose moral exhaustion leads him to commit a horrendous act without truly intending to do so – since it all began as a simple joke. The conclusion is self-evident: it is the very context of war that legitimizes Mao's rape, a crime that Meserve perhaps wouldn't have committed under other circumstances.

The ending of Gould's script gains perspective when compared to the beginning of *Rolling Thunder*, which he had written two years earlier. His version of *Casualties of War* actually concludes where John Flynn's film begins. Eriksson is packing his bags to return home when he is visited by Long, who bids him farewell and good luck. Eriksson proudly shows Long a photo of his wife, Karen. Long delivers an optimistic speech: "I'm sure she'll be happy to have her old man back in one piece. That's the important thing. The only thing you should be thinkin' about now. Everything else is over." "Seems I've ruined a lot of lives," says Eriksson, interrupting Long before he finishes. But the sergeant tries to reassure him: "Don't worry about what's already passed. You just think about goin' home, son. In two years you won't hardly be able to remember how hot it was out here, or what a corpse looks like, or how people can disappoint you."

Unlike Charles Rane's grand, heroic entrance at the start of *Rolling Thunder*, celebrated as a hero after surviving North Vietnamese prisons, Eriksson's return is more low-key. At the airport terminal, Karen waits anxiously in the crowd for her husband. When she spots him, dressed in his uniform and carrying his suitcase, she runs toward him. The couple embrace in the middle of the hall, amidst onlookers, then heads to the airport parking lot and drives off. Karen is behind the wheel. Eriksson, looking at her tenderly, has his arm around her neck. We are unsure of what she knows about Mao, and their exchange is vague on that subject. She mentions a letter Eriksson sent to his mother, which kept her awake for several days after she read it.

"You don't want to talk about it, do you?" she asks him later, to which Eriksson replies, "I'll talk about it, Karen. I'll tell you everything. But not right now…"

In contrast with Rane's arrival in *Rolling Thunder*, where his wife tells him she loves someone else, Eriksson receives a warm welcome. The living room, filled with guests, is decorated with a large banner reading "Welcome Home." Friends surround him, kissing and hugging, as his mother and wife guide him from guest to guest. And then, suddenly, in a corner of the room, he glimpses from behind a girl with long, jet-black hair flowing over her shoulders. For a brief moment he thinks he sees Mao. Memories of Vietnam rush in. Panic is evident on his face. But when the figure turns around, Eriksson realizes it is a woman introduced by Karen as her best friend. The camera moves outside the house (the lively party remains visible through the windows) and gradually moves away, suggesting that despite the joy of reunion, Eriksson will never be able to forget Mao. A brief epilogue takes us back to the courtroom during the announcement of the verdicts. A panoramic shot frames the faces of the condemned, with captions detailing the sentences they received.[112]

Gould's screenplay seems to have been well received by David Susskind and producer Freyda Rothstein. Daniel Lang, who received a copy for consultation, was expected to provide an expert assessment and drafted a seven-page typed document. Lang also expressed his thoughts to Gould in person. "He bluntly told me he didn't like my screenplay," says Gould. "He thought it was 'mannered.' I asked him how I could make it less so. 'You can't,' he said. I think he was surprised that I didn't leap to my own defense, but I respected him and was sorry he felt that way."[113]

Lang, understandably obsessed with historical detail, found himself in a rather uncomfortable position: that of the author reading, for the first time, an adaptation of his own text. One can imagine the difficulties he had in mustering the necessary detachment and momentarily relinquishing control of his work so he could be more receptive to its appropriation by Gould. Lang's written evaluation begins with a paragraph in which he outlines his intent: "The narrative may take place in Vietnam but it's not about the Vietnam War. It's about war. I knew, in 1944, in Italy, that someday I would write a piece like *Casualties*. Nor is *Casualties* an exposé, a tale of injustice in which guilty parties get off with light sentences. *Casualties* is an account of what war does to human beings, of the epidemic harm and degradation it visits on all whom it touches."[114] For Lang, Vietnam serves merely as a pretext for the more universal story of *Casualties of War*, about soldiers who might, in any conflict situation, lose their moral compass and succumb to the basest of instincts.

Lang suspected Gould of having written a screenplay specifically about Vietnam, a subject that Gould was familiar with given the reporting he did for the *New York Post*. To bolster his critique, Lang cites a line in the script from Lieutenant Reilly about Mao: "Hundreds of people die here every day. She was simply another casualty of the war." Lang found fault in Gould's use of the definite article because it clearly referred to Vietnam, thus undermining the abstract and universal nature Lang intended for his article and book title. This is harsh criticism, especially since Gould's script avoids specific references to Vietnamese politics, and there is nothing to support the suggestion that the screenplay was partly inspired by the My Lai massacre, as Lang suggests in his notes.

Lang's pointed observation exposes his ideals about what constitutes a "worthy" cinematic adaptation. Firmly attached to historical fidelity, Lang expected Gould to respect the original material and introduce only occasional liberties – much like Clayton had requested of Hamill, before having his wish partially fulfilled by Giler. But instead of strictly adhering to the original text, Gould reappropriated it, showing scant regard for the precise dialogue and situations meticulously documented by Lang. Somewhat futilely, Lang even listed obvious differences between the book and screenplay, suggesting that he didn't differentiate between reality and its representation, between journalistic investigation and its cinematic adaptation. Does keeping silent about or transforming a detail of history necessarily betray the truth? Lang thinks it does. Some of his remarks are certainly valid. Gould might have refrained from changing the names of the characters (who were already pseudonymous), and it isn't clear why he removed Rowan and replaced him with two characters, Kramer and Long. Likewise, the reasons behind making Eriksson so tall, when he was actually short, are unknown. But the most problematic distortion lies in Meserve's line, uttered at the start of the screenplay, when he suggests to his men that they take "five girls" with them instead of just one, a line mentioned by Lang in his notes but, oddly, not elaborated on, given that it has detrimental effects on the entire screenplay.

Lang focuses on Eriksson, who, he writes, "is a much more complex character than the script makes out. He may appear a saint compared to the rest of the patrol but that's not the way he looks upon himself. To this day, as I know from being in touch with him, he remains a casualty of war, condemned by himself for having failed to save Mao's life." Lang isn't convinced by Gould's overly simplistic portrayal of Eriksson who, according to Lang, "is the embodiment of conscience, which exists in us all but to a lesser degree." Lang writes of the "strange phenomenon" that drives an individual to act unexpectedly after listening to their conscience. Instead, says Lang, Gould's Eriksson is too polished, too virtuous.

Ultimately, Lang and Gould's relationship mirrored that of Clayton and Hamill. In both instances, there are conflicting visions of the screenplay. For Lang, as for Clayton, historical truth must not yield to narrative convenience. The screenwriter's creativity must serve the original text or the real story, and any modification, however minor, is a potential form of betrayal. Conversely, and akin to Hamill, Gould asserted his right to autonomy, even when adapting real events, recognizing that a screenplay remains an inherently imperfect, subjective reflection of reality.

An additional factor sheds light on Lang's attitude toward Gould. "He was disappointed not to have been allowed to write the screenplay himself," says Gould, "and I felt his disapproval, which is not unusual in the relationship between an author and their adapter."[115] On this point, Gould was vindicated, as the following year Lang began working on an adaptation of his own text.

It is difficult to predict the direction events might have taken if Susskind's project had reached its conclusion. Gould produced at least two versions of his script, so it is likely that a third – a response to Lang's notes – might have appeared. Although critical, Lang conceded that Gould's script contained some merits. He liked the opening scene, for example, because it reintroduced complexity into a story that for him could never be a simple good-versus-bad tale. One can reasonably assume that the exchanges between Lang and Gould would have continued until both parties were satisfied.

Gould had already started rewriting and casting had begun (Ron Howard was considered for Eriksson[116]) when the project was shelved. As Stephen Battaglio notes, most television projects David Susskind developed for Time-Life had been commercial successes.[117] So what happened? "They said it was too soon after the war to show American soldiers killing Vietnamese women," says Gould. "It was a 'duh' moment. People working together on a movie share a mutual fantasy, which is then blown away by a cold blast of reality. Who could ever have thought this would be a big network event?"[118]

By the end of 1979, Time-Life had struck a deal with 20th Century Fox to produce twelve feature films over the next three years. Among these projects was one of Gould's scripts, *Fort Apache, The Bronx* – but not *Casualties of War*. The contract between Lang and Susskind, then Time-Life Television Productions, had expired a few months earlier and was not renewed. Lang was now free to pursue his own interests. This provided the perfect opportunity for him to finally do what had become obvious: he would have to adapt *Casualties of War* for the screen himself.

Daniel Lang, screenwriter (1979-81)

When, at the end of 1979, Lang began his slow transformation into a screenwriter, he was less interested in writing scripts than he was in completing one specific screenplay. As far as we know, Lang never harbored Hollywood ambitions.

Between late 1979 and early 1980, he was in negotiations with Alfred Crown – producer of Frank Perry's *Last Summer* (1969) and Miloš Forman's *Taking Off* (1971) – and Jerome "Jerry" Hammer, a figure active in Broadway and television, about an adaptation of *Casualties of War*. In a letter dated May 29, 1979, Crown expressed his admiration for Lang's prose writing, praising its truthfulness in depicting the story and characters, though he felt the subject matter was more suited for television than film.[119] A meeting apparently followed, leading to an agreement signed on March 18, 1980 whereby both producers secured a one-year option on the book, extendable by six months. The contract encompassed both the production of a feature film and Lang's delivery within 90 days of a treatment.

This hybrid treatment form (a prose text with some dialogue, more akin to a short story than anything else), which likely suited Lang more than the traditional screenplay format, was meant to serve as foundation for a future professional screenwriter, who would be recruited by Crown and Hammer. Lang wrote at least three undated drafts. The first, 22 pages long, written partially in a telegraphic style and filled with corrections and notes, is unfinished (it ends during Eriksson's interrogation by the CID).[120] Lang experiments with ideas that were abandoned in subsequent versions, for example interspersing the narration with exchanges between Eriksson and an anonymous interviewer (presumably a version of Lang himself). The second draft, a dozen pages longer, is also incomplete, ending with the conversation between Eriksson and Lieutenant Reilly.[121] The third draft is a complete typed version of 80 pages, revised and corrected by Lang, with some passages, marked in black ink, removed.[122]

Reading these various versions reveals that for Lang, this exercise was a series of stepping stones toward screenwriting. His treatment aims to be more than the usual format, often detailing camera placement, movement, sound effects and sequence duration, showing his meticulous planning in translating text to visuals. He was envisioning how *Casualties of War* could evolve beyond its narrative framework to become a piece of cinema.

Casualties of War – version #4 (Daniel Lang's treatment)

How does Lang's storytelling distinguish itself from the three preceding versions? A first read of the complete version immediately gives the impression that he has attempted to resolve all the problems posed by previous versions, in part by returning to the structure of his original text. Lang clearly made use of his knowledge of the previous drafts, as well as his discussions with Clayton, to find narrative solutions. This applies to the opening, which surpasses in intensity those written by Giler and Gould, but remains inferior to the two openings by Hamill (especially the first, the deer hunting scene, which Clayton didn't care for).

Daniel Lang

Lang sets his opening along a dusty road, on the edge of the jungle. Two young children, dressed in rags, observe two North Vietnamese fighters carefully planting mines in the ground. Not far away, a convoy of three U.S. Army vehicles enters a village. Lang describes the commotion around the trucks: children begging for food and offering soldiers the favors of their older sisters, which the G.I.s crudely respond to. Among them are the Diaz cousins, Manuel and Rafe, who throw treats to the children while making obscene gestures toward local girls. (A similar moment appears in Hamill's and Giler's scripts.) Lang introduces three other characters:

Sergeant Tony Meserve, Corporal Ralph Clark and Technician Corporal Ted Crowley, specifying that the latter carries "a ten-inch hunting knife, its handle wrapped with tape decorated with a pattern of tiny diamonds," which is the weapon used in Mao's murder. Clark's cruel nature is made clear as he hurls a chocolate bar into the face of a child who is begging at the side of the road. Tears well up in the boy's eyes as Clark, perched on the back of the truck, laughs with sadistic glee. Moving away from the village, the convoy cautiously approaches the road, where North Vietnamese mines await.

Lang interrupts the sequence to introduce Private First Class Sven Eriksson, newly arrived in Vietnam with a contingent of around twenty young recruits. After listening to the customary speech from an instructor, Eriksson meets Rowan, who becomes something of a mentor to him. From their dialogue, we learn that Eriksson hails from a village in Minnesota near the Canadian border and that he has settled in Minneapolis with his young wife, who has a job there.

As a friendship begins to form between Rowan and Eriksson, the convoy carrying Meserve, Clark, Crowley and the Diaz cousins advances along the mine-laden road. Suddenly, there is a massive explosion. One of the trucks has driven over an explosive charge. Crowley is killed as a hail of bullets rains down on the convoy. The enemy, hidden in the underbrush, have sprung an ambush. A battle scene ensues, with Meserve taking command of his troops and calling Lieutenant Harold Reilly via radio for reinforcements. "As the scene ends, thick, billowing smoke envelops the screen; it is accompanied by sounds of invisible planes, helicopters – the help that Lieutenant Reilly has promised. The sounds abate and the smoke swirling on the screen begins to thin out. As it does, we see a single credit: "CASUALTIES OF WAR. An incident in Vietnam, 1967."

With this pre-credit sequence, Lang immerses the viewer directly into the relentless action, sets the scene – a country at war, consumed by poverty and violence – and introduces the five main characters. It's likely that the idea for this moment, absent from his book, was the result of exchanges between Lang and Clayton, who initially wanted a similar pre-credit sequence for his film version.

Lang's version remains largely consistent with earlier screenplays, save for one crucial difference. During the briefing, Meserve reveals his intention to "find a girl" for the group to have fun with throughout their mission, then dispose of her afterward. Here, Lang has the opportunity to re-establish a decisive detail: the premeditation of Mao's murder, which previous scripts mostly omit. The scene aligns with Lang's account as told to him by Storeby and continues with Eriksson's conversation with his friend Rowan, who, initially skeptical, eventually recounts how Meserve, once a respected and exemplary soldier, has transformed into a bloodthirsty brute, coldly executing an elderly peasant couple for no apparent reason. According to Rowan, Meserve has become "a kind of casualty of war."

Mao's murder, which is condensed into a single paragraph, occurs at the end of the first third of the treatment, unlike in the previous three scripts where it takes place a little over halfway through. While the patrol is atop Hill 192, tasked with preventing North Vietnamese fighters from reaching their cave hideout, Clark savagely stabs Mao (with Crowley's knife), but she manages to escape and crawls into the bushes. Observing movement in the tall grass, Meserve points out a bush and orders his men to shoot. All except Eriksson do. "What follows," writes Lang, "is a re-enactment of the rape scene, with bullets." Lang takes pains to indicate the calculated premeditation of the crime. As Clark pleads with Meserve to let him kill Mao, Meserve calls Reilly to report that a "VC girl is climbing the mountain." "Capture her," orders Reilly. After the crime, Meserve contacts his superior, informing him that they were unable to intercept the suspect, so had to shoot her. "Well done," responds Reilly, and the matter seems closed – at least as far as Meserve is concerned. He, for one, is satisfied with his alibi.

Lang doesn't dwell on Mao's suffering, choosing instead to show Eriksson's intense struggle to uncover the truth and condemn the four murderers. When Eriksson returns to the base after the rape and murder, he confides in Rowan. Lang retains the altercation with Clark but invents a scene between Rowan and Eriksson that isn't in the book and doesn't appear in the trial transcripts. Here is a significant passage:

ERIKSSON
I want everybody to know about her. [...]

ROWAN
You think that'll do anything?

ERIKSSON
(ingenuously, at once)
Of course – why not? *(pause, then fresh tone)* Curly, you think maybe it's a freak patrol – I mean, that the guys in it happen to be – well, psychopaths...

ROWAN
(shaking head, rueful smile)
There's nothing wrong with *them*, Sven – *you're* the problem... You don't know it – leastwise, not *yet* – but those guys *did* what most everybody here just thinks of doing...

ERIKSSON
Even you?

ROWAN
(slow nod, half sigh)
Yeah, even me...

Later, as Eriksson faces the scornful and suspicious glances of his comrades, Rowan becomes even more distant, accusing his friend of "making trouble." Their dialogue concludes with the following description: "[Rowan] looks at Eriksson, not proud of his words. Eriksson is crushed, aware he has lost his friend, his apartness from others now complete. He rises and walks away slowly. Rowan himself is far from happy. His eyes follow Eriksson's forlorn figure until it is just beyond earshot. Prayerfully, he then calls out, out of sight. 'Stay the same, Sven, don't you change!'"

In Lang's original text, Rowan appears as a straightforward and honest actor, but in the script he is transformed into a more ambiguous, almost cowardly figure. Instead of supporting Eriksson, he attempts to discourage him from testifying against Meserve and his men. This change is particularly surprising, given Lang's commitment to portraying every character in his story as accurately as possible. He allowed himself the freedom to write dialogue and actions for his protagonists that he didn't directly witness, but he was, at the same time, careful not to alter their personalities to fit the logic of his narrative. One might speculate that Lang chose to omit certain troublesome aspects of Rowan's (Pearson's) personality from his original article at Storeby's request. These aspects might have been reintegrated into his screenplay under the guise of fiction.

However, all exchanges between Eriksson and his various interlocutors (Reilly, Vorst, Greenacre, Chaplain Kirk, the CID agents) remain rigorously consistent with the testimonies collected by Lang or that appear in trial transcripts. Lang notably reintroduces the character of the chaplain, whom Gould had excluded from his screenplay, and expands on the dialogue in Giler's version. Kirk deliberately takes on the role of an investigator, recalling that he had, in reality, served ten years with the Salt Lake City police before entering the Mormon clergy: "Maybe you did the same as the others… maybe you're trying to save your hide, giving evidence…When those agents get here, Eriksson, your life's going to be changed. You'll be spending all your time making your story stick – if you can…" Then, abruptly, the chaplain asks him: "You know where that girl's body is?" Eriksson confirms that he will be able to locate it. Interrupting , Kirk interrogates him, prosecutor-style: "What time of day was the girl killed, where were you when it happened, what kind of ammo was used, you have grudges against the patrol, how near was Charlie, was it a stray bullet did it?… Come on, Eriksson, give, you playing games?"

This dialogue, inspired by testimony gathered from the chaplain by Lang, serves two purposes: it prepares Eriksson for the interview with the two CID agents and foretells how difficult it will be for him to produce all the evidence they need and to identify where Mao's body is. The confrontation with the CID agents takes place at midnight, in a steel cube-like bunker, serving as a prison within Camp Radcliff. Eriksson steps inside after one of the agents informs him of his placement in "protective custody." No further details are offered.

After an unspecified lapse of time, we next find Eriksson climbing Hill 192 with a group of inspectors. A colonel, a major, CID agents, photographers, a pathologist, and experts in firearms and ballistics accompany Eriksson, along with a squad of GIs responsible for his protection. "Eriksson has crossed a line: from a lone underground accuser, he has become a cog in a law-enforcement machine." Lang makes clear that Eriksson's position is still precarious, contingent on his ability to locate Mao's body, which he succeeds in doing only with some difficulty. Lang emphasizes a passage that occupies only a few lines in his article/book: Eriksson manages to identify the bush where the body lies, and the military-judicial machine then starts its work. In his script, Lang – like Giler – describes the incredible pressure Eriksson faces from the men in charge of the investigation. He initially makes a mistake and indicates a spot where there are no human remains. Suspicious glances converge on him, and the major says irritably, "Goddamit, soldier, Charlie's laughing up his sleeve!" Eriksson's confidence momentarily vanishes. He thinks hard, and eventually identifies the ledge where Mao's body is found.

Thus begins the collection of evidence at the crime scene. Lang devotes an entire page to describing this meticulous work, from the pathologist taking notes to the photographers flashing their cameras to the experts collecting scattered bullet fragments. Lang's rigor as an investigative journalist is revealed, with his attention to detail contributing to the overall picture. From a distance, Eriksson observes the bustle around Mao's body, which, once the work is completed, is placed in a rubberized, khaki-green bag, the kind designed to carry away the remains of fallen soldiers. Lang does not omit this detail, already present in his article, as it reflects the irony of the situation. The battlefield is transformed into a crime scene, where those meant to be honored as warriors are now the perpetrators.

The final part of Lang's script focuses on the legal aspects of the case: the military trials of the four accused. Lang introduces Eriksson's lawyer, Lieutenant Ray Moore (the equivalent of prosecutor Yelton). "Moore is no more than four or five years older than Eriksson but his skull shows not a hair; he speaks with a Maine accent." Friendly and unafraid to joke when the occasion arises, Moore warns Eriksson about how he should behave during the hearings.

"You get on that stand, answer the question only, not a word extra," he tells him. To which Eriksson replies, in his characteristic frankness: "I have nothing to hide, I know what I saw."

"That's not the way it works," Moore warns him. "You talk too much, they'll trip you up."

"Trip you up?" Eriksson questions, looking puzzled. "Sounds like a game."

"Maybe it is, but you want to win it, don't you?" the lawyer adds before taking on a more serious tone. "Look, Eriksson, this is no easy case, not the kind comes along every day of the week. I mean, who the hell goes around bringing charges, like you're doing? We've got a credibility problem." Moore isn't wrong, as the proceedings will demonstrate.

Lang's solution is similar to Hamill, Giler and Gould's: the four trials are merged into one, but key moments from the various hearings have been retained. Professor Furue, the anthropologist from Tokyo, provides all necessary details regarding Mao's autopsy. He is followed by Phan Thi Loc, who certifies that her sister's bra, stained with blood, was found at the scene of her rape. She also reveals that her mother was kidnapped by North Vietnamese for leading American soldiers to the hut, which served as a communist weapons cache.

Called to the stand by Meserve's lawyer, Lieutenant Reilly and Captain Vorst praise the young sergeant for his fighting qualities, but they become uneasy when the prosecutor goes on the offensive. Then it is the turn of the accused to be interrogated. The Diaz cousins take the stand (Chaplain Tucci is called as a witness in Rafe's favor), followed by Meserve and Clark. Lang reproduces, sometimes verbatim, the statements of the accused during the actual courts-martial. Eriksson is the last witness to be heard. He is subjected to a lengthy interrogation by Meserve's lawyer, who hopes to prove that Eriksson is far from heroic, denouncing him for not diverting his comrades' attention to allow Mao to escape, and not shooting them when they were about to rape her. When the lawyer asks, "You traded that girl's life for your own, did you not?" Eriksson erupts in despair, admitting that he "should have done *something*." Meserve's lawyer's face lights up with a scornful, triumphant smile. The proceedings are adjourned until the following day.

Lang doesn't dwell any longer than necessary on this final day of the proceedings. He revisits Meserve's testimony, already reported in his article, then focuses on the pleadings of Merserve and Eriksson's lawyers. While the former argues that the crime "did not even occur in civilization," the latter raises the question that sparked Lang's investigation – "Why didn't this fifth man act like the other four?" – before answering it himself: "It wasn't just to stay alive, but also to maintain his integrity."

As the court-martial deliberates, Lang includes dialogue between the lawyers, who congratulate each other on their respective performances – an ironic moment given the ethical stakes played out throughout the trial. The sentences pronounced are consistent with reality, except for Meserve, who here receives fifteen years of hard labor, five more than in his real trial. There is no indication as to why Lang, who is typically resistant to such modifications, chose to increase the sentence.

Cut to: four months later, July 1967. The monsoon season has begun, and rain pours down on Camp Radcliff. Lang envisions a sequence from Moore's perspective. The prosecutor, about to leave Vietnam, drives in a jeep to the military police headquarters to bid farewell to Eriksson and update him. He informs Eriksson of Manuel's release due to a technicality and Rafe and Clark's reduced sentences, the latter thanks to a petition calling for leniency from the judges. Moore promises to write to Eriksson and keep him informed about the developments in their sentences, and the two men part ways after a warm handshake.

Early December 1967. It is Eriksson's turn to return home. His plane lands at Minneapolis airport, where he is reunited with his wife, Kirsten. The young woman falls sobbing into his arms, and Eriksson wipes away her tears. Their conversation makes it clear that Kirsten is aware of Mao's murder. She has evidently sensed the mixed feelings that consume her husband – the immense joy of seeing her again tempered by the haunting memory of the young Vietnamese girl. "Dear Sven, you've brought her home, haven't you?" she asks tenderly. "She'll always be with us. I want her, too." Eriksson is soon reminded of the murderers when he receives a letter from Moore, who explains that Meserve and Clark are eligible for parole because of their family background. Meserve has promised to control his impulses, and Clark is destined for a career as a philosophy professor. "They could be out in a few months," Eriksson confides worriedly to his wife. "I don't care," she replies. "You did what you had to do. There'd have been no living with you if you had kept quiet – and it's you I want to live with."

Lang sets his epilogue the following autumn, in the cabinetmaking shop where Eriksson works. For the first time "we see him in civilian clothes." As the day draws to a close and Eriksson is still busy in his shop, his colleagues gently break his concentration. "Come on, Sven, the day's over, time to go home." Together, they leave the workshop and go their separate ways. We follow Eriksson to a bus stop, where he waits in line. When the bus arrives, he steps inside, finds an empty seat, and falls asleep. A young Asian woman (the script doesn't specify that she is Vietnamese) carrying a heavy shopping bag boards the bus and sits opposite him. The journey goes smoothly, but at one point the driver has to brake sharply and Eriksson is jolted out of his daze. His eyes half-closed, he catches a glimpse of the young passenger's face. In his mind she is transformed into Mao. Eriksson imagines her walking through the hills of Vietnam, a calming vision that is entirely in keeping with the conclusion of Lang's book.

Examining Lang's script offers a glimpse into his cinematic vision. Faithful to his original text, he takes liberties that never stray far from the essence of the tale, occasionally offering a novel perspective that illuminates it anew. Especially interesting is Lang's deliberate avoidance of hasty audience interpretations. In the pre-credits battle scene, for instance, he meticulously notes that the devastation from mine explosions "has to be done with utmost economy, almost subliminally." Lang writes adamantly, with valid concerns, that a longer, more spectacular sequence could wrongly imply that the soldiers' confrontation with North Vietnamese "is the specific cause of all else that follows." He warns against a clichéd portrayal of war's horrors, hinting at the moral decay it entails without overtly stating it. He adds: "It would also inject a bewhiskered method of demonstrating that war is hell," and, one assumes (even if Lang doesn't say it directly), the idea that the soldiers lose all sense of morality in the process.

Lang's refusal to turn the soldiers' actions into a voyeuristic spectacle is palpable throughout, notably in the rape scene as written. After removing his pants, Meserve heads toward the hut where Mao awaits, "shutting its rusty-hinged door behind him." "The camera does not go in with him," writes Lang, who describes a "piercing moan of pain and despair" from Mao, as heard by Eriksson. Later, when it is Rafe's turn inside the hut, Lang again refrains from describing the rape: "We see Rafe advance toward Mao but that is all. The camera leaves the hootch, dwelling on Clark, who remains where he is, a frenzied voyeur." It is with the same refusal to directly depict violence that Lang represents Mao's murder, partially obscured by vegetation: "We do not see Clark's face," he writes, "but we do see his hand raised high and then, the hunting knife tightly clasped, the hand plunges hard. A cry, not too loud, issues from the bushes; the cry is pathetic in quality, like the gasp a hunter draws from a deer he is gutting."

Finally, the question of suspense (or its absence) is central to Lang's work. From the start of his treatment, there is no doubt that Mao will be raped and murdered. As for the trials, they bear no resemblance to the usual Hollywood way of doing things. "It is no whodunit," Lang writes as a preamble to the lengthy court-martial sequence. "No suspense attaches to the question of whether the defendants raped and killed a girl. In a time of war, though, was that a crime? This is the sole issue on which the proceedings turn, and it is in dealing with it that the hearing derives its 'suspense.'"

Why didn't the Lang/Crown/Hammer collaboration hold together? At the end of 1979, Lang drew up a written proposal to the two producers regarding adaptation rights of *Casualties of War*.[123] Doubtless discouraged by Susskind's inability to bring the project to fruition, Lang wanted to do his utmost to ensure that the producers would be responsive and that the film would see the light of day within a reasonable timeframe. Crown and Hammer had sixteen months to sign an agreement with a director and a screenwriter, and if they failed to meet the deadline, a clause provided for the reversion of all rights to Lang.

The proposed agreement was signed by the producers only in March the following year.[124] Barely five months later, in a letter to Crown and Hammer, Sidney E. Cohn, Lang's lawyer, made mention of a dispute between the two parties and the fact that the producers were asking Lang to return the sum they had paid him for writing the treatment, thereby relinquishing the rights to adapt the book. In the letter, Cohn announced that "other sources" had expressed interest but that no agreement had yet been reached. "Your signature below constitutes a complete cancellation of all rights which you have heretofore acquired under the March 18, 1980 agreement," the document concluded.[125] Those "other sources" were probably David Rabe, who had made contact with Lang, and Brian De Palma.

In the summer of 1980, Daniel Lang was diagnosed with aplastic anemia, a blood condition. His health deteriorated, and in June the following year he developed leukemia, which turned out to be the result of his exposure to radiation while covering the first nuclear tests in the Nevada desert. Five months later, on November 17, 1981, at the age of 68, he died.

Part 2

The Making of Brian De Palma's *Casualties of War*

Revisiting *Casualties of War*

Daniel Lang never lived to see the film adaptation of *Casualties of War*, which for more than a decade he had hoped would be produced.[1] It took seven more years before Brian De Palma, backed by tenacious producer Art Linson and assisted by David Rabe, one of the finest dramatists of his generation, made his version of *Casualties of War* – nearly twenty years after first conceiving the idea.

De Palma's skills as a filmmaker alone can't explain why he succeeded where others failed. A mix of circumstances played in his favor, starting with the fact that by the late 1980s, America was perhaps finally ready to confront its demons. The decade that concluded with *Casualties of War* is, more than any other, the era of successful films about the war in Vietnam, including, most famously, *Platoon*, *Good Morning Vietnam* and *Full Metal Jacket*. But though they didn't shy away from criticizing American policy in Vietnam, none delved into the kind of real-life atrocities laid bare by Lang in *Casualties of War*.

It is no exaggeration to say that De Palma was obsessed with *Casualties of War*. The roots of his fixation date back to the mid-1960s when, of draft age, he was part of the pool of young Americans ready to be conscripted and sent to Vietnam. Influenced by Hitchcock and Antonioni, as well as French and British New Wave cinema, whose freedom of expression he greatly admired, De Palma was at the very start of his career. The year he began filming his first feature film, *The Wedding Party*, in 1963, President John Kennedy was assassinated, a trauma that left a lasting impact on De Palma and that, along with the Vietnam War, helped shape *Greetings*, his first significant film.

Far from Vietnam

Set in New York, *Greetings* is the comic story of three friends – Jon Rubin (Robert De Niro), Paul Shaw (Jonathan Warden) and Lloyd Clay (Gerrit Graham) – all looking to evade the draft. In its opening minutes, Lloyd and Jon suggest to Paul that he pretend to be gay, and they give him advice on clothing, how to move, what to say and how to talk. The screenplay, written by De Palma (with Charles Hirsch, also the film's producer), was inspired by his own tribulations, as he tried every means possible to avoid military service. "I tried everything. I pretended to be a homosexual, I imbibed any number of things to induce the allergies I was prone to, I smoked cigarettes until I was coughing and wheezing like a madman, I had a doctor's certificate stating that I was practically allergic to the air. Eventually, I found myself in front of a shrink. I looked him straight in the eye and told him I wanted to become a communist and that communism was the best path forward. They thought I was crazy and sent me home."[2]

De Palma inserted a delightful nod to his experiences in *Greetings*. Akin to a Hitchcock cameo, he appears sitting on the steps of the building where Jon is going for his army induction. Lost in thought, a cigarette dangling from his mouth, De Palma is addressed by Jon, whose own attempts to avoid the army include him pretending to be an extreme right-winger who despise blacks, Jews and gays, and wants "to kill fifty Chinese a day."

"Hey, what are you doing down here?" says Jon. "You going to be inducted?"

"You talking to me?"

"Yeah, I'm talking to you, son. You sit like that on US property? Stand up! Attention! Stand at attention! Take that cigarette out of your mouth! Stand at attention! Put your hair back. We'll make a man out of you in the army. Come on! Follow me! One, two, three, four…"

As Jon climbs the stairs, De Palma – sheepish, resigned – follows.

More than just a gag, the scene reflects De Palma's opposition to American interventionist politics. Despite his immersion in artistic circles of the era, he distanced himself from the movements that protested, sometimes violently,

Robert De Niro and Brian De Palma in *Greetings*

against the war.[3] "I think we have to speak through our works," he argues today. "If we have strong political ideas, our work is the best way to spread them, rather than marching in the streets."[4]

Of the tumultuous Sixties, De Palma retains a "very intense memory." "Every night, we watched images of Vietnam on television. The government hadn't yet learned to control what was happening, the deaths of people, children dying, and that's what triggered the pacifist movement in the United States."[5] The pre-credits sequence of *Greetings* is a static shot of a television screen broadcasting news from Vietnam. The anchor discusses the Tet Offensive engagement at Khe Sanh before introducing an excerpt from a President Johnson speech in which he justifies the war in the name of "peace" and "freedom."

De Palma doesn't depict the war itself in *Greetings*. Each scene, *à la* Godard, is more caustic than the last. Paul uses computer dating to chase women; Jon offers women a role in a movie so he can watch them undress and so satisfy his voyeuristic impulses; Lloyd, obsessed with the Zapruder film, is consumed with conspiracy theories based on his extensive readings. Of the three friends, only Jon is drafted. His particular strategy of evasion doesn't work because the army psychiatrist tells him not to worry about such violent impulses. Jon's return home from Vietnam is documented in *Hi, Mom!* (1970), the sequel to *Greetings*, in which the character – something of a precursor to Travis Bickle, the character played by De Niro in Martin Scorsese's *Taxi Driver* (1976) – turns into a voyeuristic terrorist who films his neighbors' activities from his window and eventually blows up his own apartment building.

De Palma never fully shows what happens to Jon in country, though the epilogue of *Greetings* ("Somewhere in Vietnam") briefly takes us to the frontline in the form of a fake newsreel. A correspondent in suit and tie, microphone in hand, crouching in some reeds on the Hô Chí Minh trail, explains to camera that North Vietnamese snipers are attacking American truck drivers and slowing their operations. The camera pulls back to reveal Jon, who explains that he is on a search-and-destroy mission. Pointing behind him, he claims that "at least ten VC" are hidden there, but the camera is unable to capture anything more than a shot of tall grass. After spotting a figure through the reeds and signaling Rubin, the correspondent is convinced he has an exclusive. "Private Rubin has now got the communists in sight. He's got his finger on the trigger…" But the "enemy" turns out to be a young girl, clearly occupied with washing clothes. "It's not the Viet Cong, it's a woman," concludes the journalist with a hint of disappointment, immediately contradicted by Rubin who, without any evidence, insists, "No, it's a VC – except it's a woman."

"What do you in a situation like that?"

"I'm going to have to kill her anyway," says Rubin, who quickly changes his mind when he sees how pretty his target is. Instead of shooting, Rubin approaches her, and while pointing his gun has her mime the opening of a window before telling her to undress. It is a scene about mass media, political propaganda and image-making, as well an exploration of the connection between sex and violence, something De Palma returns to again and again in the film, notably the sequence where Lloyd recreates JFK's autopsy on a nubile young woman, upon whose naked body a copy of the 1967 issue of *Film Comment* ("John F. Kennedy –Two Controversial Films") has been strategically placed. Jean-Baptiste Thoret has concluded that "the political puzzle comes with an extra twist tied to desire." De Palma is suggesting "a literal

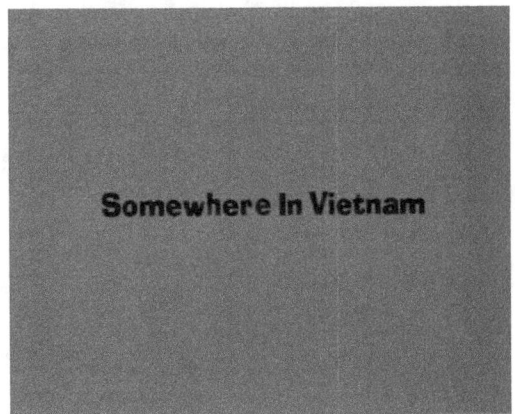

174 Casualties of War

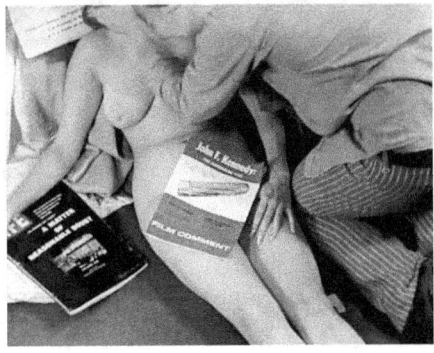

equivalence between the JFK murder mystery and that of feminine desire."⁶ However, one could just as easily see in this image a metaphor of a different kind – less about "feminine desire" and more about male domination, as represented by Rubin.

Recall Pete Hamill's lucid remark about photographs of *Playboy* playmates: "They are the rhetoric of fantasy, of perfect orgasms, of the innocent woman who is a whore in bed. They promise everything and give nothing, because of course they are not real; they are plastic fantasies. Then suddenly these young men… find themselves in a situation that is real, where they can act out their fantasies on the body of an anonymous woman."⁷ Rubin fits this description perfectly, especially when he buys a porno film from a stranger (Allen Garfield) on the street. Although he did all he could to avoid the war, the frontline Rubin we meet is as lascivious and uninhibited as ever. He has finally realized that in wartime, being a man brings just as much power – more, in fact – as carrying a rifle. The TV news report at the very end of *Greetings* cuts out before the Vietnamese woman undresses. The famous line from President Johnson that closes the film implies the obvious: "I'm not saying you never had it so good, but that is a fact, isn't it?" Rubin is clearly about to assault her.

The satirical *Greetings*, which anticipates the themes of *Casualties of War*, helps us understand why De Palma was so taken with Lang's book and why he joined the ranks of producers and filmmakers who wanted to adapt it for the screen. De Palma never made direct contact with Lang, but he did enquire about whether the rights were available, by which point Lang had already reached an agreement with David Susskind and the project was already in development at Warner Bros. Despite his Silver Bear win in Berlin, De Palma couldn't match the clout of the established filmmakers who were being considered by Lang or Susskind (Zinnemann, Schlesinger and Clayton all boasted significant commercial successes and awards). Disappointed but resigned, the young De Palma had no choice but to turn the page.[8]

A few months later, in June 1970, De Palma found himself back in Berlin as part of the official selection of the film festival, where he presented *Dionysus in 69* (co-directed with Robert Fiore and Bruce Rubin), a film of a modern version of Euripides' *The Bacchae*, as staged by the Performance Group under the direction of Richard Schechner. A kind of contemporary New York art installation, it is noteworthy because of De Palma's early use of split-screen. The critics took note, but at Berlin that year it was Michael Verhoeven's *o.k.* that captured the spotlight.[9]

Conquering Hollywood

De Palma left New York for Los Angeles in 1970 to shoot *Get to Know Your Rabbit*, his first film for a major studio (Warner Bros.), his first with a substantial budget, and his first made with a professional crew. But disaster struck when, shortly before filming was completed, De Palma was ousted by Warner Bros. executive John Calley, who at the time was coincidentally working with Jack Clayton on David Giler's *Casualties of War* script. *Get to Know Your Rabbit* was shelved for three years by the studio before eventually being released.[10]

Brian De Palma, around the time of *Carrie* (1976)

De Palma, meanwhile, made his first foray into Hitchcock territory with *Sisters* (1972), which also marked his first collaboration with Bernard Herrmann, the legendary composer of *Psycho*, who later wrote music for De Palma's *Obsession* (1976), a glorious homage to Hitchcock's *Vertigo*. From the mid-1970s onwards, De Palma was consistently compared to the Master of Suspense – too often inaccurately and superficially. In fact, his body of work, which included the rock opera *Phantom of the Paradise*, was much more diverse. *Carrie* (1976), adapted from a Stephen King novel, provided De Palma with his first major popular success. The film, which cost less than $2 million to make, earned over $33 million and made John Travolta famous. The success of De Palma's *The Fury* (1978) was more modest, and the following year he directed the low-budget, semi-autobiographical *Home Movies* (1979), which, despite Kirk Douglas' involvement and some good reviews, failed at the box office. By the end of the decade, De Palma was at a pivotal point in his career. None of his films since *Carrie* had matched its success, and he feverishly looked for a project that would satisfy his ambitions, one that might also definitively relaunch his career. The answer to his problems turned out to be *Prince of the City*, an adaptation of Robert Daley's book that he was set to direct for Orion Pictures. To write the script, De Palma called on playwright David Rabe.

From *Prince of the City* to *Casualties of War*

Unlike De Palma, Rabe had been drafted, and between 1966 and 1967, he served in Vietnam in a medical unit. Back home, Rabe was unable to write for six months. "Oddly enough," he recounts, "it was a novel rather than a play that I wanted to work on."[11]

After resuming his studies at Villanova University in Pennsylvania, Rabe secured a grant from the Rockefeller Foundation, "enough to live on for a year and a half." He recalls thinking he could "dash off some plays real quick, then focus in on the novel."[12] Four plays followed, all informed by his experiences in Vietnam: *Sticks and Bones* (1969), *The Basic Training of Pavlo Hummel* (1971), *The Orphan* (1973) and *Streamers* (1976). None depict the war directly, but instead focus on its repercussions in the language and bodies of those who fought, before their departure and after their return. Rabe's plays received public and critical acclaim, notably *Sticks and Bones*, which in 1972 was awarded a Tony Award for Best Play.

From the early 1970s, Rabe aspired to write screenplays. Building on his theater successes, he developed several film projects, but few came to fruition. *Sticks and Bones* was filmed as a TV movie in 1973, directed by Robert Downey Sr.

Rabe asked Al Pacino, who had appeared on Broadway in *The Basic Training of Pavlo Hummel*, to play the lead role in a film version, but he declined. "I tried a few other avenues and actors with that script but nothing ever came of it," says Rabe.[13] It wasn't until 1983 that another of his plays was adapted, under the direction of Robert Altman. *Streamers* features Matthew Modine (the future Joker from *Full Metal Jacket*), Michael Wright, and George Dzundza, unforgettable as John in *The Deer Hunter*.

David Rabe, Fort Gordon, Georgia, 1965

Rabe and De Palma knew each other. For one thing, Rabe was married to actress Jill Clayburgh, who had been De Palma's girlfriend in the 1960s and starred alongside

Robert De Niro in *The Wedding Party*. For nearly a year, Rabe collaborated closely with De Palma on a script of *Prince of the City* before De Palma was ousted by producer Mike Medavoy, who handed the film to Sidney Lumet. Rabe, in turn, lost control of his script, and the job was handed to Jay Presson Allen. It was then that Rabe suggested to De Palma that they work together on *Casualties of War*, which for more than a decade he was convinced would make an important film. It was a pleasant surprise for De Palma, who for years had also thought of adapting Lang's text.

David Rabe in Vietnam, 1966

Rabe had contacted Lang a few months earlier to check the availability of the adaptation rights for *Casualties of War*.[14] It is unlikely that Lang – under contract with Susskind between May 1977 and May 1979 – would have discussed the adaptation rights with anyone else, especially at the time when Heywood Gould was at work on the project. More probable is that Rabe contacted Lang once the contract with Susskind had expired and when Lang was in negotiations with Alfred Crown and Jerome Hammer.

While Meserve's transformation from war hero to rapist intrigued Rabe, he was also drawn to Eriksson's moral dilemma: refusing to be part of a collective rape while risking accusations of insubordination or desertion if he escaped with the victim. "You're out in the middle of nowhere, the only people who are going to help you out are the ones you're with, and you try to alienate them? So the whole thing was very complex and powerful and moving to me," says Rabe.[15]

Lang apparently appreciated Rabe's approach, and was likely convinced that De Palma, now free of commitments after *Prince of the City*, was the best possible choice to direct the film. But De Palma remained clear-headed about the chances of attracting producers for such a project. "I told David: 'Great! But an impossible film to make,'" he recalls.[16] Indeed, "no studio would touch it," confirms Rabe.[17] And so De Palma went off and made *Dressed to Kill* (1980) while Lang set about writing his own treatment of *Casualties of War*.

The 1980s represent a period of maturity for De Palma, during which he created some of his most accomplished films – despite critics struggling to recognize his true worth. *Blow Out* (1981), which offers a daring variation on Michelangelo Antonioni's *Blow-Up* (1966), was a resounding failure, despite John Travolta, who thanks to *Carrie* and *Saturday Night Fever* (1977) had become a major star. *Scarface* (1983), one of the major films of the decade, was disparaged by most American critics, and De Palma fought to have his cut of the film released. *Body Double* (1984), though critically acclaimed in Europe, flopped in the United States and faced a feminist backlash. *Wise Guys* (1986), a comedy starring Danny De Vito, also failed to find an audience.

Midway through the decade, De Palma found himself with his back against the wall: "After the catastrophic failure of *Wise Guys*, I was in desperate need of a hit."[18] The support of Dawn Steel, a high-ranking Paramount executive, proved decisive. "At the time," asserts Art Linson, "Dawn was the most powerful female movie executive in Hollywood… She was volatile, ambitious, supportive"[19] – but also, adds De Palma, "very stubborn."[20] It was Steel who told De Palma that Paramount was developing *The Untouchables*, based on a script by David Mamet, and arranged for him to meet Linson, the film's producer.

"When you come face to face with Brian De Palma for the first time," says Linson, "it doesn't come as some big surprise that he directed *Carrie* and *Dressed to Kill*. He is large, abrupt, and seemingly stern. You are instantly given the feeling that if he hasn't yet scared the shit out of you, he eventually will."[21] There was immediate chemistry between the two men, and within a week they had become firm friends. De Palma was hired by Paramount to direct *The Untouchables* – and the rest is history. Buoyed by a stellar cast (Kevin Costner, Sean Connery, Robert De Niro, Andy Garcia) and virtuoso direction (the film's iconic moments include the pram scene, an homage to Eisenstein's *Battleship Potemkin*), *The Untouchables* earned over $10 million in its first weekend of release – more than a third of its production costs, around $25 million. Within three weeks, the studio broke even. Profits would ultimately exceed $75 million, marking De Palma's biggest box office success to date. With a single masterstroke he had erased all previous failures, and now had a free hand to look around for his next film.

Brian De Palma and Robert De Niro
on the set of *The Untouchables*

Not long after successful test screenings of *The Untouchables*, Linson began contemplating the next steps in his collaboration with De Palma. "We had a great time working together, so it felt very natural for me to ask him, 'What do you want to do now?' And that's when he sent me Daniel Lang's article."[22] Linson had never heard of the story but immediately liked Lang's writing, even though he found it emotionally challenging and expressed surprise that De Palma, "who could have done pretty much anything he wanted"[23] after *The Untouchables*, was so interested in it. Unbeknownst to Linson, De Palma had in fact already reconnected with Rabe, letting him know that he was investigating the possibilities of adapting Lang's book.

Linson suggested to De Palma that they pitch the project to Ned Tanen, Paramount's production head, with whom they had previously developed *The Untouchables*. In his exhilarating book about his years in Hollywood, Linson depicts Tanen as a man of fiery temperament, fully invested in the projects he supported but wholly inflexible regarding financial matters. "HEAR ME, LINSON!" he said during a heated discussion about the budget of *The Untouchables*. "I want you to listen very, very carefully. We are not spending $20 million to remake a gangster movie. This picture is not green-lighted. This budget is soaring. Get it under control. Get the number down. And tell your director that he better start looking at himself in the mirror and coming up with the right answers."[24]

When Linson and De Palma expressed a desire to adapt *Casualties of War*, Tanen, reassured by excellent early feedback on *The Untouchables*, initially appeared receptive. On May 27, 1987, a few days before the U.S. release of the film, Paramount reached an agreement with Margaret Lang. The studio secured an 18-month option on the adaptation rights to her husband's book, renewable for 12 months. The letter from David Hollander, Margaret Lang's lawyer, sent to Greg Gelfan, Paramount's vice president of business affairs, specifies that this agreement is subject to a meeting between De Palma and Lang, who wanted to discuss certain aspects of the adaptation before giving her approval.[25] The excellent rapport between Rabe and Margaret Lang facilitated the negotiations. "Margaret and I met often," says Rabe, "and had dinner with my wife Jill, as I recall. I'm sure we discussed my hopes and aims for the film."[26] Rabe regularly kept Margaret informed of the project's progress and even submitted draft screenplays to her.

Casualties of War – script #5 (David Rabe)

"We discussed the subject together and then he went off to write entirely on his own," says De Palma of Rabe. "He knew he could call me if there was a problem he couldn't solve."[27] De Palma liked Rabe's first draft, which took about three months to write, though made some suggestions for rewrites. I have identified six different versions of Rabe's screenplay.

During the initial phase of my research, David Rabe emailed me an undated, 131-page version of the screenplay entitled *"CASUALTIES OF WAR II."* "It is not the last script I submitted, but it is close to what I had at the end of my work," he cautioned.[28] The "II" in the file title implies there was a previous version. Several months later, Rabe discovered a different version, five pages shorter, which he sent to me as a PDF. It is dated 1994, likely because years after the film's release Rabe did a data transfer from one computer to another. He also located older files archived on a hard drive, but for technical reasons they proved unreadable.

Three versions – 123, 127 and 134 pages, respectively – were located in the private archives of the Lang family. The 123-page undated "First Draft" is identical to the script held in the UCLA archive.[29] The British Film Institute and the New York Public Library each possess a copy of the 127-page version, dated March 15, 1988.[30] The BFI catalogue identifies it as the shooting script sent to Columbia, a detail contradicted by the version Bill Pankow, the editor of *Casualties of War*, gave me, dated March 26, 1988 and labelled on its cover as a "revised" version. It was given to Pankow by Columbia while he was working on the director's cut for the film's DVD re-release.[31] A handwritten note to the editor states: "This is the only script on file, could not find the lined script. This probably is not the shooting script. Everything highlighted is not in the feature DVD."[32] According to this note, there appears to exist a final version, amended by De Palma, which is missing from the studio archives.

Dating the three versions with absolute certainty (the two that Rabe sent me and the third he gave to Margaret Lang) hasn't been possible. We can, however, try to advance a few hypotheses.

First hypothesis: the version dated 1994 is slightly later than the initial draft. It contains minor changes in the introduction and conclusion. Rabe has not yet reached the solutions explored in the March 15, 1988 version.

Second hypothesis: the 134-page version in the Lang family's possession evidently stands as an intermediate stage, which I would place immediately after the "1994" version. The opening remains closely aligned with the preceding two versions, but Rabe introduces a variation of a sequence just before the epilogue (a nightmare), which will undergo substantial modifications in subsequent versions. (I will elaborate further on the nature of these modifications in the following pages.)

Third hypothesis: the 131-page version sent to me by Rabe, the one he claims to be "most satisfied" with, is the most challenging to position chronologically in the writing process. A detail in the introduction provides a clue: Eriksson boards a bus and dozes off, while a young passenger of Asian origin sits opposite him. From the March 15, 1988 version onward, Eriksson boards a subway, explained by the choice of filming location for the sequence, in San Francisco, which means this detail couldn't be altered in subsequent versions. And so the 131-page version predates the March 15 version. But where does it fit among the three preceding versions? We're left to speculate. I'm inclined to place it after the aforementioned 134-page version because its prologue is more refined compared with those in earlier drafts. Rabe made cuts to things that were reintegrated into later versions, indicating that at a certain stage he'd had to backtrack, evidently against his will (for reasons I will elucidate later).

For the sake of clarification, if one attempts to number the different versions of Rabe's script in their chronological order, it would go:

(I) 123-page version, "First Draft," Paramount (UCLA/Lang family)

(II) 126-page version, dated "1994," Paramount (David Rabe)
(III) 134-page version, Paramount? (Lang family)
(IV) 131-page version, Columbia? (David Rabe)
(V) 127-page version dated March 15, 1988, "~~Shooting script~~," Columbia (BFI/New York Public Library/Lang family)
(VI) "Revised" version dated March 26, 1988, incomplete, Columbia (Bill Pankow)

David Rabe's script can be distinguished from all the others. Broadly speaking, Pete Hamill, David Giler, Heywood Gould and Daniel Lang's versions contain two acts roughly equal in length (act one is from the opening scene to the murder; act two is Eriksson's struggle to uncover the truth, leading to the trials), but Lang's treatment is focused more than all the others on describing the workings of the military-legal machine. Rabe, however, opts for a three-act structure of equal length:

1) the soldiers' daily lives and the horrors of war;
2) the kidnapping, rape and murder;
3) the denunciation and condemnation of the culprits.

By relegating the legal aspects of the story to its final third, Rabe removes several situations and characters that Lang introduced in his own treatment.

The second particularity of Rabe's screenplay lies in its flashback structure, which fully explores a technique Pete Hamill only suggested in his initial outline. Recall that Jack Clayton noted how a screenplay shouldn't start with a flashback without concluding in the present. Rabe avoids this mistake, and from the outset we sense how crucial the opening and closing of the film are for him, which explains why, with rare exceptions, most noticeable changes from one version of his screenplay to another are found in their opening and closing pages.

Initial draft
The idea of an anticipatory structure was already more or less present in Lang's text, which begins with Eriksson's

demobilization and ends with his reflections on the consequences of the trials. Rabe, however, drawing inspiration from an anecdote from Storeby as reported by Lang, chooses to start his script where *Casualties of War* ends. Lang's book concludes with the following lines:

> Six months ago, he said, he had taken a Minneapolis bus home from work and, being very tired, had dozed off. When he opened his eyes, a new passenger was sitting directly opposite him – a young Oriental woman. Still in the process of waking, and not yet thinking clearly, he said, he had transformed her into a peasant woman on her way to do a day's farming, such as he had seen many times in Vietnam; he had envisioned the passenger in a broad, peaked straw hat and black pajamas, carrying the traditional stick across her shoulders, with baskets at either end for holding crops. "Those baskets could get awfully heavy," Eriksson recalled. "Sometimes I didn't see what kept the stick from snapping. They were hard workers, those Vietnamese women picking little bananas, shinnying up palm trees for coconuts. But on the bus the peasant woman across from me was going to work in paddy fields that were near Mao's hamlet, from which it was a nice walk downhill to a stream that flooded the rice fields. That's where the woman was going in the early morning, but it was peacetime and it wasn't necessary either for her or for the peasant women she was with to smell the bodies that were always rotting for miles around, no one knew where, when I was in the Central Highlands. The only thing these women had to do on their way to the stream was breathe pure mountain air."[33]

In Rabe's version, Ericksson's memory transforms into a sequence divided into two moments, between which unfolds the long flashback that occupies almost the entirety of the story. Rabe struggled before arriving at a truly satisfying version. In his first three drafts, he attempts to provide a brief overview of Eriksson's life after his return home, while suggesting that he can never really leave Vietnam behind.

Each of the three versions begins with:

> Jungle: intense, vibrant, tangled, green, still. Arching trunks, twisted vines, huge fronds, glittering beads of water. Then the camera moves over the gray metal of the interior of a wall locker, revealing the jungle to be a photo pasted on the locker. Next, the camera settles on a photograph of SVEN ERIKSSON[34] and his wife, Kirsten, both in their early twenties, both attractive, both blonde. Moving, the camera pauses at the photo of a two-year-old girl in a pink dress.

The use of photographs allows Rabe to outline the situation of the main character: married, a father, a Vietnam veteran. Rabe cuts to the photos with the sudden image of a hand (presumably Eriksson's) violently slamming a locker door (I), replaced in a later version by Eriksson's silhouette retrieving his parka to face the cold outside (II). The next sequence shows him leaving the small Minneapolis wood shop where he works with a man named Weber, who is approximately the same age. It is the end of a hard day. Snow begins to fall and the two men head home. Weber gets into his car, Eriksson takes the bus. He engages in casual conversation with the driver before dozing off, exhausted. The bus is relatively crowded, and other passengers board at the next stop. Among them, "an oriental girl, quite young, quite attractive, dressed in a big winter coat and hat. She carries two large shopping bags, and settles into a seat directly in front of the sleeping Eriksson."

When the bus enters a long tunnel, the lights dance on Eriksson's face as he moves his head from side to side, slowly awakening from his slumber. As he wakes up, he watches elongated shapes on cots around him. He is now in a tent full of sleeping soldiers, and an anonymous figure is standing opposite him. The person shines a flashlight in his face, blinding him (versions I to III). The sequence abruptly cuts, and Eriksson is back with his unit, patrolling in a village in Vietnam on a sunny late afternoon. The intermediate sequence in the tent can be interpreted in various ways. Is it the continuation of a nightmare that began on the bus, or, conversely, a "real" moment, after the murder of the young

Vietnamese girl? If so, the threatening silhouette could be that of Meserve or Clark, attempting to eliminate Eriksson under cover of night.

This opening underwent modifications in later drafts (from version V onward). The first notable change: the sequence is now situated in an unspecified location. The entire first part has been cut (no more photos or woodworking). We first encounter Eriksson and Weber descending into the subway instead of catching a bus (a second notable change, due to the production's choice of shooting location). A brief conversation between the two men is interrupted by the arrival of Weber's train. Eriksson buys peanuts, boards another train, and dozes off. The rest of the script remains largely the same as in the previous versions. Passengers crowd into the train at the next stop and a young Asian girl sits down opposite Eriksson, who is awakened by the flickering subway lights. The transition into the tent remains.

There is, however, a significant deviation between the scene as written in draft VI and how De Palma ultimately filmed it. Rabe wanted a simpler opening, both formally and narratively. Draft IV bears witness to this: Weber's character is absent, as Rabe preferred to focus on Eriksson, isolating him from his professional and social setting. In the late afternoon, as light snow falls on the streets of an anonymous city, Eriksson takes a seat on a bus and drifts off. At the next stop, a young woman – this time specified as "Vietnamese" in the script – "settles into a seat directly in front of the sleeping Eriksson, who stirs, glimpsing her with a puzzled, thoughtful gaze, as the bus plunges on and enters the dark of the tunnel." The sight of the young stranger immediately unleashes in Eriksson his memories of war, and the convoluted transition in the tent, needlessly weighing down the opening, is now gone. It is very close to the sequence that De Palma ended up shooting in San Francisco.

Act one

Every *Casualties of War* script written between 1970 and 1980 starts with an expository scene set in Vietnam, offering audiences a glimpse of the horrors of war and introducing the main characters. In this respect, Rabe's adaptation doesn't deviate from the norm. But from this point on, most previous versions shift to Meserve's announcement that his intention is to kidnap a young girl for reasons of "rest and relaxation." Rabe's script is different. Meserve's declaration, preceded by several scenes, all invented by Rabe, doesn't occur until about forty pages in. As Pauline Kael put it in her extensive review of De Palma's film, Rabe's script follows Lang's narrative closely, but also "dramatizes the story by creating several incidents to explain what led to the rape and what followed."[35] Such "incidents" serve to delve deeper into the bonds that unite the soldiers, to present a psychological portrait of them, and to illuminate their motivations.

As Heywood Gould had done, Rabe changed certain elements, including place and character names (Hill 192 becomes Hill 209, Phan Thi Mao is now Tran Thi Oanh). Alongside this handful of anecdotal alterations are more substantial modifications, including the invention of certain key (Herber, Brown) or secondary (Rasmussen, Kramer) characters. Rabe goes further than the liberties taken by Hamill and Gould in their scripts, liberties that, as we recall, had been criticized (sometimes rightly, sometimes wrongly) by Jack Clayton, then Daniel Lang, who believed that the script should deviate as little as possible from real events and Eriksson's testimony. Ultimately, the question raised by Rabe's script, more profoundly than Hamill's and Gould's: is a "good" adaptation judged primarily by its faithfulness to the original?

Immediately after the prologue, Rabe's script continues with a long flashback set in Vietnam, without specific mention of place or date. Under the command of Lieutenant Reilly, a squad of American soldiers, including Eriksson, patrols a village. The first-timer – who has been in country for barely three weeks – fraternizes with a group of children, exchanging a chocolate bar for an apple. Sergeant Meserve quickly brings him back to order: "You wanna die a sudden and horrible death, Cherry?... You eat somethin' they give you, it's got ground up glass in it, or chopped up razor blades, what are you dead of?"

"Stupidity, man," says Brown, a black soldier who quickly emerges as the joker of the group.

"I just didn't wanna be rude, Brown, but I wasn't gonna eat it," says Eriksson.

"Rude? Boy, I'll smack you upside the head you talkin' that foolishness!"

"You do somethin' rude, Eriksson, you say: 'Sorry 'bout that,'" jokes Clark. "Like for example you strangle their chickens or cop some rice or barbeque their hootch, you say: 'Sorry 'bout that.' Right, Brown? Lemme hear you say it, Cherry."

"Sorry 'bout that," Eriksson reluctantly repeats.

The sequence culminates in Meserve's aggressive interrogation of a villager.

Rabe portrays Eriksson as well-mannered and affable, perhaps naïve, who needs to be reminded by his comrades of the cunning tactics employed by the enemy. Within his unit, he is an especially introverted character, lacking Brown's humor, Clark's insolence and Meserve's charisma, seemingly quick to capitulate under group pressure.

The script transitions to a night sequence. After leaving the village, Reilly and his men are on patrol in the jungle. Perhaps to avoid stigmatizing Latinos, Rabe introduces a character named Herber (renamed Hatcher), who replaces Rafael, Manuel Diaz's cousin, and who later participates in Oanh's rape and murder. Meserve assigns Herber and Eriksson the perilous task of laying antipersonnel mines, an arduous endeavor in the thick darkness of the tropical forest. As the two soldiers toil, the distant rumble of mortars gradually draws nearer. The ill-timed shots fired by one of their squad members, who believed he has glimpsed a North Vietnamese, reveal their position to the enemy, leaving the American soldiers cornered. Suddenly, an explosion throws Eriksson to the ground, trapping him waist-deep in a hole, the entrance to a North Vietnamese tunnel. Meserve, braving enemy fire, rushes to his aid, and, once Eriksson is freed, the two men work to flush out invisible snipers, using grenades and machine-gun bursts.

This pivotal scene is yet another significant addition by Rabe – with far-reaching consequences. Nothing in Storeby's testimony, as recorded by Lang, suggests that Gervase aided his subordinate. Testimonies from other officers, however, particularly Lieutenant Collins, paint the sergeant as a valiant warrior, unhesitant to risk his life to assist his comrades. "In other connections," writes Lang, "it was brought out that the Sergeant had not waited to be drafted, that he was currently in line for the Bronze Star, and that in the course of his overseas duty he had been awarded five medals, of varying importance, and had a conduct rating of Excellent."[36] By depicting Meserve's rescue of Eriksson, Rabe complicates the relationship between the two men. Eriksson is indebted to his sergeant, making it all the more difficult for him to oppose Merserve's authority when ordered to participate in a collective rape. David Greven offers a psychoanalytic interpretation of this sequence, suggesting that Meserve can be seen as some kind of father substitute for Eriksson, a hypothesis further reinforced by Eriksson's later revelation of his father's death.[37]

De Palma chose not to include in the film the next sequence as written by Rabe. Having managed to extricate themselves from the firing zone, Meserve and Eriksson, now alongside Herber, Brown, Clark and Rasmussen, struggle through the jungle and lose Rasmussen, who vanishes into the forest. Rabe maintains the mystery of his disappearance, leaving room for the audience to imagine that he might have been abducted and killed by the enemy, thus intensifying the squad's tension through dialogue. The group heads southwest and reaches the outskirts of a village. At dawn, after finding three of their comrades carrying the corpse of one of their own (Kramer, glimpsed in the nighttime jungle sequence), the soldiers decide to take a break.

Eriksson stands out once again from his comrades after he befriends an old farmer, who teaches him how to guide a water buffalo through a rice paddy – which reveals a new and endearing side of his personality. Jack Clayton had hoped that Eriksson's interest in nature and fieldwork would come through on-screen, something that Hamill and Giler make the most of in their scripts, through dialogue about the beauty of the surrounding landscape. Rabe takes a subtler approach, though the sequence's placement in the story might be questioned. One would expect Eriksson to be more wary after the violent jungle encounter. According to Rabe, the scene should have appeared *before* the night battle: "I thought Eriksson seen plowing the fields after the battle diminished the sense of suspicion that should have been developing in him about whether or not the Vietnamese could be trusted."[38] However, despite Rabe's assertion, this scene consistently appears after the battle in every version of the script I reviewed. Perhaps there is an intermediate version, or maybe Rabe's memory is playing tricks, leading him to believe he made a change that was never implemented.

Within the logic of the screenplay, the scene where Eriksson helps the Vietnamese peasant plow his land fits with the next sequence, where Brown, observing him from a distance, with a mocking eye while smoking a joint, advises him to rejoin the rest of the troops. Eriksson complies. A lengthy dialogue scene follows in which he tells Brown that he is the father of a little girl and that he is a Lutheran. Pretending to be his chaplain, Brown, in his always colorful language, asks him to recount how Meserve came to his aid.

> BROWN
> Did you pee your pants, motherfucker!?
>
> ERIKSSON
> Sarge didn't come back for me, I sure woulda.
>
> BROWN
> Without the Sarge, you ain't nothin' but a sack a monkey shit.

Just as the two men rejoin their comrades, a burst of machine gun fire cuts down Brown. The soldiers fire back, Eriksson and Herber covering Meserve while he administers first aid. "It ain't nothin', it ain't nothin'," he says, trying to reassure Brown, pressing on the wound to stop the bleeding. "It feels like somethin', man. It feels bad," yells Brown. A helicopter is dispatched to the location, and Brown, on a stretcher, is evacuated while Meserve shouts words of encouragement.

> MESERVE
> Look into my fuckin' eyes, Brownie. Look into my eyes. I'm gonna hypnotize you!
>
> BROWN
> Good.

                          MESERVE
You're fine.

                           BROWN
I know it.

As the helicopter ascends, a lieutenant hands Meserve his orders: he and his men are to return to base and place themselves under the command of Captain Hill. Angry at the villagers, who failed to warn them about the presence of enemy forces in the vicinity, the soldiers struggle to contain their rage. "Torch the fuckin' place!" yells Clark.

At this point, Meserve is nothing like the sadistic rapist he becomes in act two. He has committed no acts of gratuitous violence but has instead established himself as a courageous and altruistic warrior, willing to risk his life to aid his comrades. Rabe refuses to represent things simplistically. This entire first section of the script prevents the characters from becoming trapped in the confines of a stark dichotomy between the "good soldier" (Eriksson) and "bad soldiers" (Meserve and his cohort). In this context, it makes little sense to compare Lang's text with Rabe's screenplay and argue that one is *better* than the other. A world of difference separates an investigative text (especially one written in the first person, where the author takes a position) from a screenplay (where the author steps back to construct a narrative). Rabe had two choices, each with its pros and cons. If he had placed Meserve's briefing earlier, Rabe's version of the story would have aligned more closely with Lang's original but might have flattened the character, immediately painting him as malevolent and cruel. By opting for the alternative, by delaying the briefing and developing Meserve's personality, Rabe pushes audiences to express a certain empathy for the soldier – a move that doesn't necessarily conflict with Lang's intentions (he paints a fairly complex portrait of Meserve), nor with the historical reality reflected in trial transcripts.

Between Brown's evacuation and the briefing, Rabe inserts four other sequences, the first of which was removed by De Palma. A truck carrying Meserve, Clark, Eriksson and Herber arrives near a village. The driver stops, claiming to need to pick up laundry from a laundromat, but instead takes his comrades to a brothel where they are propositioned by prostitutes and where a young girl is offered to Eriksson. Meserve catches the driver in the act and calls everyone to order, and the convoy leaves amid insults from the prostitutes, with Eriksson apologizing (having learned from Clark): "Sorry 'bout that!"

The next scene, however, was deemed essential, and retained. Back at the military base, Eriksson and Clark try to alleviate their boredom and negotiate for the beers Herber has patiently collected over the preceding days. Rowan, Eriksson's friend, pays them a visit and enquires about their well-being. "I nearly got killed. I went crazy!" says Eriksson, still shocked by his ordeal in the jungle. Not very talkative, Meserve, lying on a bunk, informs his men that they have the evening off. "We're gonna go shower, Sarge, whata you gonna do?" asks Herber. "I'm gonna go… to town and… get laid," responds Meserve, sitting up on the edge of his bunk. "You find anything out about Brown, Sarge?" worries Eriksson. "He's dead," says Meserve sharply.

The news of Brown's death weighs heavily on the group. In the shower, Eriksson, Clark and Herber express their frustration. Meserve, silent, takes out his anger on the beer can given to him by Eriksson. Clark, in particular, makes remarks that reveal his predisposition to violence: "WHAT I'M SAYIN' IS THESE GOOKS ARE SHIT, MAN!" he yells, throwing his canteen cup. "Every bug-eyed motherfucker in that village, every man, woman, and child knew about the mortars and they knew about the snipers and they let 'em zap Brownie. They're slugs. They're roaches and total destruction is the only way to handle 'em! They coulda warned us, but they don't care about us. They hate us."

Later that evening, the quartet heads toward the camp gate to spend a few hours at the town brothel, hoping to momentarily forget about Brown. From Herber's portable radio we hear the refrain of The Doors' 1968 song "Hello, I Love You," which Rabe says he chose for its "dark cynical" potential.[39] But the soldiers' plans are thwarted when the military policeman responsible for monitoring their movements informs them that access to the town is prohibited until further notice. "You know what this bullshit is about? The goddamn Cong is in town tonight, which is why it is off-limits. Charlie's in the whorehouse tonight!" fumes Meserve.

"No shit?" Eriksson naïvely asks. "Cong's gotta get laid, too, Eriksson. He works hard killin' us, don't he?" responds Meserve. The four soldiers have no choice but to turn around, go back to their tent, and drown their bitterness in beer and drugs.

At this stage, about a third of the way into the script, Rabe finally includes Meserve's briefing. While Herber, Eriksson and Clark languish in their tent, Meserve bursts in and introduces Manuel Diaz, freshly arrived from the third section to replace Brown. He informs them that they are requisitioned at 5:30 the next morning for a reconnaissance mission on Hill 209 to locate enemy hideouts (bunkers, food, ammunition caches). After providing them with the coordinates of the site and listing the equipment they will be bringing, Meserve adds: "I want everybody ready an hour early because" – he points to a spot on the Crayola line on a map – "at this point we're gonna detour two thousand meters south to the village of Nghia Hanh where what we're gonna do is requisition us a girl to take along with us for some boom-boom, sort of portable R-and-R, break up the boredom, keep up morale. And remember: I want nothin' but charmed people around me on this one. Bring your good luck stuff." Clark brandishes "a large hunting knife, the handle wrapped in tape and decorated with tiny diamond-like sparkles."

The lines given to Meserve by Rabe are similar to the speech the real Gervase gave to his comrades, according to testimonies collected during the court-martial proceedings. But Rabe never indicates any sense of premeditated murder, and so even though the unfolding drama is felt, the script mitigates Meserve's criminal intentions. The plan is "only" rape, and ultimately Rabe's version conveys the idea that any kidnapping is the culmination of Meserve and his men's frustration, triggered first by Brown's death and intensified by the impossibility of visiting a brothel. "I hoped to convey to a degree that the crime they committed was one they probably would not have ever committed were they not in the war zone. Not to justify it but to give it a context," explains Rabe.[40]

It is no coincidence that this issue, as reflected on by Clayton and Sims after reading Pete Hamill's script, was unresolved by both David Giler and Heywood Gould in their subsequent versions. The point here is the screenwriters' reluctance to depict Meserve as an outright rapist and killer, fearing that such a depiction would alienate the audience at this (early) point in the story and prevent any identification with the character. Moreover, let's not forget that Rabe, critical as he was of the war, was a veteran himself, and so sought to depict young American soldiers in Vietnam with some nuance, far from the "baby killer" stereotype that gripped the American press after the My Lai massacre.[41] Later dialogue between Eriksson and Meserve, shortly after Oanh's rape, reinforces this idea.

MESERVE
You probably like the army, don't you Eriksson.

ERIKSSON
No.

MESERVE
I hate the army.

ERIKSSON
This ain't the army. This ain't the army, Sarge.

Rabe is clearly intent on making a distinction between the army as an institution and Meserve's actions – those of a man who, having spent too long on the frontline, has lost his way and abandoned his moral compass to satisfy his impulses. While one might disagree with this characterization, it is important to acknowledge that Rabe wants to restore certain zones of ambiguity. His Meserve reveals a certain vulnerability, even a melancholic persona, while Eriksson leans more toward the anti-hero figure when he fails to save Oanh for want of courage. Therein lies the tragic dimension of the character.

Rabe also grasps the significance of Corporal Rowan, a pivotal character introduced just after Meserve's briefing. Eriksson approaches Rowan to recount what Meserve has just told the group. "Did he really say that?" asks an incredulous Rowan. "He wouldn't do it, would he?" responds Eriksson, as if trying to convince himself. Rowan is reassuring, noting that Meserve is to be demobilized "in less than thirty days."

>   ROWAN
> What'd the other guys think?
>
>   ERIKSSON
> Everybody was joking, you know. Clark says, "What's this, some new addition to Lurp rations?"
>
>   ROWAN
> Right. Some broad in your pack. You see how nuts it sounds? Neva happen, G.I.

Here again, Rabe alters the dialogue between Rowan and Eriksson. As reported by Lang, Rowan had confided in Eriksson that "in the last month or so, the Sergeant, apparently undergoing changes, had exhibited a mean streak toward the Vietnamese; a couple of weeks before… Meserve had shot at and wounded one of them, giving as his reason afterward that he had 'felt like it.'"[42] This detail doesn't align well with the nuanced – hence more ambiguous – portrayal of Meserve, which is why Rabe excluded it.

Act two
The segment from Oanh's kidnapping to her rape and murder occupies the second third of the screenplay. The abduction scene – seen through Eriksson's eyes, a silent witness overwhelmed by events – is intense and heart-wrenching. As Clark violently forces Oahn's own scarf into her mouth in front of her mother, Rabe describes Eriksson as "stunned, pale, shaking." While Meserve and the others quickly retreat, dragging the young woman with them, Eriksson remains momentarily frozen. "He looks at the mama-san but cannot speak. He looks at the emerging villagers. He turns and runs into the jungle." Thus begins the prisoner's long ordeal.

Rabe's dialogue illuminates one of the script's central themes (also developed by Kazan in *The Visitors*): the dangers of homosociality – namely, the perception of women strictly as sexual objects and the concurrent development of blatant homophobia (a subject at the heart of Rabe's play *Streamers*). Eriksson refuses to partake in Oanh's rape, which is portrayed as a ritual that reinforces the group's homosocial bonds. This idea is played out in dialogue immediately after the girl's abduction.

> HERBER
> It's just like Genghis Khan, right Eriksson? That's what I was thinkin'. You ever heard of Genghis Khan?
>
> ERIKSSON
> Whata you talkin' about?
>
> HERBER
> Meserve, man, he's unbelievable, I mean, what we're doin' – it's fantastic. I can't figure out how come we never thought of it before.
>
> ERIKSSON
> This is nuts, Herber.
>
> HERBER
> It ain't nuts. It's what armies do.
>
> ERIKSSON
> We ain't Genghis Khan, Herber.
>
> HERBER
> You're the one who's nuts.
>
> ERIKSSON
> We're supposed to be here to help those people. It's the twentieth century, man.

The Genghis Khan that Herber is referencing is less the historical figure and more his cinematic avatar, as portrayed by John Wayne in *The Conqueror* (1956), where the valiant warrior kidnaps the beautiful Bortai, daughter of Tatar chief Kumlek, and, with a smirk of pleasure, tears off her dress in front of his army.[43]

Later, when Meserve ties Oanh's hands before she is raped and Eriksson shows his disapproval by distancing himself from the group, Meserve and Clark explain his behavior by accusing him of having homosexual inclinations.

                    CLARK
Maybe he's queer.

                    MESERVE
You a faggot, Eriksson? Is that your goddamn problem?

                    ERIKSSON
No.

                    MESERVE
So what is it? What is your problem? Everybody else is up for this?

Eriksson is trying to make eyes contact with Diaz.

                    MESERVE
Whata you lookin' at Diaz for? Diaz is with the program. You got a problem with this, Diaz?

Diaz doesn't speak.

                    MESERVE
Will you stop lookin' at Diaz?!! I think maybe he is a queer. Herber, is Eriksson a faggot? I think we got us two girls on our patrol. IS ERIKSSON A FAGGOT, HERBER?

                    HERBER
I don't know, Sarge.

                    MESERVE
I think he is.
                    CLARK
He is a chickenshit, that's for sure. (*Pulling out his knife.*) I'll cut his fuckin' heart out.

Manuel Diaz, in reality, was married and the father of a young daughter. In Rabe's script he is a young single man, evidently inexperienced with women, a more straightforward characterization, which makes his response to the unfolding situation easier to grasp. Rabe presents every member of the patrol but Eriksson as single. If Diaz were married, perhaps his fear of being seen as gay wouldn't be quite so believable. He twice expresses to Eriksson his unwillingness to participate in the rape, and yet he succumbs to group pressure as soon as Meserve and Clark hurl homophobic insults at Eriksson. Eriksson's fear of being seen as gay is also palpable. When Meserve threatens to rape him after he's done with Oanh, Eriksson brandishes his weapon in defense, refusing – as David Greven writes – to let "the taint of homosexual identity tarnish his image."[44] This triggers a tirade from Meserve, who, as he walks into the hut where he rapes Oanh, likens his penis to a gun, an act that embodies issues of masculinity and warfare (and which is the inverse of the chant heard in *Full Metal Jacket*, as the soldiers squeeze their testicles while brandishing their rifles: "This is for fighting, this is for fun"). It is clear from Rabe's script – and even more so in Sean Penn's performance – how much Meserve's hubris cloaks a deep-seated unease about his own virility and perhaps even a suppressed undercurrent of homosexuality.[45]

Rabe essentially describes the rape from the perspective of the soldiers outside the hut, accentuating their indifference toward the victim. Herber, for example, repeatedly laments not having any beer to enhance the moment. Exiting the hut, Meserve settles for a rather surprising "better'n nothing," implying that his expectations were not fully met. (The preceding scene also suggests that he is more excited about being observed by Eriksson than actually raping Oanh. "You gonna watch?" he questions, even as Eriksson has already turned away.) Diaz is next, much to Herber's dismay. When he enters the hut, "Oanh lies on the table, naked, turned away and curled into a fetal position." Clark gags her to prevent her screams from alerting the enemy. A shot of the sky above the jungle, under a scorching sun, punctuated by the final seconds of the Doors song heard earlier, marks a brutal transition to the next scene, where, after the rape, the soldiers are seen talking outside the hut.

Meserve, at this juncture, appears to harbor no desire to kill Oanh. The idea begins to take root in his mind only once the patrol spots a group of enemy forces and he calls for reinforcements. What is immediately clear is that having Oanh with them poses a double threat for the soldiers. First, she will slow them down, and second, her presence may arouse suspicions from their superiors and expose them to disciplinary action. Before Meserve instructs his men to execute her, Rabe includes the passage, as reported by Lang, in which Eriksson finds himself alone in the hut with Oanh after Clark has ordered him to guard her and their ammunition. We witness Eriksson's futile attempts to communicate with the young woman. He notices she has a fever, feeds her, gives her water, and desperately searches for a way to help her. In his panic, he even recites the Lord's Prayer – the screenplay's only direct reference to Eriksson's faith. On paper, the scene is powerful, but it is apparent from reading the script that its strength will depend heavily on the actors' ability to embody emotions such as helplessness, pain, dread and despair. This task is compounded by the fact that Oanh says nothing, communicating only through gestures and facial expressions.

In fact, Oanh utters not a single line of dialogue throughout the entire script, which risks reducing her to a relatively anonymous figure. Deborah Thomas observes that in the film (the same applies to the script), Oanh is presented "anonymously" – "with no personal history, no audience access to her consciousness, no developed point of view."[46] However, it is important to remember that Robert Storeby described to Daniel Lang only Mao's physical behavior, not her emotions, as he didn't speak her language and didn't even know her name at the time of the assault and murder, which only came to light much later during the trials. The theme of incommunicability is central to Rabe's script, illustrating the clash between two cultures unable to understand each other. Americans, unable to speak Vietnamese, can't comprehend "the Vietnamese mentality."[47] Telling the story from the perspective of the victim would have resulted in an entirely different script. And yet, despite Oanh being reduced to a silent presence, Rabe has crafted an unforgettable character. Oanh remains a haunting figure throughout the script, from the opening lines to the conclusion – and far beyond.

Storeby confided in Lang about his inability to save Oanh, an aspect softened in Rabe's script. Moved by pity at the gaze of his captive, her health visibly fading with each passing hour, Eriksson resolves to act. Hastily gathering provisions and ammunition, stuffing his pack full, he leads Oanh out of the hut. "Okay, let's do this," he urges himself aloud. "C'mon. I'll try it. What the fuck." But when they have gone only a few feet, Eriksson suddenly grasps the weight of his decision. "Oh, shit, I'm gonna be a fuckin' deserter…" His hesitation proves fatal. Meserve and his men return to the hut. Oanh's fate is sealed.

The rest of the script largely follows Storeby's account. Meserve orders Eriksson to kill Oanh, but he refuses, as do Diaz and Herber, and Clark ultimately takes charge. After being stabbed, Oanh manages to escape, and Meserve orders his men to shoot her. Everyone fires in her direction except Eriksson, who shoots into the air, then runs toward Meserve, who hits him in the stomach with his rifle. Writhing in pain, he watches helplessly as Clark finishes off the young woman. Simultaneously, as napalm bombs fall around them, there unfolds a battle between North Vietnamese and the reinforcements called in by Meserve, followed by Eriksson's evacuation.

Act three

The transition from the second to the third act occurs through a brief sequence that might have been inspired by Rabe's own experiences in Vietnam. Inside a medevac chopper, Eriksson lies among the wounded. "Dazed, he sits, his glassy eyes staring at the faces of the wounded men around him. The floor of the chopper is filling with blood, blood washing along and over his boots." Through a window, Eriksson is witness to a "nightmare sight" below: corpses of American soldiers being hoisted aboard a huge Chinook helicopter.

Back at Camp Wolf, an agitated Eriksson seeks out Rowan and hurriedly tells him about Oanh's murder. Clark, who overhears their conversation, loses his composure and berates the private: "WHAT HAPPENS IN THE FIELD STAYS IN THE FIELD, YOU SONOFABITCH! IT'S A LAW! IT'S A MOTHERFUCKING LAW!" But Eriksson is not so easily discouraged, and with Rowan's backing decides to speak to Lieutenant Reilly. The officer tries to dissuade him by recounting his wife's childbirth story, attempting to convince Eriksson that he stands to gain nothing by confronting a system beyond his control. "I can't stop thinkin' about her," Eriksson says to Rowan. "I don't even know her fucking name!"

From this point on, the screenplay focuses on Eriksson's efforts to prevent Oanh from remaining a nameless, faceless victim. Yet his battle transcends this singular act, as he fights against the tendency to trivialize death and become accustomed to the pain of others. Rabe introduces a character called Cherry (a name given to inexperienced soldiers newly arrived in the combat zone), a pale, bespectacled young man who shivers at the sight of leeches clinging to his legs as he crosses a swamp with his unit. Cherry asks Rowan if he will trade a boneless piece of chicken for a slice of pound cake (his was stolen). When, moments later, he is cut down by a sniper's bullet, Rowan comments sarcastically on his death. This infuriates Eriksson. "Just because each one of us might at any second be blown away, everybody's actin' like we can do anything and it don't matter what we do – but I'm thinkin' maybe it's all the other way around and the main thing is just the opposite, you know, and because we might be dead in the next split second, we have to be extra careful about what we do – because maybe what we do matters more – maybe it matters more than we can imagine."

Eriksson then goes to see Captain Hill to report Oanh's murder. Rabe chooses not to include the scene where Hill summons Meserve and his men. Hill's brief appearance corresponds to Lang's original. He assures Eriksson that he has been informed of the incident by Reilly and that he is paying close attention to the matter. But that doesn't stop him from warning Eriksson about how the situation might unfold.

HILL
They'll be outa the stockade faster'n flies on shit and if I was them, I'd be pissed off, wouldn't you – I'd want some payback! And if I was you, a young man with a wife and baby daughter, I'd consider such factors very closely.

ERIKSSON

Pardon me, sir, but what's your point, sir?

HILL

No point, PFC. I'm just trying to illuminate the terrain in which we find ourselves presently deployed. You don't mind that, I hope; and fuck you if you do.

ERIKSSON

Yes sir.

HILL

Are you on my frequency?

ERIKSSON

Yes, sir.

HILL

I mean, who the fuck do you think you are?! You little scumbag! You're in this report recommending Meserve for the Bronze Star! You were out there that night. He brought the five a you outa that mess alive! I mean, this thing with the girl, it was wrong, but he is a kid. He's twenty goddamn years old! Are you gonna ruin his life?! He saved yours!

The next sequence shows Eriksson at the Longridge camp club, in a state of inebriation, looking at photos of his wife and daughter, torn between his love for them, his desire to protect them, and his determination not to let Oanh's crime go unpunished. Intrigued by his behavior, Chaplain Kirk engages him in conversation. This lengthy dialogue scene takes on an almost philosophical turn, leading to Eriksson's "confession": "I went on a long-range patrol, sir, three weeks ago, and we kidnapped a girl, sir, and the other four men raped her, sir, and they murdered her and I failed to stop them." The first-person plural ("*we* kidnapped") shows that Eriksson does not absolve himself of all responsibility. Rabe subtly informs us about Eriksson's state of mind and the guilt that gnaws at him.

From this sequence onward, Rabe's writing becomes more elliptical. Eriksson's interrogation by two agents from the Criminal Investigation Division spans four pages. The dialogue is harsh and relentless, and Eriksson's account is clearly doubted. One of the agents asks him if he would be able to locate the corpse – and we transition to Hill 209. This sequence posed an interesting challenge in previous drafts. Jack Clayton wanted it to be long, emphasizing Eriksson's difficulties in remembering where the victim's body lay. Daniel Lang opted for a similar sequence in his treatment, diverging from Storeby's straightforward account of the discovery of Mao's body. In Rabe's script, Eriksson first points to a rock, where no corpse is found, and then, quite sure of himself, indicates a second, where the investigators finally discover Oanh's corpse. The sequence ends with a brief exchange, as Captain Hill reproaches Eriksson for not being able to let the matter rest, to which Eriksson responds with a simple, "Sir… fuck you."

From the dense, suffocating jungle, we move inside the courtroom, where Rabe, like the other screenwriters, strings together a series of selected moments from the trials into one consolidated scene. Each soldier has their own line of defense. Meserve attempts to demonstrate his humanity, recounting an instance where he saved the lives of some Vietnamese children by performing mouth-to-mouth resuscitation. Diaz, admitting the act and regretting it, cites his fear of ridicule and his conflicted loyalty to his comrades as reasons for his actions. True to form, Clark maintains that Oanh was a communist and insists that he and Meserve "belong out in combat," not in a courtroom. Herber seems ashamed of the rape, but when the prosecutor asks him why Eriksson didn't enter the hut to assault Oanh, he confidently responds: "Well, sir, he was brand new. He'd just got there. I'd been there more than him. I'd been there at least three weeks longer, sir." Eriksson is then cross-examined and his sexuality questioned ("Does sexual activity always repulse you in this way?"). Lawyers even accuse him of fabricating his charges against Meserve and Clark to "avoid further combat duty." Eriksson's interrogation concludes with his admission of failure, which only deepens a sense of guilt.

> ATTORNEY
> In fact, if you wanted to save her so badly, why didn't you just shoot the other members of your patrol and...
>
> ERIKSSON
> I thought about it.
>
> ATTORNEY
> But you didn't do it, did you. Because you were watching out for your own sweet ass is why you didn't do it.
>
> PROSECUTOR
> Objection, sir!
>
> PRESIDENT
> Overruled.
>
> ATTORNEY
> In fact, you didn't do anything, except trade that girl's life for your own safety, betraying her, and then betraying your fellow soldiers with this sham of a trial! Isn't that right?
>
> PROSECUTOR
> Don't answer, Eriksson.
>
> ERIKSSON
> I probably should have shot them. I probably should have shot Meserve! And Clark! I probably should have shot them. Yes sir! Instead of what I did... which is let her die.

One notable feature is Rabe's decision to conclude the interrogations with Yen, Oanh's sister. In previous versions, including Lang's treatment, she was logically called to the stand at the beginning of the trial. Why did David Rabe reverse the order of testimonies? Possibly to place more emphasis on the victim and highlight the fact that Oanh's tragedy is also her family's. In Yen's heartbreaking testimony she recounts that her mother was kidnapped by communist forces and accused of "leading South Vietnamese forces to VC ammunition hidden on that hill."

The trial concludes with the verdict and sentencing of the guilty. The four soldiers are taken away by military police as an officer and the prosecutor discuss the outcome. "They'll all be out walkin' the streets in four years or less," says the prosecutor. "Four years max. And I mean every one of em'll be out. I know this system."

Epilogue
Rabe's epilogue opens on an airplane. Eriksson, flying home, is engaged in conversation with a man named Evans, like him newly demobilized. Tipsy with a bottle of whiskey in hand, Evans recognizes Eriksson as "the guy that turned in that patrol for wastin' that gook bitch" and asks him why he did what he did. Then, on an airport runway in Minnesota,[48] Eriksson is reunited with Kirsten and Kimberly, his wife and daughter. That evening, back home, he reconnects with the joys of fatherhood as he tucks Kimberly in and wishes her goodnight. "Will you be here in the morning, Daddy?" the girl asks him. "Sure will," he replies, before getting up and embracing his wife. It is a touching tableau of a family finally reunited, far from the horrors of war.

At this point Rabe introduces a nightmare, one that underwent several rewrites. The idea for this sequence came out of the first meeting between Rabe, De Palma and Linson. "We had trouble agreeing on the ending," says De Palma. "At one point I thought of including a rather surreal climax. In *The Visitors*, Elia Kazan, imagining what the rapists would do once they're released from prison, has them go to Eriksson's house. We played around with that – Eriksson haunted by the idea that these guys will be back for revenge."[49] (De Palma's filmmaking is full of disorientating moments like this, somewhere between dream and reality, notably the ending of *Carrie*). Ultimately a final scene on a bus (or subway) was included so as to achieve a certain symmetry with the opening and intensify the brutality of Eriksson's literal but also symbolic "awakening" – as well as that of America.

In Rabe's initial script drafts (I and II), the nightmare sequence takes place once Eriksson has returned home. After saying goodnight to Kimberly, he and his wife head to the living room, turn off the lights, and go up to their room, but as soon as they open the door, a "towering figure," dressed entirely in black, stands before them, wielding the knife used to murder Oanh. Meserve, his face covered, is back for revenge. Kirsten screams and Eriksson rushes to try and close the door, but as he turns, he sees Clark, also with his face covered, who grabs hold of Kimberly and Kirsten. Eriksson attempts to defend himself. A noise is suddenly heard and a beam of light appears. Eriksson calls for help, but Meserve puts the knife to his throat, exclaiming, "It's payback, motherfucker!" As the light draws nearer, the dialogue between Clark and Meserve recapitulates Oanh's abduction.

CLARK

Which one we gonna take?

MESERVE

Take the pretty one.

The light is now very close, and a silhouette emerges from the darkness: an avatar of Eriksson, "dressed in jungle fatigues." At which point... he abruptly wakes up on the bus. The nightmare sequence illustrates the threat looming over Eriksson and his family – the potential reprisals from Meserve and Clark upon their release from prison – as well as Eriksson's guilt that stems from his inability to prevent Oanh's murder.

But Rabe wasn't happy, thinking that there was already enough violence in the script, so he wrote an alternative which is more mysterious, almost fantastical. The family is sleeping at home. "Figures, shadowy, nearly soundless, all black, are almost floating up the stairs as if borne on a wind." Kimberly, in her bed, is startled, her eyes filled with fear, her face illuminated by a flashlight. The light moves to her parents' room. The figures move toward the bed, "murmuring in a kind of hissing foreign language," and their hands touch Eriksson's wife. Eriksson tries to get out of bed, alternating between groans and grunts, and suddenly wakes up, gasping for breath like a "drowning man bursting to the surface with a cry." The image recalls the panicked face of James Stewart's

Scottie, emerging from his nightmare in Alfred Hitchcock's *Vertigo* (one of De Palma's favorite films), except that Eriksson isn't in his bed but sitting on the same bus we saw him on at the start of the script. The figures described in the nightmare are not identified, though they presumably refer to the indeterminate silhouette that blinds Eriksson with a flashlight in the short scene following the prologue. The mention of a "foreign language" instils doubt about their true identity. It feels like Eriksson is haunted by North Vietnamese ghosts, or even Oanh herself.

This version apparently didn't convince De Palma, and Rabe quickly abandoned it. In version IV, Rabe tries another approach by integrating the nightmare into the scene (present in every draft) of the journey home on the plane. He reintroduces the idea of revenge that he had eliminated in his third draft. Immediately after the dialogue with Evans, Eriksson falls into a deep sleep. Other soldiers are on the plane. Some rise and move toward him, then suddenly throw themselves on him and immobilize him while "a figure in combat fatigues, a diamond-decorated knife clutched in the hand, the face covered in a stocking-mask," approaches him. It is Meserve. He slides his knife under Eriksson's throat and begins to cut him. The nightmare ends with Eriksson waking up on the bus.

Perhaps what De Palma didn't like in this new version was Rabe's removal of the characters of Kirsten and Kimberly. De Palma, long since drawn to scenarios in which a threatened family man has to protect his own (there are sequences like this in *Obsession* and *The Untouchables*), asked Rabe to do a rewrite that was more in line with the first draft as submitted to Paramount. In draft V, the nightmare is dissociated from the scene on the plane and occurs once Eriksson has returned home. Exhausted, he falls asleep while reading a story to Kimberly. The girl then goes to find her mother: "Mommy, Mommy, c'mon. Look what happened to Daddy." Kirsten stands in the bedroom doorway, tenderly observing her husband, explaining to their daughter that he is "so tired." After an unspecified period, Eriksson wakes up on the subway train that he boarded at the beginning of the script, and is then seen driving his car in a light rain. He arrives at his house, parks, climbs the stairs, enters, and closes the door behind him. Kirsten awaits him and a smile lighting up her face, but

Eriksson instantly sees a threatening figure behind her. It is Meserve, knife in hand. Eriksson rushes toward him, grabbing a bedside lamp and wielding it as a weapon to defend himself. The rest of the nightmare is identical to the previous version, except that Eriksson wakes up a second time on the subway – the first awakening being a false one, a technique De Palma had already experimented with in the epilogue of *Carrie*. It is assumed that these changes were due to De Palma's suggestions to Rabe, who took them up without much conviction.

There was another more significant disagreement between Rabe and De Palma concerning the final scene of the film. "I very much wanted the quiet scene on the bus," says Rabe, "and wanted it to end the film from whenever I first read the ending in Daniel Lang's book and began to think of the story in terms of a film. What I disagreed with was the tone of the ending and the setting. I wanted Eriksson, the girl, on a bus in a Midwestern landscape surrounded by farmland, it's snowing – she drops her groceries, he helps her with them, and then when they are outside in the snow, he says 'Chào cò,' 'Hello, miss' in Vietnamese and she answers 'Chào ông,' 'Hello, sir' and walks off into the snow with him watching."[50]

The version Rabe is describing appears in version IV. When Eriksson sees the young Vietnamese girl on the bus, he is spellbound, unable to look away. Even though the screenplay doesn't state it, it is clear that she physically reminds him of Oanh. A conversation between Eriksson and the driver, included in the first three drafts, was wisely excised by Rabe as it broke the melancholic, poetic and almost dreamlike aura surrounding Eriksson by pulling him back to the mundane present. Rabe also omits a line spoken by the young woman after Eriksson addresses her in Vietnamese: "You had a bad dream." Not only is this line reinstated in version V, but it is also followed by another line (highlighted in **bold** in the following excerpt) that sparked much discussion upon the film's release.

EXT: DAY: ELEVATED STATION STOP

The girl steps off, followed by Eriksson.
Snow is falling. The girl stops and waits for him.
He hands her the bag.

GIRL
                    Thank you.

          *She looks at him, smiling,
          then turns to leave.*

                    ERIKSSON
          Chào cò.

          *She stops, looks at him sharply,
          understanding.*

                    GIRL
          You had a bad dream…?

                    ERIKSSON
          Yeah…

          *She looks around at the bright air,
          the space, the falling snow.*

                    GIRL
          It's over now… I think…

          *He looks up into the falling snow.
          She reaches out to touch his arm.*

                    GIRL
          Chào ông.

          *She turns and starts walking. Eriksson watches a
          moment, then starts away himself.*

Reading this ending, so different from his original version, one grasps Rabe's reservations. The inclusion of these two lines underscores De Palma's intent to craft a positive conclusion to the film as the young woman unburdens Eriksson, steering him toward resilience. It can be presumed that she, too, had fled her country and is part of the Vietnamese community in the United States, as if the American Dream has finally eclipsed the Vietnamese Nightmare. On paper, this ending is problematic. Although well written and emotionally charged, the underlying message too hastily dismisses Eriksson's trauma, and more importantly the tragedy endured by Oanh and her family, for whom the nightmare never ended – something that the final moments of the trial, with Yen's harrowing testimony, made abundantly clear.

Lang's original text suggested redemption, but with greater subtlety: "He had yet to exonerate himself from the self-imposed charge of having failed to save Mao's life. He had no idea how long this feeling would continue, but for the present, he knew, he lived with the charge daily, often wondering how Mao might have fared in a time of peace."[51] Rabe's screenplay offers no clear timeline between Eriksson's return and the subway encounter. However, the injunction to "turn the page" is too abrupt, and clashes with Eriksson's troubled conscience, reigniting his inner turmoil rather than offering a liberating resolution.

From Paramount's apprehensions to Columbia's certainties

Eager for feedback on Rabe's screenplay, De Palma had his friend Steven Spielberg read the initial draft. Spielberg – who had just finished a film set during the Second World War, *Empire of the Sun* (1987), and was preparing a third Indiana Jones instalment – offered suggestions and expressed reservations about the nightmare at the end of the film, particularly when one of the assailants turns out to be Eriksson himself, which De Palma saw as "a kind of symbol of his guilt." "Spielberg told me that scene wouldn't work, that it was impossible," he recalls.[52]

Reactions at Paramount were divided. Dawn Steel liked the script, but Ned Tanen, whom she worked for, wasn't happy. "You can't make a movie about a bunch of soldiers raping and killing an innocent girl. No one will go see it," he cautioned.[53] Ultimately the studio, deterred by Tanen and an escalating budget (which went from $17 million to over $22 million), pulled the plug, and Rabe's adaptation, like all those before it, faced the prospect of being shelved.

De Palma didn't hesitate to invoke a clause in his contract stating that he could "offer the project to another studio if Paramount turned it down."[54] He was fortunate in his timing. Dawn Steel, who had been a supporter of his for years, was – after being fired from Paramount – now at the helm at

Columbia Studios. At 41, she had become "the most powerful woman in Hollywood."[55] Columbia executive Amy Pascal was also highly receptive to Rabe's screenplay, and together the two women took up the project. "When she came to Columbia," recalls De Palma, "the first project she greenlit was *Casualties of War* – the most depressing, miserable story you can imagine. And she let me make it precisely as I wanted. It's a rare thing to be backed by a studio executive in that way."[56]

Steel was likely reassured in her decision by the fact that every major film about the Vietnam War had done well at the box office. *The Deer Hunter* brought in $48 million on a $15 million budget, and *Apocalypse Now*, which might have turned into a fiasco due to its chaotic production, was a commercial and a critical success (the film tied with Volker Schlöndorff's *The Tin Drum* to win the Palme d'Or at the 1979 Cannes Film Festival). *Platoon*, which only cost $6 million, brought in $138 million, and was released to enormous critical success and endorsements by veteran associations. The more moderate success of *Full Metal Jacket* (which made as much as *The Deer Hunter* but with a budget twice as high) didn't dampen optimism. Steel's calculation was simple: a new film about Vietnam, with a director of De Palma's caliber in charge, had every chance of success.

Upon approval of the script, and whether or not the studio was aware of the previous legal battle between Warner Bros. and Rob Houwer and Michael Verhoeven, Columbia took steps to protect itself from potential lawsuits. Notably, Robert Storeby was sought out. He was allowed to read the script and a signed release was obtained from him, though he chose not to meet with De Palma, Rabe and the actors. Apparently in collaboration with David Rabe, Columbia made a FOIA (Freedom of Information Act) request and obtained copies of the trial transcripts, which arrived less than two months before the start of filming,[57] followed by photographs presented during the various military trials.[58] The studio then took care to request certified copies of the documents (carefully bound, to prevent any pages from being removed or inserted), which arrived at the studio in May 1988, a month and a half after filming had started.

Perhaps Columbia hoped to preempt any potential accusations of plagiarism from one of the previous screenwriters who, as Heywood Gould told me, had approached the Writers Guild of America, seeking to claim their rights. A list of all the writers involved in the project since 1970 was sent to each of the authors, including Gould, who discovered the name of Pete Hamill. Gould decided to withdraw his name from the list out of respect for his former friend, and perhaps because that WGA complaint came from Hamill. We don't know the outcome of this arbitration, but we can be sure that Columbia's foresight likely saved Brian De Palma's film from a legal quagmire.

Pre-production
October 1987 – March 1988

The Pre-production of *Casualties of War* proved to be lengthy and intense. Only a filmmaker in full command of his abilities could have overcome the endless hurdles of moving the project from one studio to another. There was a stream of problems involving location scouting, casting, accidents and soaring production costs. But luck – which seventeen years earlier had deserted Jack Clayton – now smiled on Brian De Palma. Determined to bring his vision to life, he was ready to jeopardize the cachet *The Untouchables* had won him.

Casting
Considering the film's subject matter, the production had little chance of securing necessary funds without top-tier actors attached. While the screenplay was being written, one name lingered in David Rabe's mind: Sean Penn.

At 27 years old, with several important roles already under his belt, Penn was regarded as one of the most talented actors of his generation. As the son of a veteran (actor and director Leo Penn, a bombardier and tail gunner during the Second World War[1]), he understood the kind of emotional toll endured by soldiers. The role of a G.I. seemed to align well with his profile – especially gritty Sergeant Meserve. And yet Rabe was initially convinced that Penn would make an excellent Eriksson. "I was thinking about the working-class quality Eriksson should have, and I felt having Sean there would be like Brando in *On the Waterfront*, that kind of presence at the core of the movie. But the people putting up the money weren't – because, I guess, of where Sean was at in that time."[2]

Sean Penn in *Fast Times at Ridgemont High*

In the mid-1980s, Penn became a fixture in the tabloids due to his volatile behavior and frequent run-ins with paparazzi and law enforcement. Anticipating the studio's potential reaction, Art Linson, who had already produced a film featuring Penn (Amy Heckerling's *Fast Times at Ridgemont High* [1982]), made him an offer. "I remember sending him Rabe's script and saying: 'You can play either part.'"[3] Penn himself recalls "some conversations with David Rabe about the Eriksson role."[4]

But Paramount executives vetoed Penn, insisting they wouldn't back *Casualties of War* if he were cast in the lead role. De Palma, Rabe and Linson had no choice but to acquiesce, and Penn agreed to play Sergeant Meserve, who was more in line with his combative public image. Penn was primarily motivated by the prospect of working for the first time with De Palma, a filmmaker he respected, despite not always sharing his aesthetic choices.[5] Penn has spoken of being "a sponge" when he worked with great directors, wanting "to pick up on the things that would be of value to my own tool kit as a director."[6]

With Penn on board, the production needed to find an Eriksson. "Sean was on everybody's list," explains Linson. "But Michael J. Fox's name came out of nowhere. One day, Dawn Steel said, 'We need a bigger name. We can't get Tom Cruise...' And that's how Michael J. Fox's name came up. To be honest, at that time and from my producer's perspective, I was convinced the decision had been made mainly to please the financiers. Michael came from the comedy world. He wasn't an obvious choice to play a soldier. But for Dawn Steel and the Columbia executives, his name made all the difference. Sean was excellent, but they wanted someone more glamorous."[7]

Fox was known for his light-hearted, comedic roles as Alex Keaton in the TV series *Family Ties* (1982-89) and Marty McFly in *Back to the Future* (1985). But De Palma intuited that Fox could play Eriksson with the necessary conviction and innocence, and thus reach "a whole generation of kids who have not had a direct experience with the war – to have them see the war through his eyes."[8] To convince himself, De Palma organized a dinner to which he invited the actor. "I was a little nervous," admits Fox. "Somebody said, 'He's difficult to talk to.' But [...] if you talk about movies, not about him, you can't shut him up. We hit it off okay, had a long talk."[9] De Palma didn't mention Rabe's script during dinner, but the next day Fox found a copy in his mailbox. "Later, I thought back and realized he was [...] sizing me up, casting me while we talked."[10]

Michael J. Fox in *Family Ties*

Fox's first reading of the script left him unsettled.[11] Moved by the character of Eriksson, he had no idea how to play the role. The Vietnam War had felt to him like "a scary TV show" when he was a young boy.[12] A puzzled Fox talked to his father, who had been in the Canadian Armed Forces and who explained that events similar to those in *Casualties of War* had occurred during the Korean War, which he himself had experienced, adding that "such incidents should be viewed as isolated."[13] Fox asked his fiancée, actress Tracy Pollan, to read the script because he wanted to "have a woman's perspective" and ensure that there was "nothing offensive" in it. She found the script devastating. Her reaction prompted Fox to meet with De Palma to discuss the rape and the moral issues it raised, as well as the reasons behind Meserve and his men's decision to commit the crime. In particular, Fox feared that a "circumstantial alibi" might be used to explain – even excuse – the soldiers and frame them as "victims" of war. De Palma brushed aside his doubts and convinced him to commit to the film.

Casting director Lynn Stalmaster, who had previously worked with De Palma on *Blow Out* and *The Untouchables*, set out to hire a host of supporting actors, each of whom would have to be ready and willing to spend several months in difficult climatic conditions and form sufficiently close relationships with each other to recreate a sense of military camaraderie. Don Harvey, who had appeared in *The Untouchables* and had just finished filming John Sayles' *Eight Men Out* (1988), was told by De Palma during his audition that he had the part. To save time, the production held auditions in various locations across the United States. Candidates – who were given only a brief passage from the script – recorded a scene in pairs. These tapes were then sent to Stalmaster, Linson and De Palma, who made a selection. This was how John C. Reilly was recruited, initially for the relatively anonymous role of Streibig, a soldier who loses his arm during the night battle scene in the jungle at the beginning of the film and who has just a line or two of dialogue. "I was in Chicago, doing theater and trying to get work," says Reilly. "I knew it was an important audition, so I decided to make the videotape with a friend of mine. I would read for him and he would read for me. We went to this agent's office, and we both did a much better job, I think, than if we had read with the agent."[14]

Holt McCallany, who auditioned first in front of Stalmaster, was called in a second time. "We were auditioning in pairs, and I ended up with someone I didn't know, who wasn't very good," he explains. "We hadn't rehearsed. We went in front of Brian De Palma and read something, but the guy was really bad. I genuinely thought I wouldn't be chosen. Most actors didn't even know what role they would be playing. There were dozens of roles to fill, so when I auditioned, I didn't know which role it was for."[15] McCallany ended up playing Lieutenant Kramer, who has a few lines early on in the script and dies shortly after the night battle in the jungle.

Michael Wright, who had delivered a feverish performance in Robert Altman's *Streamers*, was cast as Brown. The role of Hatcher went to Stephen Baldwin and Diaz to John Leguizamo, who recalls: "I auditioned with the end monologue of the movie and a scene or two against all the top Latin actors of the time: Benjamin Bratt, Luis Guzmán, Benicio Del Toro… I won the role and was so excited because now I could be independent."[16] Lieutenant Reilly and Corporal Rowan would be played by Ving Rhames and Jack Gwaltney, and Gregg Henry, who had appeared in *Scarface* and *Body Double*, was hired as the prosecutor in the final part of the film.

Location scouting

Where to recreate 1966 Vietnam? Eric Schwab was tasked with scouting locations. At the age of 24, a graduate of the UCLA Film School, Schwab had been eager to learn as much as he could about filmmaking, and was hired by De Palma to work on *Body Double*. Once De Palma realized he was dealing with a cinephile with encyclopedic knowledge, a strong bond formed between the two men. Impressed by Schwab, De Palma hired him to work on subsequent films and ended up giving him increasing responsibility, notably on *The Untouchables*, where he was promoted to location manager. Schwab, who quickly became De Palma's "most trusted advisor"[17] when it came to location scouting, wanted yet more responsibilities, so he gave De Palma an ultimatum: he would work on *Casualties of War* only if he could be second unit director. De Palma immediately agreed.[18]

In October 1987, De Palma, Linson and Schwab met to decide on the filming locations. "My guess is that today we would have shot *Casualties of War* in Vietnam, but thirty years ago it wasn't feasible, both for financial and political reasons," says Schwab. "In Thailand there were experienced film crews, plenty of military hardware, and extras," adds Linson. "We also received an enormous amount of cooperation from the government. I don't even know if there were film crews in

Vietnam. And the war was fresh in people's minds. It was still a deep wound."[19] The production leaned toward the Philippines, where Francis Coppola and Oliver Stone had already convincingly recreated the conflict. The country offered a triple advantage: visual (the geography resembled Vietnam), technical (the film crew could work hand in hand with the Philippine army, which was providing weapons and extras), and economic (it was less costly compared to other countries with similar geographical features).

But in late October, current events intervened, when three American servicemen were killed in an attack by communist guerrillas on a base north of Manila.[20] Fearing the situation might worsen, Columbia postponed the scouting and began looking for a different location.[21] In November, Schwab traveled to Thailand and the following month to Australia and Mexico. Studio executives suggested that the forests in those two countries might more or less be plausible stand-ins for Vietnam. Skeptical, Schwab had no difficulty convincing De Palma and Linson that Thailand was the best possible choice. It neighbored Vietnam, had similar flora and fauna, and was home to a vibrant Vietnamese community.

After spending New Year's Eve in New York, Schwab returned to Thailand in early January 1988 to continue location scouting. He received assistance from Sompol Sungkawess, who had worked on several films shot in the region, including *The Killing Fields* (1984) and *Good Morning, Vietnam* (1987). The primary filming locations were chosen – all except one.

"On every film I do," explains Schwab, "especially on De Palma's, there is usually a key scene that is visually very precise. It isn't really a matter of how it's written in the script but rather a matter of knowing what Brian is trying to get from it, and finding a way to accomplish that, both dramatically and visually."[22]

That key scene in *Casualties of War* is Oanh's death, which is a narratively intricate sequence. On a hilltop, Meserve and his men face off against communist fighters positioned below, near a river's edge. Simultaneously, within the patrol itself, Eriksson battles his comrades as he tries to prevent Oanh's murder. While the dialogue and physical movements of the characters were very specific in Rabe's screenplay, details of the location were vague, meaning that Schwab had freedom in finding a location that would amplify the scene's dramatic and cinematic potential.

During his travels, accompanied by Sungkawess, Schwab ventured into the region of Kanchanaburi, northwest of Bangkok. The two reached the bridge overlooking the River Kwai, the famed structure that inspired Pierre Boulle's renowned novel, adapted by David Lean into an equally famous film in 1957 (one of De Palma's favorites). Following the path of the railroad, nicknamed the Death Railway because of the significant number of prisoners of war and civilians who perished during its construction, Schwab and Sungkawess arrived at a section of track on a mountainside surrounded by dense vegetation, with the river below. Convinced that he had found the right place to film Oanh's death, Schwab hurriedly called De Palma to tell him the good news.

The crew

We should be wary viewing a film through a purely teleological lens that focuses solely on the omnipotent director. While the director is undoubtedly pivotal to the project, we must not diminish the significant contributions of crew members across various departments who are deeply engaged in the film's production, each playing a crucial role beyond merely the execution of the director's vision. The pre-production phase, including the recruitment of a crew, is a decisive factor in determining every film's eventual fortunes.

Co-producer and production manager Fred Caruso, who began his career in the late 1960s, was tasked with recruiting the *Casualties of War* crew. Caruso had worked on *Midnight Cowboy* (1969), *The Godfather* (1972), *Once Upon a Time in America* (1984) and *Year of the Dragon* (1985) primarily as a production manager, but also occasionally as an associate producer or executive producer.[23] De Palma, who worked with him on *Dressed to Kill* and *Blow Out*, was aware that Caruso's experience on large-scale productions would be a major asset for a film like *Casualties of War*. Caruso's job wasn't just to assemble the best possible crew but also to anticipate any problems that might arise during filming, especially since De Palma had never filmed outside the United States before, let alone in a jungle. A diverse crew gradually emerged, combining newcomers with some of De Palma's regular collaborators, notably Bill Pankow and Maurice Schell, picture and sound editor respectively. Pankow's collaboration with De Palma dated back to *Dressed to Kill*. Until *The Untouchables*, he worked in the shadow of Jerry Greenberg, the director's designated editor. *Casualties of War* was Pankow's first solo editing credit on a De Palma film.

Maurice Schell, fifteen years older than Pankow, had worked regularly alongside some of the most illustrious filmmakers of New Hollywood, including Sidney Lumet, Arthur Penn, Bob Fosse and Francis Coppola. Born in Paris in 1937, Schell was in hiding during the war before emigrating with his father to New York in 1949. His first job was as an apprentice editor for groundbreaking documentary film duo Albert and David Maysles.[24] Schell later shifted to fiction – his first experience dates back to *The French Connection* – and found a mentor in Edward Beyer, known for his work on *Scarecrow* and *Serpico*. It was thanks to Beyer that Schell joined De Palma's *Scarface* crew as a sound designer.

Cinematographer Stephen H. Burum first worked with De Palma on *Body Double*. Between 1965 and 1967, during his military service, he was stationed at the Army Pictorial

Stephen H. Burum on the set of *Casualties of War*

Center in New York, where he shot numerous training films and had his first experience working on helicopters. Twelve years later, when Francis Coppola asked him to lead the second unit of *Apocalypse Now*, Burum already had experience with aerial sequences. Hired after a devastating typhoon had destroyed a significant portion of the sets in the Philippines, Burum accepted the challenge and worked closely with Vittorio Storaro, the film's cinematographer, before reuniting with Coppola for *The Outsiders* and *Rumble Fish* (both 1983). His military experience and the harsh weather conditions he had faced, as well as his previous involvement in films set against the backdrop of the Vietnam War, made him an ideal candidate for *Casualties of War*. A number of technicians (camera assistants, grips, etc.) were placed under his direction, among them Steadicam operator Larry McConkey.

A graduate of Cornell and Temple Universities, McConkey started out as a cameraman in the 1970s. Like many, he first noticed the Steadicam when it was used by Haskell Wexler in Hal Ashby's *Bound for Glory* (1976), and quickly became so adept at using the revolutionary camera stabilization system that he caught the eye of Garrett Brown, the device's inventor. The two subsequently collaborated to develop the very first system for a camera suspended in the air, named Skycam. McConkey, whose credits include films directed by Martin Scorsese (including, later, the legendary Copacabana Steadicam shot from *Goodfellas* [1990]), Alan Parker, Peter Weir and De Palma, worked for the first time with Burum on *The Untouchables*. On one occasion, after McConkey successfully executed a complex shot, De Palma – ordinarily sparing with compliments – praised him in front of the entire crew. "That was my first clue that I might be at the start of a long working relationship," recalls McConkey.[25] His relationship with Burum was just as important. While the two proved themselves on *The Untouchables*, an entirely different challenge awaited them on *Casualties of War*, to be filmed under exceptional climatic and topographic conditions.

For assistant directors, Fred Caruso had in mind two British ADs he had met on the shoot of *Year of the Dragon*: Brian W. Cook and Michael Stevenson, regular collaborators of Michael Cimino and Stanley Kubrick. Stevenson, whose reputation is legendary, also worked as an assistant for David Lean on *Lawrence of Arabia* (1962), *Doctor Zhivago* (1965) and *Ryan's Daughter* (1970), and for Richard Brooks on *Lord Jim* (1965), an adaptation of the Conrad novel, shot in China, Cambodia and Malaysia. Cook asked a newcomer, Carl Goldstein, with whom he had already worked, to join them as the third AD. He was the youngest of the crew, and the only other Canadian next to Michael J. Fox. The other Brits who joined the crew were brought onto the project through Michael Stevenson and Brian Cook. Paul Engelen, chief make-up artist, had worked with Roman Polanski, Miloš Forman, John Boorman, Hugh Hudson and Cimino. Props master Peter Hancock, a regular collaborator of Kubrick's, recruited Dave Midson, who had worked with Steven Spielberg and Roland Joffé, and the Irishman Mickey Pugh, who earned his stripes on David Lean's *A Passage to India* (1984).

Engelen, Hancock and Pugh had all previously worked on Spielberg's *Empire of the Sun*, as had a significant portion of the special effects department, which was supervised by Kit West. Terry Cox and Yves De Bono had just finished filming another Vietnam War movie, *The Iron Triangle* (1989), in Malaysia and Sri Lanka. De Bono was also special effects supervisor on *Platoon*. Production designer Wolf Kroeger from Germany had worked on two recent films with Vietnam backdrops – Ted Kotcheff's *First Blood* (1982) and Robert Altman's *Streamers* (1983) – and had previously shot in Northern Thailand with Cimino on *Year of the Dragon*, where he met Fred Caruso. Costume designer Richard Bruno, a regular collaborator of Martin Scorsese, had the complete trust of De Palma, having worked on his two previous films. Among his crew were Julia Mansford, who worked on *Year of the Dragon*, and Laurie Riley, whose credits included Cimino's *The Deer Hunter* and *Heaven's Gate*. Sioux Richards, the script supervisor, had worked with Scorsese and on *The Untouchables* with De Palma.

It was the first time an international crew had ever been assembled for a De Palma film. As well as an office in Burbank, the production had another in London, where Sallie Beechinor oversaw significant coordination work, making sure, she explains, "that everyone was in the right place at the right time with the right equipment to do the right thing."[26] Alongside

Americans and Britons, the cosmopolitan crew included Canadians, Australians and, of course, Thais. Thanks to Sompol Sungkawess, Caruso's Thai counterpart in Bangkok, local assistants were recruited for various departments (camera, costumes, transportation). For extras, the production drew on the Vietnamese community in Bangkok.[27] "We really wanted Vietnamese and not Thais," says Eric Schwab, "because they express themselves very differently."[28]

Casualties of War's on-set photographer Roland Neveu began his career in the mid-1970s as a photojournalist, and in April 1975 documented the fall of Phnom Penh to communist forces. Holed up in the compound of the French embassy with other foreigners, Neveu witnessed the expulsion of Cambodians who had been hoping for political asylum, among them photojournalist Dith Pran, colleague and interpreter of American journalist Sydney Schanberg. Nearly a decade later, Neveu was shooting photos on the set of Roland Joffé's *The Killing Fields*, a Hollywood representation of the very events he had lived through in Phnom Penh. "I got along very well with Joffé, who cared a lot about the realism of his film and asked me many questions. Several times, in fact, I had to intervene on the set to explain that things hadn't unfolded exactly that way."[29] The production even bought some of Neveu's prints when building a version of Phnom Penh in Thailand. Two years later, Neveu found himself on the set of the film that would mark his definitive transition from journalism to on-set photography: Oliver Stone's *Platoon*, the first of several Vietnam-era films he worked on. When approached by Columbia about *Casualties of War*, Neveu accepted without hesitation. His contract stipulated that he be present throughout the filming but not pre-production, which, in hindsight, he regrets because he missed out on documenting the actors' training. On set, Neveu was given no specific instructions. "The production just hoped that I could take at least one photo as good as those I had taken on the set of *Platoon*," he explains.

Desperately seeking Oanh
Early 1988. Location scouting was complete, the crew was assembled, the cast was more or less finalized, set construction was underway. Filming was to begin in just under two

months. De Palma's biggest problem was that he hadn't yet found an actress to play Oanh. His insistence that the part be portrayed by a Vietnamese, while logical, complicated the search, as there weren't many suitable actresses available. The production conducted extensive searches across America, Europe and Asia – including China and Singapore – in major cities where there were substantial Vietnamese communities. Most auditions proved fruitless. Fred Caruso reported that "dozens and dozens" of candidates were preselected. "Some of them seemed suitable, some of them could have done the job, but they just didn't have that particular thing Brian was looking for."[30]

In early 1988, the search focused around Paris, where De Palma had connections, including his friend Régis Wargnier.[31] France was a haven for thousands of Vietnamese refugees who had fled Saigon after it fell to North Vietnamese forces in April 1975. Scattered across the country, the highest concentration was in and around Paris, especially in the 13th arrondissement. It was in February that 23-year-old Thuy Thu Le first heard about the *Casualties of War* casting through her fiancé, who had spotted an announcement posted on the window of an Asian restaurant.

Le had no aspirations to become an actress. Born in 1966, the year Phan Thi Mao was murdered, she was the youngest of ten children. In April 1975, her father, who held various high-level political positions in South Vietnam, hastily fled Saigon with part of the family, anticipating the arrival of the communists, who considered him a traitor. Le, two of her brothers and their father boarded a boat bound for the Philippines and eventually reached the United States.[32] "We needed a sponsor, someone who could vouch for us," she says. "A friend of my father who worked at the Vietnamese embassy took charge of our arrival."[33] After landing in a Vietnamese refugee center in Florida, the family settled in California. Years passed, during which Le completed her education in the United States. Then, about to turn 23, she decided she wanted to spend a year in Paris, where years earlier one of her brothers had settled as a student and where he was now preparing for his wedding.

Le would never have considered auditioning if she hadn't noticed De Palma's name. She had seen *The Untouchables*, which she loved, as well as some of the director's other films (*Carrie*, *Scarface*), and was looking forward to meeting him. The filming would also provide an opportunity to earn some money that could be used to pay for her studies. "My brother had been an extra in one or two films," she explains. "He told me about his experiences, and it sounded like a good idea. He said, 'It's easy. You don't have to do much – just stand behind the actors.' But if I had known they were auditioning for the lead female role, I would have never shown up for the casting session." The announcement that a Vietnamese woman was sought included no details of the film, not even its title. On the strength of De Palma's name alone, Le decided to show up at the auditions in an office in Paris. Fred Caruso describes the experience as "one of those magical things" that life can sometimes unexpectedly throws at you.[34]

"There were lots of young women," recalls Le. "I wondered why they were looking specifically for a young woman and not extras of all ages and sexes." While waiting her turn, she heard screams coming from behind a closed door. "That was odd," she says, "because you don't scream like that when you're an extra." When Le was finally called into the room, she was welcomed by a casting director, told to face the camera, and scream, which she did. She was then briefly thanked and her phone number taken, in case she was needed again. Three days later, an unexpected phone call from the casting director announced De Palma's arrival in Paris to meet her in person.

Le later learned that De Palma showed her audition tapes to Art Linson and Michael J. Fox. Fox, in particular, found her "very convincing." De Palma, who shared his lead actor's enthusiasm, actually had another actress in mind who happened to have the same first name – Thuy An Luu – and who had appeared in Jean-Jacques Beineix's *Diva*. Both women were asked to join De Palma and Linson for lunch at Les Deux Magots in the sixth arrondissement (one of De Palma's favorite spots). No one talked much about the film, but, says Le, De Palma "immediately made her feel at ease," and at the end of the meal he and Linson had made up their mind. The part was hers.

After being given a copy of the script, Le was immediately struck by the power of the story and Rabe's writing style, but she had reservations about filming a rape scene and appearing partially nude on-screen. "It bothered me because I wasn't an actress," she says. "I found myself with an important role in the film when I thought I was being recruited for a small part. I absolutely didn't seek to become an actress, and I wouldn't have done just anything to get the role, certainly not appearing nude." De Palma, convinced he wouldn't find a better candidate, offered a compromise: all scenes involving nudity would be shot with a body double. Le accepted. After finding an agent and signing her contract, she boarded a plane for Thailand, ready for the start of filming in April 1988.

War games
In the late 1980s, Phuket was relatively untouched by mass tourism, one reason why the production chose to recreate the Vietnamese jungle and build a military base there. "A group of about 20 actors traveled to Thailand together," says Don Harvey. "All men. It was a long trip. Everyone was wildly excited to be there. We played cards the whole way on the plane. We all drank a lot and talked about our expectations. I felt like we were actual soldiers on our way to war. We all started getting to know each other, building the relationships that would last and grow throughout the shoot."[35] For some it was their first trip abroad and their first airplane flight. They stayed at the Pearl Village Hotel – all except for Sean Penn, who with Brian De Palma and Art Linson preferred the luxurious Amanpuri Resort Hotel, situated in an idyllic setting on Pansea Beach. The crew was based at the Dusit Laguna Hotel.

Upon arrival, the actors – as would any actual military recruit – donned uniforms and got their hair cut. On the first day of rehearsals, a small group led by John C. Reilly decided to rent scooters and explore the island. They sped along the winding roads without helmets, reveling in an irresistible sense of freedom. After a few miles, they reached an intersection indicating a waterfall to the right and the town of Patong, known for its massage parlors, go-go bars and brothels, to the left. "Well, it's gonna be waterfalls or poontang!" exclaimed one of the actors. "Of course, everyone screamed 'poontang,'" says Reilly.[36]

On their way to Patong, the actors encountered a group of locals on scooters who thought they were real American soldiers and challenged them to a race. At one point Reilly was thrown from his bike, narrowly avoiding riding over a cliff. His damaged scooter was picked up off the road with the help of a Thai truck driver, and the bike's owner was paid off to keep quiet. In intense pain, Reilly thought he might have broken his collarbone. The actors boarded a van that took them back to their hotel. "As we pulled up outside the hotel, Michael Stevenson came over and handed us each a piece of paper. 'The following activities are prohibited to all cast members: motorcycling, skateboarding, surfing, roller-skating, running…' There were maybe 15 or 20 things listed. 'Anyone caught doing any of these things will be fired.'"[37]

The actors refrained from informing Stevenson about Reilly's misadventure, and upon returning to Pearl Village held a crisis meeting to try to help their comrade. "Call Michael Fox. He's cool," someone advised. Fox, who hadn't been part of the excursion, was initially staying at the same hotel as the rest of the cast (he later moved to the Amanpuri). When Reilly approached him, the actor cordially invited him into his room and asked what was happening. He then called Fred Caruso and, without telling him why, explained that the young actor had had an accident and needed to go to hospital. An X-ray eventually revealed only a sprain and Reilly was advised by a local doctor to wear a sling for a week. (When De Palma inquired during rehearsals about his mishap, Reilly claimed he had been running with Jack Gwaltney on the beach when he stumbled and fell against a log – a tale that De Palma found hardly convincing.) At the very last minute, Reilly was deemed fit enough to join the military training that the actors were about to undergo.

That training was supervised by Warriors Inc., a company created in the mid-Eighties that offered military expertise to filmmakers.[38] Its primary mission, explains founder Dale Dye, a former Marine captain and Vietnam War veteran, "was to tell the truth and correct many misconceptions about the American military in general, and the men who served in Vietnam in particular."[39] *Platoon* served as a kind of prototype for Dye. Hired by Oliver Stone as a technical adviser, he experimented for the first time with intensive training in the heart of the jungle before filming, a process designed to give actors "an idea of the hellish conditions experienced by the grunts [...] to enhance the authenticity of their performance and foster the essential camaraderie among them for the film."[40]

Dale Dye as Captain Hill in *Casualties of War*

In early 1988, Dye learned that De Palma was preparing a film about the Vietnam War. Dye had heard about the murder of Phan Thi Mao while in Vietnam but hadn't read Lang's article and wasn't familiar with the details of the case. Intrigued by De Palma's project, he used his connections to reach Art Linson, which led to meetings with De Palma, who eventually hired Warriors Inc.[41] Dye also convinced De Palma and Lynn Stalmaster to cast him in the film as Captain Hill. "I was aware that our work on *Casualties of War*," he says, "especially in making the Vietnam sequences credible, might serve to further the image in many minds that kidnaping and rape were common occurrences among American troops in Vietnam. They were not, and crimes like the one depicted in the film were certainly not the rule. That meant I was a little nervous about both providing advice and appearing in the film. But in the end, I decided that the story needed to be told and that if it was to be filmed, the least we could do was to provide some kind of context. I felt that the role of Captain Hill, and the confrontation he has with Michael J. Fox's character, provided a bit of that."[42]

During production on *Casualties of War*, Dye was also working on the ABC television drama *Supercarrier*, set on a fictional aircraft carrier, so he suggested to his friend Mike Stokey,[43] also a Vietnam veteran, that he lead the training camp in Thailand in his place. The actors were required to learn military jargon and do things like personalize their helmets with character-inspired slogans. Don Harvey's helmet, for example, bore the phrase "Your ballroom days are over, baby," a line from The Doors song "Five to One"[44] which subtly reflects Clark's passion for the California rock group as well as serving as an ironic commentary on the actor's condition, pushed beyond his comfort zone, and, in the song's title, Oanh's ordeal. After mental conditioning came physical preparation, with the actors learning how to handle weapons – notably the M-16 – and spending their days performing a series of exercises, such as attacking bunkers while carrying "forty pounds of gear."[45]

Not everyone was a novice, starting with Penn, who recounts: "When I heard the film company was offering military training, and knowing myself, I immediately felt a 'competitiveness' looming. A bunch of young actors out in the Thai jungle, each wanting to outdo the other. I'd already come to a point in my work in movies where I was very mercenary about my own personality. I also did have, though not yet fully cinematically mature, an understanding that THE REALITY of any preparation would inevitably conflict to varying degrees with fulfilling one's role in the shorthand and poetic license that film must almost always take. And, certainly this would be the case in the high art of a Brian De Palma film. So, I chose first to train independently, to understand in live-fire terms what we would be taught later under the liability of a film's training program with blanks. Still, I would be an actor learning basics. Live fire or not, I faced no real enemy. Nobody that would actually want to take my life. But at the very least, I felt the pull of a lethal trigger and heard the crack of lethal reports around me. With this, I took to Thailand. I quickly made a point of checking into a separate hotel from the rest of the cast. Most were younger than I was, and I could foresee speed competitions in blindfolded assembly and disassembly of M-4[46] series weapons. I could foresee late nights of poker, carousing drinking contests. Prostitution is also a factor for Thailand tourists. So, I generally kept to my own den. When we began the jungle training, I did find it exhilarating, despite the fact that many of my fellow actors were indulging in all the aforementioned recreations."[47]

Don Harvey and Stephen Baldwin had already undergone military training for the filming of *The Beast*, directed by Kevin Reynolds, in the Negev Desert, also under Dale Dye's supervision. But it was the very first training of this kind for the other young actors, including Holt McCallany. "We did exercises, and we had to cope with stifling heat, insects, snakes… Gradually, we began to feel a real respect for the soldiers who had to fight in such conditions. It's easier to fight in a desert, in Iraq, for example. Sure, there's heat, but it's not the humidity of Vietnam. We were constantly in the sun during training, which lasted for hours and hours at a time. Mike Stokey saw that I was suffering, and I remember him telling me that a soldier would be severely punished, even court-martialed, if he stopped because of the heat."[48]

According to Stokey, the training for the actors in *Casualties of War* was significantly less physically demanding than what the cast of *Platoon* endured, and far less demanding than what Warriors Inc. put the performers of later war films through, notably Spielberg's *Saving Private Ryan* and Terrence Malick's *The Thin Red Line*. "Usually," explains Stokey, "it's 24 hours a day, seven days a week, a week to two weeks – sometimes even three – in the field. The actors really get to walk in soldier's boots. They carry their gear and weapons, and learn how to reload and what to do about jams and malfunctions. We didn't have that luxury on *Casualties of War*. We were shorthanded, and they gave us an 8 to 5 schedule each day. But this isn't something you can teach on a blackboard. You take people into the field, immerse them in the experience of a boot camp, where they're getting very little sleep, they're hungry, they get ambushed at night, they have to go out on long-range patrols, and you watch them evolve. They really get to understand and taste the fatigue, because most of combat is just that: boredom and fatigue punctuated by moments of fear and horror."[49]

De Palma didn't see the value of more rigorous training because compared to most Vietnam films, there are few battle scenes in *Casualties of War*. "The script didn't demand all that we usually provide," says Stokey. "It was a small reconnaissance unit, so we didn't have to train scores of people and teach them all how to handle and strip down weapons. We went over those things, but it certainly wasn't an exhaustive boot camp."[50]

Sean Penn and Mike Stokey

One member of the training team was Stanley White, a Vietnam War veteran and homicide detective, who had gained a certain notoriety because of Michael Cimino's *Year of the Dragon* (the main character of the film, played by Mickey Rourke, was based on him). When assembling the *Casualties of War* crew, Fred Caruso recruited White through Brian Cook, the first assistant director on Cimino's feature.

"The first day we started training," recalls Don Harvey, "I was paired up with Sean Penn. We were instructed to face each other and alternate punching each other in the stomach. At first, everyone was a bit timid. We weren't hitting very hard. Eventually Stanley was yelling at us, telling us to hit as hard as we could. Here I am, opposite one of the greatest actors of my generation, and I'm punching him in the stomach – repeatedly. Another thing Stanley made us do was what he called The Thinker. We got down in a push-up position and then modified it so our elbows were on the ground and our hands were on our cheeks, holding our face, so you're holding up your midsection and you're basically immobile with your toes and elbows holding you up. You start shaking after a while. I think he kept us in that position for five minutes or more. This stuff was designed to toughen us up and make us feel like real soldiers. I loved it."[51]

During a martial arts session, White insisted that Michael J. Fox come at him and try to punch him in the face. Hesitant, Fox mumbled an excuse, but White insisted. When Fox eventually complied, moving forward to strike, White grabbed him, lifted him over his shoulder, and threw him to the ground.[52] De Palma was alarmed by some of the reports he was receiving about the training and worried that the physical exercises might cause serious injuries, potentially delaying the shoot.[53] White quickly became De Palma's target. "You're being too hard on them," pleaded De Palma. "They just need to *look* like soldiers."[54] His ideas about acting training clashed with White's and, more broadly, with the Warriors Inc. blood, sweat and tears philosophy.

In fact, says Carl Goldstein, one of the few crew members who participated in military exercises, the actors spent only one or two nights outdoors.[55] But De Palma, increasingly fearful that an accident might happen, was on high alert for any mishap that would give him a reason to fire White. The opportunity soon presented itself. "The guy phoned Sean Penn in the middle of the night. 'Gather your men in the perimetre at zero two hundred.' That's two in the morning. 'You're crazy!' said Sean. 'This is a movie we're making here. We aren't fighting a real war.' I ended up replacing that weirdo with Dale Dye."[56]

From that point on, the actors underwent more conventional training, distinct from any rigorous Marine regimen. This approach was more in keeping with the film's storyline, as the characters belonged to the regular army, not an elite unit. With White gone and Mike Stokey as the sole training supervisor, Fred Caruso called on someone he knew only by reputation: Major Art Smith. A Vietnam veteran and a graduate in film production, Smith had split his time between filmmaking and the military since the late 1960s, notably serving as a consultant to Robin Williams during the filming of *Good Morning, Vietnam*. "I conducted the training, teaching the actors how to be part of an infantry platoon or squad and follow the orders of their platoon or squad leader," says Smith. "They learned how to patrol, set up an ambush, day and night defense, secure their base camp, that kind of thing."[57] During downtime, each participant was addressed by their rank, "to keep unit integrity," explains

Smith.[58] For those who needed to use the radio, compass and other specialty skills, he did specialized training. Smith went so far as to give Ving Rhames a map of Thailand during the night battle in the jungle, so the coordinates he gave in his radio call were real.

Rehearsals

With Art Smith's arrival, workdays were typically structured into two parts. In the morning, the actors learned how to handle their weapons and practiced military maneuvers. After lunch, they convened in a large conference room at the hotel that had been requisitioned for rehearsals. For most of the actors, this was the first time they had read David Rabe's complete screenplay.

"Brian had brought lots of extra actors who didn't really have parts assigned to them," says Don Harvey. "During these rehearsals, guys would read different parts and every day Brian would switch them up until he found the right person to play each role."[59] One of these supporting actors quickly stood out: John C. Reilly, originally slated for a minor role.

"I was coming out of a theater background, so it felt like rehearsing a play," says Reilly. "I was very familiar with being in a room with a bunch of actors, reading a script and bringing it to life. That was really my strong suit at the time. I had been given this tiny part at the beginning of the movie. During rehearsals, as we went through the script, sometimes there would be a need for someone to play a character, like an old Vietnamese man in a village who the soldiers were interacting with. Brian said: 'Who wants to say his lines? John, read it!' Then they needed someone to play the role of a military policeman in the scene when the soldiers try to leave the base to go to the brothel. I was a hundred percent committed, and I guess Sean and the other actors were entertained and surprised by my enthusiasm and ability to completely become this elderly Vietnamese man and this military policeman. I think it sort of charmed them – even though I was not trying to charm them – and they felt like, 'Wow, this kid can do anything.'"[60]

One glitch disrupted the otherwise smooth rehearsal process. Michael Wright, in the role of Brown, had strong convictions about his character. A little too strong, according to De Palma, who, says Holt McCallany, "wanted Brown to be a cheerful character, adored by everyone, someone who made the whole troop laugh, whereas Michael Wright preferred to portray him very tormented."[61] The actor, perhaps still haunted by Carlyle, the character he had played a few years earlier in Robert Altman's *Streamers*, was fired. The role of Brown was immediately handed to Erik King, who had gone through auditions and was supposed to make a brief appearance at the very end of the film as Evans, the injured soldier who boards the plane with Eriksson to return to America. King was flown in and joined the actors in the midst of training and rehearsals. Now in need of someone to play Evans, De Palma hastily arranged an audition and asked Reilly to participate.

"In front of the entire cast, I had to audition," says Reilly. "My arm was in a sling because of my accident, which was perfect for that scene because the soldiers on that plane were supposedly injured and returning home at the end of the war." Reilly was given the part. He says that after reading Rabe's script in its entirety for the first time, and being handed a copy of Daniel Lang's original *New Yorker* article, his understanding of the film grew immeasurably. "At the start of rehearsals, I was more like, 'Let's play soldiers…,' because I grew up with G.I. Joe action figures. It was every boy's fantasy to be a cowboy or a soldier, to carry a gun. But once I read the whole script, what I was doing took on a completely different dimension. What initially was just a little boy's game transformed into a very serious endeavor."[62]

Some of the actors conducted their own research to deepen their understanding of Vietnam and the situations their characters would face. John Leguizamo read a number of books about the war[63] and Erik King spoke to family members and friends who had fought in Vietnam. "I was intrigued about the day-to-day coping mechanisms of the soldiers," he says, "and decided that my character, Brownie, would wear two rabbit feet around his neck. That came from an interview with a veteran who had worn one for good luck. In the film, I wore two, thinking that perhaps Brownie needed extra luck. But he gets killed, so perhaps they cancelled each other out."[64]

Penn struggled to get into the character of Meserve. Shortly before heading to Thailand, he confided in Rabe:

"I don't know how to *do* this guy." "I couldn't understand what he was worried about," clarifies the screenwriter, "but evidently, when he got over there he *still* didn't know."[65] Penn worked to find the right tone for the character throughout rehearsals. "I only got the character the day before shooting," he says. "It was one where I leaned heavily on a specific person I knew: an aggressive guy who had a dark secret."[66] Then came the idea to mimic his voice: "vernacular English as spoken by working-class New Yorkers."[67]

Sean Penn and Erik King

Simon Laisney, who when writing about Penn's performance has focused on the actor's vocal modulation, hypothesizes that by altering certain sounds and almost never stressing final syllables, Penn seemed to have wanted to "sketch the portrait of a young man from the social or socioeconomic category that accounted for the highest enlistment rates in the army during the Vietnam War."[68] But in light of the work of sociolinguistic founder William Labov, Laisney qualifies his remark, indicating that the New York accent "known as Brooklynese is no longer confined solely to the boundaries of those communities, having become, in the eyes of many young Americans well before the 1960s [...] a symbol of toughness, resilience and defiance against authority."[69] Consider here Gina Marie Weaver's notion that the accent chosen by Penn accentuated the social category of his character, representing him as "deviant rather than normative."[70] Penn's intentions were evidently more subtle. Once the contours of Meserve were outlined, Penn could embody the character without truly having to explain his choices to the filmmaker. "Brian gave me one of the most liberating directions I'd ever gotten. Perhaps one of the most dangerous as well," says Penn. "I'd been very understated in rehearsals, just trying to find my way in Brian's bigger picture. He said, 'You're a truth machine. There's no too far. Go too far.' If I indeed went TOO FAR, that's on me. If it worked, that's on him. Marrying both was David Rabe, as extraordinary a writer as we've had in our time."[71]

Recreating Vietnam in Thailand

Set construction was entrusted to Wolf Kroeger, who oversaw a large crew. "I couldn't tell you how many people I had under my supervision," he says. "The whole department stayed in the same hotel, and we occupied the entire dining room. That gives you a good idea of how many people there were."[72] Fred Caruso recalls a budget of $3 million for construction, with most sets – with the exception of the railroad in Kanchanaburi – having to be built from scratch.

The first significant set in the film is the North Vietnamese tunnel in which Eriksson gets trapped. De Palma saw the visual potential. He envisioned the camera moving from surface level to below ground, showing the audience what lies beneath Eriksson's feet (a communist fighter armed with a knife, ready for battle). De Palma got the idea from Tom Mangold and John Penycate's book *The Tunnels of Cu Chi*, about the 180-mile maze of tunnels around Siagon dug by the North Vietnamese. Wolf Kroeger chose to create the tunnel on the edge of the forest, in an area near a rubber plantation infested with cobras. His crew cut into a mountainside and dug an underground passage, around which was placed vegetation (trees, plants, bushes) and an artificial jungle. De Palma wanted to shoot the scene with a Chapman crane, which has a telescopic arm mounted on a wheeled base, so a track had to be built to allow the passage of the truck on which the crane was mounted.

Construction of the tunnel

The design team also built the military base camp (nicknamed "Wolf" in tribute to the production designer), the village where the soldiers patrol at the beginning of the film (which included an artificial river), the village where Oanh's family lives, the abandoned hut where she is raped and held captive by the soldiers, and the partially destroyed hillside temple where the discussion between Eriksson and Captain Hill takes place. Elephants were used to transport timber and other construction material.[73]

Arriving six weeks before filming began, Paul Engelen undertook various preparatory tasks. "I manufactured some limbs to use for the skirmishes that we were going to shoot, particularly the night attack where some soldiers are injured. One has his arm blown off at the shoulder and a couple of guys have their legs blown away. I made several leeches of varying sizes and colors that we were going to use when the cast were in the swamps. I did some tests on Thuy Thu Lee, for the scenes where her character is assaulted by the soldiers, and I met with Sean Penn to discuss the scar we decided he would have on his left brow and talk about some tattoos he wanted. As I recall, in the end, the only one we went with was one on his forearm."[74]

Construction of the tunnel

In late March 1988, the team was ready to begin filming. De Palma, a tech enthusiast, made use of a computer program called Storyboarder to plan every shot. Using simple stick figures, he defined the actors' placement within the frame and planned camera movements and the duration of each shot. Once the design work was done, the program could play back the entire storyboard, scene by scene, "keeping each sketch on-screen for the appropriate amount of time."[75]

De Palma could thus pre-visualize his film "before a single frame was shot." His method resembled that of a music composer – a comparison De Palma himself embraced: "It's like a music score. All the notes are there. I looked at this and I knew exactly how the movie would look. And if it doesn't work, you change the script to fit the storyboard. Because if something doesn't work here, it's not gonna work on the screen, and you're not gonna save it in the editing room."[76]

This statement, made by De Palma shortly after the film's release, offers insight into his relationship with Rabe's script (and, presumably, all others he has worked on over the years – including those he wrote himself). For De Palma, the screenplay can be broken open and altered to fit his visual strategy because the visual impact of a sequence outweighs its narrative plausibility. While he never modified the overall story structure, a comparison between the screenplay of *Casualties of War* and the finished film reveals that De Palma intervened in several places by eliminating characters, changing the order and appearance of certain sequences, and even inventing new ones, without necessarily informing Rabe.

The function of storyboards is to provide precise instructions to technicians regarding framing, movement and overall dynamics. "We always talked through Brian's designs and I tried to interpret them," says Eric Schwab.[77] Stephen H. Burum, not a fervent advocate of storyboarding, acknowledges that De Palma's rudimentary sketches helped him visualize key moments in the film and allowed team members to better understand his expectations. "It was very important to proceed this way," explains De Palma, "because when you're filming at night in the jungle, you're completely lost. You have absolutely no idea of where you are, so everything had to be planned in advance."[78] "For Brian," says De Palma's personal assistant, Monica Goldstein, "preparation was key. He was laser-focused, with a clear and unwavering vision of the film he wanted to make and the story he wanted to tell. By the time we shot the movie, Brian had it all cut in his head."[79]

A strategic thinker, perhaps De Palma had in mind Sun Tzu's maxim: "Every battle is won before it's ever fought." *Casualties of War* was clearly the most difficult fight he had yet faced.

Brian De Palma

Brian De Palma's Storyboards

CASUALTIES
OF
WAR

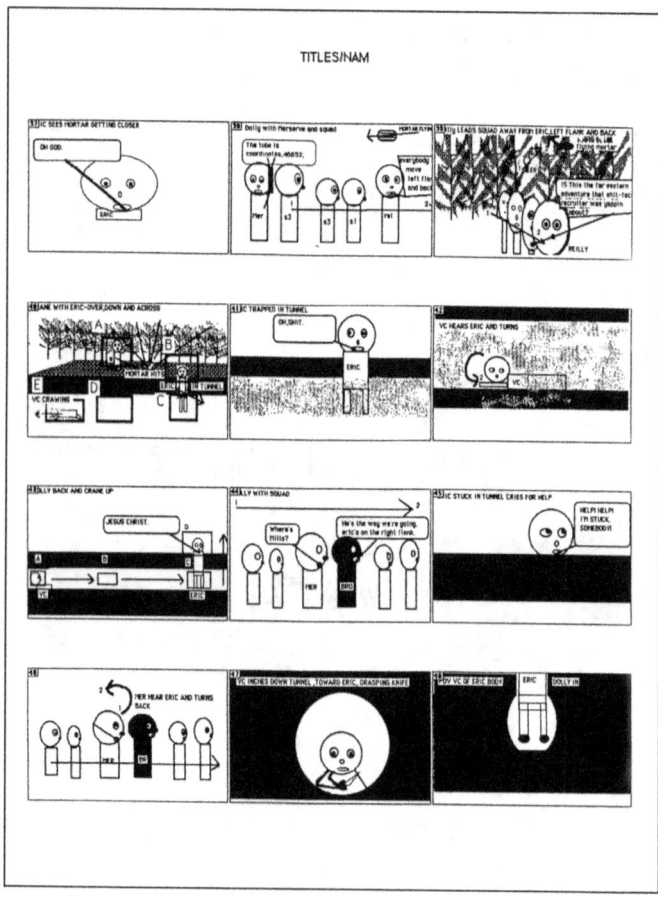

Storyboards

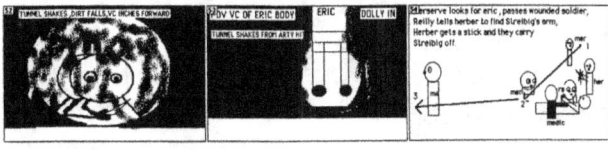
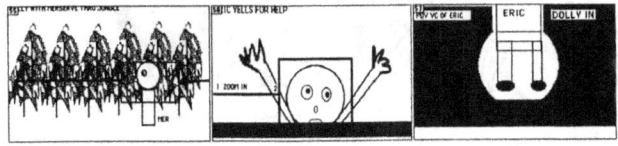

Casualties of War

Storyboards 251

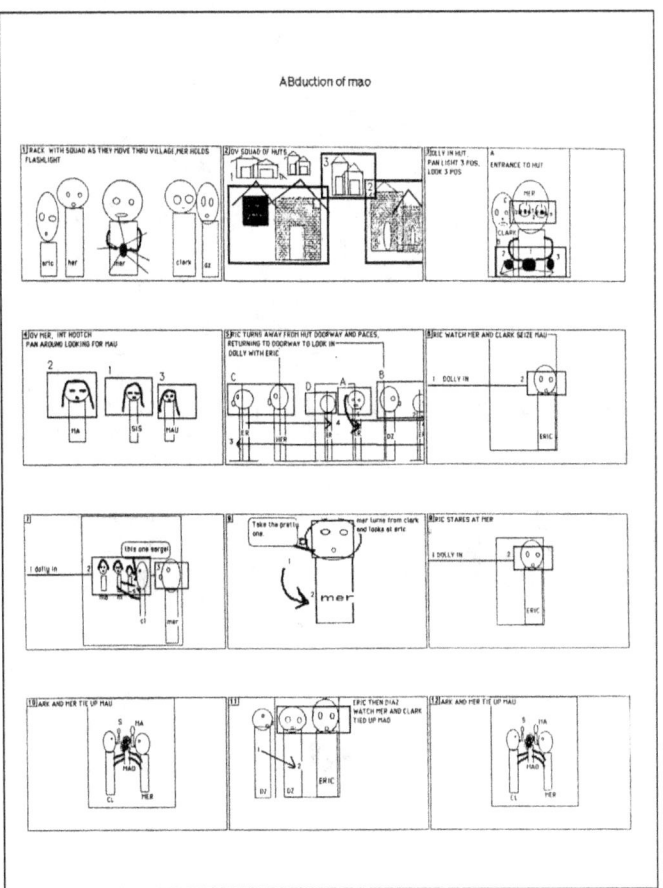

252 Casualties of War

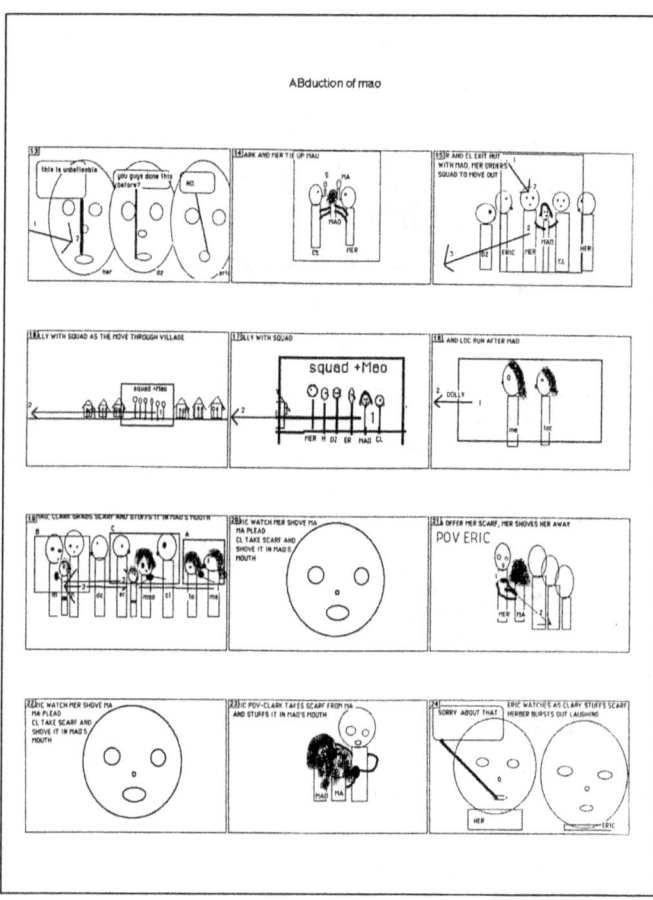

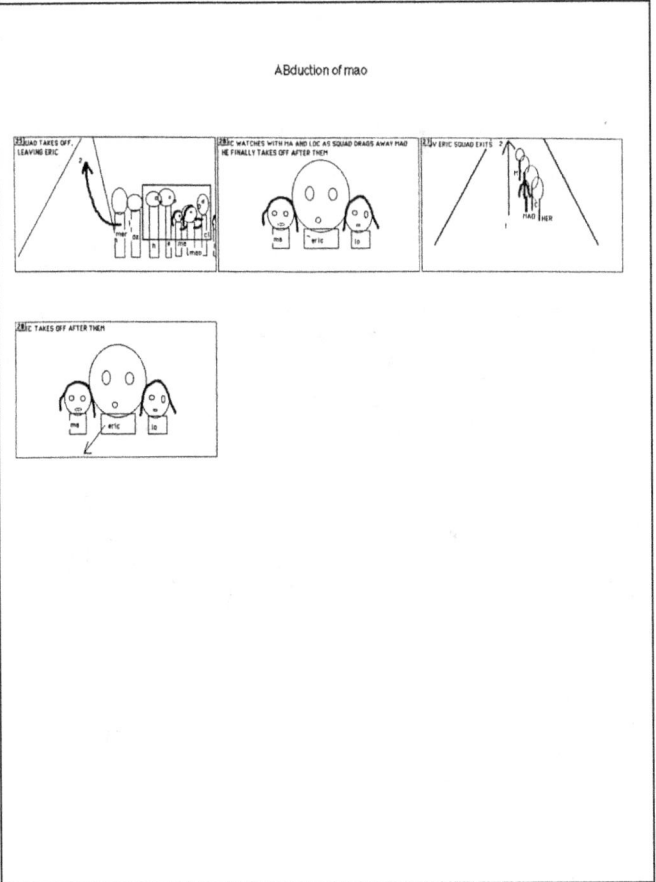

254 Casualties of War

Storyboards 255

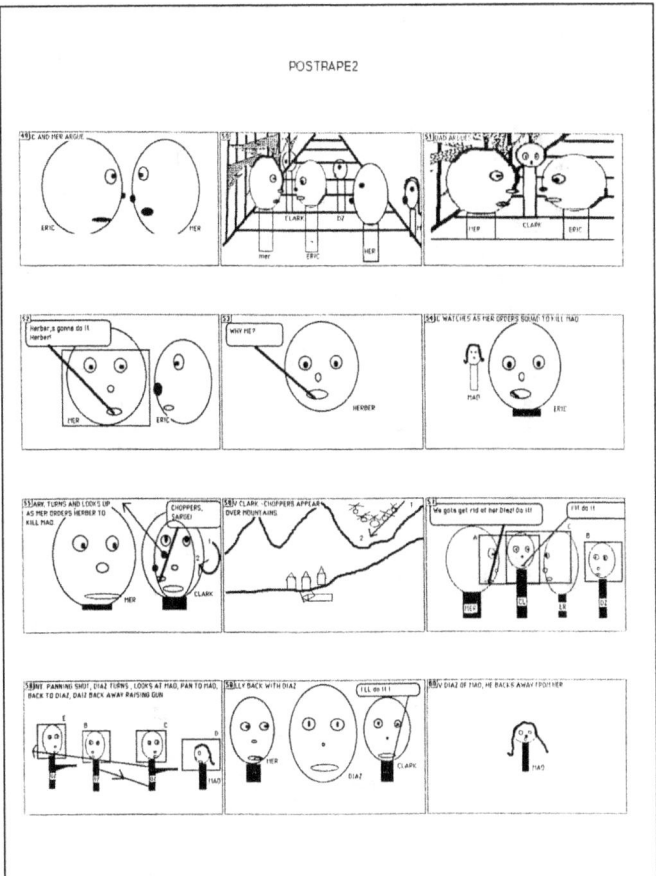

256 Casualties of War

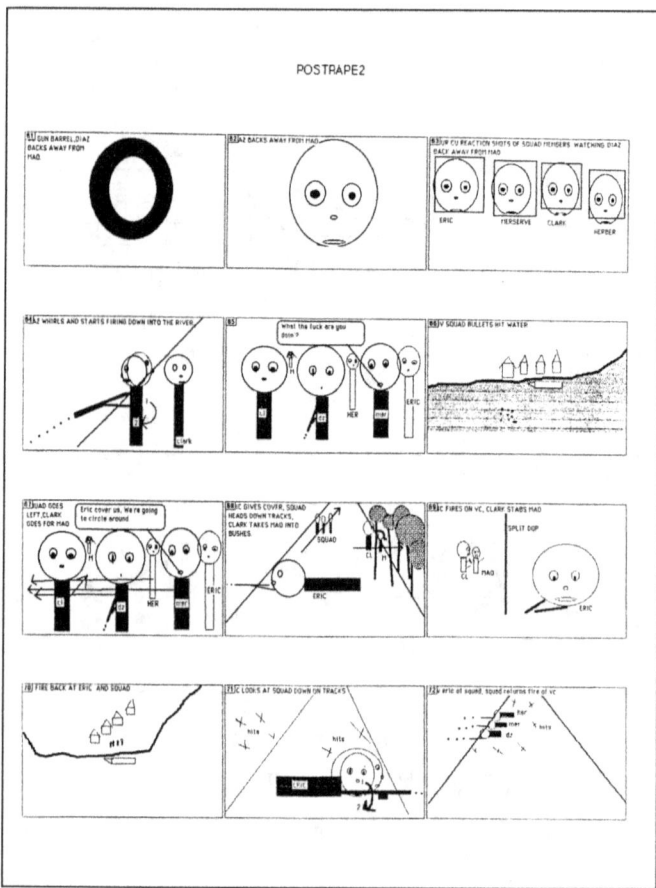

258 Casualties of War

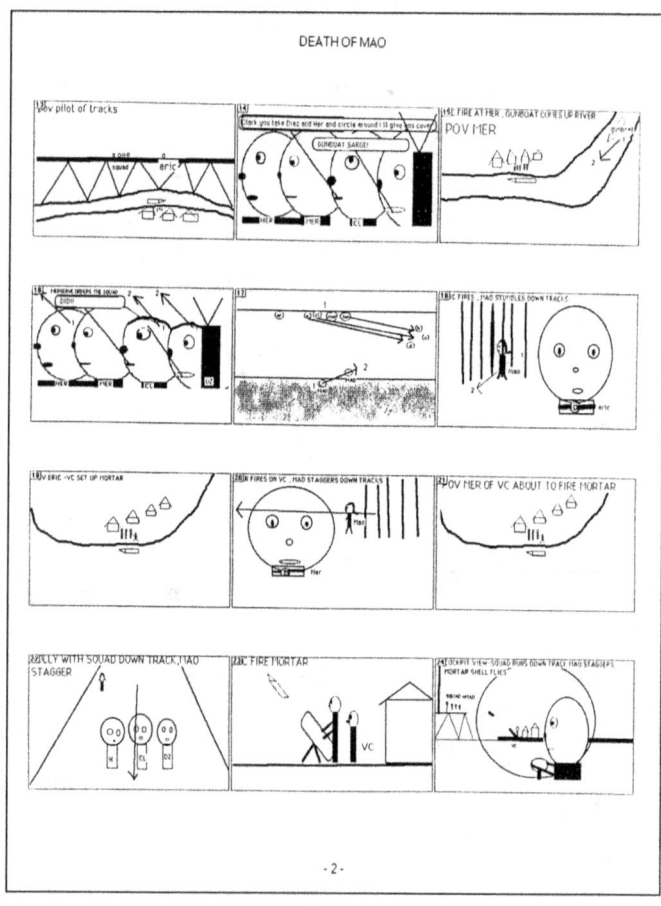

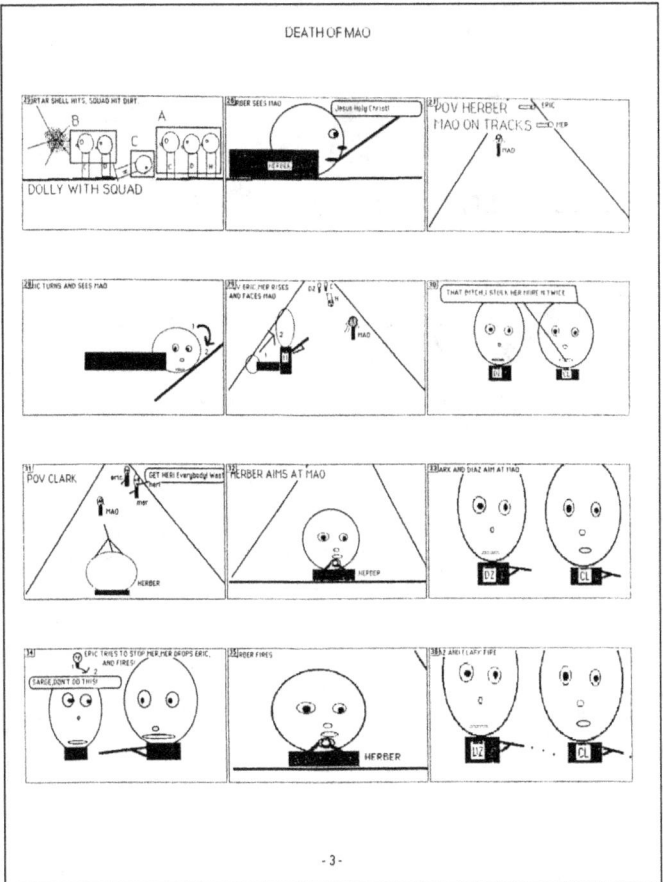

260 Casualties of War

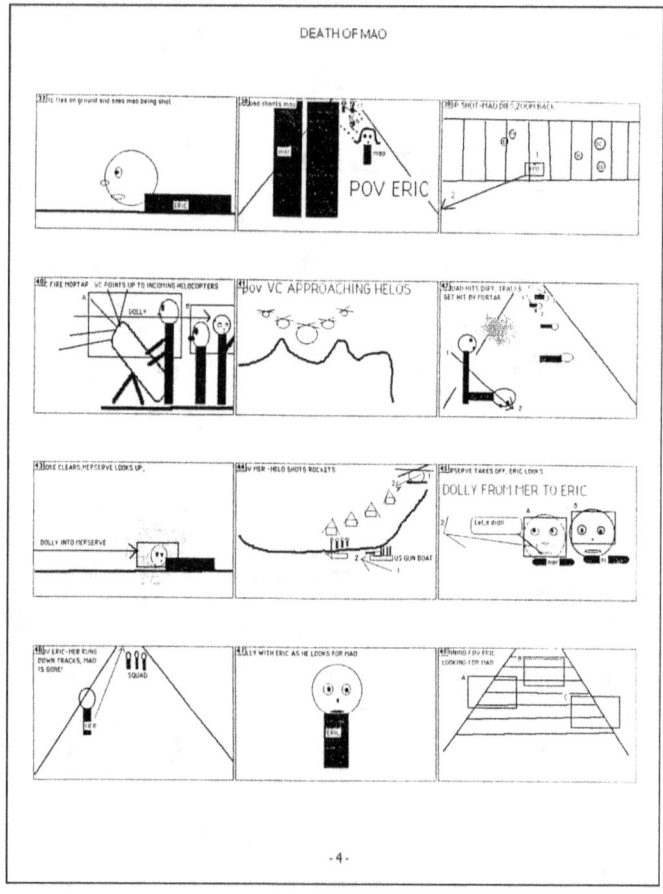

Storyboards

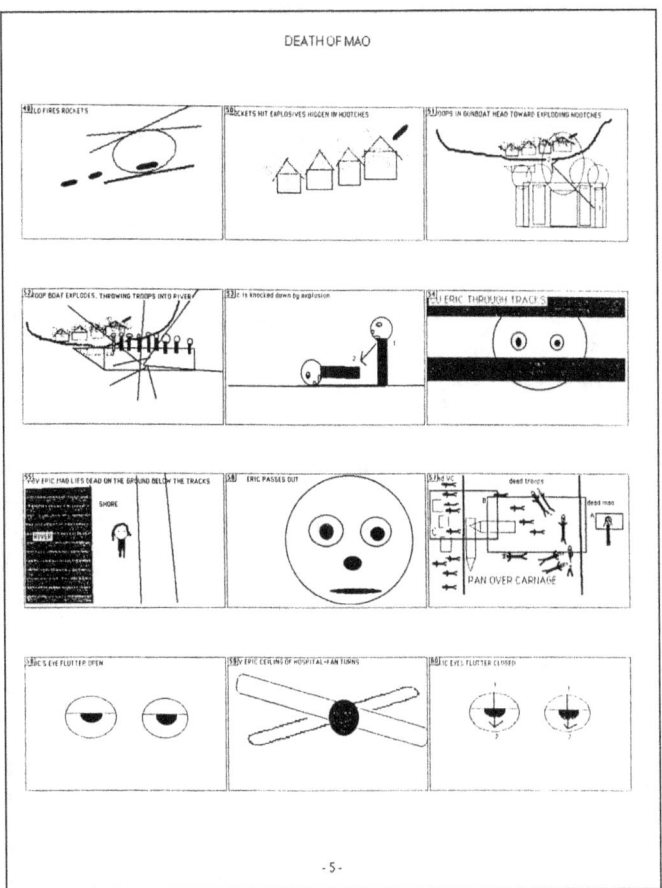

262 Casualties of War

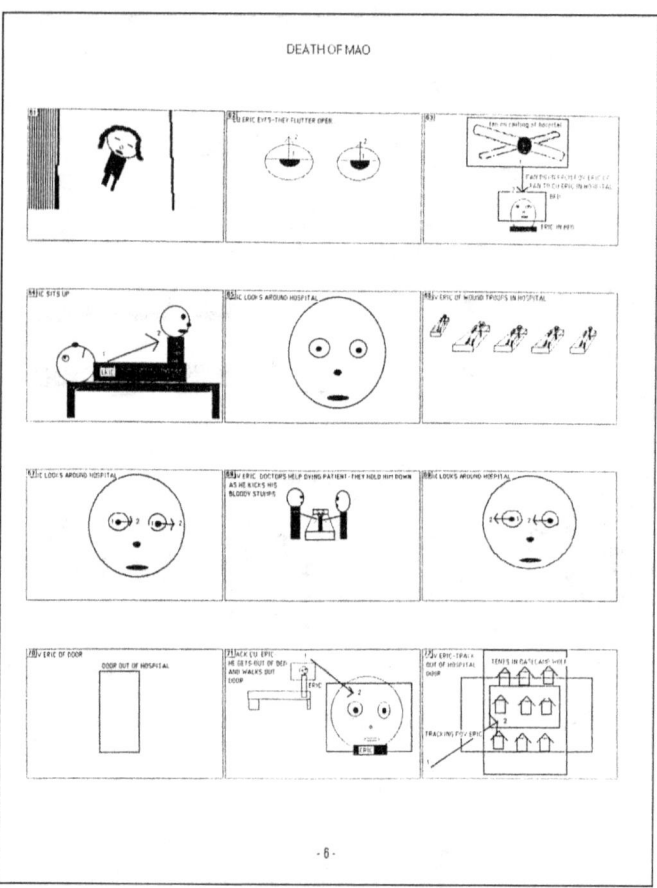

Filming *Casualties of War*:
A Ground-Level Chronicle
April – July 1988

Art Linson has compared the filming of *Casualties of War* to a military campaign.[1] For 75 days, Brian De Palma, as a general would, ensured the smooth progress of operations and strict execution of a battle plan, as carefully devised alongside Fred Caruso, Brian Cook and Michael Stevenson.

"We were shooting in a foreign country," says Caruso, "so if we ran out of equipment, we didn't have the option of calling the studio or the supplier directly and have them rush something to the set. We were deep in the jungle. If we needed something we didn't have, we had to make do without it. That's why it was absolutely necessary to be extremely precise about what we were going to do each day and how long it would take to shoot."[2] The production faced a particularly eventful initial phase. The night battle in the jungle and the sequence in the village, culminating in Brown's evacuation by helicopter, were filmed first. "It was endless," says De Palma. "Every night for a month."[3]

To preserve the unfolding of trauma and the logical flow of events from the victim's perspective, Thuy Thu Le's scenes were filmed in chronological order. But, as is often the case, other sequences weren't necessarily shot in the order they appear in the finished film. Those preceding the patrol's mission and following its return to base camp, including Eriksson's meeting with the chaplain and his interrogation by the CID agents, were scattered throughout the shoot for logistical reasons (equipment use, filming locations, actor availability, etc.). From June 11 to 15, the team focused on the trial scenes before moving to the Kanchanaburi region to film the final battle sequence. Filming in Thailand was concluded at the end of the month, at which point the majority of actors and technicians – except Fox, Le and a reduced technical team, who set about shooting the prologue and epilogue in San Francisco – went home.

The 75 days that the production spent in Thailand came to weigh heavily on some of the cast and crew. Workdays were between 12 to 14 hours, spread across six-day weeks. "We were in a remote area of Phuket, and we had to take vans to the set every day," recalls Don Harvey. "Sometimes it took hours. A lot of scenes were very physical. Running, carrying weapons, gunshots, walking through jungle terrain. There were a lot of night shoots. That really screws you up because you're staying up all night and sleeping all day. After a day or two you feel like a zombie. Then, after you start to get adjusted, you finish the night shoot and go back to days and you have to adjust all over again to a different schedule. It's brutal. As the shoot goes on, everything adds up and you get run down. You're running on adrenaline. You start doing some really interesting acting because you can't just rely on your old tricks. You have to push through to the point where you're not acting anymore. You don't have the energy to act. You just get there and make it happen. It's raw."[4]

"It was tough," says Carl Goldstein, "but at the same time really quite incredible, very formative – like getting your master's degree in filmmaking."[5] Stephen H. Burum, Fred Caruso and Michael Stevenson were an especially strong influence on the younger actors and technicians who, during the months of filming, felt symbolically as if they were living their own *Bridge on the River Kwai*. In Thailand, there was a passing of the torch from the old guard – the illustrious collaborators of David Lean, Stanley Kubrick, Francis Coppola and Michael Cimino – to newcomers who, in front of or behind the camera, each experienced decisive moments of their nascent careers. And Stevenson, with a talent for storytelling, was not stingy with anecdotes. Some evenings, crew members would crowd around him to listen as he told tales of *Lawrence of Arabia* and *Lord Jim*. "He would treat the actors as if they were coming home to Grandma's house," recalls Carl Goldstein of Stevenson's bedtime stories.

At the end of each filming day, De Palma screened rushes in his hotel, in a conference room equipped with a projector.[6]

Brian De Palma (center), Stephen H. Burum (standing)

Crew members – the director of photography, the head makeup artist, the hairstylist, and technicians from the special effects department – were often present, collectively discussing on-screen issues and finding suitable solutions to remedy them (which sometimes involved reshoots). The actors were invited: "We had to be quiet," recalls Holt McCallany. "It was very unusual because generally, directors never do that. Not everyone came because there were many distractions, but some went out of curiosity. I found the process interesting and very useful."[7]

There were no film labs in Thailand, so reels were sent abroad to be developed. "Originally, we were supposed to have the dailies developed in Australia," says Burum. "When we went to scout, I flew there to meet the people at the lab and they all seemed very competent, so I shot exposure tests and sent them over. But we couldn't get them out of customs. This mishap happened, if I remember correctly, about a week before the start of filming, so I suggested that we change labs and go with Technicolor in London, which was the most experienced lab in the world and very used to dealing with international crews. We shot another test and sent it over, and a day later I got a phone call from my contact in London saying that we would receive the rushes within a day. And the next day, we had the dailies back – so we switched over to Technicolor. There were direct flights from Bangkok to London. We would get dailies every other day."[8] Once viewed by the crew, the reels were sent back to Los Angeles for studio executives to look at.

The production resembled a Tower of Babel, with Americans, Britons, Australians, Canadians, French, New Zealanders, Thais, Vietnamese and Malays all working together. Coordination between Western and Thai crews was good, but language posed an obstacle that occasionally slowed operations. "Usually, on a shoot," says Fred Caruso, "when someone says 'Fetch the grip stand,' an assistant rushes over and brings it with no problems, but in Thailand, when the props master asks for the tripod, they first have to speak to a Thai assistant who speaks English, and then this person has to go and translate the request to the Thai props master, who then hurries to get the famous grip stand, so there were always a few seconds, or even minutes, of delay while the order was relayed."[9] To solve language problems, the production distributed T-shirts of different colors to technicians so each department could be identified at a glance (the carpentry crew had red T-shirts and the electricians wore yellow).[10]

This ingenious system didn't safeguard against every mishap. "I remember a problem that occurred while I was working with the second unit," says Pasiree Panya. "I had to prepare the costumes for the scene of the abduction, including the scarf used to gag Oanh. One day, while we were filming in the mountains, I arrived on set and realized the scarf was missing. I had set up all the costumes the night before because I needed to wake up early in the morning, around four o'clock, to leave the hotel and get to the filming location, which was quite far away. I always made sure at least twice that nothing was missing. But that morning, the scarf was nowhere to be found. It was a big issue and I had to use something else instead. Fortunately, that morning, we were shooting wide shots. I rushed back to the hotel to retrieve the second scarf that I had cleaned for the scenes the following day. I got to the bottom of it when, the next day, I discovered that the driver of our van had borrowed the scarf to clean his windshield! It looked like an ordinary rag, so he must have thought it was a piece of cloth of no importance."[11]

Compared to *Platoon*'s modest $8 million budget, *Casualties of War*, at just over $22 million, was a relatively expensive production. De Palma's modus operandi was much closer to Stanley Kubrick's than Oliver Stone's. "De Palma would have shot *Casualties of War* in a studio if he could have," says Brian Cook. "We built the exteriors as if we were in a studio. Brian wanted total control. He's like Kubrick, in a way, even though they think very differently."[12] Roland Neveu agrees: "Compared to all the shoots I've been on, *Casualties of War* was the most technical, the most Hollywood-like. Stephen Burum is the archetype of a cinematographer who uses a lot of equipment and light. Unlike Oliver Stone's films, *Casualties of War* was a complex exercise in cinematographic style. It's a bit paradoxical because you don't realize it when watching the film, which seems less ostentatious than other De Palma movies. The challenge was to portray war in a very realistic way, with technical feats that are normally impossible to achieve in the jungle."[13]

Among those feats is the sequence where Eriksson's legs are trapped in a North Vietnamese tunnel. Perched on a "hydraulic lift 20 feet in the air,"[14] De Palma, like a conductor, directed all his instrumentalists: the cinematographer, lighting technicians, set dressers, pyrotechnicians, actors, all of whom brought to life the visual symphony he had so carefully envisioned. Above where the tunnel was dug, Don Harvey recalls an incredible hallucinatory firework display. "It was utterly crazy, with people running in all directions and fireworks going off under our feet."[15]

Brian De Palma on the Chapman crane

The sequences set at base camp required even more complex logistics. Carl Goldstein, assisted by Mike Stokey, choreographed and rehearsed the extras for the shot immediately following Brown's helicopter evacuation, the first to show the camp bustling with helicopters, trucks and soldiers. "It was a huge set, with maybe a hundred tents," says Goldstein. "We were shooting in anamorphic on 35mm film, so everything was big. We spent two or three days planning the scene, then rehearsed it, setting up everything, and when it came time to shoot it, it was just magnificent, even though it was actually a very short shot – just a few seconds."[16]

Construction of the base camp set

Columbia approached the production's grand scale, bolstered by the Thai army (including jeeps, trucks and combat helicopters), with caution and concern, particularly because De Palma, known for his reputation as a filmmaker with costly demands, did not skimp on the number of takes he shot. "The studio was constantly in panic, afraid that we were going over budget," says Art Linson.[17] Allen Barra, a journalist who visited the set, wrote an extensive article for *The Village Voice* in which he mentioned rumors circulating at Columbia, and hinted that Dawn Steel, who at one point traveled to Thailand, was ready to take drastic measures if the budget crossed the fateful $30 million mark.[18] That threat was never carried out. Fred Caruso communicated daily with Columbia's executives, keeping them updated and reassuring them about the budget, which was never exceeded.[19]

The base camp set

Tropical hell

Even with the most stringent plans in place, some things were beyond anyone's control. Viruses, dehydration and intestinal parasites became a daily ordeal for cast and crew. "At one point or another, everyone ended up in the hospital," recalls De Palma.[20] Michael J. Fox, suffering from gastroenteritis during the training period, was evacuated to Bangkok and placed on an IV drip.[21]

Larry McConkey, unaccustomed to the tropical climate, had a nightmarish first day. Unlike other crew members, the Steadicam operator arrived in Phuket the same week he began filming. Jet-lagged and feeling ill, the following morning he couldn't keep anything down except a bowl of rice. Feeling slightly better, McConkey joined the rest of the crew on their journey out to the filming location. "There was a long bus ride to the army camp set, which was very bumpy, and by the time we got there, I was feeling worse than ever. I got off the bus and realized that I had big blind spots in my vision. I looked at other crew members, and they had no heads! It was very peculiar and disturbing, and I later discovered it was caused by anti-malarial pills, which I quit taking. I decided the possibility of getting malaria was less of a problem than being unable to see. I guess I was looking pretty bad because I was promptly escorted to the officer's tent and laid down on the pool table. I was only vaguely aware of what was happening, but I was given several liquids intravenously by the doctor, every once in a while waking up and hearing crew members passing by the tent: 'I heard he was dying...' After three or four hours, I started to feel good again. I learned the value of an IV."[22]

Atmospheric conditions significantly influenced the shooting process, particularly in the use of helicopters. For the shot of Eriksson unconscious on a stretcher in a helicopter mid-flight, De Palma took a chance. "It was a scene I wanted to shoot, but there were always complications. It took a long time to set up technically, and I saw the light diminishing, and even though the weather wasn't very good, I urged everyone, saying, 'Let's go, let's go...' Everyone told me it was dangerous because of the wind, the potential drift. We went for it, the sky darkened... It was risky, but it was magical."[23]

While the sets of *Casualties of War* weren't swept away by a typhoon (as happened during the production of *Apocalypse Now*), torrential rains continuously pounded the island of Phuket, occasionally accompanied by "hailstones the size of cantaloupes,"[24] which meant filming had to be halted. "The sound guy struggled to push the cart holding the Nagra because mud kept building up, covering its wheels, making it almost impossible to move," recalls Monica Goldstein. "Rain cover was set up to protect equipment. All we could do was wait it out."[25] "We stopped shooting for a couple of days," says Eric Schwab, "and at that point we were really thinking, 'My God, maybe we'll have to leave Thailand and fall back on Australia.' We almost did."[26] Philosopher Fred Caruso soothed spirits: "Let's give ourselves some time before panicking and stepping back."[27] The rains eventually subsided and filming resumed... in sweltering heat.

"There was a lot of trouble with the lenses," De Palma reported a few days before the film's release in American cinemas. "They expanded and contracted, and we wouldn't know it until we'd see rushes a month later and realize this or that scene was out of focus."[28]

The crew used WD-40 daily to prevent equipment from rusting. "Video equipment doesn't seem to last in Thailand," explained McConkey after the shoot. "The Steadicam monitor actually held up better than everything else, but it went down after about a month. The coatings on the monitor just came apart and deteriorated with all the humidity, and the tube shorted out. On my Steadicam, the cables to the monitor have connectors, so I was able to take off the monitor and put up a backup. In this case we had a Panaglide-style monitor that was being used on the 'A' camera and with a little bit of rewiring, I was able to use that. I had a little better resolution and brightness than my own backup – an external viewfinder made by Sony for ENG cameras – but still a poor substitute for the original. I ripped out the electronics in the base of the Steadicam and sent it back to John Seitz along with the monitor. He was able to repair it and get it back to me a few weeks later, but in the meantime, I went through four of the Panaglide-style monitors. One after the other they blew up, shorted out. When my monitor came back, that was a godsend."[29]

The makeup department was among the most affected by the humidity. When shooting took place during the day, the small crew led by Paul Engelen left the hotel at around five in the morning to start working on the actors before it got too hot. Engelen's expertise and knowledge of tropical environments proved invaluable. "I found, for example, that alcohol-based makeup products tend to give more resilience in such circumstances, particularly with blood and bruising effects," he says.[30]

Larry McConkey recalls problems caused by the stifling heat during the filming of the village scene at the beginning of the film. "The set had been built on a narrow dirt road, with thatched huts bordering it. It was almost 120°F in the sun, and I was tightly bound up in my Steadicam vest, which I had carefully bulked up with extra hard foam to increase the connection between my body and the device. It was like wearing a down coat. I did several long takes with the main characters down that road, and suddenly got really woozy. The Thai members of the crew quickly took off the Steadicam and vest, sat me down on an apple box, held an umbrella over my head, and slapped a bottle of water in my hand, while fanning me with a flag. Brian looked a little concerned. How was he going to shoot the scene if I couldn't carry the Steadicam? I was trying to remember where my passport was and how to get my gear back to the U.S. with me. Fortunately, I recovered after about fifteen minutes, as the entire cast and crew just waited. I was determined not to repeat my mistake.

I learned to walk slowly, always on the shady side of the street, wearing a wet cloth behind my head underneath my cap, and to take my metabolism down from New York City level to tropical level."[31] McConkey was much relieved a few weeks later when the monsoon season arrived.

One shot involved the patrol crossing a forest of charred trunks, with Oanh, barefoot, carrying Hatcher's pack. The actors rehearsed the sequence multiple times with a reduced crew, ready to film it the following day. "It was very hot, we were making a lot of back-and-forths on the hill," says Le. "When we finished, I couldn't take it anymore and nearly fainted. I usually handle heat well, but the weather conditions were really extreme."[32] Sean Penn took charge of driving Le back to the hotel. When informed of what had happened, De Palma gave her the following day off, so Eric Schwab set off with the second unit. The shot where Oanh, seen from behind, walks carrying Hatcher's pack, was actually filmed with Pasiree Panya, who served as a stand-in.[33] It was a precarious shot: a real snake crossed the path just after she had walked in front of the camera. "We had a Thai snake wrangler, an expert who brought the snakes for that day of shooting and handled them, trying to keep things safe," says Schwab. "We used a long lens, a 1000 mm, to create the illusion that the snake was closer to Oanh than it actually was. We did numerous takes before getting it right."[34] On another occasion, the crew tried to use a four-foot-long python suspended from a tree for a shot, but the animal proved uncooperative and the idea was abandoned.

"On set, everyone was scared," confirms De Palma. "My assistant director, Michael Stevenson, was frantic. A colleague of his had been bitten by a snake during a previous shoot in the same area. Despite the training they went through, the actors were always on edge. All it took was for someone to yell 'cobra!' and the set was immediately evacuated."[35] "There was a wide variety of creatures unfamiliar to an American or an English crew, whereas it didn't matter to the Thai crew," says Caruso. "They could hear, smell or see a snake which our people couldn't."[36] Locals brought large brooms to beat the ground to scare the snakes away.[37] The actors were only moderately convinced by these rather rudimentary methods. To reassure them, Art Smith explained that snakes hate noise. "And if we come across a deaf snake?" quipped Michael J. Fox.

Pasiree Panya, standing in for Thuy Thu Le

"My first day in the production office, I found myself staring at a large poster filled with images of different species of snakes," recalls Monica Goldstein. "Many had red or orange dots on them. I was told those were the poisonous ones and that many were lethal."[38] Allen Barra reported an incident where a "five-foot black-and-green snake, harmless garden snake or pit viper" caused panic during a hotel lunch shared by De Palma, Linson and Sean Penn.[39] The reptile emerged from the adjacent pool in which it was swimming to slither onto the polished teakwood floor, sneaking between the guests' legs. "Apparently choosing an ankle at random, it wrapped itself around Linson's."[40] Alerted by a waitress' screams, Linson managed to free himself from the snake's grip with a swift kick, while Penn, grabbing a bamboo chair, retreated into a defensive position. The frightened animal fled outside and disappeared into the bushes. It was Penn's second snake encounter. While climbing a steep hill, he had grabbed what he thought was a vine, only to realize he was holding onto a dangerous viper.[41]

Brian De Palma and Michael J. Fox

Bad juju

Floods, hail, heatwaves and an invasion of snakes and mosquitoes – such were the scourges that descended upon the *Casualties of War* crew. And as if that weren't enough... "I think the first shot we did," De Palma said shortly after the film's release, "the dolly fell off and clobbered one of the assistant grips, who went straight to the hospital for ten stitches. I've never worked on a movie where there were so many accidents."[42] Stephen H. Burum also fell victim to a dolly accident while setting up a shot. After his foot was twisted and severely sprained when a dolly wheel came off the track, he was forced to use a cane for the rest of the shoot.[43]

The Thai drivers who shuttled daily between hotels and filming locations were responsible for a series of unfortunate incidents. "Tons of marijuana was going back and forth between Laos and Thailand at the time," recalls John C. Reilly. "All the drivers were stoned and the roads were very dangerous." The situation inspired a great line from Michael J. Fox: "Never drive in a country that believes in reincarnation."[44] "At that time in Phuket, there was one main road," explains Carl Goldstein. "The drivers were maniacs. Every time you got into a car, you were taking your life in your hands. The trucks came around the corner at 80 miles an hour, and you had no way out. I can't count the times we went off the road and ended up in a rice field."[45] On one occasion, a driver swerved to avoid a water buffalo and crashed into another vehicle, resulting in the death of a crew member.[46] A couple of others were injured and went back to London.[47] There were also two murders early on in the shoot: a local costume designer and a massage therapist based at the Pearl Hotel, killed by her husband, tormented by the thought of her working for Americans.[48] "I felt there was some 'bad juju' going down," says Carl Goldstein. "We were all concerned. You don't want to start a film with a couple of deaths."

As the days passed, the problems piled up. Michael Stevenson was forced to leave Thailand temporarily because of the death of his mother, which meant that Carl Goldstein was left more or less alone to deal with the many tasks entrusted to him. "We were filming a scene where helicopters bomb a hill," he recalls. "Typically I wouldn't have done those sequences without at least ten other people helping. I was doing Michael's job plus my own. It was hot, it was brutal, there were 350 technicians and 150 trucks on a single road, on a side of a mountain." Goldstein's job was compounded by the behavior of a Thai assistant. "He had an ego the size of the Grand Canyon. One day, he became upset that I addressed him some way that he felt was insulting in front of the Thai crew. It was the end of a tough day, I was exhausted, and I still had two or three hours of work to do. I went back to the hotel to do paperwork and make sure everyone was ready for the next day. This guy burst into the office, pointed a .44 at me, saying, 'I could kill you right now and make you disappear into the jungle! No one would know. You insulted me!' I had no fucking idea what he was talking about. I should have had him fired, but I didn't flip out, and the next morning I told Fred Caruso and Brian Cook what had happened, and they moved him to the second unit. No one besides Fred and Brian knew – not even De Palma."

Was Goldstein right when he suggested that there was "bad juju" going around? After his hospital stay in Bangkok, Michael J. Fox learned that his fiancée, Tracy Pollan, who had flown over to visit him, was being targeted by a blackmailer threatening to kill her if she didn't call off their marriage. "I remember the phone call. It must have been 3 or 4 a.m. Phuket time when I picked up the phone and heard Tracy weeping, spilling out the surreal details. I felt helpless and angry to be thousands of miles away from this woman who, simply by falling in love with me, had apparently placed herself in jeopardy."[49] After a private detective was hired, the author of the anonymous letters to Pollan – "a lonely, disturbed young woman"[50] – was arrested. Feeling lonely and isolated, Fox developed an affection for a small dog he adopted and nicknamed Sanuk ("peace" or "welcome" in Thai) and who became his companion throughout the filming.[51]

A new Hatcher

Barely recovered from a chaotic start to filming, the production faced another hiccup. Stephen Baldwin, in the role of Hatcher, was drinking heavily, spreading false rumors about Sean Penn, and deliberately violating production safety rules by riding a motorcycle to filming locations – too often dangerously close to the minibus carrying the rest of the actors. "He was out of control," says John C. Reilly. "He probably thought, 'I'm untouchable. We've started filming, so they can't fire me.'"[52] But the production team was seriously concerned and drastic measures were contemplated.[53]

Stephen Baldwin (circled)

Baldwin appears briefly in one scene of *Casualties of War*, as part of the group of soldiers led by Penn that arrives in the village where, moments later, Brown is shot down. Easily recognizable because he is wearing a pair of large, round glasses, he is seen walking behind Michael J. Fox, Don Harvey and Erik King in the long Steadicam shot. Baldwin filmed other scenes, including the night battle and a sequence later in the film where Hatcher believes he has detected a communist, then realizes, after firing his weapon, that he has actually found a water buffalo. On the day of filming,

Baldwin informed some of his colleagues that he planned to enhance his performance with a grimace of his invention, a kind of code he used with his school friends on Long Island. "He moved his chin from side to side," remembers Holt McCallany. "It was a truly ridiculous grimace!"[54] Baldwin assumed that his friends would note his facial distortion and collapse with laughter. McCallany tried to dissuade him, but the actor insisted on going through with it.

The crew was in the middle of shooting the sequence when, at one point, immediately after one of his lines, Baldwin made his famous grimace in front of the camera, subtly enough that no one noticed it at the time. But shortly after, while watching the rushes, De Palma exploded. "I was there on the day when De Palma and Linson watched the sequence that Stephen shot with the water buffalo," confirms Holt McCallany. "When he saw him make that face, De Palma couldn't believe his eyes. He ordered the projectionist, 'Wait a minute… Stop! Go back! Play it again! What is Stephen doing with his chin? It's so BAD! What does it mean? Put in the next tape… He does it in EVERY TAKE!'"[55] The next day, De Palma, in consultation with Linson and Columbia executives, fired Baldwin and replaced him with John C. Reilly. Fred Caruso was tasked with informing the actor's agent and Baldwin himself.[56] The contract breach required the studio to compensate Baldwin, a situation not uncommon in the industry.

Reilly, set to play Evans, had already returned to the United States, since the scene he was supposed to appear in was scheduled two and a half months later. While on his way back, the young actor from Chicago stopped in Los Angeles not just to explore the city but also to visit Alison Dickey, Sean Penn's assistant, whom he had met during the pre-production phase in Thailand and fallen in love with. "I was asleep in her apartment, and I had a dream," Reilly recounts. "My agent from Chicago was calling me, saying, 'You have to go back to Thailand. You're playing a different part.' I was still sleeping when the phone rang and I heard Alison talking to someone. Then she came into the bedroom and said, 'It's your agent.' 'John,' he said, 'you have to go back to Thailand. You're playing a different part.' Exactly like in my dream!"[57] Fearing that negotiations might delay filming, the production kept Reilly in the dark about Baldwin's fate and the specifics of his newly assigned role, but he was made well aware of the urgency to reach Phuket as quickly as possible, and ended up taking a flight from Los Angeles to Phuket via Miami, New Delhi and Bangkok.[58]

In Phuket, Reilly didn't even have time to go to his hotel for a shower or change. The driver who picked him up at the airport took him directly to see Art Linson at Amanpuri, about 40 minutes from the Pearl Hotel where the actors were staying. "When we arrived at Amanpuri," says Reilly, "Art Linson came out and walked toward the car. I hadn't really spoken to him since I had started the movie. I was sitting in the back of the vehicle. He sat in the front passenger seat, turned around, and introduced himself. 'Hello. I'm Art Linson. I'm producing the film.' 'Oh, hi,' I replied. And then, in the simplest manner, he said, 'You're the new Hatcher.' I couldn't believe my ears. 'What?' 'Yeah, you're the new Hatcher,' he repeated, 'the fourth lead of the film.'"

Without time to process, prepare or even return to his hotel, Reilly was immediately taken to the set, where the costume and makeup team rushed to transform him into a soldier. They cut his hair, put him in a uniform, and presented him to De Palma. "Are you ready?" asked De Palma, after praising Reilly's outfit. "Well… sure," stammered Reilly. "Perfect. Let's film something right now," said De Palma, looking satisfied. Reilly shot his very first scene as Hatcher (also his very first on-camera scene) lying by a rice paddy, head resting on his helmet, just before Brown becomes a sniper's target. De Palma, pleased with his performance, then reshot the village scene with Reilly. For budgetary reasons (the presence of numerous Thai extras and the complexity of the shot), the Steadicam scene that includes Baldwin was not reshot by De Palma after the actor's departure. De Palma probably thought that Baldwin's presence was discreet enough to go unnoticed. Hatcher has no lines in the scene, though Meserve does mention Hatcher's name when he orders his men to deploy – a detail that escapes most viewers.

With Reilly's performance in *Casualties of War*, we are witness to the emergence of one of the most formidable actors of his generation. While De Palma's intuition was spot-on, the production took a risk by hiring a relative unknown.

280 Casualties of War

"I had to jump into this character right away," says Reilly. "Some of the actors had their own idea of how I should play Hatcher, based on what they knew of Stephen Baldwin. Of course, we were all ambitious and competitive young men,

Brian De Palma and John C. Reilly

but some people were behaving at the expense of others. Don Harvey was a bit like that. I sensed in his attitude that he was trying to influence me, as if saying, 'I'll dominate you. I have more experience, and you don't know what you're doing.' At one point, Don said to me: 'I would always hit Hatcher in the back of the head or on the shoulder. So that's what we're going to do.' I realized he was testing me, so I went to see him, looked him right in the eyes, and said, 'You're not doing that to me.' He replied, 'Okay, no problem,' then winked at me. And from that moment on, I had no more issues with Don."

An emotional black hole

Under the oppressive heat, De Palma swapped his iconic safari jacket for a loose, long-sleeved, untucked shirt, the strap of a fanny pack serving as a belt. With a bucket hat, a bushy beard and an imposing presence, he remained stoic, absorbed in the making of the film. While Caruso and Linson found solutions to the logistical and financial problems that arose daily, De Palma focused on directing. He limited his contact with the crew to essential interactions that were strictly necessary, communicating primarily with his inner circle, including Stephen H. Burum and Eric Schwab.

"Generally, Brian doesn't say much when he's shooting," says Schwab.[59] "But sometimes Sompol and I would go to the filming location with him to figure out the scenes, and he would share his thoughts with us." During pre-production, recalls Paul Engelen, De Palma was "very encouraging, and he loved looking at what I was working on. But once filming started, we rarely spoke to each other unless it was a question related to makeup. It was a very professional relationship."[60] Wolf Kroeger remembers a similarly distant relationship. He met with De Palma once before the Thailand shoot, in his office in New York, and then only once again on set. "He never gave me any instructions," says Kroeger.[61]

Unlike the relationship he developed with Oliver Stone during the filming of *Platoon*, Roland Neveu had very little contact with De Palma. "Some scenes were relatively difficult to shoot, especially on a technical level. De Palma would sometimes address the actors in the heat of the action, but it was rare. He spoke to his DP, but he wasn't the kind of director who spent time with his crew. He was alone, in his chair, under his little tent, in front of his control screens. No one dared disturb him. He didn't walk around the set constantly, he just gave orders to his technicians, who followed them. When something went wrong, the actors would go to him under his tent to talk. De Palma left me with the impression of a very focused filmmaker, completely in his own bubble, which contrasted in a certain way with the significant size of the crew, as well as the sets."[62]

Brian De Palma

"Brian is a man of few words," says Larry McConkey. "He seems to believe that you should have read the script and understood what is required for the scene before showing up on set. He would be very specific about how a scene should be set up, but then would leave it up to me to handle the details of the Steadicam shot."[63]

"Brian barely said anything on set," says Carl Goldstein, "and made only gestures. I had to look at his hands. If his right hand moved three inches to the right, it meant, 'Could you give me some coffee?' He spoke to the actors during rehearsals, but rarely on the set. That surprised me."[64]

"He wasn't like some directors, who take you under their wing and you go eat every meal with them and you become instant friends," says John Leguizamo. "He kept a friendly but professional relationship. He was encouraging and demonstrative of likes and dislikes."[65] Erik King maintains that De Palma "was very clear about his demands. He respected the actors' work and was open to them coming in with choices he could support."[66] Holt McCallany also has good memories. "He was fair with me, unlike other filmmakers I've worked with who weren't necessarily very pleasant. It's true that he didn't say much, but when he spoke, he insisted that we listen."[67]

"Brian quickly appeared to me as a kind of emotional black hole of great depth," says John C. Reilly. "There was something soft about him. In some ways, he was like a puppy dog, so kind and loving with his deep blue eyes. But he also had a sinister quality, an abyss of darkness within him. I was immediately struck by the complexity of his personality. He looked at me as if I were some strange creature, which seemed to amuse him a lot. I knew he really liked me, and he wanted to help me do well, for which I am very grateful to him, even today. Sometimes, you were just waiting for a compliment, but he was more like: 'If I'm not satisfied, you'll know it soon enough.' That's what happened with that tracking shot I'm in, the scene where Eriksson is threatened by a grenade, in the latrines.[68] It's a Steadicam shot of a few seconds, but we did it 47 times. We wouldn't move on until Brian was satisfied. Earlier during the shoot – it was the scene where I'm lying in my bed, drunk, just after the first patrol – I remember asking him, 'Could we do it again? I feel I can do it better.' I didn't know it was a big deal for an actor to ask the director for a second take. Someone like Sean Penn could ask for another take, but not a beginner like me. And yet Brian was really charmed by my attitude. He knew my request wasn't a whim, it was because I wanted to give my best for him. He responded with humor. 'Okay, everyone in position. JOHN REILLY wants to do another take. We'll do another just because JOHN REILLY is asking for it!' And I remember looking at everyone, puzzled: 'Yeah... What...? Is that wrong?'"[69]

The Phuket Film School

Stephen H. Burum shot *Casualties of War* with a Panaflex camera and Anamorphic lenses, which squeeze a wider image onto the standard 35mm film frame. "In this particular situation that worked very well," he explains, "because we were filming groups of people. We could film a conversation between several soldiers moving in and out of the frame, but we didn't have to cut with a close-up to understand the relationships between them. I prefer seeing actors all together in the same shot. It's much more stimulating and interesting than shifting from one close-up to another."[70]

When Larry McConkey asked Burum why he was using Panavision C series lenses, which are not as sharp and fast as others that were available, Burum explained he wanted to "make things look more in focus" – which at first glance seems contradictory. When pressed by McConkey, Burum embarked on a technical demonstration for him. "He explained that with the wide Anamorphic frame, there is usually more out of focus than in, especially with a close-up shot. Since depth of field is intentionally and often inevitably very shallow, the actor is generally placed in the left or right third of the frame, with the remaining two-thirds out of focus. Shooting at a generous aperture setting also helps increase the depth of field, so even on close-ups, the whole face is in focus. Stephen made sure to have enough light to allow for that, so faster lenses were unnecessary. That also avoided the undesirable edge softness that resulted from using a lower aperture stop. The softer look enhanced faces, and the transition from parts of the frame that are in focus to parts of the frame that are out of focus is less abrupt. Without any extremely sharp elements in the frame, you have nothing to compare the soft look to, so the use of soft lenses actually makes the image look sharper."[71]

The second unit, composed entirely of experienced technicians, offered second unit director Eric Schwab a privileged position. "I did a lot of scenes with the troops, when the soldiers are taking the girl and going deeper and deeper into the jungle. I was with a smaller crew, which allowed us to film in more isolated, difficult-to-access places. We spent time traveling to unusual spots, including remote villages."[72] Schwab took advantage of his autonomy to experiment. He used different types of lenses and filmed "long tracking shots through the bamboo, like Kurosawa did in *Rashomon*. Stephen spent a lot of time teaching me how to compose the image for the widescreen format since we were shooting anamorphic."[73]

After his dolly accident, Burum would sometimes use his cane to draw technical diagrams on the ground to make his concepts more concrete. Watching him one day, De Palma jokingly exclaimed, "This is the Phuket Film School!"[74]

Everyone was pushed to up their game. "Stephen was always encouraging me," says McConkey. "I had to decide whether or not I could succeed in trying his new ideas rather than rely on what I was already good at. Stephen's visual style was classic, but he was never afraid to do unconventional shots when they told the story better. He helped me in elevating my own sense of aesthetics, which means knowing the dramatic stakes and storytelling purpose of every moment of every shot. He also didn't want any apparent visual difference between dolly, crane and Steadicam work, so my goal was to disappear from the shot and let the audience feel like they're controlling what they want to see.

"Because I control every aspect of the camera's movement, and because the Steadicam responds to every movement of my body, I have to be very disciplined in how I react to the actors in the scene. I have to become very still and very attentive at the same time. When I sense a change in an actor, either something in their eyes or a change in posture or head position, I have to be able to react in such a way that makes the audience feel they are part of the scene. This might mean making very subtle or very large sudden movements, but always in response to the performers. I've noticed that great actors often react in return to my camera movements, much as they do with the other actors. This makes for a wonderful organic interaction between us. Editing, which generally refines the final result, is unnecessary here. We rely on each other to build the scene.

"For these reasons, I've always paid careful attention to rehearsals. Brian made it clear that I could adjust some of the blocking to make a shot work. He trusted my ability to intensify, rather than weaken, his intentions. In return, I had the actors' trust. They understood that what I asked of them wasn't arbitrary – although they didn't hesitate to speak up if I requested something that compromised their sense of what their character would do. I worked with the stand-ins, refining marks for them as well as for myself, so I could respond to the actors' spontaneous performances without worrying about where the camera was going to be. I studied all the obstacles I might have to work around in case I needed to adapt to the subtle differences in performance that can occur from one take to another."

The Steadicam is rarely a neutral device in De Palma's filmmaking, sometimes taking on the subjective point of view of a specific character. This technique, which has obvious ethical implications in *Casualties of War*, pushed McConkey to carefully weigh the stakes of each shot. "One of the hardest things to do is to create a convincing point of view, and in a De Palma film, it cannot seem uncertain or random. The norm in many films is to use a handheld camera as a means to convey the idea of imitating a person's vision. But it's a wildly inaccurate technique. Our brain has a very sophisticated processing system that allows us to have a very stabilized view of the world, so I try to break down point-of-view shots into a series of visual ideas, each very clearly defined, very deliberately executed."

McConkey cites the example of the sequence where Eriksson, in the latrines at base camp, is the target of a grenade attack. "At times I wanted 'my' arm to be in the shot – opening a hatch door, tossing in a grenade. On shots like this, someone else's hands need to be in perfect sync with the camera movements, which try to stimulate what that character would be seeing of his own body. That takes a lot of practice working together, like two dancers not quite touching, but in such harmony that they act as one. To achieve this, I had to come up with a plan for where to look with the camera and when. I choreographed a series of very specific ideas that would define each moment: looking up to see Michael through the window above, looking at potential witnesses, moving deliberately toward the hatch, leaning with the camera as the character would lean to reach out and up and in. I first did it by myself without a camera, analyzing what I did with my eyes, my hands, my body. Then I simplified these actions into the minimal form. Everything had to be accomplished in perfect symbiosis with the actors so I could hide when Michael turned in my direction, then move back

Filming *Casualties of War* 287

up at the right moment to keep an eye on him, and ensuring that John [C. Reilly] could see me well. It took many tries to get everything perfect. Brian kept shooting until we all thought it was perfect."⁷⁵

The opening of the sequence of Oanh's abduction from her village was also filmed using a Steadicam. "It was a subjective camera shot, quite challenging both technically and emotionally," says Larry McConkey. "I rehearsed with Laurie Shane, the gaffer, holding a flashlight which defined where and how my character was looking for the right girl to kidnap, so that my movements were convincing. I practiced myself by holding a flashlight without using the camera, and noticed how I tended to move as I search. I would often begin by moving the flashlight beam from one thing to another, then following it with my gaze. It was subtle, but for me it was an essential detail and it allowed Laurie and I to act as one mind. Sometimes it was better to have the camera start to back up and then have the flashlight turn off or swing out of view. I had to concentrate on the technicalities so that I didn't react emotionally. My character would have not been revulsed by what was happening as I was myself, so I had to adopt that cold, calculated, disciplined attitude."[76]

Another technique employed by Burum – one used by De Palma in many of his films – is the split diopter. "It allows a close-up of someone on one side of the frame while also holding someone or something else in focus on the other side," explains McConkey, "allowing for dramatic moments that otherwise could only be handled through intercuts, which would have a much less powerful impact." There are notable examples of this imagery in *Casualties of War*, including Eriksson, immediately after Brownie has been shot, staring into the distance as the enemy move about behind him; Meserve shaving in the tent with his comrades in the background, as he alerts them to their mission the following morning and tells them that Brownie is dead; and the stabbing of Oanh on the bridge as Eriksson takes aim at the North Vietnamese down in the valley. (Burum used the diopter a couple of years earlier in two memorable scenes from *The Untouchables*: Malone agreeing to work with Ness and, at the opera, Capone being told of Malone's death.) What the use of the diopter potentially injects into a narrative, and specifically a single image, are elements of dramatic irony, as we, the audience, are able to see what the primary character on-screen, often in close-up, is *not* able to see.

Split diopter shots from *The Untouchable*.

Memories of war

To ensure the historical accuracy of the film, the production enlisted the services of a researcher, Deborah Ricketts. Originally a script editor with a master's degree in Library Science, Ricketts had worked on *The Year of the Dragon* as historical researcher, location and props assistant, decorator and costumer, collaborating closely with Michael Cimino and screenwriter Oliver Stone. For *Casualties of War*, she conducted research into set design, purchased period-specific props sent to Thailand for duplication, provided information on military uniforms, and, more broadly, on the equipment used by the US army in Vietnam. "Things like period cigarette packs or playing cards like the Joker were stuck under the soldiers' helmet band. We sourced everything for the period, as every item had to be correct for the Vietnam War," confirms props master Mickey Pugh.[77] Eric Schwab recalls Ricketts recommending several documentaries that he should watch, including the 13-episode 1983 PBS series *Vietnam: A Television History*.[78] Ricketts also worked closely with military historian Russell Lee, whom she had met on *The Year of the*

Dragon. A Vietnam veteran, Lee served between 1966 and 1968 with the 14th Engineering Battalion, and provided the production with precise details about uniforms and insignias.[79]

The reconstruction of Vietnam in Thailand was also carefully scrutinized by former soldiers Mike Stokey and Art Smith, who were constantly watching for anachronisms. As a military advisor, Smith sat beside De Palma on set and also worked closely with the actors and department heads to guarantee the accuracy of even the smallest details, such as the correct placement of military ribbons on uniforms in the trial scene.[80] Paul Engelen reports that Smith and Stokey's expertise proved useful in creating the bandages that the wounded soldiers wore, particularly in the scene of Eriksson in the camp hospital after being evacuated by helicopter.

"Generally, we choreograph battle sequences," notes Stokey, "but *Casualties of War* was more a character piece. Sometimes during a shoot, when you tell the director that something isn't quite accurate, you have to be able to offer an alternative, something that will give him the same effect and be authentic. You try to give advice without interfering or getting in the way. There was a scene with Michael J. Fox getting behind a plow and romping happily with a water buffalo. The fact is that these animals in Thailand are much more domesticated than they were in Vietnam. I explained to Michael that the buffaloes we encountered in Vietnam hated us. They hated our smell and would even sometimes charge us. I told him he might incorporate a little hesitancy in his approach to the beast, but he shrugged it off, saying he was playing a character who had grown up on a farm and would naturally have an affinity with animals. Another day, I showed up on set to see this beautiful, pristine panorama of rice fields and hamlets, with every healthy animal they could assemble for the shot. Again, we were filming in Thailand – which looks very different to the war-ravaged Vietnamese countryside. In Nam, you rarely saw a cat, and only a few scraggly, diseased stray dogs that even they didn't want to eat. I cautioned Brian Cook about the reality and poverty in Vietnamese villages, and thankfully he got rid of some of the healthier stock."[81]

Stokey also recalls correcting errors in the scene where Cherry, played by Darren E. Burrows, is killed. "De Palma wanted him to wander off the side of the road and step on a mine. I told him the mine would take out any number of soldiers around him, so we changed the explosive to a makeshift toe-popper, which is essentially a shotgun shell positioned atop a nail that when stepped on explodes and shoots the toes or the foot of the soldier off – in this case sending Cherry splaying backwards into a large punji pit."[82] Burrows temporarily left the set so that Carl Fullerton could create a life-sized mold for him in California. "The head and arms were then attached to a fully articulated dummy. The difficulty was making it look like the explosion had just occurred, so I attached some monofilament nylon onto the dummy's arm, so that as we reveal the body, he is in his last death throes and twitching," says Paul Engelen.[83] But De Palma wasn't convinced by the molding of Burrows' face, so Burrows climbed into the pit himself.

Darren E. Burrows as Cherry

One detail in this sequence likely to go unnoticed is when the soldiers lean into the pit where Cherry's corpse is lying and one of them discreetly pulls out a camera and takes a photo. In Rabe's script, the character of Meyers takes pictures, but not of the corpse. It is highly probable that the military personnel suggested to De Palma to modify this detail, which corresponded to a reality of the war. Janina Struk notes that many soldiers took personal photographs when on the frontlines. With notable exceptions (like the images of My Lai), these photographs were mostly unseen, as newspapers and magazines – already saturated with professional photoreporters' images – didn't publish them.[84]

Even with all their suggestions and the adjustments made, the veterans of the war who worked on the film were worried that *Casualties of War* would portray an essentially negative image of American involvement in Vietnam. "Dale [Dye] and I talked openly about it," says Art Smith. "De Palma, Art Linson and Fred Caruso even asked me about my vision of the film at the start. I was concerned, but Linson told me, 'It's just a movie.' From that point on, I did my job as rigorously as possible to ensure that every detail was correct and consistent with what the soldiers' lives were really like in Vietnam at that time. There's a scene where Meserve joins Eriksson at his guard post at night, in the rain. He asks him, 'You like the army, Eriksson, don't you?' Eriksson replies, 'This ain't the army, Sarge. This ain't the army.' For us veterans, this was our disclaimer: what those guys did wasn't representative of the majority of soldiers, especially considering you could go into the nearer village and get a great experience for 25 piastres, even when on patrol."[85]

"They never talked about what they had experienced," says Eric Schwab of two American crew members who had served in Vietnam. "Yet they'd had a tremendous amount of experience on the frontline. They had seen extremely traumatic things, maybe even more than our military advisor. The first was the camera operator, a small guy who had served three tours of duty as a tunnel rat, and the second was our caterer. They didn't like to talk much about their war memories, but I do remember both of them telling us about filming, 'Boys, it really captured what it was.' They understood what Brian was seeking, and they felt that the film captured the war experience much more authentically than *Platoon* or any other Vietnam film."[86]

R&R

Most crew members describe the filming atmosphere as friendly and focused, with a pervasive sense of camaraderie and professionalism. But John Leguizamo has spoken of occasional tensions on set. "I was the only Latin person in the film, and the Thais thought I was Thai or half Thai. They treated me as one of their own. I had a lot more in common with the black actors than with the white cast. We saw the colonial mentality of Westerners in Thailand. Some white actors would exoticize the Thais. I and the black actors knew what that was like because we came from oppressed and marginalized walks of life in America."[87] One evening during dinner, writes Leguizamo in his memoir, an actor began saying "ugly things" about the Thais. "We had a big yelling match and were ready to throw down. 'Shut the fuck up with your racist bullshit,' I was yelling. Kind of ruined the evening for everybody. I felt like a killjoy, but I just couldn't take it anymore."[88]

"I do remember hanging with Johnny Legz, as I called him," says Erik King. "As well as Ving Rhames, John C. Reilly, Wendell Pierce, Don Harvey and others. Most of us lived together, ate together, hung together. I never heard any actors or crew being disrespectful. If it did happen, I certainly didn't hear it. And frankly, it would have been inconsistent with the guys I hung out with."[89] In 1996, Carl Goldstein encountered John Leguizamo when they were both working on projects at Warner Bros. They hadn't seen each other for years, and their conversation naturally turned to *Casualties of War*. Goldstein recalls the "great camaraderie" that bonded crew members, but notes that Leguizamo "didn't remember the experience as fondly as I did. What he says about racism on the set seems, at first glance, to be an unfair statement, but it's not necessarily untrue. Fundamentally, it was a clash of two different cultures."[90]

"I hired an American caterer for the crew," says Fred Caruso,[91] "knowing that most were American and English. We would eat scrambled eggs, bacon and hamburgers. But we also had a Thai caterer to deal with the Thai crew, who consumed very different food. Initially, both caterers cooked separately and the two crews sat separately under the tent to eat, but within three or four days the Americans and the

English started mingling with the Thais and eating their food, and the two caterers started cooking together."[92]

The three months of preparation, including military training for the actors, strengthened bonds among crew and cast members, who spent a lot of time together at the mess and off set. Card games, karaoke and jam sessions livened up evenings and days off. Michael J. Fox once even launched into a spirited rendition on electric guitar of "Johnny B. Goode," the Chuck Berry song he plays at the end of *Back to the Future*. When they had free time, people ventured into the old town of Phuket on tuk-tuks "for 45 minutes through the jungle."[93] "Eager to do our scenes and be done for the day, we'd become restless and start pounding down the local beer," writes Michael J. Fox. "The stuff was rumored to be laced with formaldehyde, but we couldn't read the labels and the locals weren't talking. That's not quite true: they were talking incessantly, but we couldn't understand what they were saying. Formaldehyde, turpentine, Drano, whatever… we'd swill it down and then – the big kick – drive out to the local snake farm and goad each other into drinking shots of a popular Thai cure-all: equal parts Thai whiskey and cobra blood."[94]

On a day off, Holt McCallany and John Leguizamo rented a jeep and set off on an excursion to Phuket. Along the way, they stopped at a place where a sign read: "House of Reptiles." A Thai cobra hunter welcomed them and offered to pick one of the snakes in cages to pit against a mongoose in a fight to the death. "Generally," says Holt McCallany, "the mongoose emerges victorious because it's a very intelligent animal – it attacks the cobra's eyes, and once the snake can't see anymore, it finishes it off. If the cobra is very large, it can sometimes overpower and beat the mongoose, but that's rather rare." After their host placed the reptile and the small mammal in a pit, the two creatures engaged in a merciless struggle, with the mongoose emerging as the victor. "The old Thai then retrieved the dead snake," says McCallany. "He spread it out on a stone and sliced it lengthwise in front of us. Then he poured its blood into two small glasses and mixed it with some kind of local whiskey before handing the glasses to John and me, stating that it was a Thai tradition. Supposedly, this concoction was meant to enhance our virility. I didn't know what to say:

'That's very kind, sir, but no thank you… Cobra blood isn't really my thing.' But John intervened: 'No, Holt, it's not right to refuse. We'll become cobra brothers, you and me!' I don't know how he managed it, but he convinced me to drink. And I can confirm there's nothing more disgusting. It's warm, it's heavy, the aroma is unbearable. I almost vomited. And it didn't have the slightest effect on my virility."[95]

Some of Phuket's most popular attractions were go-go bars, massage parlors and brothels, the boundaries between which were often blurred. After finishing their work on set, some actors and crew members, remembering that Thailand hosted the famous Rest and Recreation (R&R) bases for American soldiers during the Vietnam War, chose to visit places where sex was displayed and traded. "We were young men and always looking for love," says John Leguizamo,[96] who became a regular customer of a Phuket brothel. "The girls were behind a glass wall, and they were all dressed like they were going to a prom. Really young, beautiful girls, not like what you'd think of as hookers. And they all had numbers on their dress. You just picked the number of the girl you liked, and you'd go back with her to this sort of bathroom-bedroom, where she'd shower you, bathe and scrub you, and then you'd get busy with her."[97]

Frequenting prostitutes wasn't without risks. The spread of HIV in the 1980s led to a gradual awareness and upheaval in sexual behavior. Carefree attitudes give way to concern, to the extent that one member of the *Casualties of War* crew expressed worries to a comrade about the possible consequences of unprotected sex. Nevertheless, recounts Michael J. Fox in his autobiography, "Some members of the C.O.W. crew, many of whom were Aussies, had hired local prostitutes as companions for their entire stay in-country. One guy set up housekeeping with two women; an oddly civilized arrangement, they would accompany him into Phuket village to do his marketing. When finally asked, 'Why two?' he answered, straight-faced, as if it was obvious: 'So they can keep each other company while I read the paper in the morning.' He obviously wanted to approximate the routines of his ordinary home life but kick it up a notch by including the fulfillment of his sexual fantasy."[98] Within a week of leaving Phuket as Evans and returning as Hatcher, John C. Reilly was surprised by the change in atmosphere at the hotel. "When I came back, it was insane! Members of the crew had prostitutes living in their rooms. They were drinking and taking all these crazy drugs."[99]

The production remained unfazed by the situation, a common occurrence during location work. With characteristic composure, De Palma observed his crew's behavior, noting patterns reminiscent of those displayed by American soldiers in the Vietnam War.

Don Harvey, Sean Penn, Michael J. Fox and Brian De Palma

"The people there live and think differently," he says. "And their conception of women… It's probably nauseating to us, but prostitution is almost normal for them. People there don't see any problem with it. When you absorb this notion it's much easier to understand how those soldiers could have kidnapped that girl and done what they did. Many women in those countries end up selling themselves. We saw that ourselves in Bangkok, so you can imagine how bad it must have been during the war in Vietnam. Bangkok today is a lot like Saigon probably was during the war – an open city where anything can be bought. To understand how this atrocity happened, you have to understand the world these soldiers were living in. From that vantage point, it doesn't seem so strange. Consider the fact that these guys were wandering through a foreign country that they couldn't begin to fathom, a country where notions of morality seemed upside down, where you couldn't tell good guys from bad, the Vietcong from other Vietnamese. Everyone looked the same. These 18-year-olds, who visited brothels every night, didn't see the harm in kidnapping a village girl. 'She looks like the whore I fucked last night,' they would say."[100]

The Penn Method

One actor, Sean Penn, kept himself apart from the distractions of the rest of the cast. "Sean did all the military training alongside us," recalls Holt McCallany. "But once we started filming, he was more often seen on set than off."[101] The rest of the time, Penn kept to himself. Fond of weightlifting, he spent his free time in the gym specially set up for him at his hotel, accompanied by his physical trainer, Ray Kybartas. "He sequestered himself away like a true man of rank in the army," says Reilly. "He didn't stay with the 'privates!'"[102]

Unlike Penn, Fox stayed in the same hotel as the rest of the cast. "Michael was very friendly and remembered all the crew members' names," says Pasiree Panya. "Every time he saw me, he called me by my nickname, Noiy. Sean behaved very differently. He stayed in character most of the time and rarely spoke to anyone on set. He would sit in a corner with a book or the script."[103]

Penn had a powerful aura about him when he arrived in Thailand to shoot *Casualties of War*. More than Fox, he was the true star of the film – a status he relished. When Columbia executives made a hurried visit to the crew in the middle of filming,[104] Penn refused to take a photo with the other actors and Dawn Steel, who had asked for the picture, insisting that he was not her "trained monkey."[105] Penn may have had a bad-boy reputation, but Mike Stokey remembers him as "totally disciplined."[106] "Although Sean had the reputation of being hard to handle, I found him very cooperative, with a good sense of humor," confirms Paul Engelen. "He was always on time for his call, very aware of coming to me early to get into character."[107] Eric Schwab recalls that Penn would want to watch the rushes, and always had plenty of questions. "'How did you shoot this scene? How did you get that one?' He was learning the craft of directing. I really enjoyed working with him."[108] "Sean is a man who does not suffer fools, but he is very professional," says Mickey Pugh. "He didn't play Sergeant Meserve. He *was* Sergeant Meserve."[109]

Sean Penn, John C. Reilly and Michael J. Fox

The situation on set somehow mirrored the filmed story. Much like Sergeant Meserve, the most seasoned of the soldiers, Penn was the most experienced of the actors. He was scrutinized by his peers and consciously played on his charisma. "I think I was aware of the regard some of them held me in," he admits. "At the time, I had a pretty mercenary attitude about things and I'm sure if there was anything between weaknesses, strengths and admiration that I could exploit to serve the film or my own purposes as an actor, I did. That does not mean I look back with a certainty of sophistication in those choices. But yes, I would've made those choices."[110]

Penn quickly gained followers, including Reilly. "Sean took me under his wing in a wonderful way," says Reilly. "I ended up doing my first three films with him."[111] On the set of *Casualties of War*, Reilly keenly observed his mentor and learned from his acting method. He remembers the scene where Meserve and his men are denied their camp outing to go to the brothel. Reilly channeled the frustration of his character by giving his all during the filming of the master shot. But between takes, Penn approached him, put his arm around his neck, and whispered in his ear: "Hey, man, save some for the close-up." "It hadn't even crossed my mind," admits Reilly. "I was coming from theater, where you have to give everything, all the time. I didn't even understand how the camera worked. But Sean was very savvy."[112]

Another sequence particularly impressed the actors, where Meserve escorts Brown, lying on a stretcher, to the helicopter that evacuates him after he is shot. "That's one of my most memorable moments," enthuses Erik King. "Sean was completely present and supportive between takes, never letting go of my hand, not even after the camera stopped rolling. There was blood drying on my uniform and on my neck, my wound needed to be refreshed, and we were surrounded by a large crew, as you can imagine, but we never broke character between shots. It's a scene about friendship, about men relying on each other. Sean was there, both for my character and for me, as an actor. I learned a lot by watching him work."[113]

Holt McCallany, meanwhile, was preparing for his only appearance in the film, as Lieutenant Kramer, who gives Meserve instructions shortly after the helicopter takes off. "Something very interesting happened on the first take of the helicopter scene," says McCallany. "Erik King is lying on a stretcher and Sean is encouraging him by saying, 'Look into my eyes, man...' As the helicopters were taking off, Sean suddenly started shouting, 'Cut! Cut!' It isn't normally the actor's job to cut the camera, so De Palma comes running over and asked him what the problem is. 'When a helicopter would take off in Vietnam,' Sean said, 'there was always cover smoke.' 'Oh yeah?' said De Palma. 'What color?' And Sean replies, 'Yellow or purple.' So De Palma yells to the props master to get some cover smoke going. I was standing there, amazed, thinking: Sean has done enough research about the Vietnam War to know the color of cover smoke used in Vietnam. I was impressed. Here was an actor who had done a huge amount of preparation. I never forgot that lesson, which I've always kept as a kind of creed: an actor should do as much research as possible for their role, because it might come in handy in one way or another, even if it isn't in the script."[114]

302 Casualties of War

Pasiree Panya recalls filling the field jackets worn by the actors with items that didn't weigh much. "We faked them by putting lighter things in the pockets instead. Sean was the only one who asked us not to cheat. He insisted that we use the real equipment because he wanted to know what the soldiers would really have experienced."[115] Eric Schwab remembers being struck by Penn's behavior during the filming of the night battle in the jungle. While the technicians were busy preparing the scene, Schwab saw him walk barefoot in the tropical forest. "Even the Thais couldn't believe their eyes. They were concerned about his safety because there were snakes there. I think Sean felt he had to become one with the environment."[116]

Penn has always been resistant to discuss how he works as an actor, claiming that "it would take away all the mystery of films."[117] "This reluctance to reveal his creative strategies partially veils their true magnitude," writes Simon Laisney, who notes Penn's propensity "to frequently begin constructing a role through its externalities and contours [...] rather than its internal aspects."[118] Up until the filming of *Racing With the Moon* in 1984, Penn insisted that everyone working on his latest film, as well as his friends, "address him only by the name of the character, or else they would be ignored."[119] (He abandoned this approach with his next film, *The Falcon and the Snowman*, "because he realized that the negative reactions of some people had the opposite effect of what was intended."[120]) In his relentless pursuit of realism, Penn shuns all artifice: he performs his own stunts, holds back no punches, and "conditions his colleagues, focusing not just on his own performance but extending his influence over the entire scene."[121]

These acting techniques were extensively employed by Penn on *Casualties of War*. In the long sequence shot on and around the railroad track in Kanchanaburi, Diaz refuses to stab Oanh and Meserve slaps him once, then twice, then three times. The beatings that John Leguizamo received were not staged. "When Sean Penn slaps you, he really wallops you. It was no joke. By the thirteenth take my face was beginning to swell up so badly I couldn't even say my lines clearly."[122] The young actor had been psychologically conditioned by Penn as early as the military training phase. "When we were doing military jungle training, I was insubordinate, because I'm still a kid from the ghetto and I bristle at authority. Sean would make me drop and do 25 push-ups over and over, but it was all for the sake of getting into character."[123]

Penn sought to maintain constant psychological pressure on Fox. The two actors spoke a great deal before filming began, but then a rift developed. "Sean hardly spoke to Michael at all," says De Palma of the tension between the two performers, on set and off. "He got very seriously into character and when he wasn't shooting, he hung around with the actors playing his solders. He was determined to be the best sergeant possible. Michael, who's a really nice guy, was repulsed by Sean's behaviour. They were staying in the same hotel but never spoke to each other."[124] "During dinner at the hotel, Sean and Michael never sat at the same table," confirms Art Linson. "It wasn't because they didn't like each other, as people thought, but because Sean took his role very seriously. Meserve doesn't like Eriksson."[125]

Fox claimed that because of the intensity of the shoot, "it became too complicated to form friendships that neither of [the actors] truly wanted."[126] But according to Eric Schwab, Fox – accustomed to comedic roles – struggled with Penn's attitude, even though what appears to have been a tacit agreement seems to have been made between the two men before filming began, that they would stay in their roles throughout the shoot to maintain tension between their characters.[127] One night, alone in a hotel deep in the jungle, Fox confided in Schwab that he "didn't appreciate the atmosphere" on set. Between takes, Penn was deliberately unpleasant and aggressive toward his co-star. "He was constantly provocative," recalls Schwab. "He would even insult him to emphasize their antagonism."[128] One of the best-known anecdotes, shared by De Palma, is from the filming of the final trial sequence, as one by one the convicted soldiers pass by Eriksson and Meserve stops to whisper something in his ear. Penn reportedly said to Fox, "I've screwed your wife a few times. Now it's your time."[129] – a line that fits perfectly with his character.

In another take, Penn allegedly called him "nothing but a TV star,"[130] an insult directed not at the character (Eriksson) but at the actor (Fox), thus blurring the lines between fiction and reality. "Sean played the dangerous guy to the end. Michael never knew what he would do, and it perfectly suited the film," says De Palma.[131] One day, while preparing to shoot a scene, Penn went so far as to shove Fox to the ground after staring him down. According to De Palma, the look on Fox's face in the next scene – when Eriksson, after narrowly avoiding an assassination attempt, bursts into the tent where Meserve and Clark are playing cards with other soldiers – vindicated Penn: "He had a crazy look in his eyes, and it's captured on film."

Don Harvey, however, invites us to contextualize the animosity between the two actors: "I think Sean and Michael liked each other a lot, but they had very different styles of acting and different ways of preparing. Sean didn't get along with Michael because that's the way he wanted it. Their characters clashed, and he wanted to make sure Michael never really felt comfortable around him. Sean is an absolute gentleman. He never did anything intentionally nasty to Michael. He just didn't go out of his way to make friends with him off the set. He kicked his ass every day during the shoot – but only ever in character."[132] Harvey himself was keen on maintaining the hostility Clark feels toward Eriksson.

"Don was completely invested in his character, to the extent of wanting to embody him 24 hours a day," recalls Holt McCallany. "One night, around 2 or 3 in the morning, he calls Sean Penn in his hotel room. 'Sergeant Meserve? What are we gonna do with Eriksson?' And he kept talking as if he were in the movie, proposing a plan to eliminate Eriksson. What Don didn't know was that Sean had put the phone receiver down and fallen back asleep."[133]

Brian De Palma and Don Harvey

There is no doubt that the strategies employed by Penn – and, to a lesser extent, Harvey – impacted Fox's performance. Eriksson is nervous, perhaps terrified by Meserve's uncontrollable power, and yet is determined not to compromise his moral principles or succumb to the madness of war. Haunted by his character, Fox crossed a threshold in Thailand. "It wasn't till I got out here… that I felt I could even begin to understand what he went through… It doesn't take too much imagination to wonder what it would do to you to fight a *war* here. The humane take on what Meserve and the others did can't be anything but condemnation. But the horror is that you can almost see *why* they did it – you can almost feel that horror rising in yourself."[134]

In the language of nobody

In her critical analysis of *Casualties of War*, Deborah Thomas notes: "Unusually few clear indications are given of what [Oanh] might be feeling as she is kidnapped, raped, and later killed: fear and panic, certainly, and physical pain, but what else? Does she understand what's in store for her at every stage? Does she feel ashamed? Angry? Disillusioned? Had she welcomed the American presence in her country, and is she now feeling betrayed?"[135] Thomas laments that the film provides no answers to these questions. However, it seems to me that while *Casualties of War* doesn't provide any literal answers, Oanh's character isn't merely an empty shell or an abstract concept, the symbol of a country violated by a foreign army.[136] She is, indeed, a flesh-and-blood character whose depth embodies itself in the unspoken, in the looks and gestures of the woman who plays her on-screen.

Arriving in Thailand, Le had to find her bearings in a country she was discovering but which also reminded her of the Vietnam of her childhood. Enthusiastic and intrigued about the impending experience, she knew nothing about how films were actually made and had little time to prepare, as only a few days passed between signing her contract and boarding the plane for Phuket. "I didn't have time to be afraid, or even to realize I was in a big movie. I wasn't aware, to be honest, even though I knew who Brian De Palma was. I didn't realize how important this film would be."[137] When she stepped onto Thai soil, Le hadn't been in Asia since her dramatic evacuation from Saigon at the age of eight. One can presume the shock was significant, even more so when she began embodying her character, someone mistreated throughout almost the entire film. "After a while, I felt like her," she confides. "I was beaten, tied up, and dragged along. Sometimes I thought, 'Why am I doing this? Maybe I'm the victim.' We worked ten hours a day. I dressed like her and put on her wig. Every time I looked in the mirror, I didn't see myself... I saw her."[138]

If *Casualties of War* were made today, the production would almost certainly hire a psychologist to offer support to Le, as is now common practice on films shooting potentially traumatic scenes.[139] But in 1988, she was dropped into the shoot with almost no physical or psychological preparation.

"I'm not sure if Brian De Palma intended it this way," she wonders, "but I think that the psychological work unfolded naturally through the filming process. If a psychologist had been there to assist, I don't think I would have been able to play that character quite as authentically. With no one there to help, I found myself in challenging situations that required immediate reactions. That helped me as an actor."[140]

Nevertheless, Le could count on De Palma, who quickly developed a fatherly bond with her. "He rarely showed his emotions, but I knew he was looking out for me. I had confidence," she says. Once the cameras stopped rolling, De Palma would often ask for her opinion on a particular shot – an opinion she often hesitated to express, out of shyness, politeness or plain humility. "With the actors and technicians, we were like a family," says Le. "We ate together at the hotel, sometimes went out in the evenings. I felt cherished."

The actors all speak highly of her. "She made a very strong impression on all of us," says Penn. "A very intelligent, soulful young woman. Ahead of her years."[141]

"In today's culture," continues Penn, "there's a big sector that enjoys marginalizing the work of actors. But in my own experience, I've had the privilege of a front row seat to so many of our best actors and actresses expressing corners of our human experience as almost canaries in a coalmine. How far can you go? Even when things are staged, to make things real, you make the staging the reality, and the more experience you have, the more you realize the damage actors often come to do themselves. It can be a damaging thing to hypnotize yourself into a reality emotionally, even though you're by no means committing to a physical real one. I will leave it to others and their own process to justify or to trivialize what they do. In my case, the hero of the story was Thuy Thu Le. Not so much the character she played. But her. To be so brave, coming from the history and social expectations she came from, to be willing to share this continuing reality through the art of film. Amazing."[142]

"Thuy was always hanging out with the guys," recalls Don Harvey. "Always quiet, because she didn't speak a lot of English, but still there. Totally protected by all of us. We were all really respectful of her. She was like a fine piece of China that we were guarding with our lives. But she loved to be with us, playing cards, or going into town. She was like our mascot."[143]

Testimonies from the actors reveal a striking contrast between Le's demeanor on and off set. When it was time to film, she transformed. The cheerful and lively young woman became a frightened young peasant girl, wary of men and unable to understand what the soldiers were saying. Her commitment was absolute. Her colleagues describe her as diligent, methodical, and discreet – so much so that some, like Harvey, believed that she didn't speak English well, even though she was actually fully bilingual. "I never saw Le on set unless we were ready to rehearse and shoot," says Harvey. "She was insulated from us during filming and extremely focused. She really became the character, and I don't remember her even talking with us or being around while we were on the set. I think she needed to be alone in order to get into the right mindset."[144]

Le drew a great deal from within herself to embody Oanh. "Everything I've experienced allowed me to feed the character I had to portray because, in the script, I had no dialogue. I had to invent Oanh's words. I was on set, interacting with the actors, and based on the situations, I responded verbally in my language. I reacted as if I were undergoing these things myself."[145]

"Her performance is incredible," enthused De Palma. "She spoke Vietnamese throughout the filming. I had no idea what she was saying. She was in this terrible situation, and she was improvising."[146] Viewers of *Casualties of War* are inevitably struck by Le's intelligence as an actress – a complete novice who, with minimal guidance from Rabe's script regarding her character, delivers a compelling performance. Le portrays a violated, brutalized, dominated woman who nonetheless retains her dignity. The expressions on her face and body oscillate, sometimes very subtly, between terror, fear, hope, pain and resignation. "When I was acting, I wasn't listening to the actors speaking," she says. "I played the girl who understood nothing. I contented myself with reacting physically to what was happening around me."[147]

The sequence of Oanh's abduction from her village took several days to film, and was initially shot with Stephen Baldwin, later replaced by John C. Reilly. "Of course, I had

Thuy Thu Le

read the script and knew very well what was going to happen," says Le, "but on set, everything felt so authentic. I could only react to what was happening, to what my character was experiencing. It was the only way to do it. We shot the scene at three or four in the morning. The soldiers were brutal. They really did shove me to the ground. We were tired, drained from filming it over and over."

According to Harvey, two factors made the scene difficult to shoot: filming at night and complex logistics. "There were dolly tracks laid all the way down the village path and De

Palma did long, one-shot takes through the huts. Everything had to be perfect. It took us a few nights just to rehearse and stage the scene. We were all totally amped up because it was early in the shoot and we had a lot of energy. There was this whole bit where we are ripping Oanh away from her mother and sister, Sean is yelling at them, and they're screaming in Vietnamese. I take a rag and stuff it into Oanh's mouth. It was hard to do because you're trying to be intense but you're also concerned about safety and protecting your fellow actors. When we were leaving the hut, I had to pick up Thuy, put her on my shoulders and run with her down the path. We were all in a line, and as we started moving, someone in front suddenly slowed down a bit. Sean stopped in front of me, I stopped, Stephen Baldwin bumped into me, and I fell forward with Thuy on my shoulder. She landed pretty hard on the ground under me. I was upset because I was trying so hard not to hurt her. She was wearing protective pads, so she didn't get hurt and eventually got up, but for a moment, there was complete silence and no one knew what to expect. Everyone on the set was shocked. I felt really bad about it, but of course it wasn't my fault. It just happened. But it energized us. Everybody stepped up their game a bit."[148]

While Harvey tried to control his actions, Sean Penn, on the other hand, fully immersed in his role, was just as intentionally brutal with Le as he was with other actors. In the scene where Meserve accuses Oanh of being a communist after giving her an aspirin, he lifts the young woman by the scarf around her neck, almost strangling her. Le didn't fake the pain. "I was really suffering. I thought that De Palma, seeing that I was in pain, wouldn't do more than one take."[149]

Voyeurism

Portraying Oanh's rape placed a tremendous responsibility on De Palma, as wartime rape was a taboo subject both then and now, often glaringly absent from media.[150] This task was further complicated by De Palma's previous work, with films like *Dressed to Kill* and *Body Double* earning him a reputation for misogyny. How best to portray Oanh's collective rape without descending into excessive or unhealthy voyeurism?

Unlike with other scenes, De Palma chose not to rehearse this one, likely to protect his actress and retain the spontaneity of her performance. "I don't know if De Palma discussed it with Sean Penn," says Le. "Everything happened very naturally: he ties me up, I struggle, he slaps me. We never rehearsed. It was the hardest scene I've ever filmed. Firstly, because it's a rape context. Secondly, because Sean Penn was completely into his character, very brutal."[151] De Palma limited the crew to only essential technicians, but two Thai assistants lingered and observed the scene with a lewd eye, snickering as they watched. Le asked that they leave the set, and they were ushered away (and perhaps dismissed, as she didn't encounter them again).

Thuy Thu Le

"Oanh's rape was a very tough scene in so many ways," confirms John Leguizamo. "The actress was very uncomfortable. I was uncomfortable. It was my first nude scene. It was a horrible scenario. De Palma was very helpful in keeping it by the numbers and not letting it get out of control so that no one felt humiliated or abused. But I still felt sick to my stomach for days after. I started to understand what the war is doing to these children, these 19-year-old boys. The horrors of war are real, even when you're acting it."[152]

Le says that the scene where Meserve hits her and tears her clothes was done only once, but Pasiree Panya, in charge of her costume, remembers it differently. "For the part where Meserve had to tear the pants away from Oanh, I had to prepare five spare pairs of pants for Thuy. I had to sew them back over and over again because it took many shots and cuts."[153]

"The recreating of this crime was really disturbing," recalls Michael J. Fox. "Shattering… It was unbelievable for [Le] – not only the rape but the strenuousness, the cuts, rope burns, and blisters. The thing I'll always remember is standing outside the hut and watching Sean come in, drop his drawers, grab her, rip her clothes off, throw her on her back, and jump on top of her. I can still hear her screaming."[154] For subsequent shots, in line with De Palma's promise, Le was replaced by a body double, briefly seen naked from the back when Diaz takes his turn. Perhaps for this reason, the camera remains at a distance, neutralizing any voyeuristic effect. The viewer sees almost nothing of the forced sexual act.

De Palma then filmed one of the most heartbreaking moments of the film, the scene where Eriksson discovers Oanh after she has been raped multiple times, cowering like a wounded animal in a corner of the hut. In the script, David Rabe describes Eriksson's verbal efforts to communicate with Oanh. He urges her to leave, mimicking her flight from the hut. Feeling utterly powerless, he begins to recite the Lord's Prayer. De Palma filmed at least some of these shots before deciding perhaps that they were out of place with the rest of the sequence.[155] He condensed the action and relied mainly on Michael J. Fox's facial expressions to convey his character's distress, torn between wanting to save Oanh and his fear of disobeying orders.

Filmed largely with a Steadicam, the scene demanded a significant emotional, psychological and physical investment from both actors. As Eriksson tries to untie Oanh, she initially struggles and screams, as if her body is reactivating the memory of her rape. Once freed, she runs to seek refuge near a wooden post, resembling a bird whose wings have been clipped and revealing her beaten face, which, until now, has been hidden under her long black hair. Le uses her posture to convey a sense of stiffness, as if her bones were frozen, petrified. With her arms close to her body, she uses her fingers like claws when Eriksson offers her food, which she eagerly

devours while brushing aside strands of hair that are still covering her face. Le masterfully shows how Oanh quickly realizes she can trust Eriksson once she understands he wants to help her. She varies her facial expressions, shifting abruptly from distress, tears welling up in her eyes, to renewed hope after Eriksson stammers a few words in Vietnamese.

Larry McConkey's Steadicam expertise was essential in capturing Eriksson's emotions—since the scene was shot from his perspective—while ensuring they didn't overpower the moment. "The story of *Casualties of War* is painful in almost every aspect," he says. "There is a sense of the inevitability of terrible events that starts with the very title, but Brian never wants the camera to turn away. Michael had a terrible responsibility to portray someone who is an unwilling participant in evil. He had to somehow convey his reluctance, even revulsion, in what he is nevertheless a party to. Sean and the others had an easier time playing more villainous characters. I needed to play the same careful, agonizing role as Michael – being repulsed, but still deliberately watching what was happening, participating at times with reluctance, or occasionally sharing the same reckless thrill as the other soldiers. To be a party myself to the terrible things I witnessed, I needed to be confident that the film had a certain moral viewpoint."[156]

Knowing De Palma probably wouldn't settle for just one take, Fox dreaded shooting this particular sequence in a single long take, afraid he might not bring enough intensity. Dissatisfied with the first take, De Palma shot the scene multiple times, much to Fox's dismay. At one point, Fox asked De Palma if the last take was satisfactory. His negative response triggered the actor, who, in anger, punched through one of the bamboo walls of the hut, which, says Fox, "was like basically slamming your fist through a stack of knives," and cut his hand open.[157]

Fox wasn't the only actor struggling. Don Harvey recalls that the rape scene consumed the crew for several weeks, affecting the nerves of actors and technicians. "It was a grueling period, with day and night shoots. One day during a scene, Brian came up to me and asked, 'Don, did you not get out of bed this morning? You seem like you're still asleep. I want you to bring more intensity.' I said, 'I've been thinking about my character, and I'd like to play it with some sensitivity. I feel like I'm being too crazy. I don't want Clark to come across as a bad person. I think he's a good guy who does bad things because he's in a bad situation. But back home he has a girlfriend. His mother loves him. He was a good kid who played football and was on the honor roll.' Brian just looked at me for a while, then said, 'Don, there are two kinds of people in this movie: the ones in the white hats and the ones in the black hats. And you have the blackest hat of all. You're not a good person. Your mother doesn't love you. You don't have a girlfriend back home. You're bad. You're vicious. I want to see you get intense.' It was a turning point for me. Before that, I hadn't understood the darkness Brian was going for. His films are very human. They have compassion, romance, humor and adventure – all the elements of great storytelling. But most of them also have an element of evil, and the darkest aspects of the human character. At some point in the shooting, I understood that *I* was that element. And it scared me. I was really into the Method at that time. I wanted to live my character. When I started to understand the depth of Clark's anger, it put me in a dark place."[158]

John C. Reilly, on the other hand, preferred not to burden himself with any moral viewpoint. Not that he was unconcerned about the nature of the crime his character was involved in; he was, on the contrary, very much aware of it. But Reilly was firmly convinced that any moral judgment passed on Hatcher would have affected the accuracy of his portrayal. "I love characters like that because they aren't at all conflicted. He believes in his sergeant. And if you look at the history of warriors, that's what a warrior is: loyal to his leader. That's one of the confusing things about modern warfare for these young men. War is a tactical exercise, it's not civilian life. It's supremacy. You are supposed to defeat your enemy without any mercy. The speech I give in the film about Genghis Khan – that's how a soldier is supposed to think. So I didn't feel, 'Oh, it's not right what Hatcher is doing…' I don't believe in looking down on a character like that, thinking that I'm morally superior to him. I can always tell when actors are doing that. There's a kind of condescension that doesn't ring true somehow. When I play somebody, I completely immerse myself into what that character believes. You need to find the one facet of yourself that is exactly like the character. Then you expand that part of your personality until it's everything, and you become the character. You don't have to be a bright guy to be a good soldier. You have to be brave, you have to be tough, you have to listen to your commanding officer, and you have to want to kill your enemy. Not everybody can do that. I had no ambivalence about Hatcher."[159]

"I tried to stay vulnerable throughout the shoot," says Leguizamo. "When you do that, you can't help but become the character. You don't even intentionally try… It just happens and you start talking like Diaz in real life and the two start to blend, and the boundaries between imagination and reality blur. I was trying to show how someone who is innocent and not an abuser can become one when mob mentality takes over. It explains how nice people do terrible things when they are put into certain situations. It's that Stanley Milgram experiment: taking regular people and having them obey an authority figure who instructs them to perform acts that conflict with their personal conscience."[160]

On the bridge

As the shooting in Thailand entered its final phase, the crew left Phuket for Kanchanaburi province, where the battle against North Vietnamese forces – during which Oanh is murdered – was to be filmed. Most of the crew stayed in a hotel about thirty minutes from the location, except for Penn, who preferred to be in Bangkok and commute daily from the capital. De Palma, Fox and Schwab stayed about fifteen minutes from the location, in an old royal residence that Robert De Niro had discovered while shooting *The Deer Hunter*, deep in the jungle, on the banks of the River Kwai. "It was a beautiful place," says Carl Goldstein, "but it felt haunted. Fifteen thousand prisoners of war died at the hand of their Japanese captors in that area, and you felt a spiritual unrest. We heard strange noises and screams in the middle of the night."[161]

Casualties of War allowed Brian De Palma to follow in the footsteps of a filmmaker, David Lean, whose influence on him, less overt than Hitchcock's, tends to be forgotten. De Palma has cited Lean's dramatic climax in *The Bridge on the River Kwai* – the bridge's destruction, symbolizing the brutal absurdity of war – as his inspiration to become a director.[162] Eric Schwab even suggested filming Oanh's death scene on the actual bridge on the River Kwai (which Lean reconstructed in Ceylon, now Sri Lanka). While Lean's portrayal of war in *The Bridge on the River Kwai* was already cynical, De Palma further deconstructs its representation. Here, the bridge serves as the backdrop for a shootout, but the focus shifts from conventional combat and its associated pseudo-values – honor, bravery and sacrifice – to the war's true horror, euphemistically termed "collateral damage."

On the first day of shooting in Kanchanaburi, early in the morning, everything was in place. Technicians were at their stations, the actors were present, and the cameras were ready to roll. But where was De Palma? His silhouette eventually appeared in the distance, aboard a small motorboat. Once it docked, De Palma stepped out, looking drawn, with a scowling expression. "I can't stay here! I was up all night, hearing death in the jungle," he whispered to Eric Schwab.[163] Worried by the roars of predators and the screams of prey being torn apart, De Palma decided to pack up and stay in Bangkok, even if it meant losing five hours a day traveling to the set every morning and returning to the hotel at night.[164]

The most difficult part was yet to come. "Shooting the bridge scene was very complex," recounts Caruso. "We had to coordinate with the railroad because there was a daily transport train, back and forth, that used the track. We had to make a deal with the railroad workers, who would stop the train before the section of track where we were filming so the passengers could get off and get on a bus."[165] The scene, which was filmed with four cameras, was especially perilous due to the configuration of the location: a bridge with a train track overlooking the River Kwai. On one side, a rocky cliff overgrown with dense vegetation, on the other... the void.

Filming on the bridge

The specifics of the location pushed De Palma to rewrite the scene, which originally made no mention of a railroad. In the version as filmed, as a shootout begins with enemy forces entrenched along the riverbed, Meserve and his men move quickly onto the bridge and take cover behind the railroad, on the cliff side. This is the spot where Clark stabs Oanh. The topography of the area made shooting risky. "I remember running on that bridge, which was 50 feet above the ground, take after take," recalls Don Harvey. "I was carrying a .50 caliber rifle and trying not to step between the railroad ties. If you didn't land your foot on one of the ties, your leg would go down between the ties and you would go all the way down to your gonads. Not fun. I was trying to run as fast as I could without making any missteps."[166]

John C. Reilly, Brian De Palma and Don Harvey

Since the railroad was operational, the rails were covered in grease, making it even more dangerous for the actors to move without slipping, all while not giving the impression of slowing down. An enemy fighter's rocket-propelled grenade explosion was supposed to halt the soldiers' sprint and send them tumbling to the ground. Positioned at the front, Reilly received instructions: "Run down along the railroad track, and an explosion is going to happen right in front of you," one of the technicians told him. "Then dive to the right and land on the ground, on that embankment next to the railroad. Don't go left – or you'll die!"[167] Just as Reilly informed Carl

Goldstein that the exact spot where he was supposed to stop running was especially greasy, on the opposite side of the river the crew was getting ready to shoot. A voice echoed through a speaker: "Okay, get ready... Camera and... ACTION!"

"We go running," says Reilly, "and everyone else is behind me. I'm carrying a grenade launcher in my right hand and a vest full of grenades in the left. This fucking explosion goes off and the smoke obscures my entire peripheral vision. Everything I see is an orange blaze. There's intense heat coming at me, this huge ball of flame. My feet suddenly slip out from under me and I land on my back, very hard, then bounce to my left, toward the precipice. At the very last second, I drop the vest full of grenades, put my hand up, grip the side of the rail track and stop myself. Then I get up, a bit dazed, and shout, 'Carl, Carl, what happened?!' He looks at me and says, 'Well, you were supposed to go the other way.'"[168]

Another moment proved equally risky: the Steadicam shot from Eriksson's point of view, where he starts running after Meserve to stop him from killing Oanh, then receiving a blow to the stomach from Meserve, leaving him semi-conscious on the rails. "I had to move as fast as I could while making sure to step correctly on the crossties of the track," explains McConkey. "A mistake could have been catastrophic as there was no way to keep me safe if I stumbled. Also, Sean felt it necessary to tell me that even though the shot required me to come very, very close to him, there would be consequences if I hit his face."[169]

De Palma recalls filming the shots of Le falling from the bridge first, then wider shots of her stunt double.[170] "We did two or three takes," recalls Le. "They placed a mattress three or four meters below, but I was still scared."[171] The stuntman was injured in the fall, says John Leguizamo. "He fell through the boxes that were supposed to block him and hit a sharp rock, and was writhing on the ground."[172]

Ninety-one seconds

The bridge sequence marked the end of filming in Thailand. Originally slated to wrap by June 27, 1988, unforeseen weather and shifts in the schedule meant there were overruns.

"I remember I was supposed to have wrapped the picture in time to fill my front row seats to the Spinks vs. Tyson fight in Atlantic City," writes Penn. "But Brian's exacting nature took us just enough over schedule to where he had a grand total of three additional days shooting to go – and I would have to be in one of them. To this day, I credit Brian with my Guinness World Record of the longest flight for the shortest

fight. I drove like a bat out of hell from the River Kwai to Bangkok, immediately flew Bangkok-Paris with a 28-minute connection from Paris to JFK, jumped in a car, drove straight to Manhattan to pick up my two guests, then from Manhattan at 80 mph to Atlantic City, making it just in time for the bell. Then 91 seconds later drove back to Manhattan, dropped off my guests, made another flight in the nick of time to Tokyo, immediately connecting to Bangkok, drove the several hours back to Kanchanaburi, jumped into my gear, and shot 27 takes of my last scene. Thank you, Brian."[173]

At the end of the shoot, the actors were exhausted. "I was drained," admits Harvey. "My ears were ringing. I had lost a lot of weight in the jungle, eating all that rice. I went back to my mother's place in Detroit and spent weeks sleeping on her couch and watching baseball games. During filming, I really tried to live the part of Clark. It took a lot out of me. So much intensity, stretched over three months. As each scene was completed, there was some relief that you could now stop thinking about it, but you couldn't fall out of character. Even on days off. You had to keep the story going in your head all the time. And I had a very ugly story. I remember John C. Reilly talking about how, when you finish the last performance of a play, you take a shower and you wash off the character. That's what I did when we finished *Casualties of War*. I spent an hour in the shower, screaming and laughing, so relieved that I didn't have to be Clark anymore."[174]

The tension between Fox and Penn had dissipated, and the two actors buried the hatchet. "I can't really say it's been a pleasure," Fox wrote to Penn, "but it has been a privilege."[175] Years later, Penn acknowledged the talent of the actor who ended up playing the role he was once considered for. "By the time I'd finished shooting *Casualties of War*, I'm sure I could not have recalled any notion of anyone but Michael J. Fox in that role. He so beautifully fulfilled Brian's vision of the film. I came away liking and respecting him a lot. So that's my takeaway."[176]

Subway stranger

With a sense of duty fulfilled, the team left Thailand. Despite the trials and tribulations along the way – weather challenges, accidents, casting mistakes – the production managed to minimize losses and stayed within budget. Only the prologue and epilogue remained to be shot in San Francisco, a task that, at first glance, seemed like child's play compared to six months in the heart of the jungle.

De Palma was aware that the opening and closing scenes, subject to numerous rewrites and deliberations until they were shot, were of paramount importance. "When we arrived in San Francisco," says Eric Schwab, "we decided we weren't ready to film the subway sequence because it wasn't concrete enough in our minds. So we took a break, about a month, which allowed us to approach the scene with fresh eyes. We needed to digest the filming we had done in the jungle, after which we were able to completely focus on this scene, which was so different from the rest of the shoot, but so crucial in framing the story."[177]

According to Le, someone else was originally lined up to play the Vietnamese student in the subway. She was on set, says Le, "but Brian De Palma changed his mind. Why, I don't know."[178] De Palma asserts that he "always wanted to use Thuy, and no other actress was considered in her place."[179] The actress' version of events is plausible, since nothing in Rabe's script specifies that the young bus (or subway) passenger should be Oanh's look-alike. It is probable that the production initially chose two different actresses of similar age and appearance before De Palma, perhaps quite late in the process, decided to cast Le in this second role. If the decision had been made during pre-production, the actress likely wouldn't have been forced to make a quick round trip to New Jersey in the middle of June 1988, while the production was still in Thailand, to get a prosthetic nose made. Paul Engelen prepared dentures for her in Bangkok, then Carl Fullerton took over in San Francisco. Le recalls "long makeup sessions" before shooting. Apart from the prosthetic, she wore glasses and colored contact lenses. During post-production, De Palma completed the transformation by having her voice dubbed by Amy Irving, whom he had cast years earlier in *Carrie* and *The Fury*.

In the film, the subway stranger no longer carries shopping bags as originally scripted and is not shown as a vulnerable immigrant struggling to survive in a foreign land. De Palma represents her a young student, perhaps from a wealthy Vietnamese family who fled the country during the fall of Saigon. Her refined English, devoid of an accent, suggests complete assimilation into American society. These alterations, among others, significantly reshape Rabe's epilogue.

David Rabe's absence from the fifth and sixth chapters of this book is notable, and for good reason: from the moment Columbia greenlit the script, his relationship with De Palma took a turn. Rabe didn't visit the production in Thailand (he evidently wasn't invited), he also wasn't invited into the editing room. He saw the film for the first time only after editing was completed. Linson attributes all this to the fact that Rabe "wasn't the sort to impose his views during filming," while also being careful to add that "when Brian needed something, he didn't hesitate to call."[180]

A few phone exchanges did occur between De Palma and Rabe during the Thailand shoot, though it's hard to determine their frequency and content. What we can say for sure is that De Palma did not regularly update Rabe on the numerous modifications he was making to the script: cutting one passage, abbreviating another, swapping scenes, adding new ones. Perhaps he was worried that Rabe would create similar problems to the ones he had encountered with David Mamet when shooting *The Untouchables* – problems that ultimately forced him to write two scenes himself that weren't in the original script.[181] With 8,500 miles between Thailand and New York, De Palma and Linson were able to explore alternatives with relative freedom, a method that had already proven successful for them.

Thuy Thu Le in the final scene of *Casualties of War*

The modifications made to the Vietnamese sequences were generally acceptable to Rabe, though the San Francisco epilogue was a different story, because De Palma's conception of the finale very much clashed with Rabe's. Without rehashing what has already been outlined in chapter four, it is worth noting that De Palma never liked any of the drafts of the epilogues completed before filming began. The version approved by the studio – somewhat inspired by Kazan's *The Visitors* – involved Eriksson returning home from Vietnam and having a nightmare. He wakes up on the subway (it was just a bad dream) before glimpsing the Vietnamese woman, striking up a conversation with her, and helping carry her shopping.

At the start of the *Casualties of War* shoot, the plan was to film a scene in Eriksson's house, for which sets had been partially constructed.[182] "What I remember is being asked to rehearse and briefly show shoulder in a Steadicam shot designed to be foreboding," writes Sean Penn. "And in my mind, wrongly defining of the true nature of my character. I remember saying to Brian, 'I don't do monster shots.' As I process it today, it was an argument of competing conceits."[183] During filming, De Palma abandoned the nightmare sequence and all scenes involving Kirsten and Kimberly (Eriksson's wife and daughter). On this point, says Rabe: "I felt there was enough violence in the story without it and when it was dropped from the film, I was relieved."[184] De Palma also streamlined the action around Eriksson and the unknown Vietnamese woman in the subway (Mark Weber, the carpenter character, also disappeared). These changes appear to align with the draft script that Rabe deemed the most accomplished.

In various drafts, including later ones, Rabe envisioned a prologue and epilogue set in wintertime, a decision that offered aesthetic and symbolic strengths and a stark contrast to the suffocating heat of Vietnam, while also reflecting Eriksson's psychological state upon his return (a contrast already made explicit by Kazan in a brief flashback in *The Visitors*). The final scenes of *Casualties of War*, as scripted, take on an almost Antonioni-esque mood: a wide shot captures Eriksson and the Vietnamese passenger, in a "empty and uninhabited" white landscape, moving in opposite directions on a train platform. Eriksson walks alone, then turns to watch the young woman's silhouette gradually diminish in the distance, swallowed by the blizzard. He stands, facing the deserted horizon as heavy snow settles on his shoulders and lashes his face, before turning toward home.

Filming an epilogue in "heavy snow" would have required changing filming dates and locations (which would pose scheduling issues) or deploying fake snow in a studio (which would contrast with the film's realistic tone). De Palma chose the simpler route by setting the epilogue in the middle of the summer. The choice likely masks deeper concerns expressed by Paramount during pre-production. Rabe's original ending would have overwhelmed the audience, likely already exhausted by the film's intense journey. De Palma and Linson considered the impact of a snowy conclusion on the film's reception and commercial prospects. De Palma concluded that a more luminous (both literally and figuratively) ending, symbolizing an awakening from a nightmare and liberation from self-destructive guilt, was the way forward.

But De Palma and Art Linson suspected that even with their combined efforts, matching Rabe's writing excellence would be challenging. Linson, in particular, feared that revising the epilogue wouldn't match the quality of the rest of the script. And so he decided to force Rabe's hand. "They were preparing the shoot when Art called asking me to write something which he more or less dictated," says Rabe. "He said if I didn't write it, they would, but that they wanted me to do it because I would do a better job – or something like that."[185] Rabe complied, but it seems evident that De Palma and Linson later made adjustments to the scene.

Brian De Palma and Art Linson

Winter in Minnesota, under the snow, gives way to sunny California in full summer. In the subway, which we last saw in the prologue, Eriksson wakes up and notices a young unknown woman of Vietnamese descent. He becomes unsettled. At the next stop, the passenger gets off. Eriksson notices that she has forgotten her scarf, so he rushes to pick it up from her seat and follows her outside to return it. The woman turns around, thanks him almost without looking at him, and is about to leave when Eriksson says a few words in Vietnamese. This leads to dialogue in which the stranger asks if she reminds him of someone, then assures him that his "nightmare" is over. She says goodbye and walks away after giving him a broad smile.

She is seen crossing Dolores Park, where couples lie on the grass facing a skyline – a promise of a better future, far from the ghosts of Vietnam.

Rabe recalls being "completely surprised" when he first saw the finished film, citing elements he claims never to have written, including the substitution of a bus for the subway. Decades later, it is not easy to verify claims that documentary evidence tends to contradict. However, one hint does sow doubt: there is no mention of the subway in the two versions of the screenplay that Rabe found in his archive. Does this mean someone (De Palma? Linson? a Columbia executive?) made modifications to the script without informing Rabe? This hypothesis is not improbable and suggests that Rabe lost control of every version of his screenplay from March 15, 1988 onward.

Similarly, Rabe asserts that two lines of the final dialogue, spoken by the stranger to Eriksson, were added without his knowledge: "Do I remind you of someone?" and "It's over now… I think." The last one was already in version V of the script (dated March 15, 1988), but the second was probably added shortly before shooting in San Francisco by De Palma, who believed he had alleviated Columbia's concerns about Rabe's melancholic ending. This decision became a bone of contention, one discussed in the final chapter of this book, which takes us from post-production to the tumultuous reception of *Casualties of War* and in which I will attempt to shed light on why the film has never been as highly regarded as the great Vietnam War films that preceded it.

Post-Production to Critical Reception
August 1988 – January 1990

The visual and auditory landscapes of *Casualties of War*
Editing, for Brian De Palma, has never been as adventurous a process as filming. Structural modifications during post-production are limited, in part because of his use of long takes. Consequently, the final form of *Casualties of War* was not found in the editing room. While De Palma occasionally made adjustments in response to filming decisions, post-production primarily affirmed or unified choices made during shooting.

Bill Pankow received rushes during filming and set about assembling a rough cut, which was waiting for De Palma when he returned home to New York from Thailand. The reels, in fact, had traveled far and wide before landing in Pankow's hands. "The rushes were sent from Thailand to London for processing and synchronization before being sent back to Thailand to be viewed on set," he recalls. "After that, they were shipped to Los Angeles for Columbia executives, and finally, two or three weeks after they were shot, I received them in New York."[1] Throughout this period, De Palma communicated with Pankow to keep him apprised of developments on location and answer any questions. The distance and time difference complicated their exchanges, but a new technology – email, specifically CompuServe – made their communication instantaneous.

Due to the overwhelming volume of material, the rough cut wasn't finished by the time De Palma returned to the United States, and Pankow was given an additional four weeks to complete the job. (Editing was relatively artisanal in the pre-digital era of the late 1980s. Pankow personally cut film strips using a Rivas splicer.) As was his usual practice, Pankow's initial edit – an exhaustive overview of the material – was long. Then came a process of subtraction: cutting unnecessary sections and readjusting or reorganizing sequences as needed. "Brian always has a very clear vision," says Pankow. "The more I work with him, the more I am able to identify it. I can review a shot and understand its intention. Brian isn't someone who comes and sits next to me all day long, as some directors do. He would simply sit down and review the cut I had made, give me notes, and ask, 'How long will it take you to address these notes?' I would give him a time frame, and he would come back to review the work. This process became shorter and shorter as the project evolved."[2]

De Palma's New York editing studio, where Pankow worked, was located at 1600 Broadway. A few buildings away, at 1619 Broadway, in the iconic Brill Building, supervising sound editor Maurice Schell was crafting a soundtrack befitting a story of a heinous crime committed amidst the chaos of war, but where the conflict between Americans and North Vietnamese remains a backdrop rather than the central focus. Schell's task was to convey the auditory nature of military violence without succumbing to the excesses that often characterize Vietnam War films. The job, as he puts it, was "not to interfere with the dialogue and not to introduce superficial effects that would distract the viewer from the main story."[3]

Schell, born 1937 into a Jewish family, lived through the Second World War and the anguish of deportation, and one presumes that his memories of this troubled period were as much auditory as they were visual. *Casualties of War* inevitably plunged him a half-century back in time, to memories of occupied France. "My personal story, that of a boy hidden between the ages of four and eight during the war, made me very sensitive to atrocities similar to those described in *Casualties of War*," says Schell. "That's why certain films I've worked on – and this one especially – are of great importance to me, because they focus on the tragic horror that I myself experienced, with my childish eyes."[4]

With the exception of a few lines spoiled by background noise or technical issues, all dialogue in the finished film was recorded live on location. (Le had to make "two or three trips to New York"[5] to rerecord certain lines, but according to Eric Schwab this was an isolated case.) When it came to sound effects, most were added during post-production. At Schell's request, one of the sound recordists in Thailand captured the noises of the jungle, along with an array of ambient sounds. But Schell wasn't happy with the result, and he ended up recreating most jungle sounds – crickets chirping and frogs croaking, the splashing of water and the echoes of thunder – in the studio. The same post-production process was used for the sounds of M-16 rifles, explosions, helicopters and soldiers' boots in the marshy forest and on rocky terrain. Daniel Lang initially reported that Storeby likened the sounds of Oanh being stabbed to the gutting of a deer. Rabe's screenplay does not explicitly include this detail, but Schell and his crew explored the sonic dimension. When Eriksson delivers a blow to Clark's head with a shovel, Schell struck a pig's head (a technique he had successfully used in other films, notably *Scarface*) with a blunt object.

Revisions and regrets
Casualties of War's opening shot shows the interior of a subway car. Eriksson, a passenger in a crowd, sitting at the back of the car and dozing against the window, isn't initially discernible. The front page of the newspaper held by a passenger, announcing the resignation of President Richard Nixon, places the prologue's action in the summer of 1974 – eight years after the events recounted in the film. People get on and off the train. As it is about to leave the station, a young woman hurries into the car and takes a seat. The camera floats from its static position and navigates between the rows of seats until it frames Eriksson in a medium close-up. This is followed by a series of shot/reverse-shots, cutting from his sleepy eyes to what appears to be his point of view: the passenger who just boarded the train. As the camera tracks toward her, the suggestion is that she reminds Eriksson of someone. The transition to the first sequence in Vietnam begins with a dissolve from Eriksson, asleep again, to the darkness of the jungle, where a group of G.I.s is patrolling. The lack of temporal precision preserves doubt about the images that follow. Is this dream or reality?

Rabe's screenplay specifies that the cut from the prologue to the Vietnam flashback should be abrupt, transitioning to the village scene in broad daylight under a scorching sun, followed by the sequence of the night battle in the jungle. During filming, the sequence order remained true to Rabe's vision. A comparison between the last accessible version of

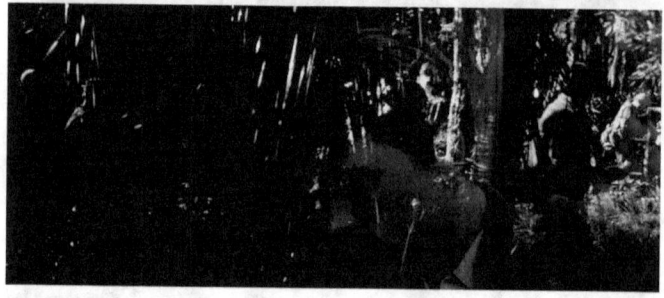

the screenplay (IV) and one of the call sheets (#2) shows that, in both cases, the battle scene is numbered 12 – with scene 11 being the village scene. During editing, De Palma informed Rabe of his intention to swap them. "I remember him telling me he did not like cutting from Eriksson sleeping on the bus to daylight in Vietnam," says Rabe. "It made more sense to him to cut to the nighttime battle."[6] This change was made for formal as well as symbolic reasons. The dissolve that connects Eriksson's sleeping face to the scene where soldiers advance in the darkness of the marshy jungle accentuates the impression that he is plunging into a nightmare.[7]

The battle sequence is indeed filmed as if it were a bad dream, constructed around a dichotomy of surface and depth. De Palma crafts the scene around Eriksson's body, symbolically trapped in the tunnel between the world of the living and the dead. In a single shot – moving from his torso above ground then descending down into the underground tunnel where it follows the silhouettes of North Vietnamese – the camera captures his extreme vulnerability. The image is of Eriksson, notes Antoine de Baecque, as "an anti-hero, a soldier on the brink of emasculation."[8] The images then alternate

Post-Production to Critical Reception

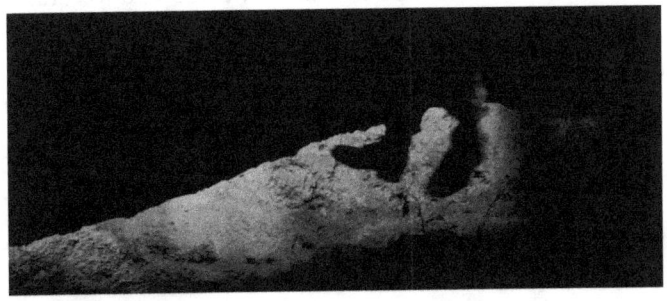

between close-ups of a North Vietnamese soldier and Eriksson, which, according to de Baecque, reflect an "unequal distribution of senses. One is able to see in the dark, the other is blinded by flashes igniting the jungle."[9] The representation of the communist fighter is something of a caricature ("crawling underground, knife between his teeth"), yet it doesn't clash with the deliberately exaggerated tone of the sequence, which mirrors the suspense of *Jaws*.[10] Iannis Katsahnias, noting this tip of the hat to Steven Spielberg's 1975 film, observes that De Palma seeks to "familiarize his audience, reassure them by demonstrating, unequivocally (a body halfway sunken into the ground, an underground threat approaching legs flailing in the void), that they are on familiar territory when it comes to Hollywood filmmaking."[11]

Then comes a role reversal. There is no emasculation. Meserve saves Eriksson at the last second by pulling him out of the hole. The enemy soldier has missed his chance. This is followed by a burst of violence, firstly when Meserve and Eriksson shoot and throw grenades at the tree where a sniper is hiding, then once the North Vietnamese soldier springs from the earth. Meserve pushes Eriksson aside and shoots the man, whose body vanishes into the tunnel from which he emerged. To accentuate this moment of violence, the camera makes a sudden rotation and frames Meserve in a low-angle shot, his face swollen and taut like an erect penis, marked by hatred and pleasure at killing. The image is deliberately obscene. Accentuated by the brutality of the editing and Meserve's panting joy, this explicit metaphor resurfaces during the rape scene when Meserve compares his penis to a weapon. The contrast with Eriksson – perceived by his comrades as "impotent and powerless,"[12] incapable of experiencing excitement in combat – becomes ever more glaring.

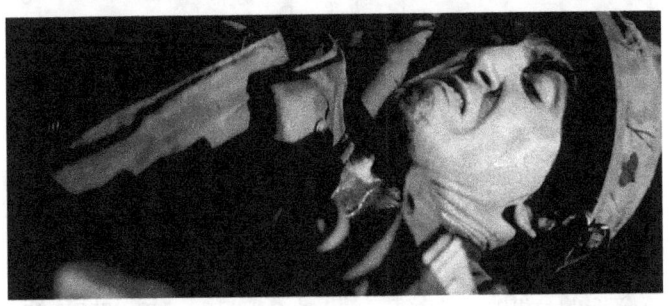

The battle scene also offers audiences a singular moment of pleasure, one unmatched throughout the rest of the film. Rabe recognized the scene's effectiveness but was uncomfortable with its juxtaposition against the village sequence. Originally placed after the village scene in the script, it suggested that the soldiers had been betrayed by the villagers, who failed to warn them about the enemy's presence. Can a soldier – in this case Eriksson – who has narrowly escaped death, genuinely fraternize with the villagers when his patrol's mission is to find pockets of communist resistance? De Palma's choice, though defying narrative logic, highlights Eriksson's innocence. Even amidst such violence, he retains his humanity in his interactions with the world around him.

This alteration in the chronology created another editing problem. John C. Reilly makes his first appearance as Hatcher during the battle, but it is Stephen Baldwin who plays that character in the village scene, which couldn't be reshot due to budget constraints. Bill Pankow attempted to minimize the discrepancy, ensuring that Hatcher's name isn't explicitly associated with shots of Reilly before the part where the soldier, dozing off, is addressed by Brown. No one mentions it during the fight. In the following scene, Penn briefly mentions it in passing while giving an order to his men, but the actor's clipped delivery makes it almost inaudible. Following the long continuous shot where the soldiers traverse the village, Baldwin disappears swiftly from the feature film (his name is absent from the end credits) and his appearance remains, in essence, anecdotal.

A matter of morality

While editing *Casualties of War*, Pankow attempted to minimize the use of cuts to preserve the integrity of one of the hallmarks of De Palma's visual style: the long take. This is evident in the village scene near the start of the film, where the immersive Steadicam follows Meserve and his troops as the sergeant chastises Eriksson for accepting fruit from the children. Once Meserve has exited the frame, Brown continues to scold Eriksson. The camera then encircles Eriksson 180 degrees before stopping so we can hear Clark berating Eriksson, then continues forward, without a cut, to Meserve, who stands in a small group that is interrogating a suspected communist sympathizer.

Post-Production to Critical Reception 345

Through his use of long takes, De Palma aims to enhance credibility in depicting both the settings and physical interactions between characters. Generally less conspicuous or performative than those in other De Palma films (with the exception of the camera movement during Eriksson's interrogation by the CID agents), the long takes in *Casualties of War* all share the same imperative: to give the viewer the impression of the least "manipulated" image possible. While the film is far from being entirely comprised of long takes, it nonetheless demonstrates a pursuit of truth in its cinematography. De Palma doesn't view cinema as "truth,"

as Godard suggested, but rather as "lying twenty-four times per second."[13] Filming with long takes is an attempt to limit the impact of editing and thus appear deceitful as little as possible. But François Niney points out, "if the long take creates a heightened sense of reality, it comes at the cost of greater artifice: executing such shots demands much more preparation and technique."[14]

De Palma often employs long takes for exposition scenes. The soldiers' arrival at the hut with Oanh is captured in a single camera movement, and later in the film, De Palma similarly opens the confrontation on the Kwai River bridge with a long, carefully constructed camera move, first capturing the North Vietnamese moving military materiel, before the camera, on a crane, gradually zooms in on the railroad tracks on the opposite side of the river, where Meserve and his men, along with their prisoner, are hiding. A long take like this captures the geography of the location and positions the characters within the landscape, so making the nascent conflict between these opposing forces clear. It is noteworthy that in both instances, these are future crime scenes. The long take thus acts as both attestation and warning. "This is where the worst will happen," the camera seems to caution.

In a similar vein, it is important to highlight De Palma's preference for long, fixed shots, which help preserve the physicality of performance and the dynamic potential of dialogue.[15] Images like these in *Casualties of War*, including the rape scene, often carry ethical weight.[16] To avoid depicting in detail the sexual abuse suffered by Oanh, De Palma positions the camera, motionless, from a distance, facing the entrance of the hut. The camera is tilted, deliberately destabilizing the frame. The image, lasting nearly three minutes, begins with Eriksson turning from the hut and walking away. Two cross-fades denote ellipses. One comes just before Meserve exits the hut. Night has fallen. Then, once the gang rape has ended, comes rain. The camera tilts up slightly only when Meserve stands and walks away, and follows him as he walks toward the lens and into a medium shot.

We might choose to reassess De Palma's entire body of work in light of this pivotal scene, sharply contrasting with the negative image of him frequently portrayed by critics: misogynistic, a purveyor of pornography and gratuitous

348 Casualties of War

violence, particularly against women. Do we need reminding of how profoundly feminist films like *Carrie* (which begins with the traumatic discovery of menstrual blood) and *Dressed to Kill* (which immerses us into the fantasies of a mature woman) truly are? On closer inspection, every inch of De Palma's cinema decries the oppression of women, whether they are being constrained in their freedoms (*Dressed to Kill*, *Scarface*), ridiculed (*Carrie*), objectified or subjected to violence (*Blow Out*, *Body Double*). Oftentimes, De Palma simultaneously assigns negative roles to men, portraying them as voyeurs, sexual obsessives, criminals and addicts. This denunciation is at the core of *Casualties of War*, within the specific context of the Vietnam War.

While in his previous films De Palma deliberately played with the voyeurism of the spectator, here he refuses to risk indulging in scopophilia. Conscious of the gaze his camera assumes, he emphasizes Eriksson's gesture of refusal, thus refusing to turn the rape into a spectacle. Contrary to some critics' arguments, the film doesn't adopt the "male gaze" just because the rape isn't shown from the victim's perspective. Instead, *Casualties of War* powerfully conveys the traumatic experience of rape, forcing audiences to feel its profound impact.

Compare this to a scene in *Platoon* where the unit, led by Staff Sergeant Barnes (Tom Berenger), destroys a village suspected of harboring communists. When Chris Taylor (Charlie Sheen) comes across a group of soldiers abusing a young woman, he intervenes, shoving one of the assailants aside. Anticipating Penn's line in *Casualties of War*, one of the rapists responds with, "What, you a homosexual, Taylor?" to which Taylor, evading the question, shouts back, "She's a fucking human being, man! Fuck you!" After being called a "fucking cherry tail," he calls out: "You're animals! All of you, you're fucking animals!" Rebuked by Sergeant Elias (Willem Dafoe), who watches from a distance, the attackers disperse. Stone concludes the sequence with a shot of soldiers evacuating the burning village, protecting women and carrying children in their arms. It is the image of these saviors that prevails and ultimately overshadows that of the assailants. Sheen – a symbol of the moral conscience of the American military – succeeds in steering his comrades back on track. Ultimately, they are not "bad guys," just men disoriented by war, and the rape is treated as a trivial incident. The scene, in light of the My Lai massacre it was inspired by, is doubly deceitful, obscuring the reality of history – the numerous rapes collectively perpetrated by Calley's men[17] – and attempts to establish a falsehood, that rapes in Vietnam were only isolated cases, blunders, certainly not premeditated acts as depicted in *Casualties of War*.

Politics and poetics of the face

In the rape sequence of the film, Meserve stands, walks in the rain toward the camera, and addresses Eriksson, who is framed in extreme close-up. Raindrops run down his face. The flash of lightning reveals a defiant gaze. Eriksson's accusing face is cut against Meserve's cynical and provocative profile, as he recites a revised excerpt from Psalm 23: "Ye, though I walk through the valley of evil, I shall fear no death, 'cause I'm the meanest motherfucker in the valley!" Penn's Mephistophelian[18] characterization is emphasized by natural elements (twilight, lightning, bluish light). Meserve's transformation, hinted at from the beginning of the film, has now been fully realized. There are few close-ups of Penn, so when they do appear, the imagery is all the more striking. His face occasionally fills almost the entire frame, creating an overwhelming presence. These close-ups highlight Penn's intense, almost histrionic performance, particularly during moments of fury, such as when Eriksson, armed with a shovel, confronts him, or when he orders his men to fire at Oanh. Penn emphasizes his character's dangerous and uncontrollable nature through exaggerated facial expressions, by contorting his mouth while chewing tobacco, widening his eyes, or tensing his jaw muscles, as seen when he slaps Diaz and shouts, "Be a man!"

Penn's performance is sometimes moderated by more restrained expressions, as evident in Brown's death scene, where his face shifts from anger and rage, as he tries to stem the bleeding, to a highly emotive expression during the helicopter evacuation of his friend. As noted by Simon Laisney, at this moment Penn is chewing tobacco, which enables him to repress Meserve's emotions while hinting at some inner turmoil.[19] Similarly, in the scene where Penn is shaving and tells his comrades of Brown's death, his performance shows signs of unease: tension in his mouth, a slight tremor in his hand holding the razor, a dignified but shaky gaze. He buries Meserve's true nature behind a mask, using the razor to smooth out his facial expressions. Penn's acting doesn't accentuate any simplistic dichotomy but instead adds complexity to Meserve. Penn isn't interested in eliciting straightforward empathy from the audience, and nor does he overplay the role (unlike Tom Berenger in *Platoon*). He maintains the complexity of his character.

Eriksson's close-ups contrast with Meserve's, highlighting the tragedy of a character grappling with an unresolved inner conflict. Although Fox's facial range might initially seem more limited than Penn's, he effectively conveys subtle nuances between distress and despair. This emotional turmoil is powerfully depicted in the abduction scene, where his gaze reflects a mix of disbelief and discomfort, stemming from his involuntary participation in the crime. His facial features appear more guarded as rebellion takes hold in him and he begins to fight back against Meserve. There follows a profound disturbance when he discovers Oanh's face covered in cuts and bruises, and later, when he attempts to administer first aid. (De Palma deftly transfers Eriksson's distress to the viewer by not subtitling Le's dialogue.) After the murder, Eriksson displays a combative yet affected demeanor, transitioning from rage (during confrontations with Clark) to emotional upheaval (when recounting his story to the chaplain, eyes brimming with tears) and even a state of dismay (overwhelmed by questions from the CID agents and the defense attorney).

Even more than in Rabe's screenplay, Eriksson's antiheroic nature is softened in the film. In real life, Storeby never physically confronted Gervase to save Mao. We see Eriksson, at the end of the abduction sequence, after the other soldiers have left, kneeling beside Oanh's weeping mother and sister. "I'm sorry," he twice repeats to them. Rabe, surprised to hear this line that had been added by De Palma, felt it accurately highlighted the soldier's "moral clarity,"[20] which isn't as evident at this stage in Lang's book. De Palma also made Eriksson's attempt to flee with Oanh after her assault more explicit. In Rabe's script, Eriksson initially plans to leave with the prisoner but quickly reconsiders, fearing accusations of desertion. De Palma felt Eriksson should take a stronger stance. In the film, he hesitates momentarily and tries to push Oanh away as she clings to him pleading for help, but ultimately decides to set aside his reservations and follows his conscience. He begins to lead Oanh away from the hut, but their escape is halted by the arrival of Clark, who orders him to rejoin the rest of the patrol. This sequence absolves Eriksson of failing to assist someone in danger and sets the stage for his later, though unsuccessful, intervention on the bridge, where he risks his life to try and prevent Oanh's murder.

Crying girl

Aside from being the most challenging to film, the bridge scene was also the most difficult to edit because, as Bill Pankow explains: "It was necessary to maintain the drama, tension, and horror of the situation. These evil men inflicted a terrible thing on this woman, but at the same time, they are American soldiers fighting against the North Vietnamese. A strange mix of emotions was at play here."[21] This conflict is similar to the one at the heart of *The Bridge on the River Kwai*, with Colonel Nicholson torn between his desire to preserve the bridge he and his fellow prisoners have built and the necessity to demolish it and so assist Allied forces. "Eriksson believes he should be loyal to his fellow squad members," writes Douglas Keesey, "but his empathy for Oahn's suffering pulls him toward siding with her against his own men."[22]

What might normally have become a typical scene in a Hollywood war film – broadly speaking, a clash between good (Americans) and bad (in this case, North Vietnamese), where there is no feminine presence – becomes something very different. In *Casualties of War*, the issues are less tactical than ethical. The film places what is usually peripheral at its center. The camera shows little interest in enemy combatants, who remain anonymous, never individualized, at a distance. Military combat recedes into the background in favor of the internal struggle between Meserve and Eriksson. The battle's opening volley comes from Eriksson, who fires his weapon not at the enemy but as a diversion to prevent Diaz from carrying out Meserve's orders and stabbing Oanh. De Palma's subversion of the codes of war films, in line with Rabe's script, means reducing issues of war to their simplest form: Eriksson is ordered by Meserve to cover him and his men as they cross the bridge.

De Palma cuts back from the soldiers to the North Vietnamese across the river, both sides exchanging fire, as Clark pulls Oanh into the bushes and leaves her for dead. The sound of his knife and her muffled screams are drowned out by the chaos of battle. Yet Oanh, still alive, emerges from the vegetation and struggles onto the bridge. The action of her slowly moving along the train tracks carries immense symbolic power, evoking the most emblematic portrayal of America's moral failure in Vietnam: Nick Ut's 1972 photograph of 9-year-old girl Kim Phuc, mistakenly bombed by South Vietnamese planes. It's not a direct quote; De Palma wasn't trying to replicate the image. Instead, he presents its negative, the missing piece.

In Ut's photograph, the girl, having removed her burning clothes, runs barefoot along the road, screaming in pain, in a pose reminiscent of a crucifixion. Alongside her run other children, including her older brother, while in the background American and South Vietnamese soldiers and photojournalists remain calm, in sharp contrast to Phuc's expression of terror. The photograph, awarded both the World Press and Pulitzer Prizes, stands out for its formal qualities. However, it is important not to forget that the iconic image is cropped, excluding the presence of *Life* magazine photographer David Burnet, who is seen reloading his camera. The cropping hints at the deep unease of a profession caught in an impossible ethical bind: to capture suffering on film rather than intervene (History records that Burnett and Ut both assisted the girl after photographing her.)

Oanh certainly isn't a little girl, nor is she a victim of a planned and consciously executed crime, but of military error. Nevertheless, De Palma's imagery of her – bloodied and longing to avoid death – holds the same symbolic value as does the image of Kim Phuc. Both Ut and De Palma depict a young, female victim metonymically representing the brutal aggression of Vietnam by the United States.[23] It's also essential to recall that Ut's photograph is "the image that should not have been shown of an event that should not have occurred," just like Ronald Haeberle's photos of the My Lai massacre, referenced by the image of Oanh's crushed body below the bridge after her execution.[24]

The end of heroism

Unlike in David Lean's film, the bridge in *Casualties of War* doesn't explode. What is shattered instead, blown apart by the brutality of four soldiers, is idealism. To further underscore the absurdity of war, Oanh's death leads to the forest's fiery destruction by helicopters, as well as collateral damage when an American patrol boat, navigating the river, is mistakenly hit. The irony is even greater since this destruction is the result of atrocities committed by Meserve and his men against Oanh rather than any genuine military engagement.

In this respect, *Casualties of War* is an inversion of *Apocalypse Now*, where the civilians bombed or strafed from helicopters are anonymous and distant figures, pulverized with a certain indifference. De Palma doesn't show the pilots' enjoyment, nor does he depict war as a "baroque dream of napalm and tropics"[25] but as a deluge of fire and steel, shifting scales, transitioning from the macrocosmic view of bombing to the microcosmic view of this small patch of greenery where, amidst red flowers, Oanh's lifeless body lies.

This sequence can once again be read as a critical commentary on *Apocalypse Now* and, more broadly, on cinematic representations of war. De Palma targets an "archetypal symbol of Vietnam": the helicopter, which he strips of its heroic dimension.[26] In the psychedelic prologue of Coppola's film, with Willard, dazed by drugs and alcohol, in his hotel room, we famously transition from the ceiling fan blades to helicopter blades, from hallucination to warlike fantasy, synchronized with the intoxicating music of The Doors. Conversely, in *Casualties of War*, the helicopter's blades merge with those of a hospital ventilator where Eriksson is being treated. He shifts from a semi-comatose state to a violent return to reality, with the background cacophony of the wounded being operated on, limbs amputated amidst their screams. The helicopter ceases to symbolize the heroism of the soldiers and becomes instead a symbol of trauma. While the script accentuates this aspect, De Palma drew inspiration from the experiences of his own father, who "served for three years on a hospital ship in the Pacific during the Second World War"[27] and could never shake the image of a soldier who had lost both legs, writhing in pain. De Palma integrated a haunting childhood horror into *Casualties of War*.

In its second half, the film leaves the battlefield to focus on Eriksson's fight for truth. He is determined that the crimes committed against Oanh do not go unpunished. The character of Rowan gains more depth, emerging as Eriksson's sole confidant, the only person who takes his story seriously. *Casualties of War* then veers into thriller territory, with Eriksson tasked with denouncing his fellow soldiers, an act which leads him successively to Lieutenant Reilly's office and the partly destroyed monastery where Captain Hill oversees troop advances.

De Palma stuck fairly faithfully to Rabe's script, but did allow for one startling addition: the attempted assassination of Eriksson in the latrines, which takes place following his exchanges with the two officers and, we presume, Meserve, Clark, Hatcher and Diaz then being told about these conversations. After surviving the latrine explosion, Eriksson, for the first time in the film, and standing in front of an incredulous Meserve, responds with violence by striking Clark in the face with a shovel. Rabe had no objections to this addition (the audience, in need of some catharsis, welcomes it[28]), and yet it further widens the gap between De Palma's Eriksson – forced by circumstances to act – and Lang's original. While the scene suggests that *Casualties of War* might become a revenge drama, that doesn't happen, and the next time we encounter Meserve and the others is in the courtroom.

Before the trial in Rabe's script is the investigation. In his 2006 director's cut, De Palma includes a nearly three-minute scene which puts Eriksson in direct conflict with CID agents, who relentlessly interrogate him and insist he is lying. Filmed in a single low-angle shot with a revolving camera, the scene heightens the intensity of Eriksson's ordeal as the two investigators attempt to break him. But he holds firm. The exchange concludes with Eriksson's assertion that he will be able to locate Oanh's body.

Cut to: a shot of the corpse, surrounded by the inspection team and forensic doctors, filmed from above, followed by a reverse shot of Captain Hill and Eriksson looking down, observing the investigation from the railroad track. "You couldn't let it rest, could you? You had to push it," says Hill. An infuriated Eriksson responds with a simple: "Go to hell... sir." A new trial awaits him: testifying before the court-martial, facing those he accuses.

The trial scene stands in stark contrast to archetypal courtroom dramas. De Palma's previous film, *The Untouchables*, also ends in a courtroom, but one which employs a very different visual strategy than *Casualties of War*. The sequence has a powerfully restrained mise-en-scène, with Meserve and his accomplices sitting in front of a static camera, distilling the essence of their characters into brief yet profound tableaux. "We each made a statement in turn, one after the other, in front of the fixed camera," recalls Don Harvey. "We each had to deliver our monologue from start to finish with no cuts. The take had to be perfect. I found that intimidating. Today, I wouldn't have any problem doing it, but after being in the jungle for months, my brain was

scrambled. I started each take worrying I was going to screw it up, but I got through it. I think it made the scene more intense and real."[29]

The trial sequence dialogue is faithful to Rabe's script, which is reproduced almost verbatim from the actual trial transcripts. Clark struggles to contain his rage; Hatcher, looking like a guilty child, sheepishly admits to the acts he is accused of, but justifies his behavior by citing the time he has spent in the field – three weeks longer than Eriksson; Diaz admits his guilt and betrays his comrades by testifying in court; and Meserve attempts to keep a cool head, offering no confession of guilt and boasting of his service record. In a moment that appears only in the 2006 director's cut, Eriksson's trial interrogation is shown. Shaken by the defense attorney's questioning and accused of cowardice, he eventually capitulates, admitting that it would have been better for him to have killed his comrades than to have let Oanh die.

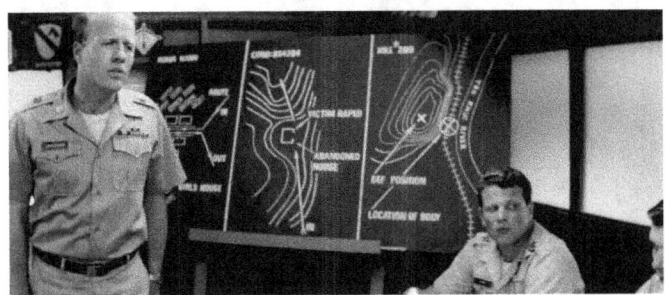

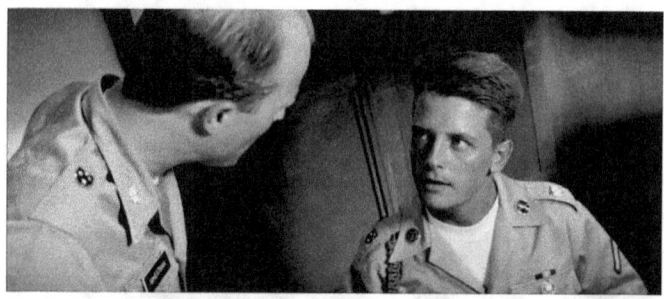

The courtroom scene took four days to shoot. De Palma, after filming the entirety of Rabe's script, decided not to include the testimony of Oanh's sister, Yen (played by Kady Tran), which he had captured in a single shot – initially framing her hands holding her sister's blood-stained scarf in a close-up, then zooming out to reveal her tear-filled eyes, unable to contain herself as she answers the prosecutor's questions.[30] This testimony is significant because in the actual trial, as in

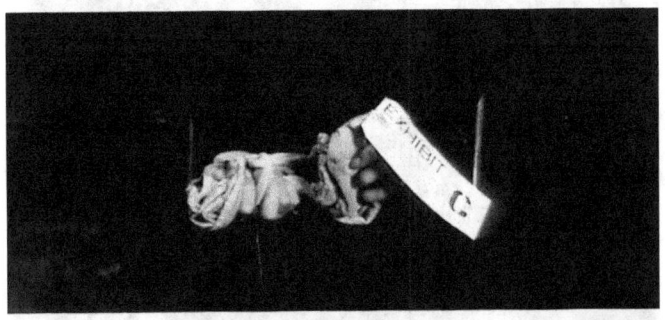

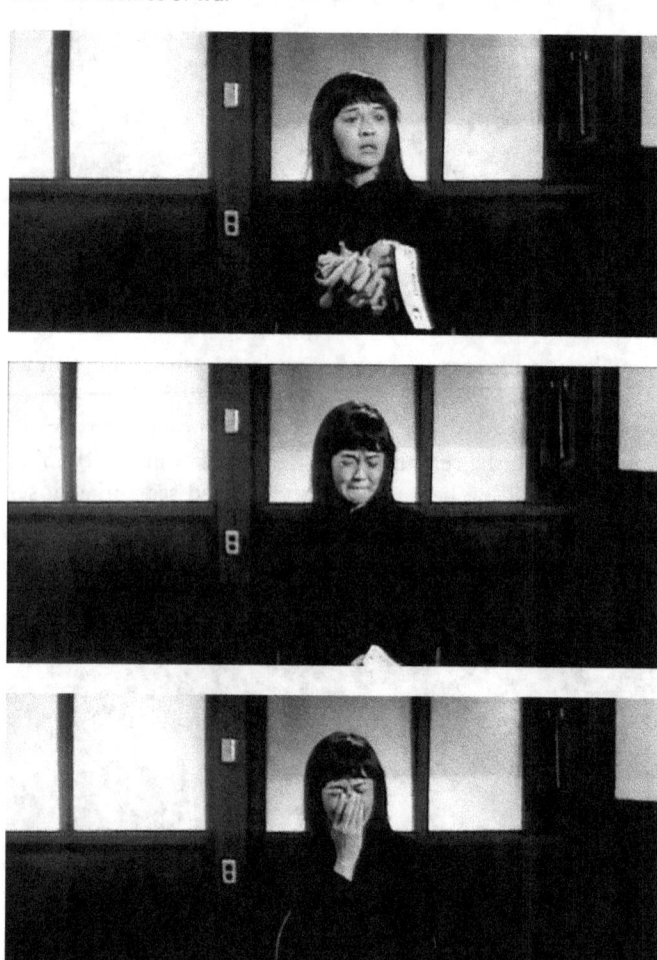

Lang's book and Rabe's script, Yen reveals before the court that her mother was kidnapped by communist troops and accused of collaborating with the South Vietnamese. "It is of course an added horror," says Rabe, "and terrible irony, and for a film we had enough of those."[31] De Palma cut the scene to avoid redundancy: "I didn't need to show Yen saying, 'I saw them take my sister…' The audience already knew."[32] While the film becomes more concise with that moment gone, it loses some of its complexity. Yen's testimony could

Post-Production to Critical Reception 367

have emphasized that the true losers of the war were civilians, who not only endured American aggression but also the brutal repression of communist forces. De Palma might also have been uncomfortable with showing the young woman's distress, as contrasted with the four accused. Perhaps it would have added unnecessary pathos to a scene that evidently didn't need it.

After the soldiers' testimony comes the verdict. Exiting the courtroom, Meserve whispers something to Eriksson, words that are inaudible to the audience but which we presume to be a threat. This impression is amplified by the soundtrack. We hear the hum of the subway and Hill's warning – "Even if these poor guys get convicted, they're not gonna do any real time. In fact, they're gonna be out of the stockade before you can flick flies off a shit, Eriksson. And if I was them, I'd be pissed off. Wouldn't you? I'd be lookin' for a little payback!" – as the scene transitions to the final sequence, the same one that opens the film.

The omission of the nightmare scene preceding Eriksson's encounter with the Vietnamese woman on the subway leads to the deletion of a scene written by Rabe, one that De Palma appears to have filmed: Eriksson's return on the plane to the United States, where the soldier engages in a conversation with a certain Evans – the role that was supposed to go to John C. Reilly. Once the actor was asked to play Hatcher, the role of Evans was given Woody Harrelson. No actors recall seeing Harrelson participate in military training, so it is assumed that he was chosen once filming had begun.[33] Bill Pankow vaguely remembers the plane sequence, but feels that had it been included, the film's narrative momentum would have been slowed.[34]

Eriksson's vertigo

Casualties of War's epilogue, which transports us back to the moment where the story began, is one reason why, for Chris Dumas, the film "is best understood as a remake of *Vertigo*."[35] Both films tell the story of "one man's failure – through indecision or handicap – to save a woman from death." In both cases, the deceased's reappearance occurs in San Francisco and the features of the lead actress are slightly altered through makeup and a change of hairstyle so she can play more than one role.[36] On these terms, Dumas suggests that *Casualties of War* succeeds where *Obsession* failed. In that film, De Palma attempted to recreate the unique atmosphere of Hitchcock's film, even to the extent of hiring the same composer, Bernard Herrmann. But with *Casualties of War*, he liberated himself from his illustrious role model and, by so doing – paradoxically, says Dumas – finally made a film as tragic and moving as *Vertigo*.

While I partially agree with this interpretation, I have reservations about the term "remake." De Palma did not consciously think of Kim Novak playing two characters in *Vertigo* when he cast Thuy Thu Le as the subway passenger, nor did he explicitly reference Hitchcock when planning and shooting *Casualties of War*. The similarities that Dumas identifies between the two films are, it seems, coincidental and unconscious. De Palma intensifies the drama by transforming the Vietnamese subway passenger into Oanh's doppelgänger (not something mentioned by Rabe in his script). As for San Francisco, it was chosen for reasons of credibility because at the time it was home to a much more significant Vietnamese community than the Minnesota countryside, where Rabe initially set the epilogue.[37]

It is important to note that *Casualties of War*, whose structure is reminiscent of *Vertigo*, diverges significantly from Hitchcock's narrative midway. When Scottie believes that he recognizes the blonde Madeleine in the brunette Judy, the film's second half begins and he goes to great lengths to resurrect the dead Madeleine in the body of the living Judy, only to discover that they are one and the same. *Casualties of War*, in which Eriksson is unable to bring Oanh back to life, follows a different path. The film's epilogue feels like a commentary on Hitchcock's masterpiece (a swan song, in fact, that *Body Double* had already sung). The Vietnamese woman and Judy ask the same question of Eriksson and Scottie: "Do I remind you of someone?" But unlike Scottie, Eriksson harbors no hopes of forging a connection with this stranger. Scottie's and Eriksson's failures are fundamentally different. Scottie loses the woman – or the image of the woman – that he fell desperately in love with, whereas Eriksson feels only a chaste, almost paternal love for Oanh, devoid of any sexual intent. He is a more positive and less ambiguous character

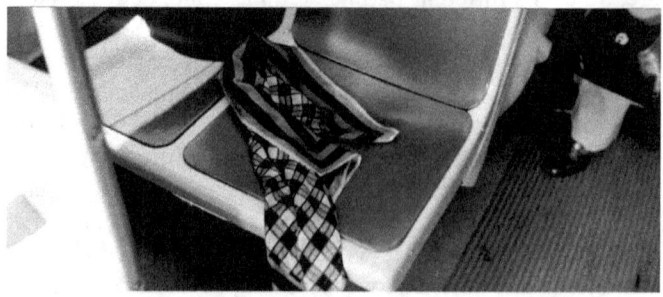

than Scottie, who turns out to be a possessive, unsettling character, and mercilessly violent.[38]

While De Palma can be blamed for some of the epilogue's clumsiness, he should be credited for adding an important detail absent from Rabe's script: the scarf that the passenger leaves on her seat when getting off the subway, a reminder of the scarf that Oanh's desperate mother handed to her daughter as she was being abducted and that was used to gag her. Eriksson rushes to pick up the scarf and follows the woman so he can hand it to her – while clearly replaying Oanh's abduction in his mind. This action might be an unconscious attempt on his part to alleviate his anguish, a way for him to unburden himself from the weight of his guilt and make for a happy ending. But, of course, as Eriksson keenly understands, the gesture is futile. Fox's facial expressions depict the veteran's abject despair. Unable to hold the woman's gaze for long, Eriksson – eight years after the events he witnessed – is incapable of looking at the world around him without superimposing the image of Oanh on it. Evidently suffering from symptoms of post-traumatic stress, he is overwhelmed by a sense of the uncanny, an intense trauma that blurs the line between dream and reality, as he reexperiences a moment that cast him into the grip of an unavoidable fate.

De Palma doesn't need a flashback of the kidnapping to convey that Eriksson is reliving something more real than reality itself. The question is not whether Eriksson will turn the page but whether he can contend with the irrepressible tension between memory and forgetfulness. Ennio Morricone's score during the epilogue invites us to explore this tension even further.

A dying bird

By the late 1980s, Ennio Morricone was a living legend, with nearly 300 film scores to his credit. His collaborations with many directors, including Sergio Leone, Pier Paolo Pasolini, Dario Argento, Bernardo Bertolucci, Gillo Pontecorvo, Don Siegel and Terrence Malick, made him one of the most respected and sought-after film composers. De Palma's collaborations with Bernard Herrmann and Pino Donaggio highlight the importance of music in his films, and his work with Morricone – which began with *The Untouchables* and continued after *Casualties of War* with *Mission to Mars* – was no exception. Morricone quickly found common ground with De Palma, who, he says, "made an excellent first impression on me, though I noticed from the start that he was a very reserved and introverted man. At any rate, his behavior concealed a sensitive and kind person."[39]

Before Morricone began his work on *Casualties of War*, De Palma gave Bill Pankow a selection of music from other films – including John Carpenter's *The Thing* and other pieces by Morricone himself – to temporarily integrate into the film and hopefully inspire Morricone.[40] This practice, fairly common in Hollywood, displeased Morricone, who preferred to work from a blank slate. De Palma says that Morricone didn't even bother to listen to the cassette he had prepared for him..[41]

Morricone flew to New York when the editing of *Casualties of War* was nearly complete. Speaking only Italian, he communicated with De Palma through his translator, Vivian Treves. "Ennio sat in the editing room with Brian, myself and the translator," says Bill Pankow, "and watched reel after reel of the film. Brian shared his feelings about each scene, and after watching the whole movie – which, if I remember correctly, took us two full days – Ennio settled in a nearby studio with a piano and composed the basic themes of the film."[42] Morricone would usually offer several alternatives to the filmmakers he worked with. "I propose four or five options for a single theme. As a result I come up with approximately twenty pieces for each film; this can be disorienting for some directors. Eventually, through reasoning, we usually find the right path. We stop, we listen patiently, and gradually things start to come along with time."[43]

In contrast to *The Untouchables*, where Morricone and De Palma had "long groped to find the two main themes," the writing of the *Casualties of War* score was done in "record time." "A very important piece had to accompany the scene where Eriksson discovers Oanh's bruised face," says De Palma, "but Morricone didn't need to listen to anything. I simply described the pieces to him one after the other, and that was enough. [...] He hit the mark right away." Several meetings followed, during which Morricone, at the piano, played the pieces for De Palma, who shared his impressions. Once Pankow had completed the editing and De Palma gave his approval, Morricone recorded the soundtrack of *Casualties of War* in Rome, at the Forum Music Village, in December 1988.

"I was fortunate to be invited to watch him record the score of the movie," reveals Monica Goldstein. "Morricone had the most discerning ear, picking up on things no one else could possibly hear. Panpipes were prominently used in one of the themes vital to expressing Oanh's innocence and sorrowful fate. Melodic, ethereal, yet eerie and gripping. Not completely satisfied, wanting a different pitch, a quick meeting took place resulting with someone taking a syringe of water and injecting it in the bamboo, causing it to swell to the sound he wanted."[44]

Casualties of War represents one of Morricone's most beautiful compositions, yet it remains one of his least known. It showcases his extraordinary talent to create poignant and unforgettable melodies, combined with a clear taste for experimentation. This tendency is evident at various points in the film, primarily passages that move away from pure emotion to focus on danger and violence, notably the sequences where Eriksson is stuck in the tunnel; Oanh, feet bloodied, back bent under the weight of Hatcher's pack, stumbling through the forest; Meserve urging Diaz to stab Oanh; and the attempted murder of Eriksson in the latrines.[45] For the musical pieces accompanying these scenes, in addition to string, brass and woodwind instruments, Morricone used a "prepared piano" (whose sound had been altered by placing various objects between or on the strings), marimba and other unconventional percussion techniques. Morricone's interest in a hybrid musical language, "applying a harmonic rationale that contradicts the tonal system,"[46] is evident in his *Casualties of War* score, which leans toward serialism without fully embracing it.

Alessandro De Rosa notes that Morricone often plays with the symbolic relationship between the score and elem-ents of the film, especially in the use of instruments. In *Casualties of War*, the choice of the panpipes to represent Oanh, coupled with the bass flute, fits this pattern. "I was struck by the symbolic figure of a Vietnamese girl who is imprisoned, abused, and murdered, riddled with bullets by a group of U.S. soldiers on a railway bridge," explains Morricone. "She buckles onto her legs like a dying bird, before tumbling down from the high ground. I imagined a theme based on just a few notes for two panpipes, which, by ping-ponging their sound, evoke the slowing fluttering of a bird's wings shortly before death. The Clemente brothers, the two pipers, amazingly rendered this idea, which was anything but ordinary for the instrument's traditional repertory. I contrasted the panpipes with a low-range brass cluster, which I believe well renders the soft and yet stifling grip of the cold ground onto which the girl's body collapses and dies. The main theme gradually emerges from this atmosphere."[47]

Oanh's theme, one of Morricone's most poignant, is first heard in the film's opening scene when the Vietnamese woman boards the subway and reappears in various forms between the moment the soldiers abduct Oanh and the epilogue.[48] Another theme is heard when Brown is dying and Cherry is killed,[49] then one final time in the epilogue, intertwined with a choral version of Oanh's theme.[50] Musicologist Todd Decker notes that this is the "only moment [in the film] when the score's two primary theme groups are juxtaposed,"[51] an observation that offers a nuanced perspective on criticism aimed at De Palma for a climax seen as consoling, in contrast to the film's overwhelmingly somber tone. And yet, the music heard during the encounter between Eriksson and the woman on the subway is a condensed reprise of variations on Oanh's theme, which suggests that Morricone is reminding us not to forget her, in the same way that Michael J. Fox's expression in the film's final seconds implies that Eriksson will be eternally ensnared by his memories. "Matching this performance," writes Decker, "nothing about the final cue suggests that the story just seen or the war just depicted is resolved. Morricone's music, together with the gradual introduction of the end titles, appeals to the viewer to stay in their seat, to not exit the theater, to not assume *Casualties of War* (or whatever is meant in American culture by the word Vietnam) is over."[52]

The soaring choir, reminiscent of the finale of Morricone's music for *The Mission*, written a couple of years earlier, steers the score toward sacred music. The panpipes have been replaced by voices repeating the word "ciao" ("chào" in Vietnamese). Oanh's theme is transformed into a universal requiem, as if the voices of every one of the war's innocent victims are mingling with hers, before returning to the panpipes as the credits end. If the audience stays for the full duration of the film's closing credits, Oanh's "voice" would be the final sound they hear. Should they, as Todd Decker proposes, interpret Morricone's score as being in conflict with the Vietnamese woman's last words to Eriksson: "It's over now"? De Palma wanted to end the film on an upbeat note, suggesting that those words somehow absolve Eriksson – and the audience – of their guilt. The ending of *Casualties of War* is therefore, to use a musical term, dissonant, torn between the desire for redemption, a call to turn the page, and, despite everything, the impossibility of forgetting. Paradoxically, its strength lies in these conflicting emotions. Morricone's music, contradicting the spoken dialogue, preserves Oanh's memory, offering a compromise between Rabe's radical vision and De Palma's more hopeful one.

Finally, it is important to highlight the originality of the music in *Casualties of War* compared to the major Vietnam War films that preceded it, notably a deliberate avoidance of rock music. At most, the music of The Doors, which became a cliché in the representation of the Vietnam conflict after *Apocalypse Now*, is ironically referenced through the character of Clark, who before he rapes her whispers to Oanh the refrain of one of the Californian group's most famous efforts: "Hello, I Love You." In Rabe's script, the song, first heard in the military base after Brown's death and just before Meserve and his men's (aborted) visit to the brothel, recurs like a leitmotif. As written by Rabe, the final seconds of the track would play during Oanh's rape, just after Diaz enters the hut. In the film, De Palma has Don Harvey sing the lyrics to the song, an illustration of his refusal to place *Casualties of War* within the conventional mythology of Vietnam War films.

Rock music in Vietnam was, for many soldiers, a way of connecting with "their homes, families, and parts of themselves they felt slipping away," a "release from the uncertainty, isolation, and sometimes stark terror" of the war zone.[53] But Meserve and his men are never carried away by the frenzy of rock or pop, nor do they consider it "the key to survival and a path to healing."[54] Songs from the 1960s in *Casualties of War* are reduced to barely audible background music, notably in the club where the chaplain speaks with Eriksson. In this respect, the film is the antithesis of *Full Metal Jacket*, in which a miniskirted Vietnamese prostitute approaches the G.I.s while swaying to Nancy Sinatra's hit "These Boots Are Made For Walkin'" (1966). Described by Antoine Pecqueur as a "symbol of female emancipation,"[55] the song also conveys a sense of "aggression and abandonment associated with both Marine boot camp and the dangerous world of sex and crime in Vietnam."[56] Vietnamese women, in Kubrick's films, are portrayed as venal and manipulative. De Palma and Rabe, in contrast, dismantle this cliché by using The Doors' song to expose Clarks' viciousness. His lecherous gaze turns an innocent woman into a "VC whore."

De Palma also chose not to use classical music in *Casualties of War*, unlike Francis Coppola or Oliver Stone, whose *Platoon* features Samuel Barber's orchestral work "Adagio for Strings," a piece often played "at times of national crisis," including after the assassination of President Kennedy.[57] "Adagio" is heard during the sequence where a village is destroyed (an evocation of the My Lai massacre), but its primary function is to illustrate the tragedy of the American soldiers in Vietnam. Heard in the opening scene, where body bags are loaded onto a helicopter, it recurs at the moment of Elias' death. Despite appearing on the soundtrack of a film about the failure of the American military, Barber's music – which has become a symbol of "the loss of innocence"[58] – also carries a solemn dimension that invites reflection, serving as a hymn honoring G.I.s who died in combat.

Morricone's music, while at times underscoring the soldiers' distress, never seeks to glorify their heroism. The night battle at the beginning of the film features polytonal and polyrhythmic music, with jarring sounds that convey the madness of war, the horror of combat. Elegies texture only non-heroic deaths, which never occur on the frontline: Brown is cut down by enemy gunfire while the soldiers rest in an apparently peaceful village, and Cherry steps on a mine. The music of *Casualties of War* lacks the commemorative qualities of *Platoon*'s score, and the film, while appearing to encourage resilience, is ultimately unable to resolve Eriksson's dilemma. He is permanently marked by his experience and can never forget Oanh. He will have to learn to live with his sense of loss – something poignantly reinforced by Morricone's score.

The test of strength

Casualties of War, shot in 35mm, was blown up to 70mm, which explains why, says Bill Pankow, "fifteen months passed between the start of filming in April 1988 and the completion of post-production in July of the following year."[59]

By early 1989, with many technical details smoothed over and the music score recorded, it was time for test screenings. In her chronicle of the filming of *The Bonfire of the Vanities*, Julie Salamon reveals that "Columbia Pictures didn't plan to release [the film] for several months."[60] This was most likely the consequence of test screenings, the very first of which was disastrous. Salamon reports that the viewers "found the film too stark, too full of sorrow."[61] De Palma had suspected that *Casualties of War* wasn't going to be a box office hit, but he certainly didn't anticipate such a harsh reception. Before the test screenings, he had shown an initial cut to Martin Scorsese, who gave his immediate impressions. Scorsese expressed some reservations about Penn's performance, which he deemed "a bit theatrical," advising him to cut a dialogue scene that is "a bit too talkative," and, notably, Eriksson's monologue in front of the body of Cherry, "which he found a bit too heavy-handed, saying it was the viewpoint of others and not really that of the character."[62] But De Palma, convinced of the importance of the speech, chose not to follow his friend's advice.

An April 1989 screening at a Boston cinema was attended by De Palma, Art Linson and Columbia executives, including Dawn Steel. Also there, to show his support for De Palma, was Steven Spielberg. *New York Times* journalist Bruce Weber noted the nervous atmosphere. Midway through the screening, half a dozen spectators got up and left, presumably because they found the film unbearable. "And when the lights finally come up, the theater is silent. Not a rustle," wrote Bruce Weber, who caught fragments of an exchange between Spielberg and a man sitting next to Dawn Steel. "You'll be thinking about this for a week," whispered Spielberg.[63] Steel didn't hide her enthusiasm, says Fred Caruso, who remembers her saying, in her usual blunt manner, "I don't give a fuck about what the press and critics might think! I'm happy I made this movie. I think it's a great film, a story worth telling, and I'm proud to have been one of those who decided to produce it."[64] The audience feedback was met by Linson and Steel with what Weber described as "wary satisfaction." De Palma was more pessimistic, concerned about the audience's irritated reactions during a key exposition scene. The evaluations proved him right. Ratings ranged from "good" to "very good," but there were no boxes ticked "excellent." For a film like this, noted De Palma, "I'm not sure testing has any relevance."[65]

Regardless, the feedback prompted De Palma to send the film back to the editing room for adjustments. He added an opening title card stating that the film was based on a true story by Daniel Lang, first published in *The New Yorker*. This addition was the result of comments from some viewers after test screenings who reportedly found the story implausible. De Palma also cut two scenes – Eriksson's interrogation by CID agents and his testimony during the trial – to make the film "more palatable to the public."[66] He felt that audiences might have a hard time digesting the fact that Eriksson had to endure further hardships and verbal abuse during the trial.[67] Nevertheless, he made these cuts reluctantly, fearing that they "wouldn't make any difference for audiences" and would compromise the film's integrity.[68] "I think he regretted it," says Eric Schwab, "because these sequences captured the intensity of the situation from Michael J. Fox's character's point of view."[69]

For seventeen years, De Palma agonized over his decision. After an initial DVD release in the early 2000s, *Casualties of War* was reissued in 2006 in a director's cut which included the two cut sequences. "Brian called me, and I went to the Columbia offices in Los Angeles to see what rushes were available," recalls Pankow. "There was actually very little material that we hadn't already used. I remember another scene with the young soldier who is killed by the mine, but there was really very little to recover."[70] According to Pankow, it was Columbia Pictures who asked De Palma to add the scenes that he had removed years earlier. Sony Pictures, which had since acquired Columbia, saw it as an opportunity to entice owners of the first DVD edition to spend money on the second, which, apart from its six minutes of new footage, did not undergo a new restoration.[71] This turn of events allowed De Palma to deliver a cut more in line with his initial vision.

Disapproval

August 13, 1989. With the release of *Casualties of War* in American cinemas just five days away, De Palma and Fox were on the press junket. While anxiously awaiting the first reviews, Michael Norman, a journalist at *The New York Times* and a Vietnam War veteran, dropped a bombshell. In an article about *Casualties of War*, he revealed that Rabe might have grievances against the film and was attempting to dissociate himself from its promotional campaign. When contacted by Norman, De Palma and Linson cited "artistic disagreements," but did not elaborate on reasons for any discord.[72]

Today, Linson prefers to downplay Rabe's reaction. "He was unhappy, but David Mamet was also unhappy when he saw *The Untouchables*, which he had written the script for. He even walked out during the screening. So it wasn't the first time this happened to us. Brian had also faced similar issues with Oliver Stone on *Scarface*. We all know how things work: you've something in mind, and somebody comes along and changes it. You no longer have any control. If that

Brian De Palma

happens, there's only one solution: keep your mouth shut and carry on, and if you can't, get out of the way, because there's no way to stop the tide. The movie business is like that, and it's always the case when we do big movies. It was unrealistic to think that Brian's vision of *Casualties of War* would perfectly align with David's. Above all, I think that David was upset about the ending."[73]

Proud of the final sequence, which he considers "extremely moving," De Palma took Rabe's reaction very badly. "I was deeply affected by the fact that David didn't like it," he was still brooding 30 years later.[74] But Rabe's complaints weren't solely about the ending of *Casualties of War*. Back in 1989, he wasn't ready to speak out publicly and disown the film, but today he acknowledges: "I was disturbed by the rearrangement of certain sequences and the addition of dialogue that I thought hurt the narrative. These things colored my overall experience of the film, though I was aware of the power of the acting and of the supremely raw and honest filmmaking in the rape sequence, and some others. I thought Ennio Morricone's music was very powerful and moving, other than at the end sequence, where it seemed excessive."[75]

When Michael Norman reached out to Rabe, perhaps he knew – through word of mouth – that the screening of *Casualties of War* had made him uncomfortable. Norman moved in the same circles as Rabe, and through a mutual friend he obtained Rabe's phone number and called to request an interview, which Rabe politely but firmly declined. Nevertheless, Rabe did agree to explain the reasons for his refusal. "After establishing, I thought, that we were talking 'off the record,' I tried to explain to him why I did not want to participate in the article he was doing. The conclusion of the conversation was basically that he would state in his article [...] that I 'had some problems with the movie but had declined to discuss them.'"[76] When Norman's article appeared, Rabe, disheartened, took it as a betrayal and requested a right of reply from *The New York Times*, which published his explanation on August 27.

While Rabe admitted to having mixed feelings about the film, he denied wanting to "dissociate" himself from it, and pushed back against Norman's claims. "I have no desire to attack this movie," he wrote, attempting to put an end to the issue without elaborating on the reasons for his frustration. At most, he succinctly conceded: "While it is true that I wish the movie were different in certain parts than it is, it is also true that Sean Penn and Michael Fox delivered daring, beautiful performances, as do so many of the other actors," before concluding with a somewhat muted statement: "Though I cannot deny that compared to some ideal movie in my head, the film is not what I had hoped for, it is also obvious to me that compared to 95 percent of what is available in the surrounding theaters, *Casualties of War* is a worthwhile achievement."[77]

A few days before Rabe's letter was published in *The New York Times*, Vietnam War veterans' associations (the same groups that had endorsed *Platoon*) railed against *Casualties of War* for its portrayal of the conflict and the American military. John P. Wheeler, president of the Vietnam Veteran Memorial Fund, was particularly vehement. "De Palma declines to tell the greater truth, that in Vietnam, the overwhelming number [of American soldiers] were decent, built orphanages, roads, hospitals and schools," he said at a press conference on August 23. According to Wheeler, *Casualties of War* "depicts vets as morally insensitive, barely competent soldiers with cynical and cowardly officers... It's a lie about what we were really like." Concluded an agitated Wheeler: "Every dollar spent to see this film is a knife plunged into the heart of some vet, his kids or others who love him."[78] Marc Leepson, a spokesperson for veterans' associations, expressed similarly unrestrained sentiments: "The unspoken message of *Casualties of War* is that the norm in Vietnam was rape and murder, and that only a brave handful of G.I.s acted humanely. This message is 180 degrees from the truth... Now, thanks to Brian De Palma, the cinematic image of those who fought in Vietnam has taken a giant step backward."[79]

"I wasn't altogether surprised," admits David Rabe many years later, "and yet I was disturbed. Some of these reactions were, of course, politically motivated."[80] In Montreal, where De Palma presented *Casualties of War* at the World Film Festival and faced a barrage of criticism, he didn't shy away from press questions, explaining: "I've got many letters from veterans who say the movie's completely accurate about the kind of things that went on there."[81] Statements like that hardly calmed the ire of veterans, for whom the response from Rabe – one of their own – seemed like a form of disavowal of the film. Mike Stokey understood such reactions. "*Casualties of War* is a tough, brutal story taken from a big headline in the news," he explains. "At least for combat vets, it felt like a punch in the stomach. It's not that anyone should pretend that the events never happened, but they are so unusual, so unrepresentative." Stokey suggests there was a sense that focusing on such "rare" incidents in a film unfairly misrepresented American soldiers.

Nevertheless, some veterans – a minority – offered support, including Jan Scruggs, founder of the Vietnam Veterans Memorial Fund. "I really felt [that *Casualties of War*] had a very important and poignant message. During times of war, everything you've learned in your life, all your morals, go out the window. This is something that really happened. Just because it's unpleasant, you can't just pretend it didn't happen."[82]

"I knew there would be some pushback from Vietnam veterans," says Dale Dye. "That was entirely predictable, but I felt then – and I feel now – that we should not avoid this type of negative story. The key for me is that the soldiers are depicted as a tragic exception to the otherwise selfless and honorable service of the vast majority of men who served in Vietnam."[83]

On September 2, 1989, Jeff Danziger, cartoonist for the *Christian Science Monitor*, who between 1967 and 1971 had fought in Vietnam, published a column in the *Boston Globe* in which he expressed his strong disapproval of *Casualties of War*. His exaggerations bordered on slander. His goal: to malign De Palma and restore the honor of his supposedly wronged comrades. By positioning himself as a crusader for justice, Danziger – who failed even to mention that the film is based on real events – sought to promote his deliberately revisionist account of the Vietnam War's history. Confessing to leaving the cinema in the middle of the film due to "being rendered helpless with laughter by the first half," Danziger described it as "poorly acted and directed," and accused De Palma of being "an opportunist hack" who had sacrificed historical truth for profit. This, he continued, "was the average soldier's experience: hard, dangerous work in a hot climate, seven days a week. He did not think of rape and pillage. He thought of home. He held pity for the villagers whose lives he was forced to dislocate, and in most cases he held a grudging respect for the VC and the North Vietnamese. Soldiers or officers who took crazy chances to satisfy a personal animus were straightened out quickly because of the danger they posed to the squad. Anyone who proposed the plot line of De Palma's film would have been ignored. Of course, Vietnam wasn't Hollywood."[84]

The following week, the *Boston Globe* published a letter from Peter C. Holloran supporting Danziger's views, and going further: "This mean and deceitful film will forever tarnish the memory of my veteran comrades who served honorably [...] and patriotically during this catastrophic Vietnam War."[85] Danziger's piece did provoke at least one counterresponse. In a letter to *The Sunday Rutland Herald*, which had republished it, Barbara Bosworth, from Vermont, denounces Danziger's untruths.

Unfortunately, the film about which the cartoonist laughed so long and hard was based on a true story. In November 1966, a squad of American soldiers on reconnaissance patrol in the central highlands of Vietnam kidnapped, gang-raped, and murdered a Vietnamese woman, Phan Thi Mao, who was about 20 years old.

I remember reading Daniel Lang's article about this crime and its aftermath in *The New Yorker* in 1969. Women and girls were raped before and during the My Lai massacre in 1968, and there were many other recorded incidences of sexual assault against Vietnamese women by American soldiers.

I don't want my friends who served in Vietnam and other wars to be regarded as rapists and murderers. On the other hand, this sort of crime should not be swept under the rug either, as Danziger seems to think it should be.

The publication of his offensive and inaccurate comments in the *Boston Globe* [...] and in *The Sunday Rutland Herald* shows that sexual violence against women during wartime is still not taken seriously.[86]

A media lynching?

The veterans' coalition cast a shadow over the reception of *Casualties of War*, which was already undermined by Michael Norman's revelations, setting the stage for a disastrous launch. Julie Salamon recounts a phone call made to De Palma by Dawn Steel announcing that the opening night's numbers were "not very promising."[87] The film grossed only $2 million from 1,486 screens across the United States. In its first week, *Casualties of War* barely hit fourth place at the box office, after James Cameron's *The Abyss* and two comedies, Ron Howard's *Parenthood* and John Hughes' *Uncle Buck*.[88] After five weeks, it had grossed less than $20 million – seven times less than *Platoon* and with a budget nearly four times higher.[89] In the end, the film lost just under $4 million.

De Palma seemed doomed to endure yet more scrutiny. "I remember reading the reviews and watching the lines in front of theatres," he says. "Ironically, it was right here in New York that I was attacked the most fiercely, by *The Village*

Voice, which even put my picture on the cover. I didn't dare leave my house because Frances FitzGerald, author of *Fire in the Lake*, a famous book about Vietnam that had won the National Book Award, dragged me through the mud. I have never received such an overtly negative review in a magazine with my picture on the cover!"[90]

Looking at the *Voice* article, with its blaring headline "Brian De Palma's Latest Outrage," it's easy to see why De Palma was so upset. But the paper did also publish two other texts about the film: a lukewarm review by J. Hoberman and an extensive and enlightening set report by Allen Barra, who called *Casualties of War* "the most openly political film about the Vietnam War since John Wayne rode off into the setting sun in *The Green Berets*," and concluded that after this film, no one could ever again accuse De Palma of misogyny.[91] Compared to Barra's nuanced article (which is full of interview quotes with De Palma, Michael J. Fox and others), FitzGerald's review (a mere half-page) seems almost insignificant. Extremely dismissive, FitzGerald didn't mince her words. The opening sentence sets the tone: "*Casualties of War* is a sadoporn film coated with sentimentality and laced with every cliché of the Vietnam War." FitzGerald reproaches De Palma for focusing on the "atrocity" of the story: "At least an hour of running time (or so it seemed to me) is devoted to the torture, rape, and murder of the Vietnamese girl. The fact that the casting director has actually managed to find a Vietnamese actress for the role makes the hour perfectly excruciating. The girl, of course, has no lines, as she does not speak English. She merely looks beautiful, half-naked and covered with De Palma gore."[92]

Other critics, some, including FitzGerald, unfairly pitting *Casualties of War* against *Platoon* (which had been such a recent commercial and critical success), were just as combative. Reminding us that De Palma is "celebrated for his over-stylized scenes involving great plasma spillage," Desson Howe in *The Washington Post* dared an improbable comparison, writing that De Palma "lingers over the grisly death of Oanh like a demented priest who's mistaken blood-letting for transubstantiation."[93] Gail Caldwell in *The Boston Globe* called *Casualties of War* "a remarkably hollow film. It's almost as though De Palma's weird voyeurism and politically correct moral posturing cancel each other out."[94] Dick Fleming accused De Palma of harboring "a perverse fascination with the seamy underside of life," lamenting that instead of contributing "to heal the wounds of Vietnam, [he] has chosen to reopen one especially ugly wound."[95]

While acknowledging the power of Rabe's screenplay, one critic lamented that "the savage treatment of the young victim by her captors is [...] extremely difficult to endure [...] The director's penchant for the use of violence to capitalize on an emotional response is apparent here, and while not necessarily gratuitous, the overt way in which he captures it does get a bit excessive."[96] Bob Strauss of *The Los Angeles Daily News* accused De Palma of using the suffering of the Vietnamese "as a springboard for the supposedly more compelling drama of American boys undergoing crises of conscience." According to *Time* magazine's Richard Schickel, the problem lay with the story itself, which is "too singular to serve as a basis for moral generalizations."[97] J. Hoberman wrote that "De Palma thrives on shock effect and surface tension, and while this bold, virtuoso flatness has tremendous verve, it serves to drain the emotional content out of whatever he touches… This isn't the first movie De Palma's made in which a nubile young woman is terrorized by a mad slasher, but it's certainly the most ambitious."[98]

For Dave Kehr in *The Chicago Tribune*, the film "follows essentially the same formula as the Hitchcockian thrillers that made him famous – charging up the audience with graphic scenes of gore and kinky sexuality, and then punishing us, like a stern priest, for having responded."[99] The *Miami Herald* critic opened his review with: "In *Casualties of War*, director Brian De Palma applies his florid, operatic style to a parable from the Vietnam War, and nearly everything goes wrong."[100] Similarly, the *LA Weekly* review ("Casuistries of War") begins: "*Casualties of War* is so relentlessly off-kilter that audiences may emerge convinced that they've seen something very powerful."[101]

A few days before the film's release, in Jay Carr's *Boston Globe* interview, De Palma asked: "What the hell were we doing there? That's always been the question in my mind about Vietnam… Obviously, the victim was a woman. Her family members were victims, too. Her mother and sister were later kidnapped by Vietcong and never heard from again. But the G.I.s were victims, too. We took a group of boys and put them into an alien universe, and in their anger and frustration they did things that are never done. We are all responsible for subjecting them to this cruel and unusual punishment. In Vietnam, you didn't know who the enemy was. There were no boundaries. There was a sense that the war had no strong moral purpose. It was a twisted, upside-down world in which the normal things you can believe in didn't apply any more. What I find in that situation was a lot of people put through hell." When asked if his film could be read as a metaphor for "America violating Vietnam," De Palma – who later encouraged this idea – hastily responded in the negative. "I see it as more of a war between themselves, not between them and the enemy."[102]

Such statements, made the day that Michael Norman's article was published, were perhaps part of a strategy to mitigate controversy and buck up box office returns. By equating the suffering of Vietnamese with that of American soldiers, De Palma was extending an olive branch to veterans, perhaps believing that his conciliatory speech would ease tensions. It did not. By labeling the soldiers victims, De Palma fueled criticisms from those who objected to the film's portrayal of rape. Columbia, not surprisingly, was on edge, worried that the focus of debate on sexual violence would damage the film's prospects. Gavin Smith recalls the studio's reaction to the images that illustrated his review of the film in *Film Comment*: three on-set photographs, freely chosen by Smith during his visit to the studio offices, showing Meserve choking Oanh with her scarf and tying her hands behind her back just before her rape, and one just before her execution. "I perhaps sensed that these were photos they would have ruled out, but someone dropped the ball," explains Smith. "When the issue was published, the publicist – with whom I had a good relationship – called me and said higher-ups were not happy to see those images in print. She seemed to be in a tight spot, and asked me to return the photos in question, which I did."[103]

Thankfully, not every review was bad. Perhaps De Palma's most influential defender was Pauline Kael of *The New Yorker*. Of all the great films about Vietnam, none truly pleased Kael. In her review of *The Deer Hunter*, she acknowledged director Michael Cimino's talent while calling out his "xenophobic yellow-peril imagination."[104] Her feelings about *Platoon* were more decisive: it was "excessive" and heavy-handed, with overly pronounced effects – "too much filtered light, too much poetic license, and too damn much romanticized insanity."[105]

A few months later, she took aim at Kubrick's *Full Metal Jacket*: "Here's a director who has been insulated from American life for more than two decades, and he proceeds to define the American crisis of the century. He does it by lingering for a near-pornographic eternity over a young Vietnamese woman who is in pain and pleads 'Shoot me! Shoot me!' This is James M. Cain in Vietnam."[106]

But Kael appreciated the filmmakers of New Hollywood, including De Palma, whom she was quick to defend. Her review of *Casualties of War* begins with: "Some movies [...] can affect us in more direct, emotional ways than simple entertainment movies. They have more imagination, more poetry, more intensity than the usual fare; they have large themes, and a vision. They can leave us feeling simultaneously elated and wiped out. Overwhelmed, we may experience a helpless anger if we hear people mock them or poke holes in them in order to dismiss them. The new *Casualties of War* has this kind of purity."[107] After briefly (and incompletely) tracing the history of attempts to adapt Lang's book, then delving into a detailed description of the film, Kael elaborates more extensively on De Palma's "virtuoso" direction, highlighting in particular camera placement and the use of the split diopter, noting that the film's general tone "shifts from realism to hallucinatory Expressionism."

A flow of praise, to be sure, but Kael nevertheless concedes that "great movies are rarely perfect movies." Her reservations about *Casualties of War* echo comments made by Martin Scorsese regarding Eriksson's leaden tirade after Cherry's death. Kael sees here the clash between the writer's method and that of the filmmaker: "De Palma works directly on our emotions. Rabe's dialogue sometimes sounds like the work of a professional anti-war dramatist trying to make us think." Still, she adds, "there's none of the ego satisfaction of moral indignation that is put into most Vietnam films and what De Palma does with the camera is so powerful that the few times you wince at the dialogue are almost breathers."

Kael was among the few to have seen *Casualties of War* as the pinnacle of De Palma's filmmaking. Her critique is not only insightful but also forward-thinking, particularly in its examination of the feminist themes woven throughout his work. "He goes to the heart of sexual victimization, and he does it with a new authority," she notes, appreciating that De Palma "has isolated us from all distractions" and has not resorted to any "plot subterfuges." Her reading of the epilogue is remarkably intelligent: "At the end, the swelling sound of musical absolution seems to be saying that Eriksson must put his experiences in Vietnam behind him – that he has to accept that he did all he could, and go on without always blaming himself. De Palma may underestimate the passion of his images: we don't believe that Eriksson can put Oanh's death into any kind of sane perspective, because we've just felt the sting of what he lived through. He may tell himself that he did all he could, but he feels he should have been able to protect her. The doubt is there in his eyes. (I hear that baby's cries after almost fifty years.) What makes the movie so eerily affecting? Possibly it's Oanh's last moments of life – the needle-sharp presentation of her frailty and strength, and how they intertwine. When she falls to her death, the image is otherworldly, lacerating. It's the supreme violation."

De Palma didn't have time to savor Kael's review. Norman's article was published the very next day, followed by the outraged reactions of veterans, before FitzGerald's attack delivered the final blow. In that media shipwreck, De Palma clung as tight as he could to Kael's lifesaver review.

There were, in fact, plenty of positive reviews. Julie Salamon, writing for *The Wall Street Journal*, described *Casualties of War* as "a Vietnam movie like no other, having neither the hyper-reality of *Platoon* nor the stylized brutality of *Full Metal Jacket*." She further noted that De Palma had found "an emotional if not a political terrain for Vietnam that resonates more powerfully with me, someone who watched the war on television, than any other movie on the subject I've seen." Her well-informed text highlights the moral, philosophical and aesthetic issues raised by the film with great finesse, and ends with a response to attacks on the film's redemptive epilogue: "the audience won't so easily shake itself loose from the event's white-hot emotional grip, especially from the final sequence, after the abduction and the march, when all the soldiers, except Eriksson, empty their automatic rifle into the girl they've raped. The sight of her bloody death march, an operatic stagger across a railroad trestle, doesn't vanish from memory."[108]

One critic found the film a "mesmerizing and unforgettable piece of moviemaking,"[109] another "a riveting, razor-sharp movie."[110] Gary Thompson of the *Philadelphia Daily News* called it the best film about the Vietnam War, with "far more dramatic complexity [...] than the simplistic good vs. evil plot that tainted *Platoon*."[111] Tom Fitzpatrick of the *Phoenix New Times* warned his readers: "It's a picture so powerful that having seen it once, you may never dare to view it again."[112] Terrence Rafferty in *Sight and Sound* described it as "the strongest, the simplest and the most painful of all the Vietnam movies,"[113] and Roger Ebert wrote of "an effective portrait of a psychopathic, bullying personality, and the ineffectiveness of an unseasoned, unsure young soldier in standing up to him. Movies this thoughtful are not often made."[114] David Ansen in *Newsweek* exclaimed that it was "as harrowing as anything" De Palma had ever made, "but in an entirely different way – straightforward, emotionally direct, even bordering on the earnest."[115] Peter Travers of *Rolling Stone* called it De Palma's "most mature, ambitious and emotionally charged work... [He] builds skillfully on a theme he's been obsessed with for years: the way male sexual fantasies link up with violence."[116]

Terry Lawson of the *Dayton Daily News* explained to his readers that "if a reputation that reviled can be rehabilitated with only one film, *Casualties of War* just may be the film," adding that "in this post-*Platoon* era, in which the war itself has been subjected to radical revisionism, *Casualties of War* is not the sort of film we would expect from any major director working for a Hollywood studio." Lawson notes that the tendency toward symbolism and formalism seen in previous films on the subject has been replaced by De Palma with a "new realism." Nevertheless, Lawson regrets the epilogue: "De Palma has made a rather half-hearted gesture to soften the horror of *Casualties of War* by framing it as a memory piece, and it's final scene seems tacked on for no other reason than to turn us out of the theater with a glimmer of hope, so that we don't tell all our friends that, yes, it's a great film, but it's a downer."[117]

The ending of *Casualties of War* was a disappointment for many critics. Philip Wuntch of *Dallas Morning News*, who found the film otherwise "riveting and haunting," wondered whether the "heartwarming" epilogue threatened "to usurp its impact. Was this embarrassing touch De Palma's idea? Or was it the handiwork of screenwriter David Rabe?" he asks, before invalidating the second hypothesis, on the grounds that Rabe had already publicly expressed regrets about certain aspects of the film.[118] Andy Seiler, despite his generally positive review, lamented a finale "which tries to simplify everything and send you out of the theater at least a little less shaken than you would otherwise be."[119] *The New York Times* critic Vincent Canby, who had defended Elia Kazan's *The Visitors* seventeen years earlier, suggested that the ending was "so stupid that one might be advised to leave the film early."[120] "De Palma spares us the real-life ending," wrote Tom Fitzpatrick, "possibly because it would make the film much too depressing to survive as a commercial venture."[121]

Besides questioning De Palma's aesthetic and narrative choices, especially the epilogue, some critics didn't think much of the acting. While Fox received generally positive notices (some suggested that the film was worth seeing for his performance alone[122]), Penn was not spared. Joyce Persico was one of the few to judge that his performance "erases the boundary between reality and spectacle" and deserved an Academy Award.[123] Most of her colleagues mocked Penn's performance, dismissing it as a caricature. Several insisted that "much of his dialogue is garbled by his constant tobacco chewing"[124] (Penn "relentlessly over-

Publicity photographs of Thuy Thu Le

masticates," wrote J. Hoberman[125]) and expressed reservations about his Bronx accent, "picked up at the Robert De Niro school of pronunciation."[126] Dick Fleming pegged it as a "poor imitation" of the *Taxi Driver* star.[127] Philip Wuntch, while conceding that Penn gives a "brilliant" performance, criticized him for "affecting a Sylvester Stallone accent at moments when he's delivering a pivotal line of dialogue."[128] Thuy Thu Le, on the other hand, won the approval of every critic going, and gave interviews about her experiences of making the film in which she spoke about her childhood in Vietnam ("I remember playing in the street with kids my age. They're dead now."[129]) and how the role awakened "painful memories."[130]

In interviews, Le spoke about De Palma's professionalism and Penn's kindness, how he took care of her when she felt unwell due to the heat,[131] and openly expressing her anxieties, especially about filming the rape scene. "I can't take my clothes off in front of the camera. Asian people are reserved. They're *very* reserved. Even after playing this role, I'm sure I will get criticism from the Asian community – 'How could she play that rape victim? How could she let them throw her around?'"[132] "I have nothing to be ashamed of," she asserted. "I am proud of doing that movie. I'm playing a victim, and it shows the whole world how a rape victim feels." Perhaps given the reaction of veterans' organizations, that's about as far as Le was prepared to go when it came to any political discussion with journalists. "It's not a documentary," she was careful to point out, "and I'm not a political activist. [...] What happened to this girl could happen anywhere, not just in Vietnam. And the movie's not about all Americans. It's about one incident."[133]

When asked about future plans, Le explained that *Casualties of War*, like so much in her life, was behind her. "The war is over for me. I just try to live in the present, concentrate on the present and the future."[134] Despite subsequent offers, some from De Palma himself, Le returned to the anonymity of everyday life. A sublime sacrifice: to reject the career that beckoned, choosing instead to remain forever in the shadows as the embodiment of Oanh. Ever since the release of the film, she has not been able to watch it.

From *Casualties of War* to *Outrages*

As American critics, intellectuals and veterans tore into each other, *Casualties of War* made a notable first appearance in France, stripped of its original title and given a new one that isn't really a translation: *Outrages*. Jean Lacouture lamented in *Le Monde* that "the moral essence is disfigured, in the eyes of the French public, by the ridiculous translation of a title that for once was worthy of the subject: *Casualties of War*. The plural here clearly indicates that war not only produces victims who are buried or decorated with posthumous laurels but also warriors transformed into beasts of hatred, oozing racism from every pore, terrified by the unbearable tension manifested by guerrilla warfare in the jungle."¹³⁵

Thuy Thu Le and Brian De Palma

While the French title deviates from the original, it retains a notable reference, to Ida Lupino's *Outrage* (1950). The subject of this little-known film resonates, in a completely different context, with Oanh's tragic story. *Outrage* centers on Ann Walton, a young woman who is stalked and raped by a man at a truck depot. The film explores the aftermath of this trauma, emphasizing how her body continues to bear the memory of the assault. The shift in the title from *Casualties of War* to *Outrages* (plural) might have prompted a shift in critical attention away from the broader concept of victims of war to the specific plight of rape survivors. This subtlety was largely overlooked by journalists, who, like Jean Lacouture, preferred to view the film as a denouncement of war and its "excesses" rather than an indictment of rape and male oppression. Some, however, did make the connection. In *Le Canard enchaîné*, for example, cartoonist Wozniak published a caricature, attached to a review of the film, that shows a Rambo-style figure wielding a machine gun with a grenade and a condom hanging from his belt.[136]

Screening as the opening film at the Festival du Cinéma Américain de Deauville, *Casualties of War* continued to divide opinions. De Palma, a guest at the festival, was accompanied by his friend Régis Wargnier, who had been given a small video camera by De Palma and asked to film his encounters with the press.[137] In interviews, De Palma faced questions that were alternately unpleasant ("What do you think of *The Village Voice*'s criticisms?") and clichéd ("Given your frequent criticism for excesses and a penchant for violence, do you think this film could alter your reputation?"), to which he responded, depending on his mood, with either annoyance or irony.[138]

When *Casualties of War* was released in French cinemas a few months later, the reviews, overall unanimous, hailed it as a "hard and tragically beautiful film"[139] that left an "impression of truthfulness"[140] and was a marked improvement on previous Vietnam films.[141] In *Positif*, Laurent Vachaud stated that the film was one of De Palma's "most accomplished works, whose scope is far more complex than a first viewing might imply."[142] *Cahiers du cinéma*, which had been mixed in its reception to De Palma's films over the years, published two texts: a brilliant analysis of the tunnel sequence by Antoine de Baecque[143] and a fascinating essay by Iannis Katsahnias, full of references to Godard, Hitchcock and Spielberg, which concluded: "Shifting from the obscenities of cinema to the sins of history, De Palma undertakes his boldest gamble: casting America itself as the voyeur, enraptured by the grim spectacle of war."[144]

Only one periodical dared devote its cover to *Casualties of War*: *Starfix*, a monthly magazine which had been publishing for only seven years, and whose editorial board included young film enthusiasts who would themselves later become directors, screenwriters and producers. The magazine's editorial line gave pride of place to genre cinema and critically maligned filmmakers, including William Friedkin, Paul Verhoeven and De Palma, whose three previous films, the largely disparaged *Scarface*, *Body Double* and *The Untouchables*, had been defended tooth and nail in its pages. Nevertheless, the lengthy analysis by Nicolas Boukhrief in the magazine leaves a somewhat contradictory impression. Its resolutely provocative title ("Is Brian De Palma Perverse?") sums up Boukhrief's view of *Casualties of War*, which he describes as "a fascinating but highly dubious film. Fascinating *because* it is so dubious." Boukhrief celebrates De Palma's audacity, the "coarse and grim" imagery and "melodramatic effects," underscored by Morricone's "bombastic and maudlin" music. Boukhrief clearly likes the film, which, he says, fits within a "distinctly Hitchcockian bad taste where voyeurism and Jesuit morality coexist harmoniously." Boukhrief's main argument is difficult to stomach (the film's one female character is reduced to a mere "plot device" as a pretext for De Palma to film "gratuitous male debauchery"), but we should nonetheless acknowledge the combative and impassioned writing of its author, who sought to demonstrate – like de Baecque or Katsahnias in *Cahiers* – that De Palma's film does at least raise genuine cinematic questions.

What passed for qualities in Boukhrief's eyes appeared as glaring flaws to De Palma's detractors, of whom there were a handful. Some labeled *Casualties of War* as "one film too many" about Vietnam and mocked its "lack of originality."[145] Michel Pérez, who had covered the scandal surrounding *o.k.* at the Berlinale twenty years earlier, found little to admire, insisting that De Palma was reaping aesthetic and commercial benefits from the very issues he was condemning.[146] In *Le Quotidien de Paris*, François Jonquet denounced both subject and treatment as "sensationalist," lambasting "a string of obscenities" that "spare us nothing, neither the shattered remains nor the alluring curves of the young victim." He concluded, bluntly: "Isn't the film's real subject De Palma's twisted, skewed, disgusting view of this war?"[147] The anonymous critic of *L'Evénement du jeudi* found the film a "heavy-handed demonstration *à la* Cayatte, poorly filmed and performed by actors... as talentless as they are popular and inevitably drawn toward melodrama by Ennio Morricone's detestable syrupy music."[148] *L'Express* also didn't hold back, suggesting, unfairly, that it looked like the film was shot in a "second-hand bamboo television jungle."[149]

On France Inter's radio program *Le Masque et la Plume*, the discussion of *Casualties of War* turned into a complete takedown of De Palma. Michel Pérez continued his attack, reducing De Palma's work to "hollow paraphrases of Hitchcock's films," characterized by "an extremely showy, flashy technique – vulgar and in bad taste." Compared with other Vietnam films, said Pérez, and despite "the authenticity of the subject," *Casualties of War* fell short.[150] Michel Ciment of *Positif* made much the same point, though more elegantly, lamenting that De Palma had abandoned the B-movie genre to tackle bigger subjects. "For the past three or four films," he explained, "you get the impression that De Palma is aiming for the Oscar, that he's become an A-list filmmaker, and that this film is his great liberal, left-wing account of the horrible war in Vietnam, where young Vietnamese women are raped. I think the film contributes absolutely nothing." Ciment topped off his review by noting that Elia Kazan had already said it all with *The Visitors*, and that compared with Kubrick's *Full Metal Jacket*, De Palma's efforts, with its simplistic good soldier/bad soldier binary, felt "outdated." Finally, Jean-Michel Frodon spoke up, describing *Casualties of War* as a "mediocre Western from another era" whose only merit was to show that the Vietnam War had become a cinematic genre in its own right. It was, he stated, a film with a "dangerous ideology," suggesting that "wars could be honorable if honorable soldiers reported dishonorable soldiers to their superiors." In the end, at this nearly unanimous gathering, where a discussion of the film turned into a brutal critique, only Jacques Siclier from *Le Monde* sought to defend De Palma's "very well-made" film which, without being a great film about Vietnam, seemed to him at the very least to be an excellent genre work.

Despite the virulence of these attacks, French journalists were rather favorable to *Casualties of War*. Many of them treated it fairly and seriously, making sure to place it both within the context of De Palma's career and the broader genre of Vietnam War films. They were surprised to see De Palma, renowned for his thrillers and fantasies, adopt a more realistic approach in *Casualties of War*, notably stripping his direction of its usual baroque excesses. Anne de Gasperi, writing in *Le Quotidien de Paris*, was happy to see that De Palma had chosen not to engage in "a fantastical-*Platoon*-esque version of the Vietnam War" and credited him for abandoning "his penchant for brutality," citing the rape scene, which she deemed "remarkably restrained."[151] "De Palma embraces raw realism, yet none of the scenes can be described as gratuitous," wrote Jean Roy in *L'Humanité*.[152] Jean-Michel Morel, in *Révolution*, similarly observed that De Palma, refraining from self-indulgence, steered clear of "flashy effects" and his "obsession with violence."[153] René Backmann, in *Le Nouvel Observateur*, went so far as to acknowledge the film's "restraint."[154] Renowned producer Daniel Toscan du Plantier saw in De Palma a "sensitive filmmaker" who, despite the "morbid indulgence with which he paints the madness of men," managed to capture "the delicate grace" of Thuy Thu Le – "so ordinary yet unforgettable."[155]

Unlike Ciment and Frodon, who felt that *Casualties of War* was a regressive step in the context of Vietnam War films, some journalists sought to highlight the uniqueness of De Palma's film. On television, famous critic Henry Chapier, who found the film "fascinating," believed it went beyond Vietnam and addressed America's discomfort with its interventionist policies.[156] In *Le Point*, Marie-Françoise Leclère wrote that De Palma was treading on "dangerous ground," as the Vietnam War film genre since Coppola is filled with "codes and clichés, like the crime thriller and the Western." But she acknowledged De Palma's courage in tackling such a difficult subject, "even if he doesn't always avoid the pitfalls."[157] While lamenting a few "heavy-handed effects," Jean-Paul Grousset, writing in

Le Canard enchaîné, conceded that "rarely has a filmmaker presented such a relentless indictment of war crimes."[158]

Jean Lacouture expressed no such reservations in *Le Monde*, noting that De Palma "also managed to show the Vietnamese. Where were they, other than as deadly insects in Cimino's and Coppola's films? The countryside at dawn, asleep in their villages, at work in rice fields – finally we see this country and its people, even if they are fierce underground fighters."[159] Several critics emphasized the film's authenticity, contrasting it with the fantasy visions of Coppola, Cimino and Kubrick, notably Bernard Ullmann, a former Agence France-Presse correspondent who covered the Korean, Indochina and Vietnam wars, and who, in the weekly *Pariscope*, praised the "hallucinatory realism of *Casualties of War*."[160]

Examples like this suggest that French critics were less influenced by historical trauma than some American reviewers. Nevertheless, they did still draw lessons from *Casualties of War*. Lacouture compared Eriksson to Georges Picquart, who in 1896 discovered that the evidence used to convict Captain Alfred Dreyfus of treason was forged. "The Americans made this film, not us," writes Lacouture. "Does this mean that from the fighters on the Chinese border to the patrols in the Aurès, we couldn't find an Eriksson – a single man who would have refused to condone rape or torture? I don't believe it. But the fact is, except for the excellent [Pierre] Schoendoerffer, who dared portray 'our' Indochina and 'our' Algeria, French cinema's silence on these subjects is deafening... Brian De Palma's remarkable film not only demands the truth from us but also throws down a challenge."[161]

This is an unfair critique. While the Indochina War is indeed a marginal subject in French cinema, even a "cursed theme,"[162] the supposed non-existence of films about the Algerian War is a "journalistic cliché that obsessively resurfaces."[163] Filmmakers like Alain Resnais, Jean-Luc Godard, Alain Cavalier and Jacques Rozier did create work about Algeria, albeit focusing more on the before and after rather than the war itself, but more for political than aesthetic reasons, their films never left "lasting, significant traces in the French collective consciousness,"[164] and in the face of censorship they faded from collective memory. It is probable that *Casualties of War* would have met a similar fate if it had been produced in the early 1970s. After all, didn't it take fifty years to rediscover *o.k.*? Contrary to appearances, as Benjamin Stora reminds us, "American cinema produced very few (fictional) films during the Vietnam War, even fewer than French cinema, in fact."[165]

Ultimately, comparing *Casualties of War* with films post-Algerian independence, like *Avoir vingt ans dans les Aurès* (René Vautier, 1972) or *R.A.S.* (Yves Boisset, 1973) would be more fitting. Boisset was savaged by far-right groups and Algerian War veterans for his supposedly biased representation of the conflict. History repeats itself, tirelessly, and at the time of its release *Casualties of War* became the latest manifestation of the contentious relationship between cinema, history and politics.

As Marc Ferro stated in 1984, since the Vietnam War, America has demonstrated a capacity for self-examination. "This questioning is a sign of freedom, a safeguard against a return to the complacency and uniformity of the mid-twentieth century."[166] Yet the reception of *Casualties of War* suggests otherwise, revealing that behind Hollywood's façade of freedom there lurks a creeping conformity, machismo and revisionism. America's refusal – or inability – to confront reality manifested in France as collective amnesia. It became easier to believe that French filmmakers remained silent on "wars of shame" than to acknowledge how they were coerced into that silence.

Maybe because it reminded French audiences of these films they didn't wish to see, *Casualties of War* generally failed to engage, pulling in only 343,611 viewers – a long way from the 2,459,380 who had paid to see *The Untouchables*. Perhaps they preferred Michael J. Fox as the eternal teenager Marty McFly in the sequel to *Back to the Future* (which had opened a couple of weeks earlier), rather than as the tormented Eriksson, a helpless witness to the horror of a crime "largely buried in the anonymity of the violence"[167] inflicted during the Indochina and Algerian wars.

Epilogue

The reception of *Casualties of War*, which Brian De Palma regards as his most accomplished work, left a deep and lingering scar. Determined to turn the page, he moved quickly onto his next film. "Making *The Bonfire of the Vanities* was a way to forget the terrible disappointment of *Casualties of War*," he says, "which had thrown me into a depression."[1] In discussion with friends, De Palma never let his bitterness show. "Brian doesn't dwell on the past, on failures, or those kinds of things," says Fred Caruso, describing a man always focused on his work, treating each new film with the same diligence as the last.[2] In the end, *The Bonfire of the Vanities* became one of Warner Bros.' biggest flops and awakened in De Palma painful memories of the reception of *Casualties of War*.

And so, in the early 1990s, he once again hit rock bottom and had to wait until *Carlito's Way* (1993) – in the vein of *Scarface* and *The Untouchables*, but on a more elegiac and melancholic note – for a return to the limelight, before achieving worldwide success with *Mission: Impossible* in 1996. Yet this newfound grace did not shine on *Casualties of War*, which remained largely forgotten until it was rediscovered thanks to screenings at the Cinémathèque in Paris in 2018 and the Institut Lumière in Lyon in 2019, as part of a De Palma retrospective.[3]

When I began researching *Casualties of War*, I never imagined that the path I was walking would lead to the many avenues explored in this book, which demanded the patience and perseverance of a prospector. At first, all I found in my sieve were mere flakes. It was only through relentless sifting, week after week, that a few nuggets finally emerged, the first signs of a documentary treasure trove. This wide-ranging exploration offers a panoramic view of all the adaptations, abortive and completed, of *Casualties of War* that preceded De Palma's film, which, in light of these failed attempts, is now ripe for reconsideration.

Pitfalls

This book explores the delicate dance required to bring a full-length movie to life. The tumultuous relationship between Jack Clayton and Pete Hamill stands as one of the reasons why David Susskind, who owned the rights to Daniel Lang's book, never got his version off the ground. Blame can be shared between director and writer because while Hamill was generally indifferent, in the end it was Clayton's uncompromising nature that led him to drop the project. Hamill chose to abandon ship in the midst of the storm, and Clayton, an otherwise admirable filmmaker, didn't perhaps have the strength to right the ship. From this perspective, Lang's first choice, Fred Zinnemann, might have offered more assurances, but the failure of *Man's Fate* left him depleted. Fault also lies with Susskind, who seemingly misjudged or didn't adequately anticipate the political and ethical issues posed by adapting a book like *Casualties of War*.

When David Giler was brought in to write a new screenplay, it was already too late. The scandal at the Berlinale had tainted Clayton's project, perhaps prompting the Pentagon to maneuver behind the scenes and prevent the film from moving forward. The military-political situation in Vietnam and America, and growing dissent at home, were also factors. A few years later, with Susskind's second attempt to bring *Casualties of War* to the screen – this time for television – it was clear that the project had stalled. Heywood Gould's screenplay had its merits, but Lang never liked it, and the producer's numerous financial problems ended up sinking the project, at a moment when the trauma of Vietnam was still fresh in people's minds.

Lang, meanwhile, bided his time. Frustrated, he continued to write for *The New Yorker* while also working on various screen adaptations of his work,[4] but *Casualties of War* held a special place in his heart. When Susskind abandoned the project a second time, Lang, following in the footsteps of Hamill and Gould, took matters into his own hands. But his treatment is the work of a journalist, not a screenwriter.

While we can't fault Lang's moral vision, it clashes with the dramatic expectations of a film adaptation. His treatment required extensive reworking by a professional screenwriter, but disagreements with Crown and Hammer prevented this from happening.

Lang's relationship with Hollywood was a troubled one, marked by missed opportunities, dashed hopes and constant doubts. His efforts to bring *Casualties of War* to the screen are profoundly moving, and he deserves credit for his relentless determination and unwavering ethics, without which the names Phan Thi Mao and Robert Storeby might have been forgotten forever.

The De Palma turning point

How was it that De Palma succeeded where others failed? How did he manage to make a film that his illustrious predecessors were unable to take beyond the pre-production or even scripting stages? There were three mail reasons.

First: context. By the late 1980s, the Vietnam War was no longer the burning or taboo subject it had been in the 1960s and 1970s. Hollywood had explored various stories and produced several major films, many of which were both critically acclaimed and box office successes. When De Palma proposed his project to Paramount and then Columbia, the Vietnam War appeared to be a subject that was both commercially viable and, following in the wake of *Platoon*, almost revitalizing.

Second: the De Palma-Linson-Rabe collaboration, at least until the eve of the film's release, encountered no roadblocks. It is important to recognize Art Linson's courage. After backing De Palma on *The Untouchables*, he agreed to get behind a challenging project despite Paramount's reservations Both De Palma and David Rabe, who since 1969 had been trying to adapt Lang's work for the cinema, were also in sync.

Objectively speaking, a comparative study of the different screenplays shows that Rabe's version is the most accomplished, the most poignant, even if it deviates in certain aspects from Lang's intentions and takes some liberties with historical truth. Although satisfied with Rabe's work, De Palma didn't entirely share the screenwriter's vision. Wary of repeating the same mistakes as with David Mamet on *The Untouchables*,

De Palma took care to avoid direct confrontation, making necessary modifications himself shortly before (or during) filming, sometimes without informing Rabe. Rabe might not have been entirely satisfied with the finished film, but De Palma's approach had the benefit of sidestepping the deadlock encountered by David Susskind during his earlier attempts to make the film with Clayton and Hamill.

Rabe only recently spoke about his experiences on the film. In February 2019, after our exchanges, and bolstered by a few positive comments from veterans that he had read online, Rabe watched *Casualties of War* for the first time in three decades, after which he sent me this lengthy message.

"I was truly rocked to my core by it, and am very proud of it. Much of what I hoped would be there is there – content I feared might have been jeopardized by certain changes in sequence still comes through powerfully. Shot by shot Brian's work is wonderful. So many striking sequences of powerful brave direction – almost too many to count. I watched the extended cut which had a scene where Eriksson was interrogated after talking to the minister, a scene I'd never seen before and which was very valuable. Also the music is profound and moving, other than the very last part of the last seconds of the movie. And the dialogue there between Eriksson and the girl still seems wrong to me – and I wish it was only him saying, 'Chào cò' and an exchange of looks and 'Chào ông' from her. But these are small concerns now, considering the major achievement that the film is, thanks to Brian, Art, Sean, Michael and all the actors. The rape sequence is raw and unbearable, and the image Brian found for Clark with the line from The Doors song is nightmarishly perfect. It could have been done a million ways, but they found the most devastating way. Same with the sequence where that poor Cherry is looking for some pound cake. And on and on…"[5]

If *Casualties of War* has stood the test of time, it is because it addresses a subject which is translatable to every war across the planet before and after Vietnam. What sets the film apart, says Larry McConkey, "is that it has a moral point of view, but without some kind of cathartic rage which is an excuse for a big violent chase scene. It's the moral battle raging inside Eriksson that is the main drama in *Casualties of War*."[6] The film is more than just a cinematic adaptation.

It is a veritable battleground where memories – those of Americans and Vietnamese, of veterans and those opposed to the war – collide.

"It's a film about power, powerlessness and control," said De Palma in 1989, "as much about how to keep the lid on the bottle as it is the mayhem inside it."[7] All the Americans who fought in Vietnam, he explained – "They're all casualties of war. That's what I feel. To me, the movie is very sorrowful. Vietnam is very unresolved. I don't think the pain will ever be completely healed."[8]

At the beginning of this book, I stressed the need to avoid mythologizing artists, as it often leads to hero worship. Nevertheless, it is essential to acknowledge the third crucial element behind the success of *Casualties of War*: De Palma himself. His expertise lay in delegating effectively, building trust, and creating a remarkable synergy among the crew, allowing everyone to do their best work. The end result is a collective success, a film that owes as much to its technicians and actors as it does to its producer, screenwriter and director. Everyone involved was fully invested in telling Lang's story, with De Palma at the helm.

"I watched the film again two years after its release," says Don Harvey, "and was even more amazed than the first time. With more distance from the filming experience, I understood how crazy intense it had been. How unapologetic. How unflinching. How impertinent. It's such a difficult subject, yet De Palma never shies away from it. He keeps you in that surreal world from start to finish. When I saw it again much later, I started to see myself less as an actor trying to play a role and more as a character in the story. I'm part of a deep experience that is so much bigger than me. I no longer judge myself according to whether I did a good job or not. I watch the movie and I'm blown away at the totality of it. I'm very proud to be a part of the tapestry. I believe so much of what I did was beyond my control. I was swept up into Brian's energy and I gave him what he needed. It took a lot out of me."[9]

From Vietnam to Iraq
De Palma's film *Redacted*, made in 2007, is the most tangible proof of his inability to turn the page on *Casualties of War*. It is, once again, a demonstration of the political dimensions

of his filmmaking, inspired by an event, not dissimilar to the one reported by Daniel Lang, which occurred during the Iraq War, on March 12, 2006, in Yusufiyah, a village west of Mahmudiyah. A 14-year-old girl, Abeer Qassim Hamza al-Janabi, was raped and murdered by American soldiers, who then proceeded to kill her entire family. The idea for the film took hold in De Palma's mind when he read a newspaper article and understood how the actions of a group of American soldiers in Iraq could serve as a metaphor for the "rape of an entire country."[10]

But from the Vietnam of the 1960s and '70s to the Iraq of the 2000s, from *Casualties of War* to *Redacted*, things had changed. Without Storeby's testimony, the collective rape and murder of Phan Thi Mao would have remained unpunished and forgotten. The atrocities suffered by the young Iraqi girl (renamed Farah) and her family, on the other hand, benefit from a substantial quantity of visual material, available on the internet, which De Palma discovered during his research: "A soldier's blog, shot with a small digital camera, video tapes from surveillance cameras, others showing interrogations, Iraqi television reports, amateur videos of opponents of the war, images shot by Al-Quaeda."[11] And yet, for legal reasons, De Palma was unable to use these sources or the real names of the soldiers in his film, and his initial documentary project was impossible to realize because the production was unable to get insurance. "Ultimately, it's a form of censorship exercised by American insurance companies," lamented De Palma, who was forced to fictionalize the story, and ended up suing the film's production company (he lost). Screened at the 2007 Venice Film Festival, *Redacted* won the Silver Lion, but the American media called for a boycott even before its release, and the film was a commercial failure in the U.S.

Redacted doesn't focus solely on the rape and murder of the young girl and one of the soldier's efforts to report the crime. Through images recorded by Angel Salazar, it examines "the gap between the war's absolute invisibility in the mainstream media and its widespread, if precarious, visibility on the Internet."[12] Salazar, an aspiring filmmaker, who films Farah's rape in close-up, symbolizes "the loss of innocence of a television media that has never ceased to transgress all moral barriers and has perverted, since the late 1960s and the Vietnam War, its initial mission: to inform and awaken consciences."[13] In this respect, De Palma raises the question of "staging a reverse shot that is virtually online but never crosses the media threshold."[14]

Zahra Zubaidi, the actress playing Farah, faced similar challenges to Thuy Thu Le during the filming of *Casualties of War*, but these were exacerbated by the cultural context in which she was operating. The rape scene she filmed had profound consequences for her private life. After members of her community accused her of participating in a pornographic film, she became a "pariah in the Muslim world."[15] De Palma eventually arranged for her to leave Jordan because it had become "dangerous for her to stay there."[16]

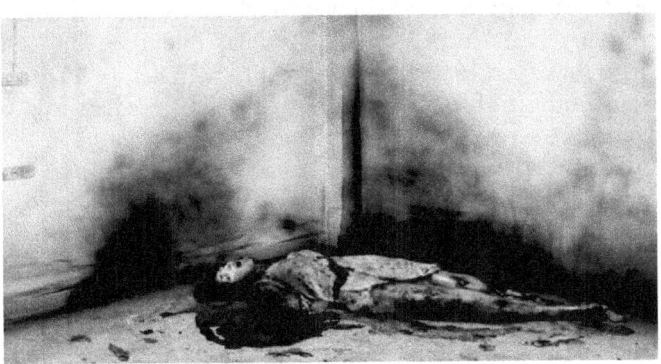

Casualties of War (top), *Redacted* (bottom)

The historical facts, the filming of *Redacted*, and Zubaidi's personal history form the basis of Taryn Simon's work *"Zahra/Farah"* (2008/2009/2011), created from the photograph made by the American artist for *Redacted*'s epilogue. The image, of the victim's corpse bathed in blood, abandoned in a corner of the room where she was raped and killed, is reminiscent of the shot of Oanh's dismembered body below the bridge in *Casualties of War*. Simon added text, silk-screened on museum walls that exhibited the photograph. "These annotations represent the changing contexts that the image and the actress who is its subject endured over the past five years. [...] The photograph and its exhibition were used to reveal a continued threat and, at the same time, to support Zahra's case for political asylum, which was granted in 2011. She couldn't go home because of the images. You could see an image's very real influence on an individual life from start to finish: from a casting call with you in Jordan to ending up in the United States and receiving political asylum."[17]

"Women in jeopardy are more dramatic than men in jeopardy," said De Palma in 1989.[18] However, his fascination with telling these kinds of stories goes far beyond his interests as a storyteller. In *Casualties of War* and *Redacted*, De Palma is challenging the pervasive culture of rape that flourishes in wartime, beyond the reach of justice and ethics. He has, not surprisingly, attempted to address violence against women in other projects, including a film – which remains unmade – about a female soldier who is raped.[19] After recent Hollywood scandals – the numerous rapes and sexual assaults for which producer Harvey Weinstein was found guilty and sentenced to many years in prison – De Palma announced in 2018 that he was working on a script entitled *Predator*. "Having been a director for 50 years," he explained, "needless to say I've come across a couple of the notorious predators in the business."[20] The project remains unproduced.

The Courage to Say No
I shall conclude this book on a personal note. In a thought-provoking essay, Pierre Bayard wonders whether, during the Occupation, he would have been a resistor or a perpetrator. *Casualties of War* leads me to similar questioning: What would I do if, like Storeby/Eriksson, I faced intense group pressure, was compelled to participate in a rape, and was urged to succumb to my impulses in a context where all moral boundaries had disintegrated? Instinctively, a small voice deep within me whispers that, like the character in

Lang's book and De Palma's film, I would categorically refuse, simply because I have an aversion to rape.

But would I have the courage to stand up to the leader and defend the victim, alone against all and with a weapon pointed at me? Bayard observes that the "becoming-resisting" – that is, "the capacity that certain beings demonstrate at certain moments in their history, contrary to what is asked of them and their objective interest, sometimes even contrary to their apparent personality, to say no" – is "rarer than becoming a perpetrator."[21] Would I, in such circumstances, have the ability to say "no" and intervene? It is a question that troubles me.

I want to say yes. I want to believe that I would act heroically and be willing to risk my life to stop the worst crime a person can commit. But faced with such a situation, what would I really do? Would I, in Storeby's place, have the strength to escape with Phan Thi Mao, to escort her back to her people, to desert my post at the risk of being caught by my comrades and killed with her, or even being shot by the enemy as the easy target I would have been? Asking this type of question, writes Bayard, necessitates "personally engaging in the response."[22] Writing this book has been, in its own way, an attempt to do just that.

Throughout my research, which gradually turned into an exercise of deep self-reflection, I tried to understand the reasons that led me to dedicate more than two years of my life to *Casualties of War*, after having successively worked, for a decade, on the destruction of the Jews of Europe and the genocide of the Tutsis, even though I don't appear to have been destined for such work. I didn't realize that the answer was actually hidden in my family history.

My childhood was marked by the absence of two grandfathers, both of whom had died before my birth, both of whom had experienced combat – the first, on my mother's side, during the Spanish Civil War, the second, on my father's side, during the Second World War. The story of my Spanish grandfather, José Pérez, was recounted to me in great detail. He enlisted on the Republican side and was gravely wounded, then held in Nationalist jails for a year under inhumane conditions before being forced to do military service after the war during the Franco regime. I knew far less about my paternal grandfather, Joseph Réra. I questioned my grandmother extensively about him, but sensed a reluctance in her to recall the details of their life together because of the tragic circumstances of his death, in her arms, after a sudden heart attack at the age of 52. There were some photographs, but very few from the era of the war. My grandmother burned all their correspondence and buried her memories deep.

Of this grandfather, born in 1922 in Souk Ahras, an Algerian municipality near the Tunisian border, to a pied-noir family of Italian origin, I had the image of an upright, courageous man, devoted to his family, who brought people together. My grandmother used to enjoy likening him to the actor Raf Vallone, which probably increased the fascination I felt for him. My grandfather was, I believe, the man I would have liked to become: an intellectual, a seasoned mathematician, a formidable chess player, and an outstanding jazz saxophonist. During the Algerian War and in the three years that followed, he lived with his wife and two sons on the outskirts of the Sahara, in Laghouat, where he held a responsible position at the French Postes, Télégraphes et Téléphones. He spoke fluent Arabic, cared little for politics, and counted among his friends both Algerians and French, supporters of independence as well as defenders of French Algeria.

I also knew that my grandfather returned to the country at the end of 1945 a hero, the sole survivor of his unit, according to family legend. The scant information I have about his journey was from his military record. Mobilized on June 25, 1942, he joined the 3rd Algerian Tirailleurs Regiment on January 7, 1943, eventually reaching the rank of corporal-chef. He twice received the silver Croix de Guerre for acts of bravery, and was wounded on June 18, 1944 during the Italian campaign, by shrapnel to the upper lip and right temporal lobe, likely during the attack on Piancastagnaio in Tuscany. His unit was involved in operations in Provence and the liberation of Lower Alsace before crossing the Franco-German border and, at the end of March 1945, the Rhine.

I vaguely knew that deep within, he carried a profound wound. Details are scarce, but it appears that at one point he and his comrades, advancing in thick fog, spotted two figures. Fearing they were facing the enemy, and there being no response to their order to halt, they opened fire. The two presumed soldiers were, in fact, a civilian couple. My grandfather had nightmares about it for years afterward. I suspected, of course, that this tragic story concealed others, that he must have witnessed atrocities and reprisals, especially in the context of the "cleansing" operations around Stuttgart in which he had likely taken part. I never discussed these events in

Joseph Réra during the Second World War

detail with my father, who himself had to rely on the few scattered memories of my grandmother while she was still alive.

As I was finishing the writing of this book, at a family meal one day I spoke of Robert Storeby, emphasizing how moving I found his story. "I have often wondered what Grandpa would have done if he had found himself in such a situation," I said to my father without any ulterior motive. His eyes suddenly lit up. "I know," he announced, his voice choked with emotion. "Your grandmother told me that he intervened when his unit was in Germany to prevent his comrades from raping women. He was thinking of his sisters, of what they would have endured if they had been in such a situation. He turned his gun against his fellow soldiers."

In an instant, everything made sense. I finally understood why Storeby's story had affected me so deeply, working its way inside me and transforming me profoundly, without me being able to express it in words. It took completing this work for me to fully grasp the precious value of the legacy passed on to me by my grandfather, who undoubtedly shared some of the same moral DNA as Robert M. Storeby. His blood runs through my veins, and I still believe that this book wouldn't have been driven by the same urgency if my grandfather hadn't been the honorable man I would have so much loved to know.

Chronology

November 17, 1966	Preparation for the reconnaissance mission led by Sergeant David Gervase toward Hill 192 (Bong Son, South Vietnam). His patrol members are Steven Thomas, Joseph Garcia, Cipriano Garcia, Robert M. Storeby. At the end of the briefing, Gervase informs his men of his intention to kidnap, rape and kill a Vietnamese woman.
November 18, 1966	Departure of the mission just before dawn. Kidnapping of Phan Thi Mao in the Cat Tuong hamlet. Rape of the latter by all patrol members, except for Private First Class Robert M. Storeby.
November 19, 1966	Murder of Phan Thi Mao.
December 8, 1966	Storeby gives testimony to CIA Agent Jimmie McClendon.
March 15-16, 1967	Trial of Cipriano Garcia (Camp Radcliff, Vietnam). Found guilty of non-premeditated rape and murder, and sentenced to 8 years of forced labor.
March, 16-17 1967	Trial of Joseph Garcia (Camp Radcliff). Found guilty of rape and sentenced to fifteen years of forced labor.
March 18, 20 and 21, 1967	Trial of Steven Thomas (Camp Radcliff). Found guilty of premeditated rape and murder, and sentenced to life imprisonment with forced labor.

March 22, 1967	Trial of David Gervase (Camp Radcliff). Found guilty of nonpremeditated murder and sentenced to ten years of forced labor.
February, 7-8 1968	Second trial (on appeal) of Joseph Garcia. Acquitted.
Autumn 1968	Daniel Lang gains access to the trial records in Falls Church, Virginia, and meets Robert Storeby.
July 1968	Conditional release of David Gervase.
October 18, 1968	First publication of "Casualties of War" in the "A Reporter at Large" section of *The New Yorker*.
15 November 1968	*Casualties of War* is published as a book by McGraw-Hill.
Nov. – Dec. 1969	Numerous producers and directors show interest in *Casualties of War*, including Brian De Palma, aged 29.
December 1969	Lang reaches a tentative agreement with producer David Susskind for a film adaptation of *Casualties of War*. John Schlesinger is in line to direct.
January 1970	Jack Clayton replaces Schlesinger. Pete Hamill writes an initial draft of the *Casualties of War* screenplay.
March 1970	Filming of *o.k.* by Michael Verhoeven in Germany, inspired by *Casualties of War*.
Spring 1970	Conditional release of Steven Thomas. Hamill delivers his completed screenplay to Warner Bros. Studio executives, which is not well received. Hamill abandons the project because of differences with Jack Clayton and is replaced by David Giler.

July 1970	*o.k.* causes a scandal at the Berlinale and prematurely ends the festival. Warner Bros. sues Verhoeven and his producer, Rob Houwer, for plagiarism.
August 1970	David Giler finalizes an initial version of his screenplay. Start of pre-production of *Casualties of War*.
September 1970	Warner Bros., having lost the lawsuit against Rob Houwer and Michael Verhoeven, decides not to appeal. Location scouting in India, where *Casualties of War* was supposed to be filmed, is canceled.
October 1970	In East Germany, DEFA produces a short film, *US-Soldat Erikson gibt zu Protokoll*, inspired by Daniel Lang's book.
March 1971	Producer Ronald Shedlo and David Giler consider a theatrical adaptation of *Casualties of War*, based on the Giler's screenplay.
April 1971	Attempt to revive the adaptation project with one of the new heads of Warner Bros., Richard Zanuck.
Summer 1971	Stanley Chais suggests to Daniel Lang that he seek funding to revive the screen project of *Casualties of War*. Conditional release of Cipriano Garcia.
October 1971	Clayton works on two other literary adaptations: *The Tenant* and *The Great Gatsby*.
February 2, 1972	Release of *The Visitors* by Elia Kazan, inspired by Daniel Lang's book.
May 1972	*The Visitors* is presented in competition at the Cannes Film Festival.

January 1975	Adaptation rights of *Casualties of War* revert to Daniel Lang.
May 1977	New agreement between Talent Associates Ltd., David Susskind's company, and Lang, for an adaptation of *Casualties of War*.
September 1977	Time-Life Films, which acquired Susskind's company, confirms the project as a television film.
End of 1978 to May 1979	Heywood Gould writes a new screenplay for *Casualties of War*. Daniel Lang expresses an initially negative opinion. Time-Life Films abandons the project.
Summer – Autumn 1979	David Rabe contacts Daniel Lang to check the availability of the rights to his book. Rabe discusses it with Brian De Palma, who shows enthusiasm. No producer expresses interest.
March 18, 1980	Producers Alfred Crown and Jerome Hammer secure a one-year option on the adaptation rights of *Casualties of War*. Lang is tasked with writing a treatment.
August 1980	Crown and Hammer terminates their contract with Lang. Lang is diagnosed with aplastic anemia.
June 1981	Lang is diagnosed with leukemia.
November 17, 1981	Death of Lang.
April – May 1987	After the immense success of *The Untouchables*, Brian De Palma sends a copy of *Casualties of War* to producer Art Linson with the intention of adapting it. He reconnects with David Rabe for this purpose.
May 1987	Paramount reaches an agreement with Lang's widow, Margaret. David Rabe is hired to write the screenplay.

Summer 1987	De Palma and Rabe consider Sean Penn for the role of Eriksson, but Paramount refuses. Penn takes on the role of Meserve. Ned Tanen finds the script depressing, and the studio abandons the project. Dawn Steel revives it at Columbia.
Sept. – Dec. 1987	Pre-production begins. Michael J. Fox is approached to play the role of Eriksson. Casting for supporting roles and assembling the crew. Location scouting in the Philippines is canceled. Eric Schwab explores Australia, Mexico, and Thailand, where filming ultimately takes place.
January 1988	Set construction begins in Thailand.
February 1988	Thuy Thu Le, then a student, auditions in Paris and is given the role of Oanh.
February – March 1988	Military training and rehearsals.
April – June 1988	Filming of *Casualties of War* in Thailand.
Summer 1988	Filming of the prologue and epilogue of the film in San Francisco. Bill Pankow delivers a first rough cut to De Palma.
Sept. – Dec. 1988	Editing, sound mixing, color grading. Ennio Morricone composes the score for *Casualties of War*.
December 1988	Morricone records the film's soundtrack in Rome at the Forum Music Village.
March – April 1989	Test screenings for *Casualties of War*. Initial audience reviews are mixed. De Palma, fearing the film is too bleak, makes some cuts in the final section.

August 1989	The film's promotional campaign begins. In *The New York Times*, Michael Norman reveals disagreements between De Palma and Rabe, stating that the screenwriter has distanced himself from the film.
August 18, 1989	*Casualties of War* is released in 1,487 cinemas across the United States. Columbia fails to recoup its costs, and the film faces harsh criticism, especially from Vietnam War veterans' associations.
September 1989	*Casualties of War* opens the Deauville American Film Festival.
January 10, 1990	*Casualties of War* is released in France.

Acknowledgements

My deepest gratitude goes to all those who agreed to contribute to this book and placed their trust in me by sharing anecdotes, archival documents and photographs. Thank you to:

Brian De Palma, for agreeing to meet and putting me in touch with some of his collaborators.

David Rabe, who supported my project without hesitation, gave me access to several versions of his script, and acted as an intermediary.

Art Linson, for our fascinating discussion, his enthusiasm, humor and humanity.

Sean Penn, who answered my questions with uncommon honesty and sensitivity.

Don Harvey, whose memories and frankness played a crucial role in the writing of this book.

John C. Reilly, for his infectious humor and stimulating ideas.

Thuy Thu Le, for her kindness, humility and dignity.

Holt McCallany, for his unwavering commitment, availability and immense generosity.

John Leguizamo, for his precious memories and goodwill.

Eric Schwab, for his love of cinema, his sensitivity and precious friendship.

Fred Caruso, for his encouragement and sense of accuracy.

Stephen H. Burum (ASC), for enriching my knowledge of cinematography.

Larry McConkey, for sharing his trade secrets.

Bill Pankow, for his remarkable editing expertise.

Maurice Schell (†), who taught me to use my ears as well as my eyes.

Monica Goldstein, for the confidence she showed in me by entrusting me with her incredible photographs and film footage.

Brian W. Cook, for sharing his vision of the filming of *Casualties of War* and for putting me in touch with Carl Goldstein.

Carl Goldstein, for speaking frankly, with a wildly contagious passion for cinema.

Paul Engelen, Mickey Pugh, Wolf Kroeger and Yves De Bono, to whom I owe a better understanding of makeup, props, set design and special effects.

Erik King, for the wonderful stories he told me.

Pasiree Panya, who offered another perspective on the filming of *Casualties of War*.

Mike Stokey and Dale Dye, thanks to whom I was able to clear up some misunderstandings and who taught me much military jargon; Art Smith, who provided valuable archival materials that had previously been inaccessible to me; Roland Neveu, who gave me access to some of his work; Sallie Beechinor, Marko A. Costanzo, Nancy Hayes, Deborah Ricketts and Charlie Sungkawess, for their insights; Heywood Gould, who kindly revisited the genesis of one of his scripts; Michael Verhoeven (†) and Rob Houwer, without whom I would know so much less about *o.k.*

I wish to express my deep gratitude to Cecily Lang, who accompanied a significant part of the journey of this book and offered crucial insights into the work of her father. Thanks also to her two sisters, Helen Lang and Frances Labaree-Lang.

My research benefited from the support of the Howard Gotlieb Archival Research Center at Boston University. I extend my warmest thanks to J.C. Johnson for the efficiency with which he provided me with remote assistance.

The welcome I received at the British Film Institute in London, from Storm Patterson in particular, enabled me to conduct my research optimally.

I owe thanks to Sato Masuzawa, Sean Penn's assistant, who endured my numerous follow-ups over a year and a half with unflagging good humor. Penn's testimony in this book owes much to her.

Special thanks to all those who, in the shadows, acted as intermediaries, took my requests seriously, facilitated my efforts, or provided me with useful information:

United States: Brian Bennett (Linson Entertainment), John Burke (Akin Gump, Strauss Hauer & Feld LLP), David Bushman (The Paley Center for Media), John Calhoun (The New York Public Library, Billy Rose Theatre Division), Laura Civiello and Julia Dye (Warriors Inc.), Shannon Fifer (Warner Bros. Motion Picture Rights), Jeronimo G. Guzman (U.S. Army Court of Criminal Appeals), Molly Haigh (UCLA, Library Special Collections), Diana L. King (UCLA Arts Library), Ashley Landay (KMR Talent), Chester B. Longcor (U.S. Army Crime Records Center), Joan Miller (The Reid Cinema Archive, Wesleyan University), Richard Pontius (The National Center for Jewish Film), Nina Rosenblum (Daedalus Productions Inc.), Lea Schell and Meryl Schutte (Film Afrika Worldwide), Gretchen Shoemaker (U.S. National Archives & Records Administration), Corey Stewart (U.S. National Archives & Records Administration), Ali Tesluk (Samuel French, Inc.), David E. Williams (American Cinematographer), Sarafin Stein, Rebecca Miller and Joannie Burstein (The Burstein Company).

England: James R. Aston (University of Hull), Nathalie Morris (BFI National Archive), Neil R. Sinyard.

Ireland: Halina Froudist (Actors and Movers).

Germany: Stefan Hornung (Sentana Filmproduktion), Donald Houwer (Edison Film), Cinzia Kattin (Deutsche Kinemathek), Herbert Klemens (FilmBild Fundus), Tim Storch (Bundesarchiv), Mirko

Wiermann (DEFA-Filmverleih/Deutsche Kinemathek), Justus Wörmann (Bundesarchiv).

Italy: Alessandro De Rosa.

France: the staff of the Bibliothèque du film and the Iconothèque de la Cinémathèque française, particularly Sandra Laupa and, for her bibliographic advice, Aude Nicolas.

Warm regards to Paul Verhoeven, who was instrumental in my contacting Brian De Palma through their mutual producer, Saïd Ben Saïd, whom I also thank sincerely.

Katja Beckel, Marlène Thomas, Ludivine Branco, Cecily Lang and Thuy Thu Lu made their linguistic skills (German, English, Vietnamese) available to me, for which I am grateful.

My research laboratory, CRIHAM (Poitiers), provided financial and logistical support for some of my travels. The University of Poitiers, as well as the UFR Sciences humaines et arts, allowed me to obtain a teaching release during the first semester of the 2019/20 academic year to work on this book. I express my gratitude to them. The enthusiasm and encouragement of my colleagues has been a source of comfort.

Some parts of the original French edition of this book were reviewed and enriched by the comments and advice of friends, whom I thank from the bottom of my heart for their availability, rigor and interest in my work: Pierre Wat, Sylvie Lindeperg, Ophir Levy, Augustin Braud, Bernard and Lydie Réra.

I express my deepest thanks to Guy Astic, who supported every stage of this project with his reassuring presence and unwavering passion. I am also very grateful to Paul Cronin for having the audacity to publish this book in English, and for the obsessive attention to detail with which he translated it.

This English edition contains a number of additions and clarifications, which owe a great deal to discussions I have had with colleagues and friends, including Jean-Jacques Manzanera, Dork Zabunyan, Aurore Maletras and Yann Bertrand, and to exchanges I had with Gavin Smith and Claude Monnier, who made his *Starfix* archives available to me. I would like to thank Eric Schwab and Graeme Watson for reading the entire translation and their helpful comments. Special thanks to Julie Salamon for her friendly support.

All my affection goes to my parents, my sisters, and my in-laws, who lent an attentive ear to my research and provided moral support throughout this adventure. Thank you to my wife and sons for continuing to light up my life.

Paul Cronin thanks Adrian Martin and, for her continued assistance and much-needed support, Stacey Knecht.

Endnotes

Introduction

1. Hence the astonishment of Art Linson, a longtime friend of De Palma and the producer of *Casualties of War*, when I recounted this episode to him. After watching it, he confirmed to me that he had never seen the filmmaker in such an emotional state.
2. Blumenfeld and Vachaud, *De Palma on De Palma*, 172.
3. Among these exceptions, the following should be mentioned: Blumenfeld and Vachaud, *De Palma on De Palma*; Keesey, *Brian De Palma's Split-Screen*; Dumas, *Un-American Psycho*.
4. For example, Lawrence H. Suid devotes just four pages to *Casualties of War* in his 700-page book *Guts and Glory*, half of which are devoted to veterans' reactions to the film's release, whereas *Apocalypse Now* and *Full Metal Jacket* are given lengthy treatment.
5. See in particular Weaver, "The Vietnam War Film, Victimized Veterans, and the Disappearing Woman" in Heberle (ed.), *Thirty Years After*; Goldensohn, "Feral Soldiers: *Casualties of War* and *In the Valley of Elah*" in ibid.; Weaver, *Ideologies of Forgetting*; Thomas, "Up Close and Personal."
6. See, for example, Tessier, *Le Vietnam*, 246-249; Jacquet, *Nuit américaine sur le Vietnam*, 16; Moury, *Flammes sur l'Indochine*, 213-215.
7. Lang, "Casualties of War"; *Casualties of War*.
8. Barra, "Welcome to the Jungle."
9. The Munich Film Museum has since released a restored version of the film on DVD, with English and French subtitles.
10. Kael, "A Wounded Apparition."
11. *The Bonfire of the Vanities* (1990), directed by Brian De Palma, adapted from a novel by Tom Wolfe, and *Parc* (2009), directed by Arnaud des Pallières, adapted from a novel by John Cheever. See Salamon, *The Devil's Candy*, and Mandelbaum, *Anatomie d'un film*.
12. This observation is by no means a value judgment. It is, of course, important to recall that journalists significantly assist in "clarifying the contours and principles of immediate history." Soulet, *L'Histoire immediate*, 31. The central role played by Daniel Lang in this book vividly demonstrates this.
13. Brian De Palma, email to the author, August 31, 2018.
14. Margarita Diaz, email to the author, October 30, 2019.
15. Blumenfeld and Vachaud, *De Palma on De Palma*, 5.
16. Brian De Palma, email to the author, March 2, 2019.

17 An essential lesson learned from historian Raul Hilberg, a specialist in the Nazi's destruction of European Jewry.
18 In the original French, this term is *provoquer*. On the topic of *l'archive provoquée*, see Philippe Joutard, "Introduction à l'histoire orale" in D'Almeida and Maréchal (eds.), *L'Histoire orale en questions*.
19 Included in this book are photos taken by Goldstein, images that were included in the book I wrote for the DVD and Blu-ray box set of the film released by Wild Side Films (2021).
20 De Rosa, *Ennio Morricone*.
21 Bloch, "Critique historique et critique du témoignage."
22 Ibid., 6.
23 Descamps, *Archiver la mémoire*, 128.
24 Ginzburg et al., "La leçon de méthode de Carlo Ginzburg."
25 Sinyard, *Jack Clayton*.
26 To borrow the title of Plutarch's famous work.
27 Kris and Kurz, *La Légende de l'artiste*.

Prologue

1 JAG officers are involved in military court-martial proceedings and army investigations.
2 Catherine Coquio, "À propos d'un nihilisme contemporain: négation, déni, témoignage" in Coquio, *L'Histoire trouée*, 24.
3 Ibid., 27.
4 Borch, *Judge Advocates in Vietnam*, 71.
5 These details appear in some sources that discuss De Palma's film. See, for example, Niemi, *100 Great War Movies*, 58-61.
6 This American law, which came into effect in 1967, guarantees anyone access to federal agency archives, with the exception of sensitive documents, including those deemed "top secret."
7 United States vs. Cipriano S. Garcia (CM 416159); United States vs. Joseph C. Garcia (CM 416160); United States vs. David E. Gervase (CM 416161); United States vs. Steven C. Thomas (CM 416162), in Army General Courts-Martial Records of Trial, 1939-1976; Records of the Office of the Judge Advocate General (Army), 1792-2010, Record Group 153; National Archives, St. Louis (RL-SL).
8 For all four trials combined there is a total of 2,914 pages, including the court-martial hearing transcripts, reports from forensic pathologists and ballistics experts, witness testimonies, convictions and appeals, as well as all correspondence related to the various cases, from 1966 to 1988.

A Test of Conscience

1 This term refers to a small patrol of up to five men, dedicated solely to observing enemy activity.
2 The reason for this desertion is unknown.
3 United States vs. Steven C. Thomas (CM 416162), Review of Staff Judge Advocate, Fort Leavenworth, Kansas, April 9, 1968, 9-11.
4 United States vs. David E. Gervase (CM 416161), Personal History of Accused, January 21, 1967; Review of the Staff Judge Advocate, June 10, 1967, 5.

5   United States vs. Cipriano S. Garcia (CM 416159), Record of Trial, Camp Radcliff, Vietnam, March 15-16, 1967, 93 (testimony of Sergeant Steven Dennis Saunders).
6   United States vs. Joseph C. Garcia (CM 416160), Record of Trial, Fort Leavenworth, Kansas, February 7-8, 1968, 167.
7   Testimony that Joseph Garcia will corroborate during his appeal. Refer to the same source, 188.
8   United States vs. Cipriano S. Garcia (CM 416159), Review of the Staff Judge Advocate, August 6, 1969, 7-8.
9   United States vs. Joseph C. Garcia (CM 416160), Record of Trial, Fort Leavenworth, 169.
10 Although not part of the mission, Soldier Emmitte Prince, a friend of the Garcia cousins, also attends the briefing, which will later make him a key witness during the various trials.
11 The purpose of this type of mission was to locate pockets of North Vietnamese resistance, neutralize and then destroy them, including stocks of weapons, ammunition and food.
12 According to the testimony of Cipriano Schulz Garcia, in United States vs. Cipriano S. Garcia (CM 416159), Statement, December 10, 1966, 1.
13 United States vs. Sergeant David E. Gervase (CM 416161), Reply to Assignment of Errors, Washington, D.C., October 31, 1967, 1-2.
14 United States vs. Cipriano S. Garcia (CM 416159), Record of Trial, Camp Radcliff, 42.
15 United States vs. Steven C. Thomas (CM 416162), Record of Trial, Camp Radcliff, Vietnam, March 18, 20 and 21, 1967, 25.
16 United States vs. Sergeant David E. Gervase (CM 416161), Record of Trial, Camp Radcliff, Vietnam, March 22, 1967, 24. This quote, along with the following ones, is taken from Storeby's interrogation by the prosecutor.
17 Ibid., 27.
18 According to Storeby's testimony during the trial of Cipriano Garcia. United States vs. Cipriano S. Garcia (CM 416159), Record of Trial, Camp Radcliff, 35.
19 United States vs. Sergeant David E. Gervase (CM 416161), Record of Trial, Camp Radcliff, Vietnam, March 22, 1967, 27.
20 Ibid., 28.
21 United States vs. Steven C. Thomas (CM 416162), Record of Trial, Camp Radcliff, 27.
22 United States vs. Sergeant David E. Gervase (CM 416161), Statement, January 19, 1967.
23 United States vs. Sergeant David E. Gervase (CM 416161), Record of Trial, Camp Radcliff, 28.
24 During Thomas' trial, Storeby specifies that they were blue glass earrings. See United States vs. Steven C. Thomas (CM 416162), Record of Trial, Camp Radcliff, 39.
25 United States vs. Sergeant David E. Gervase (CM 416161), Record of Trial, Camp Radcliff, 29.
26 See Storeby's testimony in the trial of Thomas, United States vs. Steven C. Thomas (CM 416162), as documented in the Record of Trial, Camp Radcliff, 42.
27 United States vs. Sergeant David E. Gervase (CM 416161), Record of Trial, Camp Radcliff, 29.

28 This knife actually belonged to the team leader, Butch Paszkiendtz, who was injured in an ambush six days before Mao's murder, on November 13, 1966. As indicated by Cipriano Garcia in his testimony, Paszkiendtz had purchased it in Alaska. After his evacuation, Paszkiendtz reportedly handed over his knife and M-16 rifle to Thomas. See the testimony of Cipriano Garcia in ibid., 59.
29 Ibid., 54.
30 See the testimony of Robert M. Storeby in the case of United States vs. Steven C. Thomas (CM 416162), as documented in the Record of Trial, Camp Radcliff, in the previously cited source, 70.
31 Ibid., 74.
32 United States vs. Joseph C. Garcia (CM 416160), Record of Trial, Fort Leavenworth, 135.
33 According to Storeby's testimony in the case of United States vs. Steven C. Thomas (CM 416162), as recorded in the Record of Trial, Camp Radcliff, 64.
34 Joseph Garcia, Affidavit, December 10, 1967, 3, in United States vs. Joseph C. Garcia (CM 416160).
35 According to the testimony of McClendon, in United States vs. Sergeant David E. Gervase (CM 416161), Record of Trial, Camp Radcliff, 62.
36 United States vs. Cipriano S. Garcia (CM 416159), Record of Trial, Camp Radcliff, 15-18.
37 Ibid., 22.
38 Ibid., 31-58.
39 Ibid., 49.
40 Ibid., 97.
41 Ibid., 107.
42 United States vs. Joseph C. Garcia (CM 416160), Record of Trial, Camp Radcliff, Vietnam, March 16-17, 1967, 14.
43 Ibid., 29.
44 Ibid., 113.
45 Ibid., 44.
46 Ibid., 134-5.
47 Ibid., 99.
48 Ibid., 102.
49 Ibid., 128.
50 Ibid., 134.
51 United States vs. Steven C. Thomas (CM 416162), Record of Trial, Camp Radcliff, 30-71.
52 Ibid., 23.
53 Ibid., 43.
54 The law enforcement officer repeatedly expressed reluctance, fearing that the presentation of the victim's remains might be perceived as "inflammatory." Ibid., 120.
55 Ibid., 220-1.
56 Ibid., 275.
57 United States vs. Sergeant David E. Gervase (CM 416161), Record of Trial, Camp Radcliff, 109.
58 Ibid., 110.
59 Ibid., 112.
60 Testimony of lieutenant Chester A. Collins. Ibid., 93-4.

61 Ibid., 96.
62 Testimony reiterated by Collins during Joe Garcia's appellate trial. United States vs. Joseph C. Garcia (CM 416160), Record of Trial, Fort Leavenworth, 128.
63 United States vs. Sergeant David E. Gervase (CM 416161), Record of Trial, Camp Radcliff, 48-50.
64 Called to testify in the context of Thomas' trial, Duckett revealed that he was responsible for Gervase's promotion to the rank of sergeant. Refer to United States vs. Steven C. Thomas (CM 416162), Record of Trial, Camp Radcliff, 286.
65 United States vs. Sergeant David E. Gervase (CM 416161), Record of Trial, Camp Radcliff, 99.
66 Ibid., 115.
67 Ibid., 148. This statement will later be strongly criticized. Refer to United States vs. Sergeant David E. Gervase (CM 416161), Opinion of the Board, December 22, 1967, 2; Assignment of Errors and Brief on Behalf of Appellant, undated [September 1967], 1.
68 United States vs. Joseph C. Garcia (CM 416160), Record of Trial, Fort Leavenworth, 78.
69 Ibid., 92-3.
70 Ibid., 204.
71 Ibid., 212.
72 Ibid., 309.
73 General court-martial order, number 353, Fort Leavenworth, 28 March 1968, in United States vs. Joseph C. Garcia (CM 416160).
74 United States vs. Cipriano S. Garcia (CM 416159), letter from Cipriano S. Garcia to Henry B. González, 10 April 1969; letters from Cipriano S. Garcia to Richard Nixon, April 5, 1967 and April 15, 1969.
75 United States vs. Cipriano S. Garcia (CM 416159), Record of Trial, Fort Leavenworth, June 6, 1969, 39-53.
76 United States vs. Sergeant David E. Gervase (CM 416161), Review of the Staff Judge Advocate, June 10, 1967, 5.
77 I discovered this information on the internet, where I also came across photos of Gervase's tombstone. The dates of birth and death confirm that this is the same Gervase who was on trial for the rape and murder of Phan Thi Mao. However, I could find no information about the cause of his death.
78 See "Witness in murder trial raped, killed Vietnamese," *Orlando Sentinel*, July 24, 1992; "Bloody past of witness revealed," *Florida Today*, July 24, 1992.
79 Examples from California, Florida, Massachusetts, Minnesota, Missouri, Nebraska, New Jersey, Pennsylvania and Texas newspapers: "4 Soldiers Convicted in Slaying," *Lincoln Journal Star*, March 23, 1967; "4 G.I.s Convicted on Rape Charges," *Pensacola News Journal*, March 24, 1967; "U.S. Soldiers Are Convicted in Rape-Slaying," *Lubbock Avalanche-Journal*, March 23, 1967; "St. Paul G.I. Testifies in Viet Rape," *Minneapolis Star*, March 23, 1967; "G.I.s Sentenced in Rape-Killing," *Boston Globe*, March 24, 1967; "4 G.I.s Found Guilty in Viet Rape-Slaying," *Los Angeles Times*, March 24, 1967; "Four Soldiers Sentenced in Vietnam Rape, Murder," *St. Louis Post-Dispatch*, March 24, 1967; "General Approves Sentences," *Austin American*, June 12, 1967; "Sentences of G.I.s Upheld in Viet Rape-Murder," *Record*, June 12, 1967; "S.A. G.I.s Sentence Reduced," *San Antonio Express*, June 12, 1967; "Approves Terms of Three Soldiers in Viet Girl's Death," *Evening Times*, June 13, 1967.

80   According to his daughters Cecily and Helen, Daniel Lang would have read about the trials in the military magazine *Stars and Stripes*. However, I have been unable to find a relevant article in the magazine's online archives, despite the fact that it published material the same year about other rapes committed by American soldiers in Vietnam. See "G.I. Rape Conviction Stuns Parents," *Stars and Stripes*, August 30, 1967; "5 G.I.s Sentenced for Assault," *Stars and Stripes*, August 27, 1967.
81   Shawn, "Daniel Lang."
82   Lang, *Early Tales of the Atomic Age*.
83   William Shawn in Mitgang, "Daniel Lang, 66, correspondent."
84   See Lang, "Incident on Hill 192: The 5th Man's Story."
85   Lang, "Affidavit," 2.
86   Ibid., 1-2.
87   Ibid.
88   Remarks made by a friend of Daniel Lang, reported in a note written by Helen Lang forwarded to me by Cecily Lang, in an email dated June 2, 2019.
89   Lang, "Affidavit," 3.
90   Ibid., 2.
91   Lang, "Incident on Hill 192."
92   Ibid.
93   Lang, "Casualties of War," 61.
94   Lang, "Affidavit," 4.
95   Ibid.
96   Ibid.
97   Cecily Lang, author interview, May 21, 2019.
98   Ibid.
99   Lang, "Casualties of War," 118.
100 Ibid.
101 Ibid., 111-12.
102 Lang, "Affidavit," 8.
103 The names Storeby and Eriksson share Scandinavian origins.
104 Lang, "Casualties of War," 71.
105 Ibid., 78.
106 Ibid., 100.
107 Ibid., 94.
108 Ibid., 96.
109 Ibid., 105-6.
110 Ibid., 118.
111 Ibid., 118-21.
112 Ibid.
113 Ibid., 134.
114 Ibid., 137-38.
115 Ibid., 146.
116 Ibid.
117 Margaret Altschul was a reporter for the *New York Journal-American* when Daniel Lang met her. They married in 1942.
118 Lang, "Affidavit," 7.
119 See Prados, *Vietnam*.
120 Turse, *Kill Anything That Moves*, 225-6.
121 Brownmiller, *Against Our Will*, 104-7.

122 See Ibid. Part of the third chapter, entitled "War," is devoted to the rapes perpetrated in Vietnam by Americans. Lang's book is mentioned in passing.
123 Branche et al., *Viols en temps de guerre*, 11.
124 Lilly, *Taken by Force*, 31.
125 Just, "Humanity: Another Casualty of the Vietnam War."
126 Christiansen, "A Minnesotan Who Resisted the Corruption of Vietnam."
127 Lehmann-Haupt, "Incident on Hill 192."
128 Ibid.
129 Raymond, "A Matter of Time?"
130 This was not the first title Lang had in mind. The introduction to one of his revised manuscripts includes three other titles: *An Honorable Discharge*, *Bearing Witness* and *Incident on Hill 192* (the title under which the text was published in Britain). Annotated manuscript [undated], 62, in Daniel Lang Collection, Box 13.
131 Lang, "Incident on Hill 192."
132 Lang received the Society of Magazine Writers Award for Excellence and the Sidney Hillman Award in 1969, the National Magazine Award in 1970.

From the Forests of Bavaria to the Snows of Connecticut: Variations and Extensions, 1970 – 1972

1 Muraire, *Hollywood-Vietnam*, 35-36.
2 Leo Cawley, "The War about the War: Vietnam Films and American Myth" in Dittmar and Michaud, 74. See also Tessier, *Le Vietnam*, 52-58. Readers are directed to Muraire, 38-41, and Anderegg, "Hollywood and Vietnam: John Wayne and Jane Fonda as Discourse" in Michael Anderegg, *Inventing Vietnam*, 24-25, for the numerous inconsistencies (factual, geographical) of *The Green Berets*.
3 Boutet, "Le Vietnam et l'Amérique au cinéma et à la télévision," 76.
4 See Smith, *Looking Away*, 25.
5 In the wake of Lieutenant Calley's trial, veterans were called upon to testify to the realities of war, in an attempt to demonstrate that the abuses committed at My Lai were not unique. Daniel Lang took a close interest in the activities of Vietnam Veterans Against the War. His archive contains documents and a press review of articles relating to the organization.
6 See Stefan Drössler, "Die Geschichte des Films *o.k.*," DVD booklet for the film, Munich Film Museum, 2020. I would like to thank Paul Verhoeven, Michael Verhoeven and Mirko Wiermann, without whom I couldn't have been able to locate the film, as well as Donald and Rob Houwer, who graciously allowed me in 2019 to view a copy remotely – unfortunately without subtitles.
7 I have been unable to locate this article and am relying on information provided to me by Michael Verhoeven.
8 Unless otherwise stated, all quotations from Rob Houwer in this chapter are taken from an author interview conducted on November 1, 2019.
9 Unless otherwise stated, all quotations from Michael Verhoeven in this chapter are taken from an author interview conducted on August 9, 2019.
10 Schweizer, "Bringing the War Home: Pour une politique de la représentation" in Zabunyan et al., *Martha Rosler*, 365.
11 Mignon Nixon, "What's Love Got to Do, Got to Do With It? Feminist Politics and America's War in Vietnam" in Ho et al., *Artists Respond*, 331.

12. Sontag, *Regarding the Pain of Others*, 21.
13. Michael Verhoeven told me that *o.k.* was shot on black-and-white ORWO stock, obtained in East Germany, but in an email to me (July 13, 2024), Rob Houwer, based on the memories of his cinematographer, wrote that the film was shot on a black-and-white Kodak negative.
14. Brecht, *Brecht on Theatre*, 194.
15. On the relationship between Godard and Brecht and, more broadly, the making and reception of *Les Carabiniers*, see de Baecque, *Godard*, 215-23. Rossellini's contributions to the script and the cinematography of Raoul Coutard, a former war reporter who had spent time in Indochina, give *Les Carabiniers* the air of a neorealist film or a current affairs documentary, an impression reinforced by the inclusion of genuine archival footage, particularly from the Second World War.
16. Ibid., 216.
17. Chion, *Stanley Kubrick*, 16-17.
18. Verhoeven's intention was undoubtedly to exacerbate the horror of the crime and the perversity of the rapists by making the character younger than Phan Thi Mao actually was.
19. At least not before Wes Craven's *The Last House on the Left* (1972), which is not unrelated to *Casualties of War*. In the early 1970s, a number of successful films depicted brutal rape: Stanley Kubrick's *A Clockwork Orange* (1971), Sam Peckinpah's *Straw Dogs* (1971), Alfred Hitchcock's *Frenzy* (1972) and John Boorman's *Deliverance* (1972). For an analysis of the representation of rape in these films, see Brownmiller, *Against Our Will*, 301-305. Several Italian films from the 1960s – including Luchino Visconti's *Rocco and His Brothers* (1960) and Vittorio De Sica's *Two Women* (1960) – contain graphic depictions of rape (the latter in the context of war).
20. Kraus, *The Last Days of Mankind*, 516.
21. Vander Lugt, "30 June 1970," 431.
22. Eisenschitz, *Le Cinéma allemand*, 86.
23. Ibid., 93.
24. Haim, "L'industrie cinématographique allemande après la guerre," 227.
25. de Valck, *Film Festivals*, 64.
26. Supporters of the film included student groups and left-wing activists who took the opportunity to ask for money for the North Vietnamese embassy in East Berlin and distribute political leaflets. See Picaper, "Le festival de Berlin est brutalement interrompu."
27. According to William Wyler's testimony in Sinyard, *George Stevens*, 92.
28. Berthomieu, *Hollywood classique*, 317, 326, 330.
29. George Stevens in Brianton, *Hollywood Divided*, 58.
30. Bourget, *Cecil B. DeMille*, 137.
31. Anecdote reported by Michael Verhoeven in Hans-Christoph Blumenberg and Alfred Holighaus' documentary *Trace of the Bears*. Thanks to Michael Verhoeven and Stephen Hornung for sending me a copy of the film.
32. Vander Lugt, "30 June 1970," 433.
33. Lindeperg, *Night and Fog*, 176.
34. These revelations, which emerged during the Berlinale's seventieth edition in 2020, led to the cancellation of the Alfred Bauer Prize, awarded every year since 1987 to a film appreciated for its innovative form. In the aftermath, the festival commissioned an investigation into its former director, entrusted to the Munich's Institute of Contemporary History.

35 Telegram from Dušan Makavejev, read by Alfred Bauer at the film's press conference (July 1970). Archive footage of this historic moment can be seen in *Trace of the Bears*.
36 I have retained the spelling mistake, as it appears in the original title. Special thanks to Katja Beckel for her translation of the film. There are no records of the film in the archives of the DEFA Studio für Dokumentarfilme. The only archival fragment is a letter from the East German Ministry of Culture, approving the making of the film. This information, obtained from the DR 1-Z-Zulassungsunterlagen der HV Film beim Ministerium für Kultur collection, at the Bundesarchiv, was communicated to me by Tim Storch, in an email dated December 9, 2019.
37 See Joe Madura, "Liliana Porter" in Ho, et al., 194-96.
38 Kazan, "The Cinema in America" in Ciment, *Elia Kazan*, 136.
39 Kazan, *A Life*, 754.
40 Ibid.
41 Kazan, "The Cinema in America," 140.
42 Kazan, *Kazan on Directing*, 233.
43 Kazan, *A Life*, 754.
44 Young, *Kazan*, 304.
45 The correspondence surrounding *The Visitors* mainly concerns the film's financing (letters exchanged by Kazan with his lawyers and with the executives of United Artists), its legal problems (letters from the Directors Guild and the Screen Actors Guild), and its promotion (invitation letters for the preview). There are no letters from Elia Kazan in Daniel Lang's archive.
46 Kazan, *A Life*, 754.
47 This is the amount given by Kazan in his autobiography. However, he told Michel Ciment that the film was shot for $135,000, and in *Vietnam War Films*, Malo and Williams cite a budget of $150,000 (469).
48 Kazan, *A Life*, 754.
49 Two scripts, identical in length at 75 pages, are preserved in Kazan's archives at Wesleyan University's Odgen and Mary Louise Reid Cinema Archives. One is the shooting script, annotated by Kazan. My thanks to Joan Miller for this detail, who assured me that Chris Kazan's screenplay is very close to the film version.
50 See Silver and Zuker, "Visiting Kazan."
51 Gentry, "Interview: James Woods."
52 Kazan in Silver and Zuker, "Visiting Kazan."
53 Ciment, "Entretien avec Elia Kazan sur *The Visitors*."
54 Kazan in Young, *Kazan*, 306.
55 Lilly, *Taken by Force*, 22.
56 Devlin and Devlin, *Selected Letters of Elia Kazan*, 562.
57 Canby, "*The Visitors* Portrays Ordeal of a Threatened G.I."
58 Kazan, *A Life*, 757.
59 Ibid., 758.
60 Ciment, "Entretien avec Elia Kazan sur *The Visitors*."
61 Lachaud, *Redneck Movies*, 14.
62 Ibid., 271.
63 Lowenstein, *Shocking Representation*, 120.
64 See Levy, "De la hantise des archives."
65 Szulkin, *Wes Craven's Last House on the Left*, 147.
66 Levy, *Images clandestines*, 176-177.

Casualties of War in Hollywood: On Some Inadaptations, 1970 – 1980

1. Jeannelle, *Films sans images*, 197-209, for all citations in this paragraph.
2. Willner, letter to Daniel Lang, October 21, 1969, Daniel Lang Collection, Box 17.
3. Willner's name was mentioned several times in the hearings that took place before the HUAC. See Communist Infiltration of Hollywood Motion-Picture Industry – Part 5. Hearings Before the Committee on Un-American Activities Houses of Representatives. Eighty-Second Congress, First Session, September 20, 21, 24 and 25, 1951, Washington, United States Government Printing Office, 1951, pp.1824, 1915-16, 2317.
4. Nancy Hamburger Sureck, letter to Daniel Lang, October 23, 1969; Albert Gottesman, letter to Daniel Lang, October 23, 1969, Daniel Lang Collection, Box 17. Unless otherwise stated, all correspondence quoted below is taken from the same collection.
5. St. Clair, letter to Daniel Lang, November 21, 1969.
6. Scott-Fox, letter to Milton Greenstein, December 5, 1969.
7. De Grunwald, letter to the editor of *The New Yorker*, January 1, 1970.
8. Townley, letter to Daniel Lang, February 17, 1970.
9. Todini, letter to Daniel Lang, April 8, 1970.
10. Smyth, *Fred Zinnemann*, 68.
11. Ibid., 16.
12. Helen Lang, email to the author, June 11, 2020.
13. Frances Lang, email to the author, June 11, 2020.
14. Frances Lang, email to the author, May 21, 2019.
15. Smyth, *Fred Zinnemann*, 97.
16. I have not been able to find a copy of this letter, dated October 15, 1969, which Zinnemann mentions in a letter to Lang several weeks later. Fred Zinnemann, letter to Daniel Lang, December 23, 1969.
17. Jeannelle, *Films sans images*, 321-22.
18. Ibid.
19. Zinnemann, letter to Daniel Lang, November 18, 1969.
20. Jeannelle, *Films sans images*, 335.
21. Ibid., 345-7.
22. Kael, "A Wounded Apparition."
23. This is one of the various entities the producer created from the names of his children (Paman is a contraction of the first names of his daughters, Pamela and Samantha). See Battaglio, *David Susskind*, 35.
24. Ibid., 119.
25. Ibid., 198.
26. Heywood Gould, email to the author, September 12, 2019.
27. "Agreement between Daniel Lang and Paman Productions – Norton Simon Inc.," January 1970, Daniel Lang's private archives.
28. Jerry Schatzberg is mentioned by Henri Béhar in an article published on the occasion of the presentation of Brian De Palma's *Casualties of War* at the Deauville Film Festival ("Le Vietnam ou la déraison exemplaire," *Le Monde*, August 31, 1989), though this article contains several factual errors. Having found no mention of Schatzberg's name elsewhere – neither in the Clayton nor Lang archives – I cannot certify the validity of this information. It does seem rather improbable, however, given that in 1969 Schatzberg was known primarily for his career as a photographer,

and that his first film, *Puzzle of a Downfall Child*, wasn't released until the following year.

29 Clayton's interest in *Casualties of War* might be surprising to some, as his filmography leans more toward intimate dramas and literary adaptations than historical epics and tragedies based on real events. But an examination of Clayton's numerous unrealized projects reveals that Lang's themes (war, violence, racism, justice) deeply concerned him. Throughout the 1970s he worked on *Massacre at Fall Creek*, based on the novel by Jessamyn West, about the savage murder in 1824 by seven white settlers of two Seneca Indian families, and *Silence*, based on a novel by James Kennaway, about racial violence in a Chicago suburb. See Sinyard, *Jack Clayton*, 218-22).
30 Hamill, *A Drinking Life*, 245.
31 Ibid.
32 His first "official" screenplay was for Frank Perry's Western shot in Spain, *Doc Holliday* (*Doc*, 1971), with Stacy Keach and Faye Dunaway.
33 Battaglio, *David Susskind*, 111.
34 Ibid.
35 Hamill, "An outline for *Casualties of War*. By Daniel Lang," 1970 [undated], BFI, JLC-15-35-1-2.
36 Hamill, letter to Jack Clayton, January 8, 1970, BFI, JLC-15-35-1-2.
37 Ibid.
38 Hamill, "An outline for *Casualties of War*. By Daniel Lang."
39 Lang, "Casualties of War," 61; United States vs. Steven C. Thomas (CM 416162), "Record of Trial," Camp Radcliff, 68.
40 Muraire, *Hollywood-Vietnam*, 134.
41 Clayton, letter to Pete Hamill, February 2, 1970, BFI, JLC-15-35-1-2.
42 Clayton, "*Casualties of War*. Notes on Pete Hamill's First Outline," January 28, 1970; letter to David Susskind, February 2, 1970, BFI, JLC-15-35-1-2.
43 Neil Sinyard, *Jack Clayton*, 9.
44 Ibid.
45 Sims, "*Casualties of War*. Comments on Pete Hamill's First Outline."
46 Ibid.
47 Ibid.
48 Hamill, letter to Jack Clayton, January 8, 1970.
49 Ibid.
50 See the HBO documentary *Breslin and Hamill: Deadline Artists* (2018), directed by John Block, Jonathan Alter and Steve McCarthy..
51 Sims, "*Casualties of War*. Brief Synopsis"; "*Casualties of War*. Principal Characters"; "*Casualties of War*. Main Locations"; "*Casualties of War*. Trial Verdicts & Sentences"; "*Casualties of War*. Chronological Breakdown," January 22, 1970, JLC-15-35-1-4.
52 "Questions for Military Adviser," March 16, 1970, BFI, JLC-15-35-2-3.
53 Rissner, letter to Jack Clayton, March 25, 1970, BFI, JLC-15-35-2-5.
54 Hamill, *Casualties of War*, undated [1970], Daniel Lang Collection, Box 13. Strangely enough, this version (to my knowledge the only one) of Hamill's screenplay is missing from the Clayton collection at the BFI, which leads me to the following hypothesis: the filmmaker could have given his copy to Lang in person after reading it.
55 Clayton, letter to David Susskind, April 6, 1970, BFI, JLC-15-35-2-5.
56 Clayton, "Questions for Daniel Lang," April 8, 1970, BFI, JLC-15-35-2-2.

57 Clayton, "*Casualties of War.* Notes for New York Trip: 7 April," 6 April 1970, BFI, JLC-15-35-2-5.
58 Clayton, "*Casualties of War.* Notes on Pete Hamill's First Draft Script," April 15, 1970, BFI, JLC-15-35-1-5.
59 In a letter written after his stay in New York, Jack Clayton thanked Lang for giving him an "essay" on *Casualties of War*, which he had read carefully and which had helped him to reflect on aspects he had not fully understood. Perhaps it was a commentary on Pete Hamill's script. I have found no trace of this document. Clayton, letter to Daniel Lang, April 22, 1970, BFI, JLC-15-35-1-1.
60 Clayton, "*Casualties of War.* Notes on Pete Hamill's First Draft Script."
61 Rissner, Inter-Office Memo, Warner Bros. – Seven Arts Production Ltd., to John Calley, April 20, 1970, BFI, JLC-15-35-2-5.
62 Clayton, letter to Pete Hamill, April 21, 1970, BFI, JLC-15-35-1-5.
63 Ibid.
64 Given the date and place of the meeting, it is likely that Pete Hamill was in London when the letter arrived.
65 Hamill, Telegram to Jack Clayton, April 22, 1970, BFI, JLC-15-35-1-5.
66 Although he was largely blameless for its failure, Giler's adaptation of Gore Vidal's scandalous *Myra Breckinridge* – his first screen credit – was something of a humiliating fiasco. See Froug, *The Screenwriter Looks at the Screenwriter*, 219-228.
67 Froug, 228. Unlike Hamill's script, which Clayton extensively annotated, Giler's initial draft, as located in Clayton's archive, contains no written comments. Giler, *Casualties of War*, based on the book by Daniel Lang, August 12, 1970, 113pp., BFI, JLC-15-35-1-3. This same version is in Daniel Lang's Boston archives. There is a second version, expanded by ten pages, in Clayton's archives. David Giler, *Casualties of War*, 1970 [undated], 123pp. (second draft), JLC-15-35-1-3.
68 Calley, telegram to Jack Clayton, August 14, 1970, BFI, JLC-15-35-1-1.
69 Most were second-tier television actors like Sidney Johnson and Norman Mitchell, who could have played the roles of certain middle-aged officers. Among the candidates suitable for the main roles were Timothy Craven, Louis Cabot and John Hallam, a 28-year-old who had a cameo in Tony Richardson's *The Charge of the Light Brigade*. Besides these unsolicited messages, it is possible that Clayton and his producers were considering more prominent actors for the roles of Eriksson and Meserve, though there is nothing in the archives on this. Cabot, letter to Jack Clayton [undated]; Timothy Craven, letter to Jack Clayton, July 9, 1970; Norman Mitchell, letter to Jack Clayton, July 9, 1970; John Hallam, letter to Jack Clayton [undated], received on July 20, 1970; Sidney Johnson, letter to Jack Clayton, July 20, 1970 [JLC-15-35-2-4].
70 A letter in the Clayton archives proves that the director was already thinking about putting together his crew in April 1970. At the same time, he received an unsolicited application from a British assistant director, but Clayton's secretary, Ley Zeff, told him that the production would recruit an exclusively American team. Jack Clayton, letter to Les Wiles, April 24, 1970, BFI, JLC-15-35-2-5; Ley Zeff, letter to John Francis, April 22, 1970, BFI, JLC-15-35-2-4.
71 "Scene Breakdown for Set" [undated], BFI, JLC-15-35-2-1.

72 "Brief Summary on contents picture *o.k.*," undated [1970], Daniel Lang Collection, Box 13 (for this and subsequent citations).
73 Ibid.
74 As Lang's correspondence suggests. See Warburg, letter to Daniel Lang, July 20, 1970, Daniel Lang Collection, Box 13.
75 *Variety*, July 8, 1970. The review is critical of the film for being overindulgent, particularly in its depiction of the rape, which is long and brutal, and while the film's technical virtues are acknowledged, *Variety* described it as "disgusting and embarrassing," concluding that it "must be regarded as a very doubtful enterprise."
76 Lang, "Affidavit," 10. In the original, Lang has underlined the word "stolen" and handwritten the word "exploited?"
77 Rob Houwer, author interview, November 1, 2019.
78 Lang, *Die Meldung*.
79 Shannon Fifer, email to the author, December 17, 2019.
80 Rob Houwer, author interview, November 1, 2019.
81 Ibid.
82 Ashley (Warner Bros – Seven Arts, Inc.), letter to Daniel Lang, August 5, 1970, Daniel Lang Collection, Box 13.
83 Wechsler, letter to Daniel Lang, September 3, 1970, Daniel Lang Collection, Box 17.
84 Clayton, letter to Alan Shayne, October 6, 1970, BFI, JLC-15-35-2-5.
85 In his letter, Clayton spells it "MacGuire," which seems to me to be a typo. I am fairly certain that Clayton is referring to Charles H. Maguire (1927-2001), an assistant director and then associate producer for Elia Kazan before working with Sidney Lumet, Hal Ashby, Warren Beatty and Robert Wise. Maguire, who was second unit director on *The Sand Pebbles*, would surely have been an excellent production manager for *Casualties of War*.
86 Clayton, letter to Daniel Lang, April 16, 1971, BFI, JLC-15-35-1-1.
87 Lang, letter to Jack Clayton, March 19, 1971, BFI, JLC-15-35-1-1.
88 It was probably producer Ronald Shedlo (1940-2007), who had just financed Jack Gold's *The Reckoning* (1970). Nine years later, Shedlo discovered a young actor named Michael J. Fox and offered him his first role in a CBS TV film, *Letters from Frank* (1979).
89 "Agreement made by and between Daniel Lang and Paman Productions-Norton Simon Inc."
90 Clayton, letter to Daniel Lang, April 16, 1971.
91 Chais, letter to Daniel Lang, June 16, 1971, BFI, JLC-15-35-1-1.
92 Chais, letter to Daniel Lang, July 1, 1971, BFI, JLC-15-35-1-1.
93 Ibid.
94 Ibid.
95 Chais, letter to Jack Clayton, July 13, 1971, BFI, JLC-15-35-2-5.
96 Ibid.
97 It is likely that these projects included adaptations of Roland Topor's *The Tenant* (directed by Roman Polanski in 1976) and Scott Fitzgerald's *The Great Gatsby* (which Clayton filmed in 1974).
98 "Option agreement between Talent Associates Ltd. and Daniel Lang," May 7, 1977, Daniel Lang's private archives.
99 Battaglio, *David Susskind*, 297-98.
100 Heywood Gould, email to the author, September 1, 2019.
101 Heywood Gould, email to the author, August 31, 2019.

102 See Gould, *Drafted*.
103 Heywood Gould, email to the author, August 14, 2019.
104 Gould, *Casualties of War*, from the book by Daniel Lang, draft 3/26/79, Collection of motion picture scripts 1921-1998, Box 1021, UCLA Library Special Collections, Los Angeles.
105 Gould, *Casualties of War*, from the book by Daniel Lang [undated], Daniel Lang Collection, Box 17.
106 Unsigned, undated document [handwritten notes by Daniel Lang on Gould's screenplay]; "Notes on adaptation of *Casualties of War*," May 28, 1979, Daniel Lang Collection, Box 13.
107 No doubt to distance himself from the original text, Heywood Gould changed the first names and sometimes the spelling of the characters' last names: Sven Eriksson becomes "Charles Erickson," Tony Meserve's first name is now Andrew, Clark is Clarke and his first name is no longer Ralph but Arthur, and the Diaz cousins are now Bernardo (Buddy) and Raphael Martinez. For the sake of consistency, however, I have chosen to retain the names originally chosen by Daniel Lang.
108 Heywood Gould, email to the author, September 12, 2019.
109 United States vs. Sergeant David E. Gervase (CM 416161), "Record of Trial," Camp Radcliff, 108.
110 Heywood Gould, email to the author, September 14, 2019.
111 Heywood Gould, email to the author, September 16, 2019.
112 The sentences were changed, but Gould preserves the stark contrast between the initial verdict and the subsequent commutations. In the screenplay, Meserve and Clark, initially sentenced to life imprisonment, have their sentences commuted to eight and six years, respectively, resulting in their release between 1973 and 1975. Manuel and Rafe are sentenced to 25 years but Manuel is released on appeal and Rafe is released in 1970 after serving only three years.
113 Heywood Gould, email to the author, August 14, 2019.
114 Lang, "Notes on adaptation of *Casualties of War*." All the citations that follow are taken from the same document.
115 Heywood Gould, email to the author, August 14, 2019.
116 This choice is interesting because it foreshadows that of Michael J. Fox in De Palma's version. In the 1970s, Ron Howard was, like Fox in the 1980s, a star of the small screen: he played Richie Cunningham, the archetypal American teenager, in Garry Marshall's *Happy Days* (1974-84). The series, set in the 1950s, was created at the very end of the Vietnam War to lift the spirits of Americans and make them forget the bloody media coverage of the conflict – even if it failed to avoid, in a humorous way, America's social problems. Howard had demonstrated the extent of his talent under the direction of George Lucas (*American Graffiti*, 1973) and Richard Fleischer (*The Spikes Gang*, 1974), before moving behind the camera to focus on his career as a filmmaker.
117 See Battaglio, *David Susskind*, 302.
118 Heywood Gould, email to the author, September 17, 2019.
119 Crown, letter to Mrs. Mortimer Levitt, May 29, 1979, Daniel Lang Collection, Box 17.
120 Lang, untitled and undated manuscript [1979], 22pp., Daniel Lang Collection, Box 17.

121 Daniel Lang, untitled and undated manuscript [1979-1980, "34-page treatment" in grey pencil on the first page], 34pp., Daniel Lang Collection, Box 17.
122 Lang, *Treatment Casualties of War*, undated [1979-1980], 80pp., Daniel Lang's private archives. I would like to thank Cecily Lang for sending me a digitized copy, with the agreement of her sisters Helen and Frances.
123 Lang, letter to Alfred Crown and Jerome Hammer, 1979 (rough draft), Daniel Lang's private archives.
124 Lang, letter to Alfred Crown and Jerome Hammer, March 18, 1980, Daniel Lang's private archives.
125 Cohn, letter to Alfred Crown and Jerome Hammer, August 27, 1980, Daniel Lang's private archives.

Revisiting *Casualties of War*

1 Lang was said by one of his colleagues from *The New Yorker* to be "nuts about turning the damn thing into a movie." See Barra, "Welcome to the Jungle."
2 Blumenfeld and Vachaud, *De Palma on De Palma*, 31.
3 De Palma was a regular at Andy Warhol's Factory, rubbing shoulders with Robert Rauschenberg, Frank Stella, Richard Hamilton (who makes an appearance in *Greetings*) and Allen Ginsberg. See Lagier, *Les mille yeux de Brian De Palma*, 20-21.
4 Brian De Palma, author interview, March 22, 2019.
5 Brian De Palma in Lagier, *Les mille yeux de Brian De Palma*, 29.
6 Thoret, *26 secondes*, 113.
7 Hamill, letter to Jack Clayton, January 8, 1970.
8 The thunderous claims made by Henri Béhar in an article I have already mentioned in chapter 3 ("Le Vietnam ou la déraison exemplaire") should therefore be treated with caution. Béhar claims that James Woods "pestered" De Palma for the role of Eriksson, which seems strange given that the actor hadn't yet made a film and probably didn't know the director at the time. De Palma, to whom I put this information, replied: "I don't remember having considered Woods in the role of Eriksson. It seems unlikely to me" (email to the author, June 11, 2020). In the same paragraph, Béhar indicates that the filmmaker "was thinking more of Al Pacino and Jon Voight for the roles," which seems more likely, given that they both eventually made films with him.
9 De Palma didn't see Verhoeven's film while he was at the festival in Berlin. Nearly twenty years later, when he wanted to watch *o.k.* before starting work on his adaptation of Lang's book, he was unable to locate a copy (Laurent Bouzereau interview, 2001 DVD and Blu-ray, Columbia Pictures/Sony Pictures). De Palma told me that when he did eventually see the film, he found it "very crude," with only a "vague connection with the real incident."
10 Dumas, *Un-American Psycho*, 130.
11 Rabe, *The Vietnam Plays*, XII.
12 Ibid.
13 David Rabe, email to the author, December 10, 2018.
14 "I would have met him around 1978 or 1979 I would think, though it could have been earlier," says Rabe. Email to the author, December 10, 2018.

15 Kelly, *Sean Penn*, 212.
16 Brian De Palma, author interview, March 22, 2019.
17 David Rabe, email to the author, December 10, 2018.
18 Blumenfeld and Vachaud, *De Palma on De Palma*, 150.
19 Linson, *A Pound of Flesh*, 66.
20 Blumenfeld and Vachaud, *De Palma on De Palma*, 154.
21 Linson, *A Pound of Flesh*, 123.
22 Art Linson, author interview, March 1, 2019.
23 Ibid.
24 Linson, *A Pound of Flesh*, 131.
25 Hollander, letter to Greg Gelfan, May 27, 1987, Daniel and Margaret Lang private archives. A few weeks later, Hollander drew up a summary of all the adaptation rights acquired and returned to Lang since 1970. Discussions were also held about a reprint of *Casualties of War* by McGraw-Hill. See David Hollander, "Summary of adaptation rights for *Casualties of War* (1970-1981)," September 30, 1987, Daniel and Margaret Lang private archives.
26 David Rabe, email to the author, October 22, 2019.
27 Wargnier, "Question de morale."
28 David Rabe, email to the author, September 8, 2018.
29 Collection of motion picture scripts 1921-1998, Box 0302, UCLA Library Special Collections, Los Angeles.
30 Rabe, *Casualties of War*, based on the book by Daniel Lang, 3/15/88, 127 pp.; The New York Public Library, The Performing Arts Research Collection, CTR 1844. I would like to thank John Calhoun for providing me with the information I needed to identify this copy of the script.
31 Two sequences cut by De Palma shortly after the test screenings have been added in this new cut. These will be discussed in the seventh chapter.
32 Handwritten note signed C.H. on the cover of David Rabe's screenplay, *Casualties of War*, "Revised 3-26-88," Bill Pankow private archive (incomplete version).
33 Lang, "Casualties of War," 146.
34 Eriksson's first name, Sven, has been changed to Daniel in the postdated version, as well as in the last two versions. Apart from this change, the introductory paragraph is identical in the three versions cited.
35 Kael, "A Wounded Apparition," 76.
36 Lang, "Casualties of War," 127.
37 Greven, *Manhood in Hollywood from Bush to Bush*, 63.
38 David Rabe, email to the author, January 19, 2019.
39 Ibid.
40 Ibid.
41 See Jones, *My Lai*, 3.
42 Lang, "Casualties of War," 66.
43 I am grateful to John C. Reilly, who speaks these lines about Genghis Khan in De Palma's film, and who suggested this John Wayne reference to me.
44 Greven, *Manhood in Hollywood from Bush to Bush*, 70. See also: Eberwein, *Armed Forces*, 129-132; Donald and MacDonald, *Reel Men at War*.
45 One also thinks of Nancy Spero's extraordinary series of gouaches and inks, where bombs take on the appearance of erect penises. In one of her most memorable works, *The Male Bomb* (1966), Spero represents a male

body in its phallic omnipotence but also, simultaneously, "castrated and decapitated." Mignon Nixon, "What's Love Got to Do, Got to Do with It?" 335.
46 Thomas, "Up Close and Personal," 140.
47 On that point, see Griffiths, *Vietnam Inc.*
48 The location was changed in version IV to an airport in Illinois. Presumably this was again to reveal as little as possible about where the real Eriksson lived.
49 Blumenfeld and Vachaud, *De Palma on De Palma*, 156.
50 David Rabe, email to the author, January 22, 2019.
51 Lang, "Casualties of War," 146.
52 Wargnier, "Question de morale." It is likely that Spielberg's criticism prompted De Palma to ask Rabe to rewrite the nightmare scene.
53 Blumenfeld and Vachaud, *De Palma on De Palma*, 157.
54 Ibid.
55 Taylor, "Steel Ambition."
56 Blumenfeld and Vachaud, *De Palma on De Palma*, 154.
57 Montgomery Miller (Columbia Pictures Industries Inc.), letter to the Clerk of Court, United States Army Legal Services Agency, January 22, 1988, in United States vs. David E. Gervase (CM 416161).
58 Mary B. Dennis (Deputy Clerk of Court), letter to Montgomery Miller, February 24, 1988, in United States vs. David E. Gervase (CM 416161).

Pre-production, October 1987 – March 1988

1   After the war, says Penn, his father endured "about ten years of hardcore flashbacks and sleeplessness, and used things to stay awake and things to go to sleep; and then the nightmares that were probably enhanced by those pharmaceuticals. Because there was nobody who really knew how to deal with all that stuff." Quoted Kelly, *Sean Penn*, 12.
2   David Rabe in ibid., 213.
3   Art Linson, author interview, March 1, 2019.
4   Sean Penn, email to the author, June 5, 2020.
5   Ibid.
6   Ibid.
7   Art Linson, author interview, March 1, 2019.
8   Thomas, "'*Casualties*' story electrified De Palma."
9   Barra, "Welcome to the Jungle."
10 Ibid.
11 Ibid. Fox told Laurent Bouzereau that he first read the script during the Christmas holidays in 1987, which suggests that the choice of lead actor was made at an advanced stage of pre-production, and that Fox had relatively little time to get into character. Bouzereau, "*Eriksson's War*."
12 Portman, "Fox Becomes Casualty of War."
13 Ibid.
14 John C. Reilly, author interview, October 10, 2019.
15 Holt McCallany, author interview, October 2, 2019.
16 John Leguizamo, email to the author, January 25, 2024.
17 Salamon, *The Devil's Candy*, 80.
18 For several years, Schwab had been writing screenplays with a friend, Lynn Kuwahara. One of them, first titled *Golden Triangle* (later renamed

Chasing the Dragon), was set in Thailand and revolved around an American narcotics agent who succumbs to corruption. Although it attracted the interest of an agent, the project never came to fruition. See ibid., 86.

19 Art Linson, author interview, March 1, 2019.
20 See Mydans, "2 U.S. Airmen Slain at Philippine Base."
21 Perhaps the production team was concerned about a repeat of what Francis Coppola had been confronted with on the Philippines set of *Apocalypse Now*, including a civil war and, because the government feared he might be kidnapped by rebels, the need for bodyguards. See Coppola, *Notes*.
22 Eric Schwab, author interview, April 11, 2009.
23 In a slightly different role, Caruso also produced David Lynch's *Blue Velvet* (1986).
24 Maurice Schell, author interview, May 15, 2019.
25 Larry McConkey, email to the author, November 16, 2019.
26 Sallie Beechinor, email to the author, June 4, 2019.
27 Charlie Sungkawess, author interview, May 30, 2019.
28 Eric Schwab, author interview, April 11, 2019.
29 Roland Neveu, author interview, May 7, 2019.
30 Fred Caruso, author interview, June 3, 2019.
31 A great admirer of De Palma, Wargnier first interviewed the director in 1987 at the Deauville Festival where *The Untouchables* was screened. This interview, conducted for *Studio Magazine*, marked the beginning of a friendship between the two directors.
32 See Farrell and Nolan, "In a War of Nerves"; "*Casualties* a catharsis for Vietnamese refugees."
33 Thuy Thu Le, author interview, March 19, 2019. Unless otherwise stated, all quotations from Thuy Thu Le in this chapter are taken from this interview.
34 Fred Caruso, author interview, June 3, 2019.
35 Don Harvey, email to the author, August 30, 2019.
36 John C. Reilly, author interview, October 10, 2019.
37 Ibid.
38 Dye first served in Vietnam for six months with the 3rd Marine Division as an infantryman. He then returned to the United States, changed his military specialty, became a Combat Correspondent and returned to Vietnam for service with the 1st Marine Division in 1967.
39 Dale Dye, author interview, March 29, 2019.
40 Tessier, *Le Vietnam*, 190.
41 Dale Dye, email to the author, March 29, 2019.
42 Ibid. However, the testimonies of veterans in *Winter Soldier*, gathered by Vietnam Veterans Against the War, mention numerous rapes, as well as the barbaric acts perpetrated on the bodies of Vietnamese women (genital mutilation). See also the facts and figures reported by Susan Brownmiller in *Against Our Will*.
43 Mike Stokey arrived in Vietnam in January 1967 as a Private First Class in the Marine Corps and left in April 1969, after three tours of duty, with the rank of sergeant. Like Dale Dye, Stokey also served as a combat correspondent in the 1st Marine Division (they did two tours together). He spent most of his time in the field with companies of the 5th and 7th Marine Regiments. He was in Hue during the Tet Offensive in 1968 and took part in operations during the Battle of Khe Sanh. Wounded, he was awarded the Bronze Star with "V" for heroism.

44 From the album *Waiting for the Sun* (1968). My thanks to Carl Goldstein for bringing this anecdote to my attention, and to Don Harvey for the clarification he provided (in an email dated September 28, 2019).
45 Portman, "Fox Becomes Casualty of War."
46 This type of rifle, a shortened version of the M-16, was introduced into service in 1994.
47 Sean Penn, email to the author, June 5, 2020.
48 Holt McCallany, author interview, January 19, 2020.
49 Mike Stokey, author interview, March 27, 2019
50 Ibid..
51 Don Harvey, email to the author, August 30, 2019.
52 John C. Reilly, author interview, October 10, 2019.
53 Blumenfeld and Vachaud, *De Palma on De Palma*, 158.
54 Ibid.
55 Carl Goldstein, author interview, September 25, 2019. This is confirmed by Mike Stokey (author interview, March 27, 2019).
56 Blumenfeld and Vachaud, *De Palma on De Palma*, 158. This story is confirmed by Sean Penn, who recalls White telling the actors that they weren't going to be ready for the first day of principal photography and that they needed more training. Email to the author, June 5, 2020.
57 Art Smith Jr., email to the author, October 8, 2019.
58 Ibid.
59 Don Harvey, author interview, August 30, 2019.
60 John C. Reilly, author interview, October 10, 2019.
61 Holt McCallany, author interview, October 2, 2019.
62 John C. Reilly, author interview, October 10, 2019.
63 John Leguizamo, email to the author, January 25, 2024.
64 Erik King, author interview, October 9, 2019.
65 David Rabe in Kelly, *Sean Penn*, 213.
66 Sean Penn in ibid.
67 Laisney, *Sean Penn*, 79.
68 Ibid., 80.
69 Ibid.
70 Weaver, *Ideologies of Forgetting*, 149.
71 Sean Penn, email to the author, June 5, 2020.
72 Wolf Kroeger, author interview, June 16, 2020.
73 Ibid.
74 Paul Engelen, email to the author, October 10, 2019. The Chinese symbol 力, which conveys the idea of strength and power, is clearly visible on Penn's forearm in several sequences of the film.
75 Pond, "Shot by Shot."
76 Ibid. De Palma said it took him four months to learn the storyboard "by heart." Ferney, "Bleu comme la peur!"
77 Eric Schwab, author interview, April 11, 2019.
78 Brian De Palma, author interview, March 22, 2019.
79 Monica Goldstein, author interview, April 26, 2021.

Filming *Casualties of War*: A Ground-Level Chronicle, April – July 1988

1. Art Linson, author interview, March 1, 2019.
2. Fred Caruso, author interview, June 3, 2019.
3. Blumenfeld and Vachaud, *De Palma on De Palma*, 162. De Palma is exaggerating. Call sheets make clear that the battle sequence at the start of the film took about a week to shoot. It is possible that at times the crew shot both day and night to make up for any potential delays.
4. Don Harvey, email to the author, August 30, 2019.
5. Carl Goldstein, author interview, September 25, 2019.
6. Eric Schwab, email to the author, January 14, 2020.
7. Holt McCallany, author interviews, October 2, 2019 and January 19, 2020.
8. Stephen H. Burum, author interview, June 12, 2019.
9. Fred Caruso, author interview, June 3, 2019.
10. Stephen H. Burum, author interview, June 12, 2019.
11. Pasiree Panya, author interview, January 23, 2020.
12. Brian Cook, author interview, June 7, 2019.
13. Roland Neveu, author interview, May 7, 2019.
14. Barra, "Welcome to the Jungle."
15. Don Harvey, email to the author, August 30, 2019.
16. Carl Goldstein, author interview, September 25, 2019.
17. Art Linson, author interview, March 1, 2019.
18. Barra, "Welcome to the Jungle."
19. Fred Caruso, author interview, June 3, 2019.
20. Brian De Palma, author interview, March 22, 2019.
21. Mike Stokey, author interview, March 27, 2019.
22. Larry McConkey, email to the author, November 16, 2019.
23. Wargnier, "Question de morale."
24. Carr, "De Palma confronts Vietnam."
25. Monica Goldstein, author interview, April 26, 2021.
26. Eric Schwab, author interview, April 11, 2019.
27. As reported by Eric Schwab in an email, November 27, 2019.
28. Carr, "De Palma confronts Vietnam."
29. McConkey, "Larry McConkey in Thailand."
30. Paul Engelen, email to the author, October 10, 2019.
31. Larry McConkey, email to the author, November 16, 2019.
32. Thuy Thu Le, author interview, March 19, 2019.
33. Thuy Thu Le had three body doubles. Pasiree Panya, who was only slightly younger than her and had the same body shape, is in all the scenes where her character appears from behind or from afar. A Thai wearing a wig was used as a stand-in for the scene where Oanh falls from the bridge. A third was used for nude shots.
34. Eric Schwab, email to the author, November 27, 2019.
35. Blumenfeld and Vachaud, *De Palma on De Palma*, 162-63.
36. Fred Caruso, author interview, June 3, 2019.
37. Monica Goldstein, author interview, April 26, 2021.
38. Ibid.
39. Barra, "Welcome to the Jungle."
40. Ibid.
41. Anecdote reported by Art Smith in the film's press kit, distributed at the Deauville Film Festival in 1989.

Endnotes

42 Pond, "Shot by Shot."
43 Stephen H. Burum, author interview, June 12, 2019.
44 John C. Reilly, author interview, October 10, 2019.
45 Carl Goldstein, author interview, September 25, 2019.
46 Barra, "Welcome to the Jungle."
47 Carl Goldstein, author interview, September 25, 2019.
48 As noted by Carl Goldstein and Eric Schwab, in conversation with the author.
49 Fox, *Lucky Man*, 15.
50 Ibid.
51 Bouzereau, *Eriksson's War*, and Fox, *No Time Like the Future*, 14-15.
52 John C. Reilly, author interview, October 10, 2019.
53 In various interviews that can be found on YouTube and elsewhere, Stephen Baldwin offers up a completely different version of events, never once mentioning the real reason for his being fired from the film.
54 Holt McCallany, author interview, October 2, 2019.
55 Ibid.
56 Fred Caruso, author interview, June 3, 2019.
57 John C. Reilly, author interview, October 10, 2019.
58 John C. Reilly, author interview, October 10, 2019.
59 Eric Schwab, author interview, April 11, 2019.
60 Paul Engelen, email to the author, October 10, 2019.
61 Wolf Kroeger, author interview, June 16, 2020.
62 Roland Neveu, author interview, May 7, 2019.
63 Larry McConkey, email to the author, November 16, 2019.
64 Carl Goldstein, author interview, September 25, 2019.
65 John Leguizamo, email to the author, January 25, 2024.
66 Erik King, email to the author, October 9, 2019.
67 Holt McCallany, author interview, October 2, 2019.
68 This sequence, which does not appear in Rabe's script, was added by De Palma to accentuate the danger faced by Eriksson after denouncing Oanh's rape and murder. It replaces the passage in Daniel Lang's book in which he describes what appears to be the attempted assassination of Storeby by Joe Garcia during a military operation.
69 John C. Reilly, author interview, October 10, 2019.
70 Stephen H. Burum, author interview, June 12, 2019.
71 Larry McConkey, email to the author, November 16, 2019.
72 Eric Schwab, author interview, April 11, 2019.
73 Eric Schwab, email to the author, June 17, 2019. See also Salamon, *The Devil's Candy*, 87.
74 Eric Schwab, email to the author, May 31, 2019.
75 Larry McConkey, email to the author, November 16, 2019.
76 Ibid.
77 Mickey Pugh, email to the author, December 4, 2019.
78 Eric Schwab, email to the author, May 30, 2019.
79 Deborah Ricketts, email to the author, July 19, 2019.
80 Art Smith Jr., email to the author, October 8, 2019.
81 Mike Stokey, author interview, March 27, 2019.
82 Ibid. This trap, widely used by the North Vietnamese, consisted of bamboo stakes on which soldiers would impale themselves. The stakes were covered with poison or excrement, so as to promote infection. These traps were sometimes placed in camouflage pits.

83 Paul Engelen, email to the author, October 10, 2019.
84 See Struk, *Private Pictures*, xvi-xvii.
85 Art Smith Jr., email to the author, October 8, 2019.
86 Eric Schwab, author interview, April 11, 2019.
87 John Leguizamo, email to the author, January 25, 2024.
88 Leguizamo, *Pimps, Hos, Playa Hatas*, 59.
89 Erik King, email to the author, October 9, 2019.
90 Carl Goldstein, author interview, September 25, 2019.
91 His name was Frank Woodward, owner of For Stars Catering, Inc. His partner, nicknamed Bubba, was a Vietnam War veteran, according to Eric Schwab (email to the author, June 10, 2020).
92 Fred Caruso, author interview, June 3, 2019.
93 Don Harvey, email to the author, August 30, 2019.
94 Fox, *Lucky Man*, 14.
95 Holt McCallany, author interview, October 2, 2019.
96 John Leguizamo, email to the author, January 25, 2024.
97 Leguizamo, *Pimps, Hos, Playa Hatas*, 59-60.
98 Fox, *Lucky Man*, 14.
99 John C. Reilly, author interview, October 10, 2019. It was easy to buy boxes of Valium for ten cents each. Its effects when coupled with opiates were radically increased. Holt McCallany recalls finding plenty of local marijuana. Email to the author, February 17, 2020.
100 Blumenfeld and Vachaud, *De Palma on De Palma*, 162.
101 Holt McCallany, author interview, January 19, 2020.
102 John C. Reilly, author interview, October 10, 2019.
103 Pasiree Panya, author interview, January 23, 2020.
104 According to De Palma's recollection, the visit would have lasted no more than five hours, due to the heat (in Baumbach and Paltrow, *De Palma*).
105 Carl Goldstein, author interview, September 25, 2019.
106 Mike Stokey, author interview, March 27, 2019.
107 Paul Engelen, author interview, October 10, 2019.
108 Eric Schwab, author interview, April 11, 2019. Two years later, Sean Penn stepped behind the camera to direct *The Indian Runner* (1991). The film focuses on the relationship between two brothers: Joe (David Morse), a policeman who feels guilty about killing a delinquent in self-defense, and Frank (Viggo Mortensen), a man with a violent past who has just returned from Vietnam.
109 Mickey Pugh, email to the author, December 4, 2019.
110 Sean Penn, email to the author, June 5, 2020.
111 John C. Reilly, author interview, October 10, 2019. After *Casualties of War*, Reilly co-starred with Penn in Neil Jordan's *We're No Angels* (1989) and Phil Joanou's *State of Grace* (1990).
112 John C. Reilly, author interview, October 10, 2019.
113 Erik King, author interview, October 9, 2019.
114 Holt McCallany, author interview, October 2, 2019.
115 Pasiree Panya, author interview, January 23, 2020.
116 Eric Schwab, author interview, April 11, 2019.
117 Sean Penn, *American Film*, April 1986; quoted in Laisney, *Sean Penn*, 20.
118 Ibid.
119 Ibid., 23.
120 Ibid..

121 Ibid., 24.
122 Leguizamo, *Pimps, Hos, Playa Hatas*, 61.
123 John Leguizamo, author interview, January 25, 2024.
124 Blumenfeld and Vachaud, *De Palma on De Palma*, 160.
125 Art Linson, author interview, March 1, 2019.
126 Bouzereau, *Eriksson's War*.
127 As De Palma revealed at a press conference held to mark the film's release in Beverly Hills. See Portman, "Fox Becomes Casualty of War."
128 Eric Schwab, author interview, April 11, 2019.
129 Blumenfeld and Vachaud, *De Palma on De Palma*, 160.
130 Ibid.
131 Art Linson, author interview, March 1, 2019.
132 Don Harvey, email to the author, August 30, 2019.
133 Holt McCallany, author interview, October 2, 2019.
134 Barra, "Welcome to the Jungle."
135 Thomas, "Up Close and Personal," 140.
136 Unlike, for example, Bruno Dumont's *Flandres* (2006). On the question of rape in Dumont's films, see Alligier, *Bruno Dumont. L'animalité et la grâce*.
137 Thuy Thu Le, author interview, March 19, 2019.
138 Thuy Thu Le, as reported by Cerone, "'Casualty' Newcomer Walks On as a Star."
139 For example, for films re-enacting the genocide against the Tutsi with extras who themselves lived through the events. See Réra, *Rwanda*, 329.
140 Thuy Thu Le, author interview, March 19, 2019.
141 Sean Penn, email to the author, June 5, 2020.
142 Ibid.
143 Don Harvey, email to the author, August 30, 2019.
144 Ibid.
145 Thuy Thu Le, author interview, March 19, 2019.
146 Brian De Palma, author interview, March 22, 2019.
147 Thuy Thu Le, author interview, March 19, 2019.
148 Don Harvey, email to the author, August 30, 2019.
149 Thuy Thu Le, author interview, March 19, 2019.
150 See Azoulay, *The Civil Contract of Photography*, 217. Wartime rape is a story yet to be written, note Branche and Virgili, *Viols en temps de guerre*, 26.
151 Thuy Thu Le, author interview, March 19, 2019.
152 John Leguizamo, email to the author, January 25, 2024.
153 Pasiree Panya, author interview, January 23, 2020.
154 Telander, "In Your Face."
155 The cut sequence is part of the special features of the original DVD release from Columbia Tristar Home Video (2001).
156 Larry McConkey, email to the author, November 16, 2019.
157 Bouzereau, *Eriksson's War*.
158 Don Harvey, email to the author, August 30, 2019.
159 John C. Reilly, author interview, October 10, 2019.
160 John Leguizamo, email to the author, January 25, 2024.
161 Carl Goldstein, author interview, September 25, 2019.
162 Julie Salamon, *The Devil's Candy*, 94.
163 Eric Schwab, author interview, April 11, 2019.

164 This anecdote was told to me by several different people, including Art Linson and Carl Goldstein, who were still laughing about it on the phone. It brightened the crew's conversations during the final weeks of shooting.
165 Fred Caruso, author interview, June 3, 2019.
166 Don Harvey, email to the author, August 30, 2019.
167 John C. Reilly, author interview, October 10, 2019.
168 Ibid.
169 Larry McConkey, email to the author, November 16, 2019.
170 Brian De Palma, author interview, March 22, 2019.
171 Thuy Thu Le, author interview, March 19, 2019.
172 John Leguizamo, email to the author, January 25, 2024.
173 Sean Penn, email to the author, June 5, 2020.
174 Don Harvey, email to the author, August 30, 2019.
175 Bouzereau, *Eriksson's War*.
176 Sean Penn, email to the author, June 5, 2020.
177 Eric Schwab, author interview, April 11, 2019. It is possible that this break also allowed Michael J. Fox to marry Tracy Pollan on July 16, 1988, and go on his honeymoon.
178 Thuy Thu Le, author interview, March 19, 2019.
179 Brian De Palma, author interview, March 22, 2019.
180 Art Linson, author interview, March 1, 2019.
181 See Art Linson's instructive and scathing account in his book, *A Pound of Flesh*, 65-75.
182 As revealed to me by Stephen H. Burum, author interview, June 12, 2019.
183 Sean Penn, email to the author, June 5, 2020.
184 David Rabe, email to the author, November 8, 2019.
185 David Rabe, email to the author, December 9, 2019.

Post-Production to Critical Reception, August 1988 – January 1990

1 Bill Pankow, author interview, April 11, 2019.
2 Ibid.
3 Maurice Schell, author interview, May 15, 2019.
4 Ibid.
5 Thuy Thu Le, author interview, March 19, 2019.
6 David Rabe, email to the author, January 19, 2019.
7 This hypothesis was confirmed to me by Brian De Palma during our interview in Paris on March 22, 2019.
8 De Baecque, "Le cauchemar d'Eriksson."
9 Ibid.
10 Douglas Keesey notes that De Palma films Diaz in the same way, crawling and holding a knife, when Meserve asks him to kill Oanh. He concludes that "Americans can be as shark-like as the Vietcong." *Brian De Palma's Split-Screen*, 195.
11 Katsahnias, "Le spectacle de la guerre."
12 Girard, "Victimes du Viêt-Nam."
13 Brian De Palma in Lagier, *Les mille yeux de Brian De Palma*, 30.
14 Niney, *Le documentaire et ses faux-semblants*, 109.
15 Examples include the shot where Meserve, while shaving, tells his comrades about Brown's death; the scene in the showers where Clark, framed by Hatcher and Eriksson, explodes in anger; and the discussion

between Eriksson and Rowan, just before the departure of the mission commanded by Meserve.

16   In the interview he conducted with De Palma on the film's release, Régis Wargnier asked if he agreed with Godard's famous line that "tracking shots are a matter of morality." True to form, he replied: "It's French stuff! You're not going to start talking to me again about content and form, and all that... It's a nice-sounding formula, but what does it mean? When you film a chair, the truth is the chair, nothing else. [...] Cinema is just a way of telling a story with images, with 24 frames per second... You can't give yourself a moral justification for something that's purely aesthetic." (Wargnier, "Question de morale.") Regardless of De Palma's claims, the depiction of rape on screen involves not just aesthetic choices but also significant ethical considerations. In this respect, *Casualties of War* is an important case study.

17   Among Ronald Haeberle's photographs documenting the My Lai massacre, one in particular shows a group of terrified women. In the background, a young girl (later nicknamed the Black Blouse Girl), holding a small child in her arms, is rebuttoning her garment. This often overlooked detail provides information on when the photograph was taken, the moment between sexual assault and mass slaughter. See Wieskamp, "Sexual Assault and the My Lai Massacre."

18   Viviani, *Le Magique et le Vrai*, 141.
19   Laisney, *Sean Pen*, 74-8.
20   David Rabe, email to the author, January 19, 2019.
21   Bill Pankow, author interview, April 11, 2019.
22   Keesey, *Brian De Palma's Split-Screen*, 194-204.
23   Sturken, *Tangled Memories*, 93.
24   Hariman and Lucaites, "Public Identity and Collective Memory in U.S. Iconic Photography."
25   Baudrillard, *Simulacres et simulation*, 90.
26   Spark, "Flight Controls," 86.
27   Keesey, *Brian De Palma's Split Screen*, 196.
28   Telander, "In Your Face," *Premiere*, October 1989.
29   Don Harvey, email to the author, August 30, 2019. Compare the sequence of Clark during the trial with outtakes on the DVD release.
30   See the DVD extras mentioned above.
31   David Rabe, email to the author, January 2, 2019.
32   Brian De Palma, author interview, March 22, 2019.
33   Harrelson's part would have been a cameo. He was already a television star, with a regular role on *Cheers*, for which he won an Emmy the year *Casualties of War* was released. Holt McCallany is quite adamant that Harrelson filmed the scene in question. Shortly before, McCallany had replaced Woody Harrelson on Broadway in Neil Simon's *Biloxi Blues* (1984).
34   Bill Pankow, email to the author, December 7, 2019.
35   Dumas, *Un-American Psycho*, 141
36   Ibid.,142.
37   As David Rabe confirmed to me (email to the author, December 20, 2019).
38   See Esquenazi, *Vertigo*, 267.
39   De Rosa, *Ennio Morricone*, 76.
40   Bill Pankow, author interview, April 11, 2019.

41 Blumenfeld and Vachaud, *De Palma on De Palma*, 170.
42 Bill Pankow, author interview, April 11, 2019.
43 De Rosa, *Ennio Morricone*, 82.
44 Monica Goldstein, author interview, April 26, 2022.
45 Morricone, *Casualties of War*, CBS Records, 1989, tracks 2, 5, 9 and 10: "Trapped in a Tunnel" (4'37"), "No Hope" (2'31"), "The Fragging" (1'20"), "Waste Her" (3'40").
46 De Rosa, *Ennio Morricone*, 214.
47 Ibid., 77.
48 Morricone, *Casualties of War*, tracks 3, 4, 6, 7 and 8: "No Escape" (7'01"), "The Abduction" (4'47"), "The Rape" (4'00"), "The Death of Oanh" (2'31") and "The Healing" (2'14").
49 Ibid., tracks 11 and 12: "Elegy for a Dead Cherry" (1'16") and "Elegy for Brown" (3'43").
50 Ibid., track 1: "Casualties of War" (9'24").
51 Decker, *Hymns for the Fallen*, 249.
52 Ibid., 250.
53 Bradley and Werner, *We Gotta Get Out of this Place*, 1-2.
54 Ibid., 2.
55 Pecqueur, *Les Écrans sonores de Stanley Kubrick*, 36.
56 Cocks, *The Wolf at the Door*, 136.
57 Decker, *Hymns for the Fallen*, 214.
58 Tessier, *Le Vietnam*, 194.
59 Bill Pankow, author interview, April 11, 2019.
60 Julie Salamon, *The Devil's Candy*, 31.
61 Ibid., 33.
62 Wargnier, "Question de morale."
63 Weber, "Cool head, hot images."
64 Fred Caruso, author interview, June 3, 2019.
65 Weber, "Cool head, hot images."
66 Salamon, *The Devil's Candy*, 33.
67 No doubt a similar argument also explains the curiously euphemistic end card: "Although this film is based on an actual incident, the names of the participants have been changed. Herbert Hatcher was found not guilty of murder. On appeal, Hatcher's rape conviction was reversed and on retrial he was acquitted, his confession having been disallowed on constitutional grounds." When the film was released, a number of critics pointed out that many more sentences had been commuted than the film suggested, and that none of the four convicted soldiers spent much time in jail.
68 Salamon, *The Devil's Candy*, 33.
69 Eric Schwab, author interview, April 11, 2019.
70 Bill Pankow, author interview, April 11, 2019.
71 Wild Side's 2021 Blu-ray release of the film in France includes the theatrical and director's cut versions. In addition to a book containing Monica Goldstein's never-before-seen photographs of the shoot, I produced two special features: an interview with Eric Schwab and a edit of 8mm footage shot by Monica Goldstein on the set of the film.
72 Norman, "Brian De Palma Explores Vietnam and Its Victim."
73 Art Linson, author interview, March 1, 2019.
74 Brian De Palma, author interview, March 22, 2019.
75 David Rabe, author interview, December 10, 2018.

76. Rabe, "*Casualties of War*: Types of Ambiguity."
77. Ibid.
78. Reppert, "Vets criticize message in *Casualties of War*."
79. "Vietnam vets protest *Casualties of War*," *The Burlington Free Press*, August 25, 1989.
80. David Rabe, author interview, January 2, 2019.
81. "De Palma says nothing wrong with his movie," *Arizona Daily Sun*, August 30, 1989.
82. Kastor, "*Casualties* takes flak from vets."
83. Dale Dye, author interview, March 29, 2019.
84. Danziger, "The real casualties of Hollywood war films."
85. Holloran, "Hollywood casualties."
86. Bosworth, "Women's Safety A Casualty Of War."
87. Salamon, *The Devil's Candy*, 34.
88. "*Uncle Buck* tops box-office list."
89. To fully appreciate the scale of De Palma's commercial failure, note that Ron Howard's film took in over $100 million in the U.S., John Hughes' over $65 million, and James Cameron's just under $55 million (boxofficemojo.com).
90. Blumenfeld and Vachaud, *De Palma on De Palma*, 171.
91. Barra, "Welcome to the Jungle."
92. "Brian De Palma's Latest Outrage," *The Village Voice*, August 22, 1989.
93. Howe, "*Casualties of War*."
94. Caldwell, "Vietnam in Film."
95. Fleming, "*Casualties* shocks, but doesn't enlighten."
96. Futterman, "Powerful, Draining Insights On Vietnam."
97. Schickel, "Vice and Victims in Vietnam."
98. Hoberman, "Jungle Love."
99. Kehr, "*Casualties of War* exploitation, not moral nobility."
100. Cosford, "De Palma, Fox, Penn lose this *War*."
101. Carson, "Casuistries of War."
102. Carr, "De Palma Confronts Vietnam."
103. Gavin Smith, email to the author, May 23, 2024.
104. Kael, "The God-Bless-America Symphony."
105. Kael, "Little Shocks, Big Shocks."
106. Kael, "Ponderoso."
107. Kael, "A Wounded Apparition."
108. Salamon, "De Palma in the Moral Quicksand of Vietnam."
109. Fitzpatrick, "There Is Yet More to *Casualties of War*."
110. Seiler, "Fox superb in powerful 'Nam tale."
111. Thompson, "War Story Tells Shameful Truth."
112. Fitzpatrick, "There Is Yet More to *Casualties of War*."
113. Rafferty, "Vietnam's Agony."
114. Ebert, "De Palma unjustly receives flak over *Casualties of War*."
115. Ansen, "In the Valley of the Shadow."
116. Travers, "*Casualties of War*."
117. Lawson, "*Casualties of War*."
118. Wuntch, "Director's Restraint Shows Growth."
119. Seiler, "Fox superb in powerful 'Nam tale."
120. Canby, "In *Casualties of War*, Group Loyalty vs. Individual Conscience."
121. Fitzpatrick, "There Is Yet More to Casualties of War."
122. See, for example, Bentley, "*Casualties of War* worth seeing because of Fox."

123 See Smith, "Body Count. Rabe and De Palma's Wargasm"; Persico, "Penn, Fox aren't film *Casualties*"; Strauss, "*Casualties* misses mark."
124 Thomas, "*Casualties* mirrors grim reality."
125 Hoberman, "Jungle Love."
126 Seiler, "Fox superb in powerful 'Nam tale."
127 Fleming, "*Casualties* shocks, but doesn't enlighten."
128 Wuntch, "Director's restraint shows growth."
129 "*Casualties* star recalls war's horrors," *Times Colonist*.
130 See, for example, "*Casualties* a catharsis for Vietnamese refugees."
131 "*Casualties* star recalls war's horrors," *Times Colonist*.
132 Cerone, "*Casualty* Newcomer Walks On as a Star."
133 "Movie vented times of pain," *Calgary Herald*.
134 "*Casualties* star recalls war's horrors," *Times Colonist*.
135 Lacouture, "Le défi du vrai."
136 "Outrages," *Le Canard enchaîné*.
137 Images showing De Palma with his eye glued to his camera were broadcast on French television. See, for example, "Soir 3," FR3, September 3, 1989.
138 Colmant, "Brian De Palma, saigneur de la guerre."
139 "*Outrages*," *VSD*.
140 "*Outrages (Casualties of War)*," *France Soir*.
141 Fabre, "*Outrages*. Tous coupables sauf un."
142 Vachaud, "Promenade avec la mort et la honte."
143 De Baecque, "Le cauchemar d'Eriksson."
144 Katsahnias, "Le spectacle de la guerre."
145 See Quenin, "*Outrages*,"; Diastème, "Retour vers le Viêt-Nam."
146 Pérez, "Navets incontournables."
147 Jonquet, "*Outrages* de Brian De Palma."
148 "*Outrages*," *L'Événement du Jeudi*.
149 "De Palma au napalm," *L'Express*.
150 *Le Masque et la Plume*, France Inter.
151 De Gasperi, "Une guerre d'aujourd'hui."
152 Roy, "Un meurtre est un meurtre."
153 Morel, "Le courage de dire non."
154 Backmann, "Héros et salauds."
155 Toscan du Plantier, "La belle et les bêtes."
156 "Soir 3," FR3, January 7, 1990.
157 Leclère, "*Outrages*."
158 Grousset, "*Outrages*."
159 Lacouture, "Le défi du vrai."
160 Ullmann, "*Outrages*."
161 Lacouture, "Le défi du vrai." This observation is shared by other critics, including Bernard Ullmann et al., "Le Viêt-Nam, toujours."
162 Robic-Diaz, *La Guerre d'Indochine dans le cinéma français*. The author lists a corpus of "51 films over 65 years," acknowledging that this hardly compares with the hundreds of films about the Vietnam War made by American filmmakers.
163 Stora, "La guerre d'Algérie dans les médias: l'exemple du cinéma."
164 Ibid.
165 Stora, "Le cinéma américain pendant la guerre du Viêt-Nam: le mythe de 'l'avalanche.'"

Endnotes 455

166 Marc Ferro, "Aux États-Unis, cinéma et conscience de l'histoire" [1984], in *Cinéma et histoire*, 237-238.
167 Branche, "Des viols pendant la guerre d'Algérie."

Epilogue

1 Blumenfeld and Vachaud, *De Palma on De Palma*, 173.
2 Fred Caruso, author interview, June 3, 2019.
3 Quentin Tarantino, who considers *Casualties of War* to be "the greatest film about the Vietnam War," has repeatedly cited it as one of his major influences (see "Les films de guerre qui m'ont inspire," *Le Monde*, August 16, 2009). His statements come as a surprise, given that his films, stories of revenge and ultraviolence, are a world away from any message *Casualties of War* might have. In France, Bertrand Tavernier was one of the film's most ardent defenders, calling it De Palma's "greatest film," one which, he wrote in his dictionary of American directors, avoids "almost all the pitfalls (voyeurism, exploitation of violence) inherent in the subject" (Tavernier and Coursodon, *Cinquante ans de cinéma américain*, 136). Jean Douchet also honored *Casualties of War* as part of his annual course at the Institut Lumière in 2013, stating that "the more time passes, the more remarkable the film remains" (see "À propos du film *Outrages*," Lyon, Institut Lumière, March 16, 2013, a recording of which is available on YouTube).
4 See a letter to Daniel Lang from Robert Lantz (1914-2007), one of Hollywood's most important agents (Robert Lantz, letter to Daniel Lang, March 24, 1980, Daniel Lang Collection, Box 17), sent in response to a letter from Lang which was accompanied by copies of two of his *The New Yorker* articles: "AWOL" (October 21, 1972) and "The Bank Drama" (November 18, 1974). The subjects were, respectively, the years-long desertion of a young man from the Navy to escape the Vietnam War, and a famous hostage-taking incident in a Stockholm bank over six days in 1973. Lang obviously wanted to know whether these two stories would be of interest to a major studio. Although he found both articles "brilliant," Lantz was hesitant. According to Lantz, the story reported in "AWOL" would be "outdated" ever since the release of films like Hal Ashby's *Coming Home* (1978) and Francis Coppola's *Apocalypse Now*, which he regarded as the "definitive statement on the subject." As for "The Bank Drama," he rightly pointed out its strong kinship with a film released a few years earlier, Sidney Lumet's *Dog Day Afternoon* (1975). Lang's story, whose French translation was published by Editions Allia in 2019, was adapted by Canadian director Robert Budreau in 2018 as *Stockholm*, starring Ethan Hawke and Noomi Rapace.
5 David Rabe, email to the author, February 25, 2019.
6 Larry McConkey, email to the author, November 16, 2019. See Cojean, "Le viol, arme de destruction massive en Syrie"; Méheut, "New Evidence Found of Rape and Torture"; Pronczuk and Petriczko, "No One to Talk to."
7 Freeman, "Brian De Palma Goes to War."
8 Carr, "De Palma confronts Vietnam."
9 Don Harvey, author interview, August 30, 2019.
10 Blumenfeld and Vachaud, *De Palma on De Palma*, 261.
11 Ibid., 260.
12 Boyer and Zabunyan, "Don't hurt me."
13 Lagier, *Les mille yeux de Brian De Palma*, 184.

14 Zabunyan, "Politiques de l'impureté."
15 De Palma and Simon, "Blow-Up."
16 Blumenfeld and Vachaud, *De Palma on De Palma*, 266.
17 De Palma and Simon, "Blow-Up."
18 Freeman, "Brian De Palma Goes to War."
19 Blumenfeld and Vachaud, *De Palma on De Palma*, 269.
20 "De Palma talks Weinstein, #MeToo, Snakes, Dahlia," March 15, 2020, on the unofficial Brian De Palma website www.angelfire.com
21 Bayard, *Aurais-je été résistant ou bourreau?*, 17.
22 Ibid., 13.

Bibliography

PRIMARY SOURCES

Phan Thi Mao's Rape and Murder
Military archives
> United States vs. Cipriano S. Garcia (CM 416159); United States vs. Joseph C. Garcia (CM 416160); United States vs. David E. Gervase (CM 416161); United States vs. Steven C. Thomas (CM 416162); in Army General Courts-Martial Records of Trial, 1939-1976; Records of the Office of the Judge Advocate General (Army), 1792-2010, Record Group 153; National Archives, St. Louis (RL-SL)

Daniel Lang's texts and archives
> Lang, Daniel, "Casualties of War," *New Yorker*, October 18, 1969
> — "Incident on Hill 192," *Observer*, November 16, 1969
> — *Casualties of War*, New York/St. Louis/Toronto, McGraw-Hill, 1969
> — *Die Meldung. 16 November 1966, Vietnam*,
>   Hamburg: Hoffmann und Campe, 1970
> — Annotated manuscript [undated], 62pp., in Daniel Lang
> Collection, Box 13, Howard Gotlieb Archival Research Center,
>   Boston University
> — "Incident on Hill 192: The 5th Man's Story,"
>   *San Francisco Examiner* (supplement), December 7, 1969
> — "Affidavit," undated [1970], in Daniel Lang Collection, Box 13,
>   Howard Gotlieb Archival Research Center, Boston University

Newspaper articles
> "4 G.I.s Convicted on Rape Charges," *Pensacola News Journal*,
>   March 24, 1967
> "4 G.I.s Found Guilty in Viet Rape-Slaying," *Los Angeles Times*,
>   March 24, 1967
> "4 Soldiers Convicted in Slaying Vietnamese Girl Raped,"
>   *Lincoln Journal Star*, March 23, 1967
> "Approves Terms of Three Soldiers In Viet Girl's Death,"
>   *Evening Times*, June 13, 1967
> "Bloody past of witness revealed," *Florida Today*, July 24, 1992
> "Four Soldiers Sentenced in Vietnam Rape, Murder,"
>   *St. Louis Post-Dispatch*, March 24, 1967
> "General Approves Sentences," *Austin American*, June 12, 1967
> "G.I.s Sentenced in Rape-Killing," *Boston Globe*, March 24, 1967
> "S.A. G.I.s Sentence Reduced," *San Antonio Express*, June 12, 1967
> "Sentences of G.I.s Upheld In Viet Rape-Murder," *Record*, June 12, 1967
> "St. Paul G.I. Testifies in Viet Rape," *Minneapolis Star*, March 23, 1967

"U.S. Soldiers Are Convicted in Rape-Slaying,"
  Lubbock Avalanche-Journal, March 23, 1967
"Witness in murder trial raped, killed Vietnamese,"
  Orlando Sentinel, July 24, 1992

Other atrocities committed by the U.S. military in Vietnam
Poirier, Normand, "An American Atrocity," *Esquire*, August 1969
"5 G.I.s Sentenced for Assault," *Stars and Stripes*, August 27, 1967
"G.I. Rape Conviction Stuns Parents," *Stars and Stripes*, August 30, 1967

Casualties of War film adaptations
Daniel and Margaret Lang private archives
Scripts and treatments
> Lang, Daniel, *Treatment "Casualties of War,"* 1980 [undated], 80pp.
> Rabe, David, *Casualties of War*, based on the book by Daniel Lang, 1988 [undated], 127pp.
> — *Casualties of War*, based on the book by Daniel Lang, 1988 [undated], 123pp.
> — *Casualties of War*, based on the book by Daniel Lang, 1988 undated], 134pp.

Correspondence
> Cohn, Sidney E., letter to Alfred Crown and Jerome Hammer, August 27, 1980
> Hollander, David, letter to Greg Gelfan, May 27, 1987
> Lang, Daniel, letter to Alfred Crown and Jerome Hammer, 1979 (draft)
> — letter to Alfred Crown and Jerome Hammer, March 18, 1980
> Time-Life Television Productions Inc., letter to Sidney Cohn, to the attention of Daniel Lang, September 15, 1977

Legal documents
> "Agreement made by and between Daniel Lang and Paman Productions – Norton Simon Inc.," January 1970 [signed by David Susskind].
> "Option agreement between Talent Associates Ltd. and Daniel Lang," May 7, 1977
> Furie, Daniel, "Option agreement," Paramount, August 1987
> Hollander, David, "Summary of adaptation rights for *Casualties of War* (1970-1981)," September 30, 1987

Daniel Lang's archives, Howard Gotlieb Archival Center, Boston University
Scripts
> Giler, David, *Casualties of War*, 1970, 113pp. [Box 13]
> Gould, Heywood, *Casualties of War*, from the book by Daniel Lang [undated], 142pp. [Box 17]
> Hamill, Pete, *Casualties of War*, undated [1970], 125pp. [Box 13]

Notes
> Lang, Daniel, "Notes on adaptation of *Casualties of War*," May 28, 1979 [Box 17]
> — Unsigned and undated document [handwritten notes on Gould's script] [Box 13]
> — Untitled and undated manuscript [1979], 22pp. [Box 17]

— Untitled and undated manuscript [1979-1980, "34 page treatment" in grey pencil on the first page], 34pp. [Box 17]

"Brief Summary on contents picture *o.k.*," undated [1970] [Box 13]

Correspondence

Ashley, Alfred (Warner Bros – Seven Arts, Inc.),
letter to Daniel Lang, August 5, 1970 [Box 13]

Crown, Alfred, letter to Mrs. Mortimer Levitt, May 29, 1979 [Box 17]

De Grunwald, Nicholas, letter to the editor of *The New Yorker*,
January 1, 1970 [Box 17]

Gottesman, Albert, letter to Daniel Lang, October 23, 1969 [Box 17]

Hamburger Sureck, Nancy, letter to Daniel Lang, October 23,
1969 [Box 17]

Lantz, Robert, letter to Daniel Lang, March 24, 1980 [Box 17]

Scott-Fox, Judy, letter to Milton Greenstein, December 5, 1969 [Box 17]

St. Clair, John, letter to Daniel Lang, November 21, 1969 [Box 17]

Todini, Bruno, letter to Daniel Lang, April 8, 1970 [Box 17]

Townley, Peter P., letter to Daniel Lang, February 17, 1970 [Box 17]

Warburg, Fredric, letter to Daniel Lang, July 20, 1970 [Box 13]

Wechsler, Nancy F., letter to Daniel Lang, September 3, 1970 [Box 17]

Willner, George, letter to Daniel Lang, October 21, 1969 [Box 17]

Zinnemann, Fred, letter to Daniel Lang, November 18, 1969 [Box 17]

Zinnemann, Fred, letter to Daniel Lang, December 23, 1969 [Box 17]

British Film Institute Archives

Scripts and drafts

Hamill, Pete, "An outline for *Casualties of War*. By Daniel Lang," 1970
[undated], 14pp. [JLC-15-35-1-2]

Giler, David, *Casualties of War*, based on the book by Daniel Lang,
August 12, 1970, 113pp. (1st draft) [JLC-15-35-1-3]

— *Casualties of War*, 1970 [undated], 123 pp. (2nd draft) [JLC-15-35-1-3]

Notes on scripts and drafts

Clayton, Jack, "*Casualties of War*. Notes on Pete Hamill's First
Outline," January 28, 1970 [JLC-15-35-1-2]

— "*Casualties of War*. Notes on Pete Hamill's First Draft Script,"
April 15, 1970 [JLC-15-35-1-5]

Sims, Jeanie, "*Casualties of War*. Comments on Pete Hamill's First
Outline," January 27, 1970 [JLC-15-35-1-2]

— "Casualties of War. Brief Comments on First Draft Script,"
April 4, 1970 [JLC-15-35-1-4]

Working papers

Clayton, Jack, "Questions for Daniel Lang," April 8, 1970
[JLC-15-35-2-2]

— "*Casualties of War*. Notes for New York Trip: 7 April,"
April 6, 1970 [JLC-15-35-2-5]

Sims, Jeanie, "*Casualties of War*. Brief Synopsis," January 22, 1970
[JLC-15-35-1-4]

— "*Casualties of War*. Principal Characters," January 22, 1970
[JLC-15-35-1-4]

— "*Casualties of War*. Main Locations," January 22, 1970
[JLC-15-35-1-4]

— "*Casualties of War.* Trial Verdicts & Sentences," January 22, 1970 [JLC-15-35-1-4]
— "*Casualties of War.* Chronological Breakdown," January 22, 1970 [JLC-15-35-1-4]
"Questions for Military Adviser," March 16, 1970 [JLC-15-35-2-3]
"Scene Breakdown for Set" [undated] [JLC-15-35-2-1]

Correspondence

Cabot, Louis, letter to Jack Clayton, 1970 [undated] [JLC-15-35-2-4]
Calley, John, Telegram to Jack Clayton, August 14, 1970 [JLC-15-35-1-1]
Chais, Stanley, letter to Daniel Lang, June 16, 1971 [JLC-15-35-1-1]
— letter to Daniel Lang, July 1, 1971 [JLC-15-35-1-1]
— letter to Jack Clayton, July 13, 1971 [JLC-15-35-2-5]
Clayton, Jack, letter to David Susskind, February 2, 1970 [JLC-15-35-1-2]
— letter to Pete Hamill, February 2, 1970 [JLC-15-35-1-2]
— letter to David Susskind, April 6, 1970 [JLC-15-35-2-5]
— letter to Pete Hamill, April 21, 1970 [JLC-15-35-1-5]
— letter to Daniel Lang, April 22, 1970 [JLC-15-35-1-1]
— letter to Les Wiles, April 24, 1970 [JLC-15-35-2-5]
— letter to Alan Shayne, October 6, 1970 [JLC-15-35-2-5]
— letter to Daniel Lang, April 16, 1971 [JLC-15-35-1-1]
Craven, Timothy, letter to Jack Clayton, July 9, 1970 [JLC-15-35-2-4]
Hallam, John, letter to Jack Clayton [undated], received July 20, 1970 [JLC-15-35-2-4]
Hamill, Pete, letter to Jack Clayton, January 8, 1970 [JLC-15-35-1-2]
— Telegram to Jack Clayton, April 22, 1970 [JLC-15-35-1-5]
Johnson, Sidney, letter to Jack Clayton, July 20, 1970 [JLC-15-35-2-4]
Lang, Daniel, letter to Jack Clayton, March 19, 1971 [JLC-15-35-1-1]
Mitchell, Norman, letter to Jack Clayton, July 9, 1970 [JLC-15-35-2-4.
Rissner, Danton J., letter to Jack Clayton, March 25, 1970 [JLC-15-35-2-5]
— Inter-Office Memo, Warner Bros. – Seven Arts Production Ltd., to John Calley, April 20, 1970 [JLC-15-35-2-5]
Zeff, Ley, letter to John Francis, April 22, 1970 [JLC-15-35-2-4]

UCLA Library Special Collections, Los Angeles

Gould, Heywood, *Casualties of War*, from the book by Daniel Lang, draft 3/26/79, 116pp., Collection of motion picture scripts 1921-1998, [Box 1021]
Rabe, David, *Casualties of War*, based on the book by Daniel Lang, "First draft," undated [1987], 123pp., Collection of motion picture scripts 1921-1998, [Box 0302]

The New York Public Library

Rabe, David, *Casualties of War*, based on the book by Daniel Lang, 3/15/88, 127pp., The New York Public Library, The Performing Arts Research Collection [ctr1844]

David Rabe private archives
Rabe, David, *Casualties of War*, based on the book by Daniel Lang, 1988 [undated], 126pp.
— *Casualties of War*, based on the book by Daniel Lang, 1988 [postdated 1994], 131pp.

Bill Pankow private archives
Rabe, David, *Casualties of War*, based on the book by Daniel Lang, "Revised 3-26-88"

Daniel Lang's *Casualties of War*
Christiansen, Richard, "A Minnesotan Who Resisted the Corruption of Vietnam," *Star Tribune*, December 7, 1969
Just, Ward, "Humanity: Another Casualty of the Vietnam War," *Sunday Record Call*, December 14, 1969
Lehmann-Haupt, Christopher, "Incident on Hill 192," *New York Times*, November 14, 1969
Raymond, John, "A Matter of Time? War Incident Raises Disturbing Questions," *Atlanta Constitution*, November 16, 1969

Michael Verhoeven's *o.k.*
Pérez, Michel, "Berlin 70, une révolution de cuisine," *Positif*, no. 121, November 1970
Picaper, Jean-Paul, "Le festival de Berlin est brutalement interrompu à cause d'un film contre la guerre du Vietnam," *Le Monde*, July 7, 1970
"War film dropped by Berlin Festival," *New York Times*, July 4, 1970
"*o.k.*," *Variety*, July 8, 1970

Elia Kazan's *The Visitors*
Canby, Vincent, "*The Visitors* Portrays Ordeal of a Threatened G.I.," *New York Times*, February 3, 1972
Ciment, Michel, "Entretien avec Elia Kazan sur *Les Visiteurs*," *Positif*, May 1972
Silver, Charles and Joel Zuker, "Visiting Kazan," *Film Comment*, Summer 1972

Brian De Palma's *Casualties of War*
U.S. press
Ansen, David, "In the Valley of the Shadow," *Newsweek*, August 21, 1989
Barra, Allen, "Welcome to the Jungle," *Village Voice*, August 22, 1989
Bentley, George, "*Casualties of War* worth seeing because of Fox," *Leader-Post*, August 19, 1989
Bosworth, Barbara, "Women's Safety A Casualty of War," *Sunday Rutland Herald*, October 29, 1989
Caldwell, Gail, "Vietnam in Film: The Catharsis Continues," *Boston Globe*, August 25, 1989
Canby, Vincent, "In *Casualties of War*, Group Loyalty vs. Individual Conscience," *New York Times*, August 18, 1989
Carr, Jay, "De Palma Confronts Vietnam," *Boston Globe*, August 13, 1989
Carson, Tom, "Casuistries of War," *LA Weekly*, August 31, 1989

Cerone, Daniel, "'*Casualty*' Newcomer Walks On as a Star,"
  Los Angeles Times, August 18, 1989.
Cosford, Bill, "De Palma, Fox, Penn lose this *War*,"
  Miami Herald, August 18, 1989
Danziger, Jeff, "The real casualties of Hollywood war films,"
  Boston Globe, September 2, 1989
— "Hollywood's Vietnam Short on Truth," *Sunday Rutland Herald*,
  September 17, 1989
Ebert, Roger, "De Palma unjustly receives flak over *Casualties of War*,"
  Chicago Sun-Times, September 3, 1989
Farrell, Mary H. J. and Cathy Nolan, "In a War of Nerves, First-Time
  Actress Thuy Thu Le Relives Vietnam in *Casualties of War*,"
  People, August 28, 1989
FitzGerald, Frances, "Casualties of Cinema. De Palma Runs Amok,"
  Village Voice, August 22, 1989
Fitzpatrick, Tom, "There Is Yet More to *Casualties of War*,"
  Phoenix New Times, August 30, 1989
Fleming, Dick, "'*Casualties*' shocks, but doesn't enlighten,"
  Daily Times, September 1, 1989
Freeman, David, "Brian De Palma Goes to War," *Newsday*, August 13, 1989
Fuchs, Cindy, "Casualties of War," *Cinema*, no. 3, 1990
Futterman, Ellen, "Powerful, Draining Insights on Vietnam,"
  St. Louis Post-Dispatch, August 18, 1989
Hoberman J., "Jungle Love," *The Village Voice*, August 22, 1989
Holloran, Peter C., "Hollywood Casualties," *Boston Globe*,
  September 12, 1989
Howe, Desson, "*Casualties of War*," *Washington Post*, August 18, 1989
Kael, Pauline, "A Wounded Apparition," *New Yorker*, August 21, 1989
Kastor, Elizabeth, "'*Casualties*' takes flak from vets,"
  Honolulu Advertiser, August 26, 1989
Kehr, Dave, "*Casualties of War* exploitation, not moral nobility,"
  Chicago Tribune, August 18, 1989
Lawson, Terry, "*Casualties of War*," *Dayton Daily News*, August 18, 1989
Norman, Michael, "Brian De Palma Explores Vietnam and Its Victims,"
  New York Times, August 13, 1989
— "Michael Norman replies," in "*Casualties of War*: Types of Ambiguity,"
  The New York Times, August 27, 1989
Persico, Joyce J., "Penn, Fox aren't film *Casualties*,"
  Honolulu Star-Bulletin, August 18, 1989
Pond, Steve, "Shot by Shot: Brian De Palma's *Casualties of War*,"
  Premiere, September 1989
Portman, Jamie, "Fox Becomes Casualty of War," *Windsor Star*,
  August 18, 1989
Rabe, David, "*Casualties of War*: Types of Ambiguity," *New York Times*,
  August 27, 1989
Rafferty, Terrence, "Vietnam's Agony," *Sight and Sound*, Winter 1989
Reppert, Barton, "Vets criticize message in *Casualties of War*,"
  Cincinnati Enquirer, August 24, 1989
Salamon, Julie, "De Palma in the Moral Quicksand of Vietnam,"
  Wall Street Journal, August 17, 1989
Schickel, Richard, "Vice and Victims in Vietnam," *Time*, August 21, 1989

Seiler, Andy, "Fox superb in powerful 'Nam tale,"
  Central New Jersey Home News, August 18, 1989
Smith, Gavin, "Body Count, Rabe and De Palma's Wargasm,"
  Film Comment, July/August 1989
Strauss, Bob, "'*Casualties*' misses mark; Penn acts better than Fox,"
  Advocate-Messenger, September 7, 1989
Taylor, John, "Steel Ambition," *Chicago Tribune*, July 9, 1989
Telander, Rick, "In Your Face," *Premiere*, October 1989
Thomas, Bob, "'*Casualties*' mirrors grim reality,"
  Corvallis Gazette-Times, August 18, 1989
— "*Casualties* story electrified De Palma," *Pottsville Republican*,
  August 19, 1989
Thompson, Gary, "War Story Tells Shameful Truth,"
  Philadelphia Daily News, August 18, 1989
Travers, Peter, "Casualties of War," *Rolling Stone*, August 18, 1989
Weber, Bruce, "Cool head, hot images,"
  New York Times Magazine, May 21, 1989
Wuntch, Philip, "Director's Restraint Shows Growth,"
  Daily Press, August 19, 1989
"McConkey in Thailand," *Steadicam Letter*, vol. 1, no. 3, December 1988
"*Uncle Buck* tops box-office list," *Messenger*, August 23, 1989
"Vietnam vets protest *Casualties of War*," *Burlington Free Press*, August 25, 1989
"Casualties star recalls war's horrors," *Times Colonist*, August 29, 1989
"De Palma says nothing wrong with his movie," *Arizona Daily Sun*,
  August 30, 1989
"*Casualties* a catharsis for Vietnamese refugees,"
  Edmonton Journal, August 31, 1989

France press
Backmann, René, "Héros et salauds," *Le Nouvel observateur*,
  January 4-10, 1990
Béhar, Henri, "Le Vietnam ou la déraison exemplaire," *Le Monde*,
  August 31, 1989
Boukhrief, Nicolas, "Brian De Palma est-il pervers ?" *Starfix*, January 1990
Colmant, Marie, "Brian De Palma, saigneur de la guerre,"
  Libération, September 4, 1989
Coppermann, Annie, "Le Vietnam, toujours," *Les Échos*, January 10, 1990
De Baecque, Antoine, "Le cauchemar d'Eriksson," *Cahiers du cinéma*,
  January 1990
Diastème, "Retour vers le Vietnam," *7 à Paris*, January 10-16, 1990
Fabre, Maurice, "*Outrages*. Tous coupables sauf un," *France Soir*,
  January 15, 1990
Ferney, Frédéric, with Marianne Ruuth, "Bleu comme la peur!
  Rencontre avec Brian De Palma," *Le Figaro*, September 1, 1989
De Gasperi, Anne, "Une guerre d'aujourd'hui,"
  Le Quotidien de Paris, January 17, 1990
Girard, Martin, "Victimes du Vietnam/*Casualties of War*," *Zoom out*,
  November 1989
Grousset, Jean-Paul, "*Outrages* (Forfait d'armes),"
  Le Canard enchaîné, January 10, 1990

Jonquet, François, "*Outrages* de Brian De Palma,"
    Le Quotidien de Paris, January 10, 1990
Katsahnias, Iannis, "Le spectacle de la guerre," *Cahiers du cinéma*,
    January 1990
Lacouture, Jean, "Le défi du vrai," *Le Monde*, January 12, 1990
Leclère, Marie-Françoise, "*Outrages (Casualties of War)*
    de Brian De Palma," *Le Point*, January 8, 1990
Morel, Jean-Michel, "Le courage de dire non," *Révolution*, January 19, 1990
Pérez, Michel, "Navets incontournables," *Le Nouvel Observateur*,
    January 18, 1990
Quenin, François, "*Outrages*, Un film de Brian de Palma,"
    Témoignage chrétien, January 8-14, 1990
Roy, Jean, "Un meurtre est un meurtre," *L'Humanité*, January 13, 1990
Toscan du Plantier, Daniel, "La belle et les bêtes," *Figaro Magazine*,
    January 13, 1990
Ullmann, Bernard, "*Outrages (Casualties of War)*, le sale repos du guerrier,"
    Pariscope, January 24, 1990
Ullmann, Bernard, Marie-Françoise Leclère and Annie Coppermann,
    "Le Viêt-Nam, toujours," *Les Echos*, January 10, 1990
Vachaud, Laurent, "Promenade avec la mort et la honte,
    sans espoir de retour," *Positif*, January 1990
Vecchi, Philippe, "Motherfucker. Vietnam: l'avis de Brian,"
    Libération, January 10, 1990
Wargnier, Régis, "Question de morale," *Studio Magazine*, December 1989
"*Outrages*," *VSD*, January 4, 1990.
"*Outrages (Casualties of War)*," *France Soir*, January 10, 1990
"*Outrages* de Brian De Palma," *L'Événement du Jeudi*, January 11, 1990
"De Palma au napalm," *L'Express*, January 12, 1990

France - radio
Le Masque et la Plume, France Inter, January 14, 1990

Other newspaper articles
Kael, Pauline, "The God-Bless-America Symphony,"
    The New Yorker, December 18, 1978
— "Little Shocks, Big Shocks," *The New Yorker*, January 12, 1987
— "Ponderoso," *The New Yorker*, July 13, 1987
Mitgang, Herbert, "Daniel Lang, 66, correspondent and author
    for *New Yorker*, dies," *New York Times*, November 19, 1981
Mydans, Seth, "2 U.S. Airmen Slain at Philippine Base,"
    New York Times, October 29, 1987
Shawn, William, "Daniel Lang," *The New Yorker*, November 30, 1981

Press kit
Outrages/Casualties of War, Deauville, 1989

Filmed interviews
"Michael J. Fox Interview," Reelin' In The Years Archives, YouTube (1989)
Bouzereau, Laurent, "The Making of *Casualties of War*" (2001)
— "Eriksson's War: A Talk with Actor Michael J. Fox" (2001)

Interviews by the author
Beechinor, Sallie, email correspondence, June 2019
Burum, Stephen H., June 12, 2019
Caruso, Fred, June 3, 2019
Cook, Brian C., June 7, 2019
Costanzo, Marko A., email correspondence, October 21, 2019
De Bono, Yves, November 12, 2019
De Palma, Brian, March 22, 2019
Dye, Dale, email correspondence, March 29, 2019
Engelen, Paul, email correspondence, October 10, 2019
Goldstein, Carl, September 25, 2019
Goldstein, Monica, April 26, 2021
Gould, Heywood, email correspondence, August-October 2019
Harvey, Don, email correspondence, August 2019
Hayes, Nancy, email correspondence, October 23, 2019
Houwer, Rob, email correspondence, November 1, 2019
King, Erik, email correspondence, October 9, 2019
Kroeger, Wolf, June 16, 2020
Lang, Cecily, May 21, 2019; email correspondence, May 2019-July 2020
Lang, Helen, email correspondence, May and December 2019, April 2020
Lang, Frances, email correspondence, August and December 2019, April 2020.
Le, Thuy Thu, March 19, 2019
Leguizamo, John, email correspondence, January 25, 2024
Linson, Art, March 1, 2019
McCallany, Holt, October 2, 2019, January 19, 2020, June 12, 2020
McConkey, Larry, email correspondence, November 2019, October 2024
Neveu, Roland, May 7, 2019
Pankow, Bill, April 11, 2019, email correspondence, April 2019-July 2020
Panya, Pasiree, January 23, 2020
Penn, Sean, email correspondence, June 5, 2020
Pugh, Mickey, email correspondence, December 4, 2019
Rabe, David, email correspondence, August 2018-July 2020
Reilly, John C., October 10, 2019
Ricketts, Deborah, email correspondence, July 19, 2019
Schell, Maurice, May 15, 2019, email correspondence, May 2019-July 2020
Schwab, Eric, April 11, 2019, email correspondence, April 2019-July 2020
Smith, Art, email correspondence, October 2019 and June 2020
Stokey, Mike, March 27, 2019
Sungkawess, Charlie, May 20, 2019
Verhoeven, Michael, August 9, 2019

SECONDARY SOURCES
Brian De Palma
Books and Articles
Blumenfeld, Samuel and Laurent Vachaud, *De Palma on De Palma* [2001], Sticking Place Books, 2024
Boyer, Frédéric and Dork Zabunyan, "Don't hurt me," *Trafic*, Winter 2009
De Palma, Brian and Taryn Simon, "Blow-Up," *ArtForum*, Summer 2012
Dumas, Chris, *Un-American Psycho: Brian De Palma and the Political Invisible*, Chicago, 2012

Keesey, Douglas, *Brian De Palma's Split-Screen: A Life in Film*,
   Mississippi, 2015
Lagier, Luc, *Les mille yeux de Brian de Palma* [2003],
   Cahiers du cinéma, 2008
Salamon, Julie, *The Devil's Candy. The Bonfire of the Vanities
   Goes to Hollywood*, Delta, 1991
Thomas, Deborah, "Up Close and Personal: Faces and Names in
   Casualties of War," in Christine Gledhill (ed.), *Gender Meets
   Genre in Postwar Cinemas*, Illinois, 2012

Audiovisual sources
Baumbach, Noah and Jake Paltrow, *De Palma*, 2015
Brian De Palma's Master Class, June 2, 2018, Paris,
   Cinémathèque française [online]

Elia Kazan and *The Visitors*
Briley, Ron, *The Ambivalent Legacy of Elia Kazan*, Rowman & Littlefield, 2017
Devlin, Albert J. and Marlene J. Devlin (ed.), *The Selected Letters of Elia
   Kazan*, Vintage, 2016
Gentry, Ric, "Interview: James Woods," *Post Script*, Summer 1998, 2-23
Kazan, Elia, "The Cinema in America" [1971], in Elia Kazan, *An American
   Odyssey* (ed. Michel Ciment), Bloomsbury, 1988
— *A Life*, Knopf, 1988
— *Kazan on Directing*, Knopf, 2009
Neve, Brian, *Elia Kazan: The Cinema of an American Outsider*,
   I.B. Tauris, 2009
Young, Jeff, *Kazan: The Master Director Discusses His Films*,
   Newmarket, 1999

Michael Verhoeven's *o.k.*
Vander Lugt, Kris, "30 June 1970: A Faltering Berlinane Founders on *o. k.*
   Controversy," in Jennifer M. Kapczynski, Michael D. Richardson
   (eds.), *A New History of German Cinema*, Camden House, 2012
Audiovisual sources
Blumenberg, Hans-Christoph and Alfred Holighaus, *Spur der Bären
   [Trace of the Bears]. 60 Jahre Berlinale*, Zero Fiction Film, 2010

Autobiographies and interviews
Fox, Michael J., *Lucky Man: A Memoir*, Hyperion, 2002
— *No Time Like the Future, An Optimist Considers Mortality*,
   Flatiron, 2020
Froug, William, *The Screenwriter Looks at the Screenwriter* [1972],
   Silman-James, 1991
Gould, Heywood, *Drafted: A Memoir of the '60s*, Tolmitch Press, 2021
Hamill, Pete, *A Drinking Life: A Memoir* [1994], Back Bay Books/
   Little, Brown and Company, 2012
Kelly, Richard T., *Sean Penn. His Life and Times*, Faber and Faber, 2004
Leguizamo, John, *Pimps, Hos, Playa Hatas, and All The Rest
   of My Hollywood Friends. My Life*, HarperCollins, 2007
Linson, Art, *A Pound of Flesh. Perilous Tales of How to Produce
   Movies in Hollywood*, Grove, 1993

De Rosa, Alessandro (ed.), *Ennio Morricone: In His Own Words* [2016], Oxford, 2019

Representations of the Vietnam War

Anderegg, Michael (ed.), *Inventing Vietnam. The War in Film and Television*, Temple, 1991

Boutet, Marjolaine, "Le Vietnam et l'Amérique au cinéma et à la télévision : du traumatisme au déni," *Hermès*, no. 52, 2008

Bradley, Doug, Werner Craig, *We Gotta Get Out of This Place: The Soundtrack of the Vietnam War*, Massachusetts, 2015

Coppola, Eleanor, *Notes* [1979], Faber and Faber, 1995

Decker, Todd, *Hymns for the Fallen. Combat Movie Music and Sound After Vietnam*, California, 2017

Dittmar, Linda, Gene Michaud (ed.), *From Hanoi to Hollywood: The Vietnam War in American Film*, Rutgers, 1990

Heberle, Mark (ed.), *Thirty Years After: New Essays on Vietnam War Literature, Film and Art*, Cambridge Scholars, 2009

Ho, Melissa, Thomas Crow, Erica Levin *et al.* (ed.), *Artists Respond. America Art and the Vietnam War, 1965-1975*, Smithsonian American Art Museum/Princeton, 2019

Jacquet, Michel, *Nuit américaine sur le Vietnam. Le cinéma U.S. et la "sale guerre,"* Parçay-sur-Vienne: Anovi, 2009

Malo, Jean-Jacques, Tony Williams, *Vietnam War Films*, McFarland, 1994

Moury, Francis Albert Louis, *Flammes sur l'Indochine. Les classiques du cinéma de la guerre du Viêt-Nam*, Les Éditions Ovadia, 2019

Muraire, André, *Hollywood-Vietnam. La guerre du Vietnam dans le cinéma américain : mythes et réalités*, Michel Houdiard, 2010

Smith, Julian, *Looking Away: Hollywood and Vietnam*, Scribner's, 1975

Spark, Alastair, "Flight Controls: The Social History of the Helicopter as a Symbol of Vietnam" in James Aulich (ed.), *Vietnam Images: War and Representation*, Macmillan, 1989.

Suid, Lawrence H., *Guts and Glory: The Making of the American Military Image in Film*, Kentucky, 2002.

Tessier, Laurent, *Le Vietnam, un cinéma de l'apocalypse*, Cerf-Corlet, 2009

Weaver, Gina Marie, *Ideologies of Forgetting. Rape in the Vietnam War*, SUNY, 2010

Zabunyan, Elvan, Valérie Mavridorakis and David Perreau (eds.), *Martha Rosler, sur/sous le pavé*, Rennes, 2006

The Vietnam War

Bilton, Michael and Kevin Sim, *Four Hours in My Lai* [1992], Penguin, 1993

Borch, Frederic L. (III), *Judge Advocates in Vietnam: Army Lawyers in Southeast Asia 1959-1979*, United States Army Command and General Staff College, Combat Studies Institute/CGSC, 2003

Hallin, Daniel C., *The "Uncensored War": The Media and Vietnam* [1986], California, 1989

Jones, Howard, *My Lai: Vietnam, 1968, and the Descent into Darkness*, Oxford, 2017

Penycate, John, Tom Mangold, *The Tunnels of Cu Chi: The Untold Story of Vietnam*, Random House, 1985

Prados, John, *Vietnam: The History of an Unwinnable War, 1945-1975*, Kansas, 2009

Sturken, Marita, *Tangled Memories: The Vietnam War, the AIDS Epidemic, and the Politics of Remembering*, California, 1997

Turse, Nick, *Kill Anything That Moves: The Real American War in Vietnam*, Picador, 2013

Wieskamp, Valerie, "Sexual Assault and the My Lai Massacre: The Erasure of Sexual Violence from Public Memory of the Vietnam War," in Jennifer Good, Paul Lowe, Brigitte Lardinois, Val Williams (ed.), *Mythologizing the Vietnam War: Visual Culture and Mediated Memory*, Cambridge Scholars, 2014

Sexual Violence in Wartime

Branche, Raphaëlle, "Des viols pendant la guerre d'Algérie," *Vingtième siècle: Revue d'histoire*, no. 75, 2002/3

Branche, Raphaële, Fabrice Virgili and Isabelle Delpha et al. (eds.), *Viols en temps de guerre* [2011], Payot et Rivages, 2013

Brownmiller, Susan, *Against Our Will. Men, Women and Rape*, Simon & Schuster, 1975

Cojean, Annick, "Le viol, arme de destruction massive en Syrie," *Le Monde*, March 4, 2014

Lilly, J. Robert, *Taken by Force: Rape and American GIs in Europe during World War II*, Palgrave Macmillan, 2003

Méheut, Constant, "New Evidence Found of Rape and Torture by Russian Forces in Ukraine," *New York Times*, October 21, 2023

Pronczuk, Monica and Ada Petriczko, "'No One to Talk to': The Lingering Trauma of Russian Rape in Ukraine," *New York Times*, July 27, 2024

War and Genocide (History, Testimonies, Representations)

Coquio, Catherine (ed.), *L'Histoire trouée: Négation et témoignage*, Librairie l'Atalante, 2003

Diaz, Delphine, *La guerre d'Indochine dans le cinéma français. Images d'un trou de mémoire*, Rennes, 2015

Donald, Ralph, and Karen MacDonald, *Reel Men at War: Masculinity and American War Film*, Scarecrow, 2011

Eberwein, Robert, *Armed Forces: Masculinity and Sexuality in the American War Film*, Rutgers, 2007

Levy, Ophir, *Images clandestines. Métamorphoses d'une mémoire visuelle des "camps,"* Hermann, 2016

— "De la hantise des archives. Le réinvestissement fictionnel des images d'archives de la déportation dans le cinéma des années 1960," *Cahiers du CAP*, "Au-delà de l'art et du patrimoine. Expériences, passages et engagements," no. 4, 2017

Lindeperg, Sylvie, *Night and Fog: A Film in History* [2007], Minnesota, 2007

Niemi, Robert, *100 Great War Movies. The Real History Behind the Films*, ABC CLIO LLC., 2018

Réra, Nathan, *Rwanda, entre crise morale et malaise esthétique. Les médias, la photographie et le cinéma à l'épreuve du génocide des Tutsi (1994-2014)*, Les Presses du réel, 2014

Stora, Benjamin, "La guerre d'Algérie dans les médias : l'exemple du cinéma," *Hermès*, no. 52, 2008/3
— "Le cinéma américain pendant la guerre du Vietnam : le mythe de 'l'avalanche,'" *Vingtième siècle. Revue d'Histoire*, January- March 1996
Struk, Janina, *Private Pictures: Soldier's Inside View of War*, I.B. Tauris, 2011

Cinema

Alligier, Maryline, *Bruno Dumont. L'animalité et la grâce*, Rouge Profond, 2012
Battaglio, Stephen, *David Susskind: A Televised Life*, St. Martin's, 2011
Berthomieu, Pierre, *Hollywood classique. Le temps des géants*, Rouge Profond, 2009
Bourget, Jean-Loup, *Cecil B. DeMille, le gladiateur de Dieu*, Presses universitaires de France, 2013
Brianton, Kevin, *Hollywood Divided: The 1950 Screen Directors Guild Meeting and the Impact of the Blacklist*, Kentucky, 2016
Chion, Michel, *Stanley Kubrick. L'humain, ni plus ni moins*, Cahiers du cinéma, 2005
Cocks, Geoffrey, *The Wolf at the Door: Stanley Kubrick, History, and the Holocaust*, Peter Lang, 2004
De Baecque, Antoine, *Godard. Biographie*, Grasset, 2010
De Valck, Marijke, *Film Festivals. From European Geopolitics to Global Cinephilia*, Amsterdam, 2007
Eisenschitz, Bernard, *Le Cinéma allemand* [1999], 2e edition, Armand Colin, 2016
Esquenazi, Jean-Pierre, *Vertigo. Hitchcock et l'invention à Hollywood*, CNRS, 2011
Ferro, Marc, *Cinéma et histoire*, new and revised edition, Gallimard, 1993
Greven, David, *Manhood in Hollywood from Bush to Bush*, Texas, 2009
Haim, Monica, "L'industrie cinématographique allemande après la guerre... froide: année zéro, deuxième prise," *Cinémas*, Autumn 1996
Jeannelle, Jean-Louis, *Films sans images. Une histoire des scénarios non réalisés de La Condition humaine*, Éditions du Seuil, 2015
Lachaud, Maxime, *Redneck Movies. Ruralité et dégénérescence dans le cinéma américain*, Rouge Profond, 2014
Laisney, Simon, *Sean Penn. La fébrilité au cœur du jeu*, Éditions Scope, 2010
Lowenstein, Adam, *Shocking Representation. Historical, Trauma, National Cinema, and the Modern Horror Film*, Columbia, 2005
Mandelbaum, Jacques, *Anatomie d'un film*, Paris: Grasset, 2009
Mann, William J., *Edge of Midnight: The Life of John Schlesinger*. Hutchinson, 2004
Niney, François, *Le documentaire et ses faux-semblants*, Klincksieck, 2009
Pecqueur, Antoine, *Les Écrans sonores de Stanley Kubrick*, Éditions du Point d'exclamation, 2007
Sinyard, Neil, *Jack Clayton*, Manchester: Manchester University Press, 2000
— *George Stevens: The Films of a Hollywood Giant*, McFarland, 2019
Smyth, J.E., *Fred Zinnemann and the Cinema of Resistance*, Mississippi, 2014
Szulkin, David A., *Wes Craven's Last House on the Left: The Making of a Cult Classic*, FAB Press, 1997
Tavernier, Bertrand and Jean-Pierre Coursodon, *Cinquante ans den cinéma américain* [1991], updated and revised version, Nathan/Omnibus, 1995

Thoret, Jean-Baptiste, *26 secondes: l'Amérique éclaboussée.*
L'assassinat de JFK et le cinéma américain, Rouge Profond, 2003
Viviani, Christian, *Le Magique et le Vrai. L'acteur de cinéma, sujet et objet*,
Rouge Profond, 2015
Zabunyan, Dork, "Politiques de l'impureté: Interview with Nathan Réra,"
Tierce, no. 8, 2024

Photography

Azoullay, Ariella, *The Civil Contract of Photography*, Zone Books, 2008
Hariman, Robert and John Louis Lucaites, "Public Identity and Collective
Memory in u.s. Iconic Photography: The Image of 'Accidental
Napalm'," *Critical Studies in Media Communication*, vol. 20, no. 1, 2003
Griffiths, Philip Jones, *Vietnam Inc.*, Collier, 1971
Neveu, Roland, *The Fall of Phnom Penh* [2007], Asia Horizon, 2015
Sontag, Susan, *Regarding the Pain of Others*, Picador, 2002

Theatre

Brecht, Bertolt, *Brecht on Theatre* (ed. John Willett), Methuen, 1974
Kraus, Karl, *The Last Days of Mankind* [1919], translated by Fred Bridgham
and Edward Timms, Yale, 2015
Rabe, David, *The Vietnam Plays. Volume One. The Basic Training of Pavlo
Hummel, Stick and Bones* [1969-1972], Grove, 1993

Philosophy

Baudrillard, Jean, *Simulacres et Simulation*, Galilée, 1981
Bayard, Pierre, *Aurais-je été résistant ou bourreau?*, Les Éditions de Minuit, 2013

The Writing of History

Bloch, Marc, "Critique historique et critique du témoignage," *Annales.
Économies, sociétés, civilisations*, January-March 1950
D'Almeida, Fabrice and Denis Maréchal (ed.), *L'Histoire orale en questions*,
na Éditions, 2013
Descamps, Florence, *Archiver la mémoire. De l'histoire orale au patrimoine
immatériel*, Éditions Ehess, 2019
Ginzburg, Carlo, Patrick Boucheron and Séverine Nikel, "La leçon
de méthode de Carlo Ginzburg," *L'Histoire*, no. 360, 2011/1
Kris, Ernst and Otto Kurz, *La Légende de l'artiste. Un essai historique*
[1934], Éditions Allia, 2010
Soulet, Jean-François, *L'Histoire immédiate. Historiographie, sources et
méthodes*, Armand Colin, 2009

Photo Credits

opposite 1 © Cinémathèque française
29, 30, 31, 37, 41 © National Archives, St. Louis
48 © Daniel Lang private archives. Courtesy of Cecily, Helen and Frances Lang
69, 70, 71 © Edison Filmgesellschaft mbH. Courtesy of Herbert Klemens
156 © Carl Mydans. Daniel Lang private archives. Courtesy of Cecily,
    Helen and Frances Lang
179, 180 © David Rabe private archives
225, 265 © Roland Neveu. Courtesy of ASC Archives
236 © Mike Stokey private archives
240, 245, 275, 282, 298, 305, 306, 381 © Roland Neveu/Columbia Pictures
242, 243, 268, 269, 270, 280, 300, 308, 322, 323, 324, 333
    © Monica Goldstein private collection
247-262: Brian De Palma storyboards © Monica Goldstein private collection
274 © Pasiree Panya private collection
312, 314, 327, 330, 331 © Roland Neveu/Columbia Pictures.
    Source: Filmbild Fundus Herbert Klemens. Courtesy of Herbert Klemens
415 © Bernard Réra private archives.

Index

Altman, Robert, 179, 222, 227, 239
Anderson, Robert, 128
Andersson, Bibi, 104
Ansen, David, 393
Antonioni, Michelangelo, 169, 181, 332
Apocalypse Now (Coppola), 2, 128, 214, 226, 271, 357-58, 377, 427n, 444n, 455n
Arendt, Hannah, 60
Argento, Dario, 373
Ashby, Hal, 226, 439n, 455n
Aubrey, James 117

Backmann, René, 401
Back to the Future (Zemeckis), 219, 404
Baldwin, Stephen, 222, 235, 277-80, 311, 313, 344, 447n
Barber, Samuel, 377-78
Barra, Allen, 269, 274, 386
Battaglio, Stephen, 154
Bauer, Alfred, 83-85, 434n
Baumbach, Noah, 5
Bava, Mario, 113
Bayard, Pierre, 412-13
Bayrhammer, Gustl, 68
Bazin, André, 113
Beatty, Warren, 439n
Becker, Hartmut, 68
Beechinor, Sallie, 6, 227
Béhar, Henri, 436n, 441n
Beineix, Jean-Jacques, 230
Benoliel, Bernard, 1, 5
Berenger, Tom, 349, 351
Bergen, Candice, 64
Bergman, Ingmar, 106
Berry, Chuck, 296
Bertolucci, Bernardo, 80, 373
Bloch, Marc, 9

Blow Out (De Palma), 1, 181, 221, 224, 349
Blumenfeld, Samuel, 1, 5
Body Double (De Palma), 181, 222, 225, 313, 349, 369, 399
Bogarde, Dirk, 121
Boisset, Yves, 403
Bonfire of the Vanities, The (De Palma), 378, 405, 427n
Boorman, John, 227, 434n
Borch, Frederic L., 14-15
Bosworth, Barbara, 385
Boukhrief, Nicolas, 399, 400
Boulle, Pierre, 224
Bouzereau, Laurent, 5, 443n
Brakhage, Stan, 106
Brando, Marlon, 113, 217
Bratt, Benjamin, 222
Brecht, Bertolt, 72, 434n
Breed, Putnam P., 28
Bridge on the River Kwai, The (Lean), 264, 320, 356
Brooks, Richard, 227
Brown, Garrett, 226
Brownmiller, Susan, 60, 434
Bruno, Richard, 227
Budreau, Robert, 455
Burnett, David, 357
Burrows, Darren E., 292-93
Burrows, Larry, 67
Burum, Stephen, 6, 225-26, 244, 264-67, 275, 281, 284-85, 289

Cabot, Louis, 438n
Caldwell, Gail, 389
Calhoun, John, 442n
Calley, John, 131, 135, 139, 176
Calley, William, 59, 101, 350, 433n
Cameron, James, 385, 453n
Canby, Vincent, 104, 394

Carlito's Way (De Palma), 405
Carpenter, John, 373
Carr, Jay, 389
Carrie (De Palma), 1, 177-78, 181-82, 208, 211, 230, 329, 349
Caruso, Fred, 6, 224, 226-30, 232, 236-37, 241, 263-64, 266, 269, 271, 273, 276, 278, 281, 294-95, 321, 379, 405, 444n
Castell, Rolf, 68
Cavalier, Alain, 403
Cayatte, André, 400
Cazale, John, 455
Chais, Stanley, 140-41, 419
Chapier, Henry, 402
Chayefsky, Paddy, 128
Chicago, Judy, 59
Cheever, John, 427n
Christiansen, Richard, 60
Chunko, George, 58
Ciment, Michel, 400-403, 435n
Cimino, Michael, 2, 123, 226-27, 236, 264, 291, 391, 402, 476n
Clayburgh, Jill, 179
Clayton, Jack, 3, 11, 119-36, 139-41, 143, 145, 152-53, 155-56, 158, 176, 186, 190, 192, 197, 206, 217, 406, 408, 418-19, 428n, 436-41n, 459-60n, 470n
Clift, Montgomery, 114
Coffin, William Sloane, 119
Cohn, Sidney E., 142, 166
Collins, Chester A., 21, 26, 30, 32, 38-40, 52, 55, 63, 191
Connery, Sean, 182
Cook, Brian W., 6, 226-27, 236, 263, 267, 276, 292
Cooper, James Fenimore, 123
Coppola, Francis, 2, 223, 225-26, 264, 358, 377, 402, 444n, 455n
Costanzo, Marko A., 7
Costner, Kevin, 182
Coutard, Raoul, 434n
Cox, Terry, 227
Craven, Timothy, 438n
Craven, Wes, 105-107, 110, 434n
Crenna, Richard, 64
Crown, Alfred, 154-55, 165-66, 181, 407, 420
Cruise, Tom, 219

Dafoe, Willem, 349
Daley, Robert, 178
Danziger, Jeff, 384-85
De Baecque, Antoine, 340, 342, 399-400
De Bono, Yves, 7, 227
Deer Hunter, The (Cimino), 2, 123, 179, 214, 227, 320, 390
De Gasperi, Anne, 401
De Grunwald, Nicholas, 113
De Niro, Robert, 170-72, 180, 182, 320, 396
De Palma, Brian, 1-7, 10-14, 45, 60, 64, 80-81, 143, 166-67, 169-172, 176-84, 189-90, 192, 195, 208, 210-11, 213-15, 217, 219, 221-27, 229-35, 237-39, 241, 243-45, 247, 263, 265, 267-76, 278-83, 285-87, 289, 292-94, 298, 301, 306-15, 218, 320-22, 325-36, 340, 342, 344, 346-47, 349, 353, 355-59, 361, 365-66, 368-69, 372-74, 376-81, 383-86, 388-92, 394-403, 405-413, 418, 420-22,427n, 428n, 436n, 441-43n, 445n, 447n, 448n
De Rosa, Alessandro, 8, 375
De Sica, Vittorio, 434n
De Valck, Marijke, 80
De Vito, Danny, 181
Decker, Todd, 376
Del Toro, Benicio, 222
Dellinger, David, 143
DeMille, Cecil B., 81-82
Des Pallières, Arnaud, 427n
Dickey, Alison, 278
Dionysus in 69 (De Palma), 176
Donaggio, Pino, 373
Douchet, Jean, 455n
Douglas, Kirk, 178
Downey Sr., Robert, 178-79
Dressed to Kill (De Palma), 181-82, 224-25, 313, 349
Dreyfus, Alfred, 402
Duckett, Douglas, 26, 35, 40, 431n
Dumas, Chris, 368-69
Dumont, Bruno, 449n
Dunaway, Faye, 437n
Durniok, Manfred, 82
Dye, Dale, 7, 232-33, 235, 237, 294, 384, 424, 444-45n
Dzundza, George, 179

Ebert, Roger, 393
Eckhardt, William, 38-40
Eisenschitz, Bernard, 80
Eisenstein, Sergei, 182
Empire of the Sun (Spielberg), 213, 227
Engelen, Paul, 6, 227, 242, 272, 281, 292, 293, 299, 329
Euripides, 176

Fassbinder, Rainer Werner, 68, 80
Fear and Desire (Kubrick), 74
Fengler, Michael, 80
Ferro, Marc, 403
Fifer, Shannon, 137
Filo, John, 106
Finck, Pierre, 28-30, 37-38, 52
Fiore, Robert, 176
Fischer, Wolfgang, 68
Fitzpatrick, Tom, 393-94
FitzGerald, Frances, 386, 388, 392
Fitzgerald, Scott F., 439n
Flaherty, Robert, 113
Fleischer, Richard, 440n
Fleming, Dick, 389, 396
Flynn, John, 143, 150
Forman, Miloš, 154, 227
Fort Apache The Bronx (Petrie), 143
Fox, Michael J., 2, 8-9, 219-221, 227, 230, 232-33, 237, 264, 270, 274-77, 292, 296-300, 306-08, 315, 318, 320, 328, 353, 372, 376, 380, 382, 386, 395, 404, 421, 439-40n, 443n
Frazee, Robert, 42-43
Friedkin, William, 399
Fullerton, Carl, 293, 329
Full Metal Jacket (Kubrick), 2, 169, 179, 201, 214, 281, 377, 391-92, 401, 427n
Furue, Tadao, 28-29, 37, 52, 162
Fury, The (De Palma), 178, 329

Garcia, Andy, 182
Garcia, Cipriano "Chip", 19, 21-27, 29-30, 32-36, 40, 44, 46, 52-53, 56, 417, 419, 429n
Garcia, Joseph "Joe", 19, 21, 22-25, 27, 33-35, 42-44, 46, 52, 56-57, 418, 447n
Garfield, Allen, 175
Gates, Larry, 64

Gelfan, Greg, 183
Genghis Khan, 199, 319, 442n
Germany, Pale Mother (Sanders-Brahms), 68
Gerry, Alexander, 127-28
Gervase, David, 19-27, 32-36, 38-46, 51-52, 61, 146, 191, 196, 355, 417-18, 431n
Get to Know Your Rabbit (De Palma), 176
Giler, David, 132-35, 139, 143, 152, 156-57, 160-62, 176, 186, 192, 197, 406, 418-19, 438n
Ginsberg, Allen, 441
Ginzburg, Carlo, 10
Godard, Jean-Luc, 72, 106, 171, 347, 399, 403, 434n, 450n
Gold, Jack, 439n
Goldman, William, 128
Goldstein, Carl, 6, 227, 237, 264, 268-69, 275-76, 282, 295, 320, 323-24, 449n
Goldstein, Monica, 6, 244, 271, 274, 374, 452n
Good Morning Vietnam (Levinson), 169, 223, 237
Gould, Heywood, 119, 142-54, 156, 160, 162, 180, 186, 190, 197, 215, 406, 420, 440n
Goya, Francisco de, 53, 116
Grable, Betty, 126
Graham, Gerrit, 170
Grantham, Lucie, 105
Green Berets, The (Wayne), 63, 386
Greenberg, Jerry, 225
Greenstein, Milton, 112
Greetings (De Palma), 64, 169-76
Greven, David, 192, 201
Grousset, Jean-Paul, 402
Guerra, Ruy, 80
Guzmán, Luis, 222
Gwaltney, Jack, 222, 232

Haeberle, Ronald, 60, 357, 451n
Hallam, John, 438n
Hamill, Pete, 121-33, 142-43, 152-53, 156-57, 162, 175, 186, 190, 192, 197, 215, 406, 408, 418, 437n, 438n
Hamilton, Richard, 441
Hammer, Jerome, 154-55, 165-66, 181, 407, 420

Hancock, Peter, 227
Hardy, Oliver, 105
Harrelson, Woody, 368, 451
Harvey, Don, 7, 221, 231, 234-36, 238, 264, 267, 277, 281, 295, 298, 307-308, 310, 311-13, 318, 322, 328, 361, 377, 409, 412
Hawke, Ethan, 455n
Hayes, Nancy, 7
Hayworth, Rita, 126
Hebecker, Klaus, 82
Heckerling, Amy, 218
Henry, Gregg, 222
Herrmann, Bernard, 177, 369, 373
Hersh, Seymour, 59
Herzog, Werner, 68, 80
Hesse, David, 105
High Noon (Zinnemann), 113, 115
Hilberg, Raul, 427n
Hill, Walter, 132
Hi, Mom! (De Palma), 64, 172
Hirsch, Charles, 170
Hitchcock, Alfred, 169-70, 177, 210, 320, 369, 389, 399, 400, 434n
Hô Chí Minh, 117, 172
Hoberman, J., 386, 389, 396
Holighaus, Alfred, 343
Hollander, David, 183
Holloran, Peter C., 384
Home Movies (De Palma), 178
Hong Bui Thi, 58
Houwer, Donald, 433
Houwer, Rob, 10, 65-66, 68, 83, 137-38, 214, 419, 433
Howard, Ron, 154, 385, 440n, 453n
Howe, Desson, 388
Hudson, Hugh, 227
Hughes, John, 385, 453n
Huston, John, 113, 121

Innocents, The (Clayton), 121, 125
Irving, Amy, 329

James, Henry, 121
Jaws (Spielberg), 342
Jeannelle, Jean-Louis, 111, 116, 117
Joanou, Phil, 448n
Joffé, Roland, 227-28
Johnson, Lyndon, 20, 58, 81, 87, 171, 176
Johnson, Sidney, 446n

Jonquet, François, 400
Jordan, Neil, 448n
Joyce, Patricia, 90, 97
Just, Ward, 60

Kael, Pauline, 3, 118, 190, 390-92
Kai-shek, Chiang, 117
Katsahnias, Iannis, 342, 399-400
Kazan, Chris, 89-91, 435n
Kazan, Elia, 3, 11, 63-64, 88-90, 92, 97-98, 101-5, 115, 199, 208, 331, 332, 394, 401, 419, 435n, 439n
Keach, Stacy, 437n
Keesey, Douglas, 356, 450n
Kehr, Dave, 389
Kennaway, James, 437n
Kennedy, John Fitzgerald, 28, 169, 172, 377
Kerr, Deborah, 113, 121, 125
Kilgallen, Dorothy, 119
Killing Fields, The (Joffé), 223, 228
King, Erik, 7, 239-40, 277, 283, 295, 301
King, Stephen, 178
Kirchner, John, 43-44
Korda, Alexander, 121
Kotcheff, Ted, 227
Kraus, Karl, 79
Kroeger, Wolf, 6, 227, 241, 281, 424
Kubrick, Stanley, 2, 74, 226-27, 264, 267, 377, 391, 401-402, 434n
Kumai, Kei, 80
Kurosawa, Akira, 285
Kuwahara, Lynn, 443n

Labov, William, 240
Lacouture, Jean, 398, 402
Laisney, Simon, 240, 304, 351
Lancaster, Burt, 113
Lang, Cecily, 10, 50, 431
Lang, Daniel, 3, 10, 11, 13-15, 19, 46-65, 68, 72, 78-79, 86-91, 102, 107, 110, 112, 113, 115-19, 122-25, 127-31, 133, 135-44, 146-47, 151-66, 169, 176, 180-81, 183-87, 190-94, 196, 198, 202-204, 206, 208, 211, 213, 233, 239, 337, 355, 359, 366, 379, 385, 391, 406-407, 409-10, 413, 418-20, 427n, 431n, 433n, 435-38n, 440-42n, 455n

Lang, Frances, 10
Lang, Helen, 10, 431
Lang, Margaret, 58, 183-85, 420, 432n
Lantz, Robert, 455n
Last House on the Left (Craven), 105-10, 434n
Laurel, Stan, 105
Lawrence of Arabia (Lean), 227, 264
Lawson, Terry, 394
Le Thuy Thu, 1, 7, 229-31, 242, 263-64, 273, 309-17, 325, 329-30, 353, 369, 395-97, 402, 411, 421, 446n
Le Van But, 30-31
Lean, David, 224, 227, 264, 320, 357
Leclère, Marie-Françoise, 402
Lee, Russell, 291
Leepson, Marc, 383
Leguizamo, John, 7, 222, 239, 283, 295-97, 304, 315, 319, 325
Lehmann-Haupt, Christopher, 60
Leone, Sergio, 373
Les Carabiniers (Godard), 72-73, 434n
Levy, Ophir, 106, 110
Lilly, J. Robert, 60
Lillywhite, David, 27
Lincoln, Fred, 105
Linson, Art, 4-6, 169, 181-83, 208, 218-19, 221-23, 230-31, 233, 263, 269, 274, 278-79, 281, 294, 306, 330, 332-34, 379-81, 407, 420, 427n, 449n
Loden, Barbara, 88
Loeb, George, 45
Lord Jim (Brooks), 227, 264
Losey, Joseph, 104
Lowenstein, Adam, 106
Lucas, George, 440n
Lumet, Sidney, 180, 225, 439n
Lupino, Ida, 398
Luu Thuy An, 230
Lynch, David, 444n

Madoff, Bernard, 140
Maguire, Charles, 139, 439n
Makavejev, Dušan, 82-4, 434n
Malick, Terrence, 235, 373
Malo, Jean-Jacques, 64
Malraux, André, 116-17
Mamet, David, 182, 330, 380, 407
Mandelbaum, Jacques, 4
Mangold, Tom, 241

Mankiewicz, Joseph L., 81
Mann, William J., 120
Mansfield, Harold, 45
Mansford, Julia, 227
Marshall, Garry, 440n
Martay, Oscar, 80
Martínez, Chico, 90
Mason, James, 121
Masuzawa, Sato, 7-8, 424
Mattes, Eva, 68, 72, 78
Maysles, Albert, 225
Maysles, David, 225
McCallany, Holt, 7, 221-22, 235, 238, 265, 278, 283, 296, 297, 299, 301, 308, 448n, 451n
McCarthy, Joseph, 104, 112, 115
McClendon, Jimmie, 27, 37, 417
McConkey, Larry, 6, 226, 270-73, 282, 284-86, 289, 317, 325, 408, 423
McKenna, Richard, 128
Medavoy, Mike, 180
Men, The (Zinnemann), 113
Mercurio, James, 30-31
Midson, Dave, 227
Miers Jr., Sheppard, 44
Milius, John, 128
Miller, J.P., 128
Miller, Jeffrey, 106
Minogue, Katherine, 47-48
Mission: Impossible (De Palma), 405
Mission to Mars (De Palma), 373
Modine, Matthew, 179
Monicelli, Mario, 113
Morel, Jean-Michel, 401
Morse, David, 448n
Morricone, Ennio, 8-9, 373-76, 378, 382, 399-400, 421
Mortensen, Viggo, 448
Muraire, André, 63
Murphy, Eugene W., 34

Neveu, Roland, 6, 228, 267, 281
Ngô Dinh Diêm, 116
Nguyen Thi Tron, 67
Night and Fog (Resnais), 83
Niney, François, 347
Nixon, Mignon, 67
Nixon, Richard, 44, 58, 337
Norman, Michael, 380, 382, 385-86, 390, 392, 422
Novak, Kim, 369

Obsession (De Palma), 177, 210, 369
o.k. (Verhoeven), 3, 10, 11, 63-79, 81, 84, 136-38, 400, 418-19, 433n, 441n
Ono, Yoko, 59
On the Waterfront (Kazan), 92, 217
Outrage (Lupino), 398

Pacino, Al, 179, 441, 455n
Paltrow, Jake, 5
Pankow, Bill, 6, 7, 184, 186, 225, 335, 336, 344, 355, 368, 373, 374, 378, 380, 421
Panya, Pasiree, 7, 266, 273-74, 299, 304, 315, 446n
Parker, Alan, 226
Pascal, Amy, 214
Pasolini, Pier Paolo, 373
Paszkiendtz, Butch, 429-30n
Peabody, Sandra, 105
Pearson, Randy, 22, 26, 52, 54, 160
Peck, Gregory, 116
Peckinpah, Sam, 434n
Pecqueur, Antoine, 377
Penn, Arthur, 225
Penn, Leo, 217
Penn, Sean, 1, 7-8, 178, 201, 217-9, 231, 234, 236-37, 239-42, 273-74, 277-78, 283, 298-301, 304, 306-8, 310, 313-14, 320, 325-26, 328, 331, 344, 349, 351, 353, 378, 382, 395-96, 421, 423-24 443n, 445n, 448n
Penycate, John, 241
Pérez, José, 413
Pérez, Michel, 400
Perl, Arnold, 142
Perry, Frank, 154, 437n
Petri, Elio, 104
Petrie, Daniel, 143
Phan Thi Mao, 22-35, 37-40, 42-44, 49, 51-58, 60-61, 64, 66-68, 72, 75-77, 79 86-88, 107, 110, 122-24, 127, 129, 131, 133-36, 146-48, 150-53, 157-58, 160-65, 187, 190, 202, 213, 229, 233, 355, 385, 407, 410, 413, 417, 429n, 431n, 434n
Phan Thi Loc, 22, 31, 33, 134, 162, 190
Phantom of the Paradise (De Palma), 1, 178

Phuc, Kim, 356-57
Picquart, Marie-Georges, 402
Pierce, Wendell, 295
Platoon (Stone), 2, 123, 169, 214, 227-28, 232, 235, 267, 281, 294, 349, 351, 377-78, 382, 385, 388, 391-94, 401, 407
Poirier, Normand, 58, 112
Polanski, Roman, 227, 439n
Pollan, Tracy, 220, 276-77, 450n
Pontecorvo, Gillo, 373
Porter, Liliana, 86
Pran, Dith, 228
Precht, Ewald, 68
Pressburger, Emeric, 116
Presson Allen, Jay, 180
Prince, Emmitte, 429n
Proferes, Nicholas, 90, 103
Pugh, Mickey, 7, 227, 291, 300

Qassim Hamza al-Janabi, Abeer, 410

Rabe, David, 4-6, 10, 12, 143, 166, 169, 178-81, 183-199, 201-204, 206-211, 213-15, 217-19, 223, 230, 238-39, 241, 244, 293, 311, 315, 329-34, 337, 340, 344, 355-56, 358-59, 363, 365-66, 368-69, 372, 376-77, 380-83, 389, 391, 394, 407-408, 420-22, 443n, 447n
Rafferty, Terrence, 393
Railsback, Steven, 90-91
Rain, Jeramie, 105
Rapace, Noomi, 455n
Ratliff, Lee, 36-38, 40, 56
Rauschenberg, Robert, 441n
Ray, Satyajit, 80
Raymond, John, 60-61
Redacted (De Palma), 2, 409-12
Reilly, John C., 221-22, 231-32, 238-39, 275, 277-80, 283, 287, 295, 298, 299, 300-301, 311, 319, 322-24, 328, 344, 368, 442n
Réra, Joseph, 414-15
Resnais, Alain, 83, 403
Reynolds, Kevin, 235
Rhames, Ving, 222, 238, 295
Richards, Sioux, 227
Richardson, Tony, 438n
Ricketts, Deborah, 7, 291

Ridenhour, Ron, 59
Riley, Laurie, 227
Rissner, Danton, 128, 131
Rolling Thunder (Flynn), 143, 150-51
Rosi, Francesco, 104
Rosler, Martha, 67
Rossellini, Roberto, 113, 434
Rothstein, Freyda, 151
Rourke, Mickey, 236
Roy, Jean, 401
Rozier, Jacques, 403
Rubin, Bruce, 176

Salamon, Julie, 3, 378, 385, 392
Sanders-Brahms, Helma, 68
Sand Pebbles, The (Wise), 63, 117, 128, 439n
Sann, Paul, 121
Sayles, John, 221
Scarface (De Palma), 1, 181, 222, 225, 230, 337, 349, 381, 399, 405
Schaffner, Franklin J., 143
Schanberg, Sydney, 228
Schatzberg, Jerry, 436n
Schechner, Richard, 176
Schell, Maurice, 7, 225, 336-37, 423
Schickel, Richard, 389
Schlesinger, John, 3, 118-20, 176, 418
Schlöndorff, Volker, 80, 214
Schmieding, Walther, 83
Schneider, John, 86-87
Schoendoerffer, Pierre, 402
Schwab, Eric, 6, 222-24, 228, 244, 271, 273, 281, 284, 291, 294, 299, 304, 306, 320-21, 328, 336, 380, 421, 443n, 452n
Schweizer, Nicole, 67
Schweizer, Richard, 115
Scorsese, Martin, 172, 226-27, 378, 391
Scott, Frank J., 28, 37
Scott, George C., 121
Scruggs, Jan, 383
Search, The (Zinnemann), 113-15
Seiler, Andy, 394
Seitz, John, 272
Shane, Laurie, 289
Shawn, William, 46, 58
Shayne, Alan, 139
Shedlo, Ronald, 139, 419, 439n
Sheen, Charlie, 349
Sheffler, Marc, 105

Siclier, Jacques, 401
Siegel, Don, 373
Signoret, Simone, 121
Simon, Neil, 451n
Simon, Norton, 119, 141-42
Simon, Taryn, 411-12
Sims, Jeanie, 125-27, 133, 197
Sinatra, Nancy, 377
Sinyard, Neil, 11, 125, 425
Siodmak, Robert, 113
Sisters (De Palma), 177
Smith, Art, 7, 237-38, 274, 292, 294
Smith, Gavin, 390
Sontag, Susan, 67
Spero, Nancy, 59, 442
Spielberg, Steven, 213, 227, 235, 342, 379, 399, 443n
Spigelmire, Michael, 26-27, 30-31, 34, 38, 40, 52, 55-56
Spinks, Michael, 326
Spock, Benjamin, 143
St. Clair, John, 112
Stalin, Joseph, 115
Stallone, Sylvester, 396
Stalmaster, Lynn, 221, 233
Steel, Dawn, 181, 213-14, 219, 269, 299, 379, 385, 421
Stella, Frank, 441
Stevens, George, 81-84
Stevenson, Michael, 226-27, 232, 263-64, 273, 276
Stewart, James, 210
Stokey, Mike, 7, 233, 235-37, 268, 292, 299, 383, 444n
Stone, Oliver, 2, 106, 123, 223, 228, 232, 267, 281, 291, 349, 377, 381
Stora, Benjamin, 403
Storaro, Vittorio, 226
Storeby, Robert, 19, 21-30, 32-34, 36-44, 49-59, 61, 119, 122, 127, 147-48, 158, 160, 187, 191, 202-203, 206, 214, 337, 355, 407, 410, 413, 416-18, 447n
Strand, Paul, 113-14
Strauss, Bob, 389
Streamers (Altman), 179, 198, 222, 227, 239
Struk, Janina, 293
Sungkawess, Charlie, 7, 224
Sungkawess, Sompol, 223-24, 228

Susskind, David, 118-21, 124, 128-29, 136-37, 139, 141-43, 151, 153-54, 165, 176, 180-81, 406, 408, 418, 420
Suyin, Han, 116

Tables (Verhoeven), 66
Tanen, Ned, 183, 213-14, 421
Tarantino, Quentin, 455n
Tavernier, Bertrand, 455n
Taxi Driver (Scorsese), 172, 396
The Doors, 195, 202, 234, 358, 376, 408
Thich Quang Duch, 116
Thing, The (Carpenter), 373
Thomas, Deborah, 202, 309
Thomas, Steven, 19-20, 22-30, 32-40, 45-46, 52-53, 123, 417-18, 429n, 431n
Thompson, Gary, 393
Thoret, Jean-Baptiste, 172
Todini, Bruno, 113
Topor, Roland, 439n
Toscan du Plantier, Daniel, 401
Townley, Peter P., 113
Tran, Kady, 365
Travolta, John, 178, 181
Treves, Vivian, 373
Turse, Nick, 58
Tyson, Mike, 326

Ullmann, Bernard, 402
Ulmer, Edgar, 113
Uncle Buck (Hughes), 385, 453n
Untouchables, The (De Palma), 182-83, 210, 217, 221-22, 225-27, 229, 289, 291, 330, 361, 373-74, 381, 399, 404-405, 407, 420, 444n
Ut, Nick, 356-57

Vachaud, Laurent, 1, 5, 399
Vallone, Raf, 414
Vautier, René, 104, 403
Vecchio, Mary Ann, 106
Verhoeven, Michael, 3, 10-11, 63-68, 72-73, 78-79, 81-86, 136-38, 176, 214, 399, 418, 424-25, 433-34n, 441n
Verhoeven, Paul, 399, 433n
Vertigo (Hitchcock), 177, 210, 368-69

Vidal, Gore, 119, 438n
Vidor, King, 113
Visconti, Luchino, 434
Visitors, The (Kazan), 3, 11, 63, 88, 90-105, 198, 208, 331, 332, 394, 419, 435n
Voight, Jon, 441
Von Thun, Friedrich, 68

Wargnier, Régis, 229, 398, 444n, 450n
Warhol, Andy, 441n
Wayne, John, 199, 386, 433n, 442n
Weaver, Gina Marie, 240
Weber, Bruce, 379
Wedding Party, The (De Palma), 169, 180
Weinstein, Harvey, 412
Weir, Peter, 226
Wenders, Wim, 80
West, Jessamyn, 437n
West, Kit, 227
Wexler, Haskell, 226
Wheeler, John P., 383
White, Stanley, 236-37, 445n
Williams, Robin, 237
Williams, Tony, 64
Willner, George, 112
Winter Soldier, 64, 444n
Wise Guys (De Palma), 181
Wise, Robert, 63, 117, 439n
Wolfe, Tom, 427n
Woods, James, 90-92, 103, 441n
Woodward, Frank, 448n
Wozniak, 398
Wren, Christopher, 143
Wright, Michael, 179, 222, 228, 239
Wuntch, Philip, 394, 396

Year of the Dragon (Cimino), 224, 226-27, 236, 291
Yelton, James, 33, 35-37, 40, 42, 51, 161, 191

Zabriskie Point (Antonioni), 64
Zanuck, Richard, 139, 419
Zapruder, Abraham, 171
Zeff, Ley, 438n
Zinnemann, Fred, 113-118, 139, 176, 406, 436n
Zubaidi, Zahra, 411-12

www.ingramcontent.com/pod-product-compliance
Lightning Source LLC
Chambersburg PA
CBHW070123080526
44586CB00015B/1536